Kelly

COMMUNICATION SKILLS *for the* HEALTH CARE PROFESSIONAL

Concepts and Techniques

Gwen van Servellen, RN, PhD, FAAN
Professor
University of California, Los Angeles
Los Angeles, California

AN ASPEN PUBLICATION®
Aspen Publishers, Inc.
Gaithersburg, Maryland
1997

Library of Congress Cataloging-in-Publication Data

van Servellen, Gwen Marram.
Communication skills for the health care professional: concepts
and techniques/Gwen van Servellen
p. cm.
Includes bibliographical references and index.
ISBN 0-8342-0766-4
1. Allied health personnel and patient. 2. Interpersonal communication.
I. Title.
R727.3.V36   1996
610′.69—dc20
DNLM/DLC
96-26915
CIP

Orders: (800) 638-8437
Customer Service: (800) 234-1660

About Aspen Publishers • For more than 35 years, Aspen has been a leading professional publisher in a variety of disciplines. Aspen's vast information resources are available in both print and electronic formats. We are committed to providing the highest
quality information available in the most appropriate format for our customers. Visit
Aspen's Internet site for more information resources, directories, articles, and a search-
able version of Aspen's full catalog, including the most recent publications: **http://
www.aspenpub.com**
        Aspen Publishers, Inc. • The hallmark of quality in publishing
            Member of the worldwide Wolters Kluwer group

Editorial Resources: Jane Colilla
Library of Congress Catalog Card Number: 96-26915
ISBN: 0-8342-0766-4

Printed in the United States of America

2   3   4   5

Table of Contents

Preface

Effective communications are at the core of quality patient care. Patients require the help and support of other people. Every contact with a patient or potential patient requires courteous, considerate, respectful, and helpful communication. When patients get the responses they want, they feel good about their encounter with health care providers and their need for positive interaction is satisfied. When they feel good about their experience, they are more willing to cooperate and are more likely to repeat their contacts with us. If their experience is negative, however, they are likely to avoid and limit further contact. Depending on what is required to complete their care, their avoidance may have very serious consequences. It may cause them to avoid getting needed help, or it may cause them to ignore the health care directives they have been given.

Negative communication experiences cause anger and resentment. If patients come to a health care facility, for example, and get routed to several providers without getting any real help, they will feel resentful about their encounter. One negative experience like this may require many additional positive interactions before its effects are completely erased.

The value of a positive provider-patient relationship cannot be underestimated. In addition to its being the doorway to quality care, the patient-provider relationship is regarded as the most crucial component of the health care delivery system. Del Mar (1994), in an assessment of related literature over a 35-year period, showed that providers' good communication skills are associated with better care and even better health.

Teaching communication skills to students is regarded as a priority because these skills have been associated with better patient care. It is generally substantiated that practitioners can improve their care to patients by paying attention to their communications and the dynamics of the provider-patient relationship. Despite the importance attributed to communication skills in the health care professions, deficiencies in practice abound.

Instruction in the principles of interpersonal communication with particular emphasis on teaching students skills for interviewing patients and their families is found in most health professional training programs. Sometimes the content is provided in preclinical course work; in other cases, during general practice and/or family and community rotations. In a few cases, communication skills are taught at multiple levels and with a variety of teaching aids, e.g., role-playing, process recordings, small-group tutorials, and audio tape recordings of actual patient-provider interactions. Student evaluations of courses aimed at teaching communication skills are usually positive, indicating that students do feel that their interviewing and communication skills are improved with course work. Moreover, listening to and evaluating one's own process recordings or tape recordings have been judged as the most helpful aspect of a course in communications and interviewing (Usherwood 1993). Undergraduate and graduate health care professional training programs that deny students formalized instruction in communication skills and principles produce an incompletely trained provider. A variety of skills are needed and should be in place if students are to effectively practice in today's complex health care environment.

The purpose of this textbook is to inform the reader about basic communication knowledge and skills, particularly those that are relevant in today's complex and challenging health care arena. Becoming proficient in communicating with patients and their families is a requirement of all health care professionals. Practicing effective communicative behavior with other health professionals is also mandated in this era of increased interdisciplinary collaboration. The literature is replete with examples of how communication can or did make a critical difference in the care that patients and their families received.

Just reading about communication is not sufficient, however. Despite the abundant literature on communication and therapeutic response modes, communication knowledge and skills cannot be learned from textbooks alone. The critical test of providers' competency is how they put these principles and skills into practice with patients. Because of this, laboratory experiences in which students test out and practice therapeutic responsiveness is critical in their professional role development. Practice, patience, and feedback can significantly impact providers' attitudes about their abilities to put these skills effectively to work for them. Laboratory practice allows providers time to blend these important skills and knowledge with their own personal proclivity to be helpful to others. Because patients may have different communication styles than do providers and have different expectations of our encounters with them, skills and knowledge must always evolve from a specific context and specific set of patient circumstances. These different styles, while initially anxiety-provoking for providers, must be embraced and integrated into our approach. With experience and practice, providers will recognize that patients' differentnesses contribute to the depth and richness of patient encounters. Therapeutic response modes are valued in the generic sense but do not completely describe what these interactions are or should be.

Teaching staff who use this text will find the material detailed and informative. The text is intended to be applicable to upper-division undergraduate students as well as first-level graduate students and practicing health professionals. Most universities with health professional schools have an undergraduate core curriculum where communication content and experiential learning is a requirement, therefore, the text is extremely useful to students who are entering the health professions but who have not yet encountered many client-provider contacts. The text is designed to be used by many health professional groups because all of these disciplines are in need of more formal and specific education in communication skills. The importance of effective communication skills in all health care professions is undeniably important.

The importance of human communication in the health professions has not changed. However, as technology advances the practice of contemporary health care, training in interpersonal communications may not be accorded the level of recognition necessary to support professional practice. This text is dedicated to basic communication skills and concepts that are foundational to the health care professions. The chapter on human communications was enhanced by the analysis and synthesis of Gazda, Childers and Walters (*Interpersonal Communications: A Handbook for Health Professionals*). I thank Dr. Rose Vasta for her contributions in elucidating the nature of selected therapeutic response modes. Completion of the text was facilitated by the word processing assistance of Janice Pride and the editorial services of Bonnie Lawhorn.

Introduction: Managing Care in the Current Context for Health Care Delivery

The healthcare system's new tools will permit it to transfer both power and moral responsibility to families and individuals to manage their own health more effectively.

Jeff C. Goldsmith

CHAPTER OBJECTIVES

- Identify factors affecting the current delivery of health care in the United States.
- Discuss health-promotion models that may establish and maintain health for the largest numbers of individuals in need.
- Identify how self-care, community-based programs, and interdisciplinary coordination are needed in today's health care climate.
- Discuss models of client-provider communications and how these may reflect the current health care crisis.
- Identify typical stressors in client-provider relationships.
- Identify potential client responses to these stressors.

Powerful new tools emerging from the biotechnological revolution may soon render health care unrecognizable as we know it today. These changes will be felt in our methods of communicating with patients. Health care communications are expected to be, on the one hand, more focused and, frequently, less direct as episodes of care are managed on the outskirts of the provider-patient relationship. Still, care may be more comprehensive than ever before. The compelling push in the opposite direction for managing patients' wellness over time and the need to actively engage patients in health-promoting behaviors emphasize a holistic approach. Providers' needs for skills in engaging, persuading, and facilitating change will remain critical.

Emerging in this biotechnological revolution are two primary issues: How will care be delivered and what will be required of providers in these new delivery systems? How will communication between providers, clients, and families take shape? The first issue deals with health care delivery systems; the second, with the prevailing mode of interaction between provider and client.

Just what shapes health care and health care delivery systems and how these factors play a role in the evolution of health care in the United States will be addressed. A paradigm for viewing health care from a health-promotion model will be presented. Implications for provider-patient and provider-provider relationships and communications will be discussed. The role of communications in the provision of care will be examined and needs for commitment, caring, and partnership will be highlighted. This text is addressed with multiple health care disciplines in mind. The rigid boundaries that previously existed between professionals and professional training programs are no longer appropriate, and this text attempts to transcend assumptions of dissimilarity on such basic issues as patient-provider communications and therapeutic communications.

In this section of the text, the history of the American system of health care is briefly summarized. The current crisis in health care delivery is discussed in detail, enumerating the basis for needed health care reform. It is important to understand potential threats to patient-provider communications as system barriers to adequate health care. The prerequisites for therapeutic alliances today include reassurances that problems at the system level will not govern the character of interaction between patient and provider. Encounter conflicts surrounding the availability and sensitivity of providers reflect generic problems with health care delivery.

HEALTH CARE DELIVERY IN THE UNITED STATES—1600s TO 1990s

If we were to trace the evolution of health care in the United States from its inception in the early 1600s to today's system of health care delivery, we might first conclude that because of so many differences—then and now—any comparison of these periods is impossible. Nonetheless, with closer examination, we can perceive certain common threads along with many differences.

The evolution of health care delivery over the last 300 years is indeed significant. The health care system in the early colonial days (1620) was very different from the system we have today (1990s).

Factors Influencing Health Care Delivery Systems

Those who study trends in health care delivery usually identify at least four elements that account for the character of delivery systems through time. These elements are: (1) societal influences, (2) public health programs, (3) existing health problems, and (4) levels of technology. Forces impacting the evolution of systems of care in hospitals are depicted more specifically as: (1) advances in medical science, (2) the development of specialized technology, (3) the development of professional training, (4) the growth of health insurance, and (5) the role of government (Lewis 1994).

For example, if we took a trip back in time to the colonial period (roughly 1620–1781), we would observe several factors that would account for the direction of health care. Society in the colonial period reflected small agricultural communities. Trade was important and several port towns (Boston, New York, Charleston) were the chief points of entry for intercontinental trade. There were distinct health problems that reflected this social structure; epidemics were of concern and the port towns were seen as avenues for significant communicable diseases, e.g., yellow fever. Physicians and nurses were few but participated in initiating quarantine standards. The clergy played a significant role in caring for the ill, visiting patients and their families at home. Voluntary boards of concerned citizens were involved in public health concerns, but governmental involvement was negligible. Medical technology was insufficient to control health problems. However, ordinances were passed to control problems of sanitation, waste disposal, and public markets in the port towns.

In the 300 years that have ensued, vast changes in society and in health care make the problems and issues articulated above vastly outdated. Important social events such as the Civil War, and later, WWI and WWII influenced greatly what our health care delivery system became.

From the close of WWII through 1965, the delivery of care shifted dramatically to become the care of the infirm in hospitals. Urban areas became more prominent fixtures and rural areas shifted to large farms. Housing improved and immunizations continued to improve our ability to fend off disease—this time, polio. With acute problems and infectious diseases more under control, chronic diseases came to the forefront. Diseases such as arthritis, heart failure, asthma, and diabetes drew our attention. In 1950 the government made its first significant contribution to health care, investing $73 million in medical research. While hospitals tended to dominate the delivery system, community programs were staffed to help patients and their families cope with chronic illness; these agencies included public health department programs and visiting nurses' associations.

The Vietnam War, extending from 1964 through 1973, influenced not only our social-political structure but also the structure of our health care system. Prevention of chronic diseases was still important, but the realization that these diseases would not be eradicated without significant changes in the health habits of the population prevailed. Health promotion programs to control smoking, diet, and substance abuse were stressed. By 1985 there were a total of 6,872 hospitals; the majority (5,784) of them were designated short-term acute-care hospitals. The federal government administered a mere 343 hospitals, while state and local governments administered a little over 1600 of the hospitals. While acute-care hospitals predominated, long-term care and nursing-home facilities also existed but in much smaller numbers. Home health agencies continued to deliver care to the chronically and terminally ill patient in the home.

Changes occurring from 1984 to the 1990s reflect tremendous shifts in health care. Public health problems continue to include environmental threats, e.g., pollution, but health problems once defined as disease and injury have shifted to include societal problems. What were once considered society's problems—teen pregnancy, drug abuse, domestic violence—are now being classified as significant threats to our nation. Along with the continual focus on the maintenance of the quality of life of those with chronic illnesses and disabilities, an environment for healthy living has become increasingly critical to the effective management of health care problems.

Present Health Care Crisis

For most of this century, the American health care system has been organized around acute illnesses; the role of the health care system was to rescue us from these illnesses and take custody of us until we were well (Goldsmith 1992a, p. 19). In the last 15 years this focus has been significantly shaken by our ability to manage health care on an ambulatory basis. The travesty is that we have built a vast and costly apparatus around this acute-care focus. Thus, the fit between health care needs and health care services has worsened significantly.

While Americans may disagree about issues related to the social problems that face our nation—including violence, homelessness, drug abuse, and teen pregnancy—there is general consensus that these social problems both affect and reflect the state of our nation's health and will have a significant impact on the future ability of Americans to stay healthy.

Most Americans agree that the health care system that exists in the United States today needs to be reformed. Public opinion polls have shown that only a quarter of the American public has faith in the current delivery system to meet our nation's health care needs. Health care reform was one of the major issues of the 1990 Conference of Governors (Kaplan 1991). Health care reform was a major focal point in the 1992 presidential campaign. Legislators continue to study and search for solutions to needed reform and acknowledge three basic deficiencies in our health care system. These basic deficiencies or problems are: (1) affordability, (2) accessibility, and (3) accountability (Kaplan 1991).

Affordability

To understand the problem we face in affordability of health care in the United States, it is important to examine how the costs of health care have escalated and how they are predicted to soar over the next quarter of a century. In 1940 the nation spent $4 billion on health care. By 1950 these costs had tripled. Some estimates suggest that health care spending could reach three-quarters of a trillion dollars in 1992, and that 1990 expenditures are expected to triple by the turn of the century (Kaplan 1991). The present situation is characterized by restricted growth, limited resources, and regulating restrictions that shape our ability to deliver care. Before 1940 there were fewer than 40 types of health care providers. Today (1990s) there are over 200 different types of health care providers on record with the U.S. Department of Labor. As different providers enter the system and promise to control costs, they also threaten to create further fragmentation, duplication, and gaps in service.

What seems to be at the heart of the problem is the ability of insurance programs to deliver on the basis of need and recommended level of service. Those who pay for health care (frequently, employers) can no longer afford the same level of service formerly provided. The cost of care is exceedingly high in the United States. It is estimated that if some form of health care reform to reduce the costs of care does not occur in the United States, the economic viability of the United States will be significantly threatened in the twenty-first century.

Accessibility

The enormous costs of health care are only part of the problem, albeit, a very serious part. A second significant challenge is health care accessibility. Despite the enormous costs of care, our current system of health care delivery does not equally provide for everyone. It is estimated that on the average, approximately 32 to 38 million people in the United States are denied access to care because they lack insurance coverage annually (Short, Monheit, and Beauregard 1989; Short 1990).

Economists describing the problem of accessibility estimate that up to 38 million people may be uninsured despite the fact that the United States spends more of the Gross National Product (GNP) on health care than any other country in the world.

How can this be? Despite the fact that the American health care system is one of the most technically advanced in the world and so much is spent on health care, a substantial proportion of the population is locked out of the system. This problem is described as one of both the uninsured and underinsured. This, however, is not the only basis for the problem of access. Surely the lack of health care services in rural areas, and even in some urban areas, contributes to the problem of accessibility.

The first and extremely invalid assumption that the public makes is that these people are largely the unemployed. This assumption is incorrect. Those people who are locked out of health care are employed, often at very low wages, but the employers cannot afford the high costs of health insurance.

The problem is also not distributed over all groups. The elderly, for example, do not fall into this group. Since 1965, they have been covered under Medicare. Neither do the indigent. Medicaid provides coverage to the poor, blind, and disabled. Although Medicaid helps the indigent, the services provided under Medicaid are being curtailed, and fewer poor people are assisted.

It is alarming to realize what constitutes a Medicaid eligibility case, i.e., what constitutes "poor" under federal and state guidelines. "Poor," under Medicaid, is defined as 50 percent of poverty-level income. A family of three with an annual income of $5,800 is still too "rich" to receive assistance from Medicaid. Recognizing that this family's budget would include not more than $200 per month for housing, we can understand that fewer of the poor receive aid than we would anticipate. Under these conditions, if one were concerned about health, it would pay to be homeless.

The criticism around Medicaid has included arguments that some groups are favored over others, and the favoritism that exists may further enhance the nation's social problems. Consider, for example, teenage pregnancy. In 1980 the only way to obtain health insurance (through Medicaid) if you were poor was to become pregnant. Most states allow low-income families eligibility if those families support small children. The issue of inequities in the provision of services has become a political football more than once.

What appears to be the case, or at least the argument that many legislators give in citing the need for health care reform, is that health care is a *luxury*. This luxury is provided only to certain groups. And the luxury that does exist makes the absence of care appear even more unfair.

Accountability

The third and less frequently discussed issue surrounding health care delivery today is the problem of accountability. It is shocking to realize that despite the extremely large amounts of money expended for health care, we know relatively little about its outcomes. Is it effective? Is it even safe? And, is it efficient? (We already know that it is too costly!)

Can you imagine the Chrysler Corporation not knowing the quality of its product or IBM not improving on its products and services? Not very likely, you would say. Well, why does the health care industry not know what a successful product is or how much it should cost to deliver the best product to the most people?

The most difficult piece of evidence to explain is the great variability in health care provisions with the resultant outcomes being the same, or at least much the same. We observe variation in practices. For example, some patients are provided more tests, but they don't necessarily survive any longer than less-tested individuals with the same health care problem. For example, at a Veterans' Administration hospital in California, 40 percent of the patients received an angiogram following myocardial infarction (MI). Those MI patients in the same geographical region, but privately insured, were reported to receive angiograms 80 percent of the time. It was reported that there was no evidence to suggest that those who were treated more aggressively (with angiograms) were any better off, given the survival rates of these patients (Kaplan 1991). Other examples have shown that more frequent hospitalizations, or hospitalizations that cost more, are not more effective in prolonging life. We have even been shown the contrary, that certain medical intervention was not only unnecessary but could have put the patient at significant risk for other problems.

As absurd at it seems, especially in light of the high costs of care and the advancement in technology that has occurred, we cannot establish with more exactness what treatment yields what outcome.

Those who predict or try to influence the shape of health care reform usually recognize that any change that does occur will have to address all three elements—affordability, accessibility, and accountability—simultaneously. Most important, we are now not only faced with health care problems as we've known them for years, we are faced with a "sick" system as well. Altering the sick system will be as important as treating illness and promoting health.

A PARADIGM FOR ASSURING BETTER HEALTH TO LARGER NUMBERS AND EMERGENT DELIVERY SYSTEMS

The challenge of assuring better health to larger numbers of people raises several complex issues: What is health? How is it established and maintained? How is this objective met with the largest numbers of Americans?

Needs for Reform and Health-Promotion Models

Older notions of public health and individual entitlement tend to deemphasize the dynamics of several factors that affect the health status of most persons. A social ecological orientation to health considers the interaction of numerous social, political, and environmental as well as physical and emotional conditions that affect individuals' quality of life. At the risk of being too abstract, a paradigm that ensures better health to larger numbers includes all of these factors and affects and is affected by public policy.

A basic assumption behind such a paradigm is that health is a multifaceted phenomena encompassing emotional well-being, physical health, and social integration. It is a model that recognizes the interplay between individuals, families, and groups that are set within particular socioculturally defined fields. It is a model that views health and illness on a continuum and estimates years of health based on projections of life span. When years of health are the aim, the effect of medical treatment on everyday functioning and a person's quality of life must be evaluated. We should then be able to assess the particular impact of a drug or surgical procedure on the quality of life of the patients we see.

A critical departure in the adaptation of a health-promotion model is the adherence to concepts that are foreign to more traditional medical approaches. For example, the traditional medical model stresses pathophysiology. Specific disease processes, characteristic of both illness and injury, are judged in relation to body systems and specific clinical evidence, such as lab tests and blood pressure. Opinions about intervention based upon these clinical measures may produce different, even contradictory, conclusions. Medical interventions, for example, medications to lower blood cholesterol, aim to reduce death due to coronary heart disease. Biological models are used to justify this choice of treatment, and the model argues that there is a benefit to this treatment because it reduces deaths from coronary heart disease. Interestingly enough, in controlled experimental studies, the overall outcome—morbidity—for this group of patients (from all causes) is not affected. A clearer example of the problem of the traditional medical model becomes apparent when the issue is surgical intervention. The benefits of surgery are usually stressed without equal attention being given to the complications that can occur. In contrast, a quality-of-life health-promotion model will give significantly more weight to a variety of factors, including treatment benefits, estimates of the relative value of treatment versus no treatment, and side effects that occur in relation to the treatment chosen. Decisions about treatment become quite specific with clarification of what intervention is essential, very important, or only valuable to certain groups of individuals.

The Promotion of Self-Care and Community-Based Programs

The demand for inpatient care is predicted to decrease, not disappear. The U.S. hospital use rates, now the lowest in the world, will continue to decline from the low eight hundreds to the low six hundreds in days per thousand by the early part of the next century (Goldsmith 1992b, p. 40). Acute care will not remain the model for the American health system; the ultimate focus will be outside the hospital. Goldsmith (1992b) points out that planners and public health policy makers have come to realize that community-based systems, whether founded on a public health model or medical group practice (or some combination of the two) are the foundation for an effective new system of care. This model will stress health promotion and active participation on the part of patients who are no longer the passive recipients of health care.

An outcome associated with newer health-promotion models is the achievement of high levels of self-care capabilities among our citizens. Self-care refers to the actions performed by patients (or their significant others) directed at alleviating the effects of illness and its treatment. These actions, taken with the interest of protecting and promoting health and well-being, reflect many sociocultural interpretations that the patient places on his current illness and future goals. Self-care activities may differ from provider interventions in three ways. First, they may lack a scientific basis. Second, they reflect the specific knowledge and motivational resources of the patient. Third, they are directly related to the patient's formal connections (or lack of connections) with traditional medical care. One of the variables repeatedly cited in providing quality of care through health promotion is the character of the patient-provider relationship, particularly that between physician and patient. Features of this relationship that were associated with positive patient behaviors were: (1) the friendly and accepting attitude of the provider, (2) patients' perceptions that the physician had spent time with them, (3) patients' feelings that they had control in the interaction and input in their treatment programs, (4) patients' satisfaction with the care they received, (5) a treatment program that was actually tailored to them as individuals, (6) situations where patients felt that information was willingly shared with them, (7) absence of formal disagreement with patients, and (8) continuity of the specific provider-patient relationship. Although the largest proportion of these data focused specifically on patient-physician encounters, the conclusions have validity for encounters between other providers and patients.

It is clear from current projections of trends in health care source delivery that not only the patient will be instrumental in deciding the impact of health care reform, whole communities will shape the manner in which this care will be rendered. Less care will occur in acute-care hospitals, more care will occur in brief urgent-care centers. An increasingly significant proportion of the care of the very ill will occur in the home. Providers will be asked to assist in this transition. In truth, the American system has few alternatives; inpatient hospitalization is too costly and the advent of Diagnostic Related Groups (DRGs) no longer permits the extended hospital stays enjoyed a little more than a decade ago. The deinstitutionalization of health care delivery will characterize the major shifts in delivery systems in the next quarter of a century.

Managed Care and Interdisciplinary Collaboration

Adapting a health-promotion model of care has direct implications for the collaborative relationships of health providers.

If we endorse a broad concept of health and recognize the value of the quality of our patients' lives, we depart from tendencies to view patients through the narrow channel of disease or illness. Once open to health in the broader context, not just the absence of disease, we automatically recognize the importance of multiple health and human service providers. The overall goal—maintaining the patient's optimal level of health and increasing the patient's years of freedom from disease—forces us to think not only of formal approaches to cure and care administered by physicians, nurses, dentists, pharmacists, and many other providers, but we are also provoked to consider the multitude of alternative health care approaches and strategies that lie outside scientific medicine.

This health-promotion perspective emphasizes both the advantages and the appropriateness of multilevel interventions. Many of these interventions are complementary. Reducing stress, for example, can occur through meditation; it can also be impacted through medications. Others are synergistic, building on one another to produce the desired results.

What concept of interdisciplinary teamwork is appropriate? Under the old disease-oriented approach, providers were relegated to positions of importance with respect to their role in ridding individuals of disease. Physicians, under this model, are at the top of the hierarchy for several reasons. They, and no one else, have the authority to treat disease. In relation to other disciplines: they prescribe the medications that pharmacists will issue; they diagnose emotional disorders that legitimize psychological intervention; and they prescribe actions to be carried out by nursing professionals. Under this model, since disease is paramount in directing health care providers, physicians automatically assume the primary leadership role.

Managed care has been considered as a potential solution to containing health care costs, and at the same time, ensuring equitable care to all Americans. The managed care model is expected to be the prevailing form of health care delivery in the future. According to many providers, managed care of the ill will require, at the very minimum, multidisciplinary teams consisting of physicians, nurses, home care, and ambulatory care practitioners. Under managed care, the aim is to provide a range of services in such a way that these services and their costs will be scrutinized and controlled. Three basic managed care programs exist at present: health maintenance organizations (HMOs), preferred provider organizations (PPOs), and fee-for-service plans.

HMOs and PPOs have been criticized for their drawbacks. Despite the fact that they were designed to provide preventive health care services and to improve the continuity of quality of care, the results reveal problems. Healthier individuals are favored by managed care systems over those who are at high-risk, those who require high-cost procedures, and those who are chronically ill and need long-term care. Managed care has also been criticized for overlooking quality of care in order to meet the basic aim of cost-containment. Also, low-income populations are often not served by these plans.

Managed care systems and case management are being hailed as the primary solution to needed health care reform. Skills and knowledge that are necessary to function in these systems of care are being defined. The real and potential importance of effective communication skills is clear, particularly as they relate to health care assessments, disease management, and multidisciplinary collaboration. The outcomes of health care are clearly a reflection of the provider's command of effective communication skills and knowledge as they are executed in new roles.

Managed Care versus Case Management

Managed care is a system of managing and financing health care delivery to ensure that services are needed, are efficiently provided, and are appropriately priced. Through a variety of means, including preadmission certification, concurrent review of necessity of services, and financial incentives, managed care attempts to contain costs, ensure optimal patient outcomes, and maximize the efficient use of service utilization.

As previously indicated, managed care is one system of delivery that is proposed to correct the problems in health care delivery that were, and continue to be, out of control. Managed care is rapidly changing traditional approaches to health care. The managed care industry can be understood by segmenting the industry into three distinct options. These three options are (1) HMOs, (2) PPOs, and (3) fee-for-service plans that are managed through mandatory utilization review. In the very early 1990s it was estimated that by 1994, approximately 90 percent of those with health insurance would be enrolled in managed care plans. Thus, the entire managed care industry has grown, and will continue to grow, making traditional fee-for-service medical care outdated. This later system dominated the way care was delivered in the 1980s; in the 1990s it is the exception to the rule.

Frequently associated with the concept of managed care is the term *case management*. Although managed care and case management are sometimes used interchangeably, they refer to distinctly different phenomena (see Figure I–1). Managed care generally denotes the way care is structured for reimbursement. Case management, however, is a technique used to monitor and coordinate treatment, usually for specific diagnoses. Traditionally a utilization review process, case management means that care is closely monitored and coordinated particularly with regard to high-cost service-intense diagnoses. Case management includes activities of assessment, treatment planning, referral, and follow-up to ensure that comprehensive and continuous services are provided. Case management oversees reimbursement for care in that it ensures that the coordinated payment and reimbursement of services is properly executed.

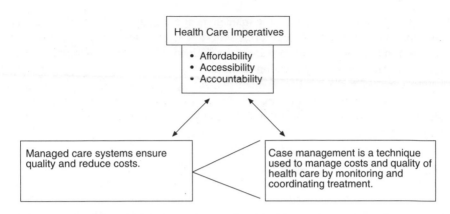

Figure I–1 Needs for Health Care Reform and Managed Care Systems

The emergence of managed care is congruent with case management since both aim to ensure quality and control costs. Managed care systems have been widely endorsed as necessary options in health care reform. The goals of these organizations—to ensure maximum value from resources—is congruent with the basic philosophy of health care professionals (Hicks, Stallmeyer, and Coleman 1992). This philosophy holds in high esteem a focus on the total needs of an individual, not just on the disease process and on maintaining health to minimize the need of future expensive health care intervention.

Underlying Problems and Issues with Managed Care and Case Management

Health care reform is not new and different; reform can be traced back in time to the health initiatives of President John F. Kennedy's New Frontier and President Lyndon B. Johnson's Great Society. Because health care reform spans several decades, we can safely conclude that reform in the United States is a continuous process.

Managed care, though, has come under severe criticism. Primarily, this criticism is leveled at the premise that accessibility, affordability, and accountability in health care is realistic. Some providers claim that addressing any one of those three elements will inevitably compromise another (Kissick 1994). Choices need to be made, and these choices may preclude the possibility of simultaneous significant improvement in all areas.

Managed care is not altogether new but neither is case management. Case management is not new to our concept of professional practice because disease management has been a familiar approach of providers in their caregiver roles. Controlling costs is also not a unique idea, since providers have been historically motivated toward this aim. Case management, though, has undergone wide criticism. The case manager is sometimes viewed as an extension of an already extensive bureaucratic system, adding yet another layer to the health care delivery system. It is felt that quality of health should be provided and managed by health care professionals. The reliance on those other than health care professionals, particularly clerks in insurance offices who in some cases decide treatment options, defies our ability to ensure quality.

These issues have generated a great deal of debate. There are three areas of debate. (1) What professional is best suited to be a case manager? (2) What added expertise is needed to function in this role? (3) What approach is best suited to execute the role with arguments for and against direct contact versus telephone triaging of patients.

In part, concerns about case management have surfaced because of the rapid proliferation of case management systems. The current managed care industry is criticized because it is felt that case managers were needed before adequate planning for their preparation could occur. Essentially, the professionals managing care may not have the expertise to execute their roles. No real data, however, is available to judge the quality of care under case management. While data about patients' responses to case management is limited, patients are said to value the system because it eases their burden in managing their own care.

Shifts in Care Delivery

In keeping with the need for health care reform and the methods used to secure access, affordability, and accountability, certain predictable trends are shaping health care. These trends have particular implications for provider encounters with patients and their families.

Community Ambulatory Care

Diminishing hospital use and vast expansion of ambulatory care are occurring. Health promotion and disease prevention—high-priority aims in health care reform—are achieved largely in community ambulatory care settings.

Health Futures, Inc., (reported in Goldsmith 1992b) reveals U.S. health care system changes in the year 2002. These changes include: (1) the declining use of inpatient hospitalization in general (as much as a 20–30 percent decline by 2002); (2) the declining use of inpatient hospitalization among the elderly (as much as a 40–50 percent decline by 2002); (3) the increasing use of managed care among publicly funded health programs (an increase of 50 percent); (4) the decreasing length of stay for patients receiving transplants (a decrease of 70 percent); (5) the declining surgical rates (age adjusted); and (6) the declining cancer death rates.

Additionally, it is predicted that ambulatory surgery will account for 85 percent of all surgeries.

Disease Management

These predicted shifts in the focus of care clearly indicate that the majority of services will occur in the community ambulatory care setting. This does not, however, mean that disease in no longer a concern. A new term, *disease management*, describes a community approach to treating chronic conditions. Diseases such as HIV and other chronic, severely debilitating conditions are examples. The care processes of disease management include prevention and health promotion. Early identification of disease; assessment of problems secondary to disease; and development, implementation, and evaluation of a plan of care are encompassed in this approach to disease management (Wolfe 1995).

Disease management consists of taking a single problem such as AIDS, cancer, diabetes, and cardiac and psychiatric conditions (conditions known to be chronic) and applying regular interventions for consistent outcomes. Early identification is critical to patients who can benefit from early detection. The individual's unique needs are understood to be an essential part of assessing the problem as well as developing care plans. In plan development, the protocol for care is based on defined medical practices that promote health rather than those that simply treat disease. The plan is put into action using health-promotion strategies prior to such anticipated periods and routine illness treatment. Plan evaluation occurs regularly but is not confined to measures of treatment. Rather, evaluation also includes measures of the level of health maintained over time.

Interdisciplinary Collaboration and Consultation

Interdisciplinary collaboration and consultation are necessities of both managed care and case management. To develop and implement successful managed care approaches, support from key participants—administrators, physicians, nurses, and other health care providers—is required. The ability to work with other individuals on a continuous basis is essential to the success of case management. Case management within hospitals requires consultation with finance personnel, administrators, and various providers, for example, dietitians, physicians, social workers, physical therapists, and nurses, to obtain relevant information about potential problems. The idea is to collaborate with many in order to design strategies for solving problems. Ideally, case managers are professionals—nurses or physicians. These professionals communicate with provider groups to identify problems, plan strategies, and evaluate progress within patient care critical pathways as well as to evaluate the overall impact of these actions. Within case management, therapeutic relationships with patients and families are important. Case managers rely on those relationships to derive mutually acceptable outcomes.

Consultation with patients and families and the development of a collaborative relationship with these individuals is said to be as important as the collaboration and consultation that occurs within colleague relationships.

THE SKILLS AND KNOWLEDGE OF PROVIDERS IN A MANAGED CARE ENVIRONMENT

Generic to All Providers

The skills and knowledge that are necessary for providers who work in managed care environments are defined in part by the expected outcomes of managed care and case management approaches.

Managed care includes a commitment to reduce cost, make services accessible, and control and monitor quality. Managed care should: (1) positively impact the cost of service, (2) improve provider consultation and communication, (3) engage other key providers in participating in care planning, and (4) improve continuous quality improvement through the design of critical-care pathways.

Additionally, patients should be positively affected in that their care is coordinated for them and that there is a reduction in unpredictable outcomes. Thus, they should be more knowledgeable and better prepared to understand and collaborate in their care.

Although there are a variety of case management models, common to all are the following service components:

- client identification and outreach
- individual client assessment and diagnosis
- service planning and resource identification
- linking clients to needed services
- actual service implementation and coordination
- monitoring service delivery activities
- patient advocacy to reduce problems of access to care
- evaluation of these activities and their expected outcomes (Allred et al. 1995).

To accomplish these goals, providers need to function as both multidisciplinary and multiservice integrators. Integrators operate at the hub of the wheel as they bring together and coordinate broad-based services.

Specific to Case Manager Roles

Case managers in managed care organizations steer, guide, and track patients through a variety of care activities, thus enhancing continuity of care. A major instrument in this tracking process is the critical-pathway analysis imbedded in the patient's plan of care. Critical pathways and critical-path tools were so coded based on the Critical Path Method, a part of the Program Evaluation Review Technique (PERT) developed by the United States Navy and Lockheed Aircraft Corporation.

The patient-care plans that are developed identify a "critical pathway" of key events (activities and interventions) that must occur as projected if the desired patient outcomes are to be achieved within a specified time period. The case manager oversees these pathways and facilitates interventions to ensure that patients progress appropriately and satisfactorily. The coordination and collaborative consultation that occurs requires skillful assessment and negotiation.

The specific facets of the case manager role have been detailed in the literature. A thorough account of this role for nurses is presented by Hicks et al. (1992). Patient advocacy, patient education, resource and risk management, benefits interpretation, and provider liaison are all aspects of this role.

Communication and Managed Care

Exploring the issue of the importance of communication skills and knowledge to providers in managed care environments is somewhat like discussing the need for eyes in order to see. Most providers would not argue either the relevance or importance of these skills and knowledge. The issue is rather what communication skills and knowledge are needed. In this text dimensions of the phenomena of human communication and more specifically, health care communication, are explored in depth. Essentially every provider needs a foundation in the basic anatomy and physiology of communication. Providers need to know the variables that effect reception, processing, and expression. They also need to understand the multicultural context in which communication occurs. Providers deliver health care services, all of which—disease prevention, health promotion, health screening, and health education—require foundations in therapeutic communications. Therapeutic response modes are needed not just to successfully assess individuals and families, they are needed to manage care and to increase client awareness and capacity for personal health management and self-care. Specialized knowledge and skill are needed to relate effectively in these capacities when crisis or prolonged chronic illness are the subjects of health care management. To participate fully in interdisciplinary managed health care teams that are collaborating with other providers and patients and their families, knowledge of the dynamics of group- and family-communication patterns is required. Communicating effectively with all relevant constituencies—patients, providers, and regulatory agencies—calls for effective negotiation skills. Finally, the ethical precepts of communicating in managed care, particularly in regard to patients' rights to informed choice and informed consent, must serve to critically guide our practice in these emerging models that now dominate health care delivery.

The Shape of Provider-Client Communications in the Era of Managed Care

The patient-consumer is generally well-aware of all the problems facing health care delivery today. They recognize the need for reform not only at the macro level, for example, in inequitable access of service but also at the micro level in the moment-to-moment encounters between themselves and their providers. Problems at the macro level will affect those at the micro level. Left untreated, problems at the micro level also have particular consequences for macro health-delivery systems. The problem of access and affordability will influence the quality of the encounters of patients with providers. Additionally, insensitive cavalier treatment of patients at the encounter level, particularly if practiced systematically, will influence the quality of care at the macro level.

Patient Stressors Related to Communicating with Providers

Patient dissatisfaction with providers has a substantial history. Consistent themes that emanate from these complaints include lack of human warmth, failure to demonstrate real caring or concern, failure to inform them about their care, and unprofessional conduct. Many patients change providers on these bases, regardless of how knowledgeable and skilled the provider, or how prestigious the health care institution. Patients are also critical of inpatient care.

In a detailed survey of the stressors that inpatients experienced with hospital care, van Servellen (1986–1988) highlighted several themes. These related to (1) lack of caring, (2) poor exchange of information, (3) absence of communication about responsibility for caring, (4) fear of retaliation if providers are burdened with unnecessary requests, and (5) observations of unprofessional conduct that raise serious concerns for patients. These concerns reflect patients' verbatim remarks in Exhibit I–1.

After surveying this list of patient statements, it is clear that the technical quality of the care received is not the primary focus of patients' dissatisfaction. Rather, the way in which care is provided is the issue. There is a great deal of literature to support the importance of provider interpersonal communication (Del Mar 1994). A good many of these complaints depict feelings of depersonalization that are exaggerated by poor communication. A lack of privacy; a sense of physical "imprisonment"; and a loss of personal power, identity, and dignity will always be exaggerated when the communication between staff and patients or between staff and patients' families is poor.

Exhibit I–1 Patients' Descriptions of Difficulties in Communicating with Providers in Inpatient Settings: Verbatim and Implied Reactions

---

"Having to tell my story over again."

Please save me the energy and humiliation.

"Not having doctors get together on their opinions—each one telling me something different."

If my doctors are not together, how can I trust what they do?

"The RNs, doctors, and physical therapists communicate poorly (to one another) . . . and they do not follow-up on the information they give."

Do they think I don't notice this and worry?

What is difficult is "wanting to speak to someone who really cares (and not having anyone)."

I'm lonely and isolated, somebody recognize me.

"I get frustrated, irritated when nurses are not able to respond because they are 'overwhelmed.'"

What is their work if it isn't to care for me?

"When nurses say, 'I'll be back in 5 minutes' and don't come back at all or it takes a long time."

How can I trust what they say to me?

"Having nurses lie to me (e.g., about not having blankets)."

What can I really believe?

"The nurses didn't involve my family (in discharge planning)."

My family needs support and counseling—I'm afraid they won't get it.

"I rarely ask for a nurse unless I really need one—nurses don't come when you call them—I ask the nurse for minor things and don't get them."

Will I always know when I need a nurse?

"I don't know what is expected of me— I don't want to be a bother."

If I ask them what is expected will I bother them?

"Night nurses don't answer call lights."

Sometimes I wonder if there really is someone out there behind the door.

"I'm beginning to feel like an inmate— not a patient . . . staff are more concerned about hospital procedures than patient needs."

I feel locked up, punished by the way they treat me.

"People are nonentities—I feel like a prisoner, alone in my room."

Nonentities are not entitled to anything.

"People come into your room without permission." "People come in and don't identify themselves. I feel like a guinea pig."

How can I tell if they should be here or not, what they're going to do to me?

"Some nurses are more professional than others—some bring their problems to work. Their attitudes are reflected in their work . . . causes you to wonder if they really care about you. You feel dependent and worry if they really care. You feel helpless."

If they can be both professional and unprofessional, how can I make sure I get the professional one?

"When I ask one member of the medical team a question, he *always* answers, 'You'll have to ask Dr. D.'—don't get information when I want it."

Does he know the answer—why is he withholding it?

continues

Exhibit I–1 continued

"(Staff) were not present to support my wife with the stress she is experiencing due to my illness."

I don't think they realize how she must feel.

"Medical students who don't know what they are doing—come in at 2:00 A.M. to take my blood, drops equipment, says 'my resident/teacher will probably tell me to go back and try it again.'"

Are medical students given experiences they can do right?

"(I worry about) morale and high turnover. I don't want to worry about my care—but some nurses work two or three shifts in a row."

How can they be up to speed? Will I suffer because of this?

"Lack of communication between doctors, hospital, and volunteers. More competition than cooperation." "Too many different doctors and nurses are involved in my care . . . I worry that they might not be communicating . . . that orders from one doctor might conflict with orders from another." "It is very bothersome when I have to fill a doctor in on the aspects of my care."

What would happen if I wasn't able to monitor my own care?

"Not always understanding doctor's answers to my questions, I ask a question and get a nonanswer for an answer. I am supposed to be satisfied with that!"

Do they think they are really helping by treating me that way?

"When you push the call light and the nurse doesn't come—a volunteer comes instead. This happened with my roommate: My roommate yelled all night for the nurse."

What does it take to get a nurse?

"I've tried to get a vegetarian diet. I'm still getting a regular diet despite five days of asking for a change, talking to the dietitian, etc."

I can't get through to them no matter what.

"The nurses do not think about how it must feel to be a patient."

They are insensitive to my needs.

"I'm afraid my doctor is not telling me the truth (cancer diagnosis)."

I can't trust what he says.

"The nurse got mad when I told her I couldn't take my pill with water."

Why is she mad at me? Doesn't this ever happen with other patients?

"There is really only one nurse who takes the time to talk to me."

I must make sure I get that nurse.

"Not having answers about why I'm sick."

Do they know and are just not telling me?

"Too many different nurses; hard to form a relationship with a nurse—causes you to hesitate to open up and confide (in them)." "Doctors not knowing what's wrong with me—not taking my symptoms (diarrhea) seriously."

My communications don't count. I don't count.

Patient Response to Deficiencies in Patient-Provider Relationships

Patients have a vote in the treatment they receive. They react, and those reactions are well-known to providers, particularly those in the private sector. Four major ways in which patients express dissatisfaction, and even retaliate, are in their refusal to pay bills, in their filing malpractice suits, in their resorting to less-expensive alternative health care options, and in their lack of compliance with prescribed regimens.

Providers in the private sector may lose a substantial amount of income because patients either refuse to pay their bills at all or only pay partially. It may be that providers who have fewer problems with collections also are the best at managing communications with their patients. This is not to imply that providers should pay attention to their communications with patients because they collect more money. Rather, it is poor communication that is one explanation for patients' refusals to pay their medical bills.

Malpractice suits have increased substantially in the last quarter of the century, causing malpractice insurance rates to reach astronomical heights. What has been observed repeatedly is that the basis for these claims may not be technical error at all. Rather, factors present in the provider-patient (physician-patient) relationship underlie the discontent that stimulates a patient to sue. The breakdown in the patient-physician relationship may indeed be the major provocation for these malpractice suits. Unfortunately, providers tend to arm themselves with defenses that have little to do with whether they will be sued. Ordering additional diagnostic tests is a defensive response but will not affect the character of the patient-provider relationship. Most certainly, however, a reliable outcome of this kind of defensive response is an increase in medical care costs.

Patients also "vote" by changing providers. Sometimes these shifts are to less-reputable health care providers or programs. While they may display inadequate technical competence, they do assure the patient the humanistic aspects of care these patients were searching for. The psychological aspect is the driving force. Patients draw a sharp comparison between the personal attention they receive in the alternative approach and the lack of attention that they received in traditional medicine. It is quite clear that the impersonal treatment that they initially received in reputable physicians' offices, clinics, and teaching-research settings falls short.

One solution to the problem of inadequate patient-provider relationships is improved relationships and responsive communications. Patients who enter into good relationships with providers will not only be more satisfied, they will generally be more cooperative and take more responsibility for their care. In turn, the provider will be more effective, achieve better treatment results, and consequently experience greater satisfaction. The practice of good interpersonal communications, more than ever before, should be viewed in light of patient outcomes. If providers' communication and interpersonal skills improve patient compliance and patients' abilities to cope with and recover from illnesses and injuries, then the need for communication-skills training becomes imperative. Research on patient satisfaction has shown that providers lack important communication skills despite the fact that these skills are valued and are linked to successful patient (treatment) outcomes. We would be remiss if we neglected that part of the current health care delivery crisis that reflects our own one-to-one encounters with our patients. Under the current health care climate, our ability to relate effectively with our patients, patients' families, and our colleagues will make a difference.

CONCLUSION

In summary, vast changes have occurred in the American health care system over the last 300 years. These changes have reflected many factors, including the advancement of medical technology, the American social structure, and the threats to health that have plagued us over time. With a seemingly unwavering belief in the American system of health care, the American dream became one that included absence of disease and, if that was not possible, remarkable chances of recovery from extraordinary debilitating conditions. This American dream is quickly becoming a significant nightmare as we attempt to assure all Americans of the privilege of health and absence of disease. Recognizing our goals and concomitantly restructuring our delivery systems while containing costs is the challenge for health care reform.

Affordability, accessibility, and accountability are major recurrent system barriers to the delivery of effective health care services. They are not isolated problems; they impact providers' one-to-one encounters with patients. Patients' reactions to providers reflect their fears and concerns that basic health care is costly, may not always prove adequate, and is frequently administered by a nonresponsive system. These fears and concerns are translated into communication difficulties where patients mistrust providers' intentions and the system as a whole.

Attitudes of mistrust and fear of neglect, if they do exist among patients, are not without basis in reality. Previously, they may have been described as an anticipated set of concerns felt by most patients but without much substance. Still, there is a new context for patient anxiety and it can hardly be ignored. Thus, it becomes even more imperative that providers be guided by sound principles of interpersonal communication.

Health care reform will include new goals for health promotion where patients fulfill certain self-care behaviors never before expected of them. Reform will occur outside the hospital, in neighborhoods, and in community settings. It will require new concepts of interdisciplinary collaboration. Finally, it will require a growing sensitivity and awareness of patient-provider encounters that work and do not work. Certainly the trust, confidence, and security that providers evoke in their encounters—an element of professional practice always held in high esteem—will play a critical role in the reform that takes place at the system level. To this end, the parameters of good interpersonal communications is the "handbook" for all health professionals. Provider-client communications are both a determinant and a byproduct of successful health care delivery.

PART I

Theoretical Foundations for Understanding Communications

There is much to know about the phenomena of communication. Interpersonal communication is one of the most important of the basic life skills (Gazda, Childers, and Walters 1982). Effective interpersonal communication skills are said to be the gateway to the development of other important life skills. Successful professional role development depends on our grasp of communication principles and concepts. In no other profession are interpersonal communication skills more important than in the health profession. As such, they have been studied extensively. Knowing which communications promote health behaviors is basic to provider role development. But, there are principles and concepts of communication that are even more generic and critical to patient-provider relationships.

Chapter 1, Principles of Human Communication, addresses the "anatomy" and "physiology" of human communications. The sensory modalities, information processing functions of the brain, and the role of memory and concentration are reviewed. The verbal and nonverbal dimensions of communications; the meta-communicative value of messages; and the basis for deficits in perception, processing, and transmittal of messages are discussed.

Chapter 2, The Nature of Therapeutic Communications, addresses the inevitable consequence that provider communications can either be therapeutic or nontherapeutic. How to distinguish between these phenomena, enlisting therapeutic response modes and resisting nontherapeutic responses, is addressed. Therapeutic and nontherapeutic response modes have either helpful or deleterious outcomes; the rationale behind certain therapeutic response modes is presented.

Chapter 3, Cultural Differences and Communication, discusses the process of effectively communicating in cross-cultural contexts. In this chapter the importance of cultural competence is stressed. Examples of specific responses are discussed as they carry different interpretations across groups. Communication fluency across groups is presented as a continuum; cultural incompetency being the negative end of the spectrum and cultural competence, the valued opposite end of the spectrum.

It is not necessary to deliberate very long about the importance of communication to our roles as providers. What providers generally do not comprehend is that communication is a science as well as an art. It is inconceivable that any text on applied communications would ignore the basic principles that have been culled from years of study of human communication.

CHAPTER 1

Principles of Human Communication

It is obvious that communication is a conditio sine quo non of human life and social order. It is equally obvious that from the beginning of his (her) existence a human being is involved in the complex process of acquiring the rules of communication, with only minimal awareness of what this body of rules, this calculus of communication, consists of.

Paul Watzlawick, Janet H. Beavin, and Don D. Jackson

CHAPTER OBJECTIVES

- Identify and describe the sensory modalities.
- Describe the process of sensory awareness and sensory receptivity.
- Describe how the sensory modalities transmit messages to the brain.
- Describe ways in which perceptions affect the emotional experience of individuals.
- Describe how learning is a stimulus-processing activity.
- Discuss the function or utility value of interpersonal communication.
- Discuss ways in which communication is an outcome of interpersonal processes.
- Discuss the principle of the multidimensionality of communication, i.e., the levels of communication.
- Describe how human communication is inevitable.
- Identify how punctuation functions in the delivery of interpersonal messages.
- Discuss how interpersonal communication may be either symmetrical or complementary.

Human communication is the product of a combination of numerous physiological, psychological, and environmental influences. Patterns of communication are indeed difficult to understand without knowing the origins and intricacies of communication in their relationship to neurological functioning—particularly

---

Note: Portions of this chapter were reprinted from G.M. Gazda, W.C. Childers, and R.P. Walters, *Interpersonal Communication*, pp. 21–37, © 1982, Aspen Publishers, Inc.

the workings of the central nervous system but also the dynamics of communication in the interpersonal context.

Several principles and concepts of human communication increase our knowledge of this high-level capability. From the standpoint of biophysiology, these include how sensory reception of information occurs, the basis for distortions of sensory experience, the processing function of the brain, and sensory and feedback mechanisms and learning. Axioms of human communication that address the origins of communication in interpersonal interactions will also be discussed.

SENSORY AWARENESS AND SENSORY RECEPTIVITY

The Sensory Modalities

Recognition that sensory awareness and sensory processing is critical to understanding human communication leads us to consider basic concepts and principles about sensory modalities. While all senses play a role, the most salient sensory modalities to a complete understanding of human communication are the visual, auditory, and kinesthetic. Some individuals are particularly adept with the use of one modality, i.e., are better at picking up visual rather than auditory clues; others are multimodal, exhibiting strength in more than one modality.

Studies of the relative strength of one modality over another suggest that age and maturation influence whether individuals are strong in only one modality or have mixed modality strength (Gazda, Childers, and Walters, 1982). The debate continues with some researchers declaring adults to be primarily visually oriented versus their being multimodal.

Goldman (1967) conducted a well-designed experimental study comparing individual preferences for a sensory modality: visual, auditory, or haptic (defined as a combination of kinesthesis, pressure, and tactile sensation). He concluded that adults, as well as first and third grade children, preferred an auditory modality; the adults chose the visual over the haptic; the children were equally divided between the visual and the haptic.

More recently, children have shown a developmental sequence of modality strengths (Barbe and Milone 1980). In the early grades, children have more well-defined strengths and tend to be auditory rather than visual or kinesthetic. As they progress through elementary school, their modalities become mixed and interdependent, shifting toward the visual and kinesthetic. By adulthood, many people have mixed-modality strength. Other researchers, however, have implied that vision is the dominant modality of the species (MacLean 1973).

Of course, in the process of communication all modalities work together to influence self-expression and understanding of the environment. A clear delineation of the strength or weaknesses within a given person may be difficult to establish.

Still, researchers, particularly educators, are interested in the issue of modality variability and dominant modality in hopes of being able to predict patterns of communication and patterns of problem solving.

Perhaps one of the most misunderstood aspects of sensory awareness is the assumption that the purpose of our sensory apparatus is to give us complete information about all the stimuli in our environment. In truth, our sensory capabilities are *not* designed to give us information in this way; the major purpose is to give us a very select range of feedback that is most useful to us. From studies of nonhumans, for example, bees and other insects as well as bats, we know that some sights and sounds that are perceived by other species are not available to us. And, like many animal species, humans tend to be sensitive to only a certain range of stimuli, the stimuli most useful to their way of life. What distinguishes humans from other species is that humans can generally access a wider range of stimuli.

Even humans, however, have been shown to have selective perceptual abilities despite the fact they may have a broader range. For example, we can taste the sweetness in certain foods and the bitter taste of some poisons (at low concentrations), but we fail to be able to discern other tastes that are neither harmful nor helpful. Our sense of smell is highly attuned to many gases but insensitive to others such as nitrogen. In short, our capacity to perceive through our senses is biologically regulated, and these capacities are largely determined by the information that would be most helpful to us.

This principle of utility also applies to how and why we become selective throughout our lives. Consider for a minute the infant's capacity to perceive separation from a nurturing figure. While other stimuli are not meaningful, distance or nearness of the nurturing figure is critical to the infant. Our training and occupations can also influence our perceptual range. Law-enforcement professionals are keenly aware of and even exceedingly perceptive about certain environmental threats. These capacities are not inherent in others; however, repeated exposures to life-threatening conditions reinforce the need to accurately and quickly perceive environmental clues that may suggest danger.

Another important example of selective perception among groups of humans is that of pain. We know that the sensation of pain has strong motivational properties. In general, pain is to be avoided. Still, the perceived intensity of pain varies a great deal. We know that pain stimuli can be the same, yet they affect people differently. We also know from observations of athletes that serious injuries may be experienced with little pain. There are still other people who report extreme levels of pain when the injury or illness does not seem to justify it. We also know that the same pain stimuli will be perceived differently by the same person, depending on time and context, even when the stimulus for pain has not changed at all. We also know that health care professionals can manipulate patients' experiences of pain by changing patients' perceptions of the stimuli. When dentists say to a patient, "You're doing fine—just a little more (drilling)," they are manipulating the patient's perception of the character of the stimuli. The suggestion is that the pain will subside and the patient will experience relief; this suggestion affects the patient's perception of whether the pain stimulus is overwhelming. Understanding that the pain is not out of control enables the patient to relax. Relaxation reduces the negative experience of the pain.

PROCESSING STIMULI AND THE BRAIN

Through the Sensory Modalities to the Brain

When physical energy such as light, sound, heat, or cold reaches the sense organs, it must be converted to a form that can be processed in the brain. The information processing that goes on within the brain has three distinct steps.

The first step is simply reception; reception is the absorption of physical energy. Transduction is the second step and refers to the conversion of physical energy to an electrochemical pattern in the neurons. Finally, coding takes place (Figure 1–1).

Coding is the one-to-one correspondence between some part of the physical stimulus and some aspect of the nervous system. For example, light rays that strike retinal receptors (reception) are converted due to a change in the receptors' membrane polarization (transduction). The resulting train of impulses in the optic nerve has a frequency that increases as the intensity of light increases. This is evidence of coding. It should be remembered that sensory information is coded so that the brain can process it, and, interestingly enough, may have little resemblance to the original stimuli. The idea that what is perceived is not exactly what actually is, is an extremely important principle of human communication. The proverb: "Believe half of what you see and nothing of what you hear" has some basis when we consider the fact that we always perceive selectively.

It is possible, for example, to create optical illusions. Optical illusions exist because what is perceived is actually different from what is actually there. One very common example of an optical illusion is provided in Figure 1–2. If one looks at one line with one eye and the other line with the other eye, the illusion is apparent. This optical illusion, the Müller-Lyer illusion, suggests that one line may be longer than the other; usually line B is reported to be longer than line A. In fact, these lines are of the same length. Various theories used to explain optical illusions generally agree that what causes optical illusions is within the brain, not within the sensory organ (eye).

The important principle to understand is that our perceptions are not the same thing as the stimuli that are picked up by our sensory receptors. When sensory information reaches the brain, higher and more complex processing takes place.

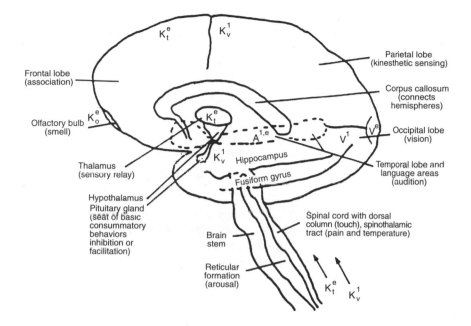

This medial aspect of the brain and spinal cord of the central nervous system includes a surface view of the temporal lobe, with language areas illustrated in dotted lines. Projection sites for receiving information through the sensory modalities are plotted with the following abbreviations:

$A^{1,e}$ = auditory input, both internal and external.

V^{e} = visual input in the occipital lobe, external.

V^{1} = visualization in the deeper striate layers of the occipital lobe or temporal lobe.

K_{o}^{e} = kinesthetic input from sense of smell, external.

K_{t}^{e} = kinesthetic input from touch, external. The nerve signals move up the spinal cord in the dorsal column, are relayed through the thalamus, and are projected to the sensory cortex of the parietal lobe.

K_{v}^{1} = kinesthetic input from pain and temperature, internal, visceral. The nerve signals move up the spinal cord in the spinothalamic tract, are processed in the hypothalamus, and are projected to the sensory cortex of the parietal lobe.

Source: Nancy A. Haynie, unpublished doctoral dissertation, 1981, reprinted with permission.

Figure 1–1 Medial View of Brain and Spinal Cord. *Source:* Reprinted from G.M. Gazda, W.C. Childers, and R.P. Walters, *Interpersonal Communication—A Handbook for Health Professionals*, p. 30, © 1982, Aspen Publishers, Inc.

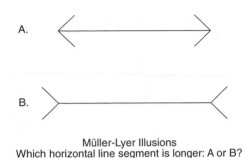

Müller-Lyer Illusions
Which horizontal line segment is longer: A or B?

Figure 1–2 Optical Illusions—Perceptions Are not Direct Reflections of Stimuli

The human brain is complex, consisting of neurons numbering in at least the tens of billions, with some estimates being at least 30 billion (Kalat 1988). These neurons are not haphazardly arranged; however, they are assembled in discrete areas of the brain and these areas have their own specialized function. Still, we have the experience of unity. Thus, although our brains are divided into many parts, each containing many neurons, our consciousness is as one. The unity of consciousness comes from the many connections between various brain parts.

The brain performs its information processing primarily in two domains. It is concerned with (1) language-related elements or the theoretical symbols and (2) thought-related elements or the qualitative symbols (Nullally 1977). Our processing the different types of symbols is dependent on functions that occur within the left and right hemispheres of the brain.

The theoretical symbols, such as visual-linguistic elements or the written word, auditory-linguistic elements or the spoken word, visual-quantitative elements or written numbers, and auditory quantitative elements or spoken numbers, are processed primarily in the left hemisphere of the brain. Qualitative symbols of a sensory nature such as sounds, taste, or visual pictures, are associated with cultural codes or the meanings that are received from observing nonverbal expressions. These symbols are processed primarily in the right side of the brain.

The bilateral symmetry of the brain provides that sights and sounds, which bring information in from the external environment, are processed by using both hemispheres together. The two hemispheres are connected by the corpus callosum for the transfer of information of different sensory modalities (Brodal 1981). In the normal brain, it appears that any information reaching one hemisphere is communicated regularly to the other, largely to corresponding regions.

Scientists and researchers have reported anatomical, physiological, and behavioral discoveries about the specialization of the cerebral hemispheres. Bakan (1971) discusses the directions of conjugate lateral eye movement (CLEM) and the inherent duality of human behavior and experience. The neurological pathways that come from the left side of both eyes (the left visual field) are represented in the right cerebral hemisphere and vice versa. Thus when parts of the left cerebral hemisphere are stimulated, the eyes move to the right; when parts of the right hemisphere are stimulated, the eyes shift to the left.

Day (1964) identified right-movers and left-movers—persons who tend to look to the right or left while reflecting, respectively. Right movement presumably activates the left cerebral hemisphere and its specialized functions that are verbal, analytic, digital, and objective. Left movement is presumed to activate the right cerebral hemisphere with its special functions that are preverbal, synthetic, analogic, and subjective.

Individuals tend to look up and away when a question has been posed and the answer must be retrieved (Gur 1975). Singer (1976) reports experimental research findings to support the conclusion that if an individual is involved primarily in attending to visual images and fantasies, the person is less likely to be accurate in detecting external visual cues. Similarly, if internal processing is primarily oriented around auditory fantasies, that is, imagined conversations or music, then the person is less likely to be accurate in detecting external auditory signals.

In both cases, the individual is better at detecting external cues in the modality other than the one in which the person is attending to internal images and fantasies. Such experiments suggest that a private internal image or fantasy in a given modality uses the same brain structures or pathways as does the processing of an external stimulus in that same modality.

Individuals look to the side or down to eliminate visual stimuli, especially the meaningful and reinforcing face of another person that might interfere with a train of thought. Dilts et al. (1979) in their book *Neurolinguistic Programming* illustrate the eye positions for visual, auditory, and kinesthetic accessing of information. Dilts identifies each eye position with its particular body posture, breathing pattern, and hemispheric specialization (see Figure 1–3).

The right movements of the eyes access the left hemisphere for constructed images (V_c), for visualization of novel and abstract patterns, or for constructed auditory (A_c), putting an idea into words. The eyes looking down and to the right access an awareness of body sensations (K_{vto}) and kinesthetic information, including the visceral, tactile, and olfactory. The left movements of the eyes access the right hemisphere for remembered images (V_r), for visualization of eidetic patterns from past experiences, or for remembered auditory experiences (A_r) and sounds and tape loops of messages from past activities. The eyes looking down and to the left are representative of an internal auditory dialogue (A_{id}), talking to oneself, probably in short cryptic commands and suggestions and simple sentence messages (see Figure 1–3).

The left cerebral hemisphere is associated with the development of speech and language. The temporal lobe is larger on the left side than on the right in about two-thirds of the brains examined (Geschwind and Levitsky 1968; Witelson and Pallie 1973). The left side is best developed in the brain of the fetus and newborn

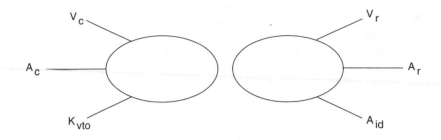

V_c V_r

A_c A_r

K_{vto} A_{id}

Figure 1–3 Eye Positions for Accessing Information. Visual accessing cues for a normally organized right-handed person: V_c = visual constructed; A_c = auditory constructed; K_{vto} = kinesthetic visceral, tactile, or olfactory; V_r = visual remembered; A_r = auditory remembered; A_{id} = auditory internal dialogue. *Source:* Adapted with permission from R.B. Dilts, J. Grinder, R. Bandler, J. DeLozier, and L. Cameron-Bandler, *Neurolinguistic Programming I,* © 1979, Meta Publications .

infants, suggesting that asymmetry does not result from environmental or developmental factors after birth.

Electrophysiological experiments using auditory (click) and visual (flash) stimuli were designed to measure the evoked responses in the brains of both adults and five-week-old infants (Wada 1977). The results show that auditory responses are significantly greater in the left hemisphere and visual in the right. It appears that the fundamental auditory neurocircuitry needed for the growth of speech and language is biologically and asymmetrically designed for its acquisition and development.

The right ear outperforms the left ear in hearing and identifying competing digits, a reflection of left-brain dominance for language (Kimura 1961). The right ear has better access to the left hemisphere because of the crossed auditory pathways. While the right ear connects directly to the left hemisphere (language area), the left ear's route to the same area first must go to the right hemisphere and then cross over to the left side and the language area. However, a clear left-ear advantage was found for all melodies and environmental sounds (Krashen 1977). The left ear has direct access to the right hemisphere, and the right brain is dominant for music, chords, and nonverbal sounds.

It is evident from studies with patients who have suffered brain damage to the right hemisphere that the right brain makes an important contribution to human performance, having functions complementary to those of the left hemisphere. The right side of the brain probably processes information differently from the left, relying more on visual imagery than on language and being more synthetic and holistic than analytical and sequential in handling data. The right hemisphere specializes in perceiving and remembering faces, unfamiliar and complex shapes for which there are no ready names, and drawings of incomplete gestalts in which part of the contour is missing. Its importance to spatial orientation and visuospatial relationships is well-documented. It also probably provides the neurological basis for the ability to take the fragmentary sensory information received and to construct from it a coherent concept of the spatial organization of the outside world— a sort of cognitive-spatial map by which individuals plan their actions (Nebes 1977).

Ordinarily, the left and right hemispheres exchange information when each hemisphere has access to the information that passed initially to the opposite hemisphere. All this occurs through the corpus callosum and several smaller bundles of fibers. What happens if the corpus callosum is injured? Clearly, any damage to the corpus callosum will result in impaired exchange of information. We know from those who have had surgery to interrupt severe epilepsy that epileptic seizures can be limited to only one side of the body. When seizures are so severe that they cannot be controlled by customary antiepileptic drug treatment, surgery has been performed to cut the corpus callosum. This results in preventing seizures from crossing from one hemisphere to another. Thus, when seizures occur, they are less severe because they affect only one side of the body. Interestingly enough, these surgeries have brought unexpected positive results because the seizures not only occur with less severity, they also occur less frequently.

The marvels of coordination between right and left hemispheres is also seen in other cases where split-brain phenomena has been observed. Observations of the roles of right and left hemispheres have led to many speculations: Is one sphere more important or more dominant? When it was first determined that the left hemisphere controls speech, the right sphere was viewed as subordinate. Its role was seen as one of support to the left sphere. Through further research, however, particularly with studies of patients whose corpus callosum was damaged (commonly referred to as split-brain patients), it became clear that the right hemisphere is capable of many more functions than was first thought. The right hemisphere does understand simple speech although it cannot control speech. It can also perform certain functions better than the left hemisphere, such as the control of emotional expression. It has been shown that after damage to the right hemisphere people not only have trouble forming facial expressions that depict emotions, but they also have trouble understanding others' emotions. Also, people who have suffered damage to the right hemisphere speak with less-than-normal amounts of inflection. The right hemisphere seems also to be specialized for complex visual and spatial tasks. It has been known for some time that people who have damaged their right hemisphere have difficulty finding their way from one place to another and have trouble recognizing faces.

Perceiving to Emoting

You have been asked to care for young children, 7 to 12 years of age, who, you have been told, possess inhuman destructive capabilities. They have superhuman powers and perceive themselves to be on an important mission. They have been placed on earth for the specific purpose of destroying the existing social structure so that a new system can be established. Their eyes are opaque; they have platinum hair, and they look characteristically alike. Although they have faces, they have no recognizable facial expressions. Do they have emotions?

The question is not whether they have emotional experiences similar to other humans, such as anger, happiness, or sadness. You cannot know what it feels like to be like them. Indeed, they may not have any conscious experience of feelings. You are looking for displayed behaviors that suggest that they have emotions. Emotion, for you, is defined as a temporary change in the intensity of behavior. Thus, if they attack another person and increase the intensity of their behavior to do this, they are showing emotion. Movement, which shows no change in intensity, is, for you, lacking emotion. You observe that they attack people, but the intensity of their movements stays the same. This scenario may sound like a script from a science fiction movie; still, the question is relevant: How do we know whether this group of children (or any human beings, for that matter) has feelings and emotions?

Emotion has been studied as a function of autonomic arousal. The intensity of behavior is largely governed by the functions of the autonomic nervous system. Within this large system, the sympathetic nervous system prepares the body for intense vigorous response while the parasympathetic system increases digestion and other responses associated with relaxation. The most compelling reason for the arousal of the parasympathetic system is frequently the removal of a stimulus that excited the sympathetic system. The example of people fainting after intense arousal illustrates this point. When something life threatening happens, for example, almost getting run over by a car, the sympathetic nervous system is excited. When the threatening stimulus is removed, a rebound effect, overactivity of the parasympathetic system, occurs. Thus, some people collapse or faint.

Reaction from the sympathetic nervous system occurs not only because of initial stimulus to the sympathetic system but also as a result of the individual's interpretation of the stimulus. This is why it is difficult to predict reactions when people perceive a threat or challenge. For example, predicting stress levels by simply counting stressful life events may be highly unreliable. More accurate measures are those that factor in a valence. For example, changing jobs is generally regarded as stressful. Just how stressful can vary a great deal from one person to another. Because of this we need the patient to tell us how he perceives it on a continuum from +7 (being extremely positive) to −7 (being extremely negative).

The power of individual interpretations of stimuli has also been shown and described in certain cognitive approaches to counseling. In the field of psychology, attribution theory suggests that stimuli or events are not only perceived to be negative but also judged to be global (affect many parts of one's life). Recurring or enduring stimuli produce feelings of hopelessness. Conversely, when these same events or stimuli are perceived as manageable, they elicit feelings of hopefulness. We know that the way in which stimuli or events are interpreted has a great deal to do with the way in which people respond. People who engage in actions of "mind over matter" are using their abilities to master challenges by reinterpreting the meanings of the stimuli. Making the stimuli less threatening is their way of modulating stress-related reactions. Thus, any given event or stimuli may produce a great deal of sympathetic nervous system arousal, a moderate amount, or very little. It depends on the individual's interpretation of the event.

For a long time it was thought that it was impossible to exert direct control over stress, including heart rate and other biologic processes affected by the autonomic nervous system. With the advent of biofeedback, it has been learned that people can control their responses to stress by progressively relaxing their skeletal muscles—as their muscles relax, their emotions become calmer. Voluntary control over responses like heart rate does not seem to be possible; however, indirect effects through the process of the progressive relaxation of skeletal muscles—e.g., with biofeedback—do seem to reduce stress and promote calmness.

Emotions and the expression of emotions depend largely on an area of the brain called the limbic system. MacLean (1970) used this concept to refer to this area of the brain; "limbic" comes from the Latin word *limbus,* which means "border." Parts or structures of the limbic system form a border around certain midline structures. The brain area most important for emotions and emotional expression, the limbic system, is a circuit that includes the amygdala, the hypothalamus, parts of the cerebral cortex, and several other structures.

MacLean (1973) identified this enlarged lobe as the connecting structure between the visual system and the limbic system of emotional behaviors. He suggests that the fusiform gyrus gives rise to the weepy feelings that people may experience upon witnessing an altruistic act:

> Primates, above all other animals, have developed a social sense which in man becomes conspicuous for its altruistic manifestations. As evidence that a charitable social sense is still in evolution we need only recall that the word *altruism* was coined as lately as 1853 by the philosopher Comte . . . and that the word *empathy* was introduced into our language by Lipps . . . about 1900. Altruism depends not only on feeling one's way into another person in the sense of empathy. It also involves the capacity to see with feeling into another person's situation. (p. 42)

Emotional behavior may be understood in part by studying the behaviors that are necessary for self-preservation and procreation. One list of such behaviors (modified from Denny and Ratner 1970) is resting, eliminating, water balance, thermo-regulation, feeding, aggressive-defensive behaviors, sexual behaviors, and care of the young. Animals, including humans, fulfill their basic needs in cycles that include an appetitive phase, a consuming phase, and a postconsuming phase (Denny and Ratner 1970). Feeding is an example of the process. Thomas (1981, p. 27) describes it this way:

> When individuals have not eaten for a time, they begin to be aroused and behaviors become directed toward acquiring food; this is the appetite phase. This phase continues and merges with the consummatory phase when food actually is eaten. Individuals then engage in behavior that terminates the feeding process (e.g., belching, going for a walk, etc.); this is the postconsummatory phase. Ordinarily, eating behavior is not thought of as particularly emotional, but it is possible to imagine situations where eating (or lack thereof) may be very emotional (e.g., lost in the woods).

Even under the most normal circumstances there is a rise and fall in body activities (brain, digestive system, senses of taste and smell, etc.). This cyclical rise and fall is referred to as facilitation or inhibition, respectively; emotional behavior may be represented as exceptional states of facilitation or inhibition. Each of the several basic consuming behaviors has its own normal range of arousal and may also show a range of overreaction (extreme facilitation) and underreaction (extreme inhibition). The language used to describe feelings and emotions usually refers to these extremes. Examples of inhibitory words for underreaction are *depressed*, *helpless*, *lonely*, and *discouraged*; facilitory words for overreaction are *excited*, *angry*, *panicked*, and *passionate*.

The limbic system is said to consist of the structures in the brain that are essential to emotion. It has been described as a response-modulation system on a continuum of inhibition to facilitation for consuming behaviors that meet physiological needs (McCleary 1966). The visual structures of the brain have connections to the limbic system in the prefrontal cortex and in the occipitotemporal lobe and the fusiform gyrus. There is evidence that these connections function to help individuals gain insight into the feelings of others—to see with feeling. MacLean (1962, p. 300) writes that in the complex organization of these evolving structures "we presumably have a neural ladder, a visionary ladder, for ascending from the most primitive sexual feeling to the highest level of altruistic sentiments."

MacLean (1973) also suggests that these large evolving territories of the brain may be incapable of being brought into full operation until the hormonal changes of adolescence occur. If this is so, it would weigh heavily against the claims of those who contend that the personality is fully developed and rigid by adolescence, if indeed not by the age of five or six.

Each individual learns to depend on one sensory system or another as a means of perceiving and understanding the world. This dependence on particular sensory modalities is characteristic of human beings and generates patterns of experience that differ between and within individuals.

All normal humans are endowed with essentially equivalent sensory organs and structures, both anatomically and physiologically. The neurological pathways and projection areas that serve the sensory mechanisms also are presumed to be similar in all human brains. Yet, despite the similar equipment, no two individuals understand a particular occurrence in exactly the same way because of the differences that are learned through selective attention to sensory input channels and with variations of experience with the senses (Bandler and Grinder 1975; Bateson 1972; Korzybski 1958).

"Selective attention to sensory input" means that at any one time individuals usually attend to (are conscious of) one, or possibly two, of their sensory channels, and their attention is limited to only seven "bits" of information. Miller (1956) reports that the span of absolute judgment and the span of immediate memory impose severe limitations on the amount of information people are able to receive, process, and remember.

"Bits" and "chunks" of information have been measured and quantified by several researchers to ascertain how much individuals can know at any one time. The number of bits of information (7 ± 2) is constant for the absolute judgment of inputs into one sensory channel. The number of chunks of information (also 7 ± 2) is also constant for immediate memory. Immediate memory is limited to 7 ± 2 chunks at any moment, but the number of bits that each chunk contains, up to 7 ± 2, can be increased simply by building larger and larger chunks, each chunk containing more information than before.

Since the bits are received through sensory channels, it is advantageous to attend primarily to the input from one critically important channel. The research indicates that the channel for making visual judgments is more accurate than those for auditory and gustatory judgments. However, each individual learns to depend on one sensory system or another as a means of perceiving the world and recoding an understanding of it into language and memory. Information from the other sensory systems may be ignored temporarily as irrelevant. This ability to focus attention in 7 ± 2 chunks protects the brain from the bombardment of too much information and a resulting state of confusion.

Learning from internal sensory representations includes how to pay attention to the feeling states of emotion, the visceral and proprioceptive cues for breathing and digestion, and the visual imageries of day and night dreams. Individuals "turning on" to their own bodies are knowing themselves through internal kinesthetic sensory information (K^i). People can pay selective attention periodically to the responses occurring in the deeper recesses of the brain. They can monitor the rise and fall of emotional responses connected with consuming acts, particularly aggressive-defensive or sexual behaviors. They can identify gut reactions and catching the breath as kinesthetic-sensory responses to stimuli. They can develop a facility for remembering night dreams and embroidering daydreams into useful visual information emanating from the deep internal gyruses of the brain (V^i). By "listening" to messages and melodies that are still being played on the internal auditory tape loops (A^i), individuals can learn how to erase any harmful or outdated messages and how to magnify the comforting and useful sounds.

So, one reason that individuals have different experiences despite similar genetic endowments of brain and body and despite similar environments is that characteristically each one attends to different aspects of the self and of the environment. "It is something like a cooking class. Since each of us selects some similar and some different ingredients in similar and varying proportions, we each end up with something different to put into the oven" (Gordon 1978, p. 215).

Several factors affect any one individual's attention and processing of stimuli. Some of these factors have been mentioned previously, including damage, injury, or even irritation such as that caused by epileptic seizures. However, both drugs and diet can have an effect as well, and because they can decrease the synthesis or release of serotonin, they are potentially mood-altering substances. This is one reason why drugs and diet are seriously considered when explanations of violent outbursts, anxiety, and the inability to experience pleasure are studied.

Learning: A Stimulus-Processing Activity

Sensory information taken into and processed by the brain may have long-lasting effects on individuals' behaviors. How do patients, for example, remember to take their medications on time? Once instructed, what process is responsible in making a patient take on this new behavior?

Many theories of learning have been put forth. Perhaps one of the most well-known is that by Pavlov. Ivan Pavlov discovered the theory of classical conditioning. He proposed that learning consists of transferring a reflex from one stimulus to another; in this way a stimulus that would normally elicit a response could be replaced with a new stimulus that would, in turn, elicit the same response. This theory, merely an inference, suggested that pairing a conditioned stimulus with the unconditioned stimulus caused the growth of a new or strengthened connection between a conditioned stimulus center in the brain and an unconditioned stimulus center in the brain. However, neither Pavlov nor his colleagues actually observed the growth of any connections in the brain.

Pavlov's theory, like those of many other theorists of the time, was oversimplistic in many ways. First, it presumed that learning about stimuli was not related to those stimuli, i.e., learning about tastes is the same as learning about temperatures. Second, the immediacy of the learning experience was viewed as important but was not examined in the context of the situation. It is known that certain learning, for example, regarding eating foods and getting sick, happens with a single instance. It does not take several trials to realize one should avoid this food. Also, learning to avoid the food that caused you to become sick can happen even if the taste of the food and illness are separated by short or long durations. In sum, learning can occur differently depending on what is to be learned.

It is generally believed that during learning some change must take place in the neurons in the brain. But, this change could take many forms, from the growth of a new axon, to new connections among neurons, to increased or decreased release of synaptic transmitters, and so on. And, it is generally believed that the mechanisms differ depending on the particular learning task. That is, the mechanisms are not the same for all instances of learning.

Despite the difficulties of discovering which mechanisms occur at the cellular level, one principle seems to hold true. Many stimuli rapidly (less than one second apart) received by a certain number of neurons in the hippocampus can change the property of neurons for weeks.

In summary, learning is often attributed to changes made over large areas of the nervous system. However, for certain tasks this is not true; learning is more circumspect, more localized in the brain. No matter how much of our brains participate in the process of learning, what is always required is change at the cellular level. For learning to occur, cells (neurons) must change their properties. Studies that address single-cell changes attribute changes to biochemical changes. Impaired learning is often associated, then, with chemical deficiencies in the brain. Theories of this kind have demonstrated that certain drugs might impair or improve learning through different biochemical processes. Studies of memory, for example, suggest that certain proteins must be synthesized. Some drugs and hormones have been shown to facilitate memory; and while the specific action is not known or well-understood, the biochemical transmission at synapses is the focus of attention.

As has been shown in this discussion of the biophysiologic dimensions of communication, several processes and structures are involved, ranging from small, molecular changes to larger regions of the brain and the entire central nervous system. These dynamics, in and of themselves, are exceedingly complex and are addressed in a great deal of depth in other discussions of brain topography and brain chemistry. The reader is encouraged to explore the fascinating world of neurophysiology and the progress that has occurred in understanding perception and learning. Neurolinguistics is a specialized science that studies how people receive information through the senses, process the information in neurons and neural pathways in the brain, and express the information in language and behaviors. Still to be described are the interpersonal and relationship principles of communications that come to us largely from the behavioral science fields.

INTERPERSONAL FOUNDATIONS FOR HUMAN COMMUNICATION

Communication has been said to be a *conditio sine quo non* of human life and social order (Watzlawick, Beavin, and Jackson 1967). Communication (see Figure 1–4) occurs on three levels—intrapersonal (or that which goes on within an individual), interpersonal (referring to that between individuals or within groups), and mass communication (that which is transmitted publicly).

It is also clear that from the beginning of our existence, we are not only refining our neurophysiological capacities to communicate, we are equally engaged in the process of acquiring the social rules of communication. Historically, much of what we know from science comes from the study of communication as a one-way phenomena. Knowledge of communication was largely gleaned from studies of speaker-to-listener communication; communication as a function of the process of interaction was virtually ignored. Now we operate with a much higher level of understanding about communication. We no longer think of communication singularly, as a single communicational unit or message. We think of communication as a series of messages (interaction) and as patterns of interaction (transactions). The principles and concepts presented in this discussion will address aspects of communication that are interpersonal and interactive.

Human communication is of two types: digital and analogic (Gazda et al. 1982). When we refer to something by name we are employing digital communication. The same object can also be described as a representation or likeness; this represents analogical communication. The following example may help us to differen-

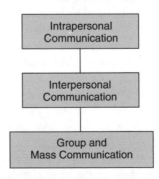

Figure 1–4 Human Communication Contexts—Within, Between, and Across People

tiate these two types. When we are visiting a foreign country and we listen to people speak, we may not understand any of the language. However, if we watch the people while they are speaking, for example, their intentional movements, we may understand at least some of what the communication is about. This latter form of communication, which often includes the nonverbal content, and the context of the interaction is analogic communication. Humans are the only species known to use both digital and analogic communication. Although we rely heavily on digital communication, there are times in which we rely almost exclusively on analogic communication. With messages that we perceive and send to define relationships, we predominantly use analogic communication. Some say that emotionally disturbed children and animals are keenly aware of analogic communication. The special intuition that these groups are believed to possess makes it very difficult to deceive them. Because we use and receive both types of communication, we are constantly translating from one to another. It is like having two languages—Spanish and French—and as sender or receiver having to flow between them. Our abilities to translate from one mode to another is vital. To talk about our relationships we must translate largely analogic data to the digital form, e.g., by choosing words to describe our feelings for another person. And, when we translate from the digital to the analogic we risk the loss of information that cannot be communicated symbolically.

The Principle of Function or Utility

As in the biological sciences, the study of communication in the social sciences has led to understanding communication by the identification of its function. This is to say, what people perceive and express is influenced by their need to perceive and express.

Everything we learn, for example, is relative unless it has a point of reference. The point of reference may be described as human needs. We know, for example, that survival and, from an interpersonal standpoint, security are basic needs. What is generally agreed is that this principle of function holds true for virtually all perceptions and expressions. Sensory and brain chemistry suggest that only relationships and patterns of relationships can be perceived and that these form the basis of human reality. So, in one way or another, functionality is predominant in our communications; we do not just perceive an event, we scan an event looking for meaning related to our needs. In this way, objects or people are not the target of our perceptions, rather they are functions. This is an important principle since it depicts the fact that our perceptions are not random events but are organized around our perception of meaning. Thus, it is possible to say that our initial awareness, and any subsequent rectification of this awareness, is highly influenced by our awareness of ourselves and the needs we experience.

The Principle of Process

The second major concept of human communication in an interpersonal context is that of process. When we think about how communication occurs in relationships, we observe that no statements can accurately reflect a communicative exchange if it is not first analyzed from the standpoint of function, and second, analyzed from the standpoint of an ongoing and ever-changing process. Messages sent and received are products of a continuous process; they are not independent of other stimuli in the interpersonal environment. Communication, then, is a mutually interdependent activity among two or more individuals in a changing environmental context.

The interpersonal communication process consists of a dynamic exchange of energy among two or more individuals within a specific socio-cultural context. Literally, communication is a process whereby individuals share something of themselves, whether it is feelings, thoughts, opinions, ideas, values, or goals. This process, when it happens in effective interchange, helps make individuals feel more human, more in touch with reality, and more capable of social intimacy. Also, the ability of individuals to influence one another and thereby exercise power, and even control, should be considered an important impetus for interpersonal communication. The communication process has frequently been depicted in a linear fashion but has now been replaced by more complex conceptual models. Figure 1–5 illustrates this phenomena.

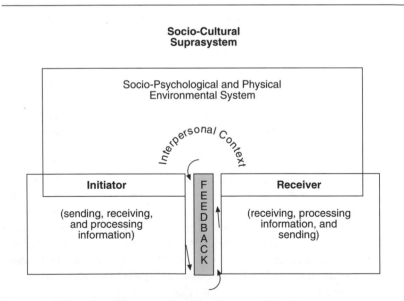

Figure 1–5 Functional Components of the Communication Process.

A concept critical to understanding communication as a process, then, is that of feedback. Feedback is a series of responses that depicts change. It is not a linear chain of events, e.g., event A affects event B, and B affects C, C, in turn, affects D, and so on. Rather, D leads back to A. Therefore, the process is circular. Feedback plays an important role in establishing, modifying, and stabilizing relationships. The concept of feedback is frequently addressed as a loop; that is, in relationships, the behavior of each person affects and is affected by the behavior of each other person. Systems that engage in feedback are distinctively different from those that do not; they generally display higher degrees of complexity. In open systems theory, open systems are generally differentiated from closed systems by the process of fluidity and permeability achieved to a great extent through the process of feedback (see Figure 1–6).

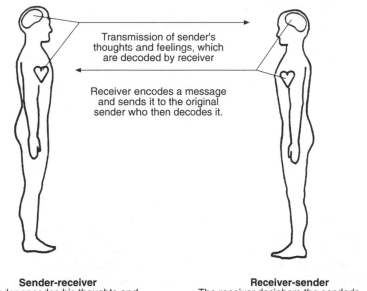

Sender-receiver
The sender encodes his thoughts and feelings into words and gestures and transmits them to the receiver via sound, touch, sight, and smell. At the same time, the sender is receiving messages from the person with whom he is communicating.

Receiver-sender
The receiver deciphers the sender's transmission. He determines what request the sender is making of him after he decodes the sender's cognitive and affective messages. Simultaneously, the receiver is sending messages to the other person.

Feedback
Feedback refers to the circular process by which
Sender and Receiver influence one another.

Figure 1–6 The Reciprocal and Circular Nature of Interpersonal Communication. *Source:* Adapted with permission from S. Smith, *Communications in Nursing*, 2nd edition, p. 5, © 1992. Mosby Yearbook.

We know that some very closed systems, for example, cults, restrict feedback, both within the system and between the system and the larger suprasystem—society-at-large. It can be postulated that the reason that feedback is not allowed is that feedback and the exchange of information across the boundaries of the system would result in the disruption of the system. Thus, to maintain homeostasis, the cult (system) disallows open exchange with the external environment. There is no feedback. This scenario can be contrasted with the open system. Functional families, for example, display intricate levels of feedback and information processing. Family decisions may require members to voice their preferences to one another in ongoing, continuous ways. These decisions are a direct result of multiple views—not the opinions of one or two members. Decisions occur as a result not only of people's voicing their views but also because these views are reactions to the views of others. Fluidity is one characteristic of these systems, and information can flow easily from member to member and between the family and its external environment. This process is transactional because individuals in an interaction affect others and are affected themselves.

When looking at theories of causality, it is appropriate to speak about the beginning statement and the results (at the end of the chain). When applying the principle of the feedback loop, this explanation is faulty: A may not cause B; the beginning is arbitrary and depends on where one enters the loop.

The Principle of Multidimensionality‎

A third important principle of interpersonal communication is that it is multidimensional (see Exhibit 1–1). What does this mean and what are the dimensions? Usually when speaking of the multidimensionality of communication, we perceive two distinct levels. They are: (1) the content dimension, and (2) the relationship dimension. Watzlawick et al. (1967), recognizing that communication has at least two dimensions (content and relationship aspects), suggested that we cannot fully understand communication until we know something about both aspects. The relationship aspect may be more hidden, while the content aspect more transparent (Crowther 1991). Some clinicians describe three levels, i.e., (1) the content level, (2) the feeling or emotional level, and (3) a level that describes the perceived relationship of one communicant to another. This model incorporates the idea that every message has a separate emotional quality that further clarifies both the content and the relational levels of the communication. Regardless of whether we differentiate two or three levels, it is clear that communication is used not only to exchange information, e.g., facts or ideas, it is also used to address the interpersonal relationship dimension.

Let us consider the command: "Take this pill now with this water." The explicit message or content aspect of this expression is the obvious: You need to take the

Exhibit 1–1 Multidimensionality of Human Communication

- the Content Dimension
- the Feeling or Emotional Dimension
- the Relationship Dimension

---

pill. However, suggested here, through both verbal and nonverbal clues, is evidence about the relationship and even what feelings one holds about the other. The command communicates authority: One person (provider) perceives herself in an authority relationship with the other (patient or client). One has power over the other and this is enacted in the exchanges that occur. Somewhat subtle is the underlying attitude: *I have expectations of you, and if you do not do as I say, you will let me down. Further, my expectations are legitimate.*

Said in a somewhat different way: One aspect of a message conveys information; this is synonymous to the content of the message. It may be about anything regardless of whether it is true or false, valid or invalid, or even indecipherable. The command quality of the message, however, describes how the message should be received and, therefore, describes the relationship of the communicants. Putting these relationship aspects in words, they would say: "This is how I see myself in relationship to you, you in relationship to me or how, at least, it should be." Consider these two expressions that seemingly communicate the same directive: "Take this pill with water—it'll be easier," and "If you refuse the water, you won't be able to take this pill." While these statements communicate approximately the same content, i.e., you need to take this pill with water, they define somewhat different relationships with the patient. The first example suggests a supportive, facilitative relationship, while the latter suggests a supervisorial, somewhat skeptical relationship.

Sometimes the distinction between levels of communication are depicted in descriptions of metacommunication and metainformation. Metacommunication is a term frequently used to identify communication about the communication. It is communication about how a message is supposed to be received. The report aspect of the communication conveys the data; the command (metacommunication or metainformation) describes how this communication should be taken. "You better take me seriously" is one verbal translation of the metacommunication in this message: "If you think I'm going to take out the garbage, you're crazy!" The relational or metacommunicative aspects can also be expressed nonverbally, by frowning or piercing looks, or through the context of the encounter, when people criticize each other in front of strangers.

Communication about the relational aspects, or feeling dimension, sometimes occurs at the nonverbal level. This brings us to still another important axiom of human communication: Communication is both verbal and nonverbal (see Figure 1–7). Sometimes verbal communication is the term used to describe the content level of a message. Otherwise, what did the sender say? This is the information or direct message intended. Nonverbal aspects of communication—facial expressions, gestures, positioning—are perceived by those who receive our messages and are considered part of the communication or interaction. Nonverbal aspects frequently disclose the feeling or relational dimension of the communication as evidenced in photographs of individuals' facial expressions (see Figure 1–8).

Can you imagine being in a relationship where you cannot have access to the nonverbal content of the interaction? Facial expressions, posture, and movement would not be available data. How would you draw conclusions about the emotional and relational aspects of the interaction? You would need to rely almost exclusively on the spoken word together with evidence of inflection, pace of speech, and tone of voice to establish the other person's feelings about you. Would you be secure in your judgments or satisfied with your data? Most likely the answer is, "Not really." What is characteristic of human communication is that metacommunication (communication that classifies the relationship) is extremely important. A great deal of what is communicated through nonverbal channels is symbolic. Facial expressions or body movements are symbolic representations of the nature of the relationship between communicants. Not only do humans rely heavily on nonverbal aspects, they are trained to use these aspects to communicate more effectively and efficiently.

Discrepancies between verbal and nonverbal communication (messages) is generally picked up in human dialogue. Discrepancies can occur in many ways, for example, in different verbal reports or in differences between verbal and nonverbal messages. Consistency in communication is important because it provides a foundation for trust. Should communication be inconsistent or two opposing messages be delivered, there is reason to mistrust the other person and the relationship. In most relationships we do not look for or search for inconsistencies, across

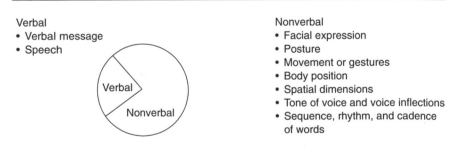

Verbal
• Verbal message
• Speech

Nonverbal
• Facial expression
• Posture
• Movement or gestures
• Body position
• Spatial dimensions
• Tone of voice and voice inflections
• Sequence, rhythm, and cadence of words

Figure 1–7 Categories of Verbal and Nonverbal Communication

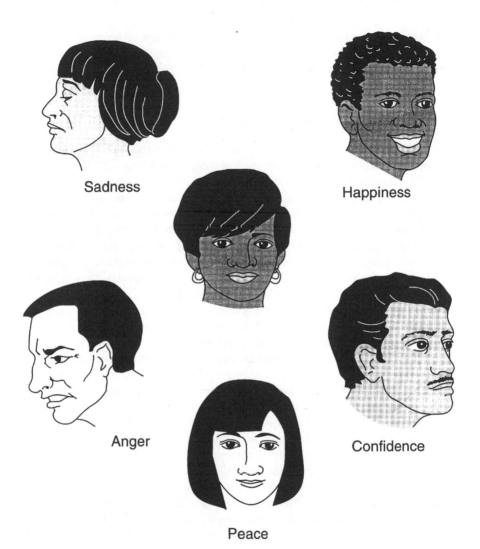

Sadness

Happiness

Anger

Peace

Confidence

Figure 1–8 Humans Rely Heavily upon Nonverbal Aspects of Communication, e.g., Facial Expressions.

verbal messages or between verbal and nonverbal messages. However, if given a reason to mistrust someone, we have the capacity to fine-tune our perceptions and be observant of mixed messages whether they are blatant or only somewhat apparent.

The Principle of Communication Inevitability

The idea that communication occurs on both verbal and nonverbal levels brings us to the next important axiom of interpersonal communication. That is, the impossibility of not communicating. Watzlawick et al. (1967, p. 48) first referred to this idea as a major property of behavior. That is, there is no such thing as nonbehavior. Putting it in simpler terms: One cannot not behave and one cannot not communicate. If we understand communication as behavior, then we can also say that no matter how much a person tries, he or she cannot not communicate. Drawing from our previous discussion of nonverbal and verbal communication, we find that words or silence, activity or inactivity, all have message potential. They influence others and, therefore, others, too, cannot not respond to these communications. To express this idea in brief: We are always communicating whether we are exchanging words or not. The nurse who looks straight ahead and avoids eye contact when passing by a patient's family or the physician who reads the patient's chart, moves in front of a nurse to return it, and checks his beeper without acknowledging anyone's presence are both communicating even though no words are exchanged. The mere absence of talking does not mean communication has not occurred. In both cases, what is communicated is that the providers are busy and do not want to speak to anyone or to be spoken to. Family members and staff, respectively, usually get the message and behave, in turn, by leaving them alone. Is this any less of an interchange of information than the most animated conversation?

It is also true that communication may not be intentional. Much of what is communicated is, in fact, unintentional, unplanned, and even unrealized. When we understand that messages are multileveled and include nonverbal behavior, this idea is quite plausible. Consider, for example, that a physician has a particular negative attitude about a nurse. Nothing said can substantiate this suspicion. Nonetheless, it is understood, and if people around them were asked about their relationship they would confirm this assumption. Still, there is no data, or is there? The data is largely in the nonverbal communication that is exchanged between nurse and physician. Therefore, when we think of communication units, we do not mean simple verbal messages but rather multifaceted occurrences where several factors are involved—verbal, tonal, postural, and even contextual aspects. Likewise, these factors have varied ways of impacting communication as well as several permutations. Permutations and variance can often be a function of cultural differences. At other times, it is a reflection of the mental or emotional stability of the sender. Some of these permutations appear in behaviors of the mentally ill or functionally impaired. A case in point is an emotionally disturbed patient who is mute and whose withdrawal and immobility expresses anger at those around him. Some people intentionally avoid verbal exchanges to sever commitment. A sequence of avoidance behaviors may also be interlaced with willingness to communicate. Because human relationships are complex, the explicit and implicit use of communication, which includes both verbal and nonverbal dimensions, is also very complex. Many impasses in communication relate to the complexity of relationships and the involvement of communication channels.

The Principle of Punctuation

The complexity of human relationships is also reflected in the cause-effect patterns that communicants claim exist. This notion is especially observed in communications where conflict exists. The principle of punctuation and sequence of events, though not a major communication principle, is relevant to our understanding of the circularity of communications. When we ask two or more people to report on the patterns of their communication, we may get two very discrepant stories. Looking in from the outside, we would say that the communication we observe, from A to B to C and to D is an uninterrupted series of exchanges. However, to those participating in the dialogue, there is a beginning, a middle, and an end. The participants see a cause-and-effect relationship and behave as though this were reality. They may punctuate their remarks at any one time in the series to depict their believed status or their desired status. These perceived beginnings, middles, and ends depict a pattern of responses that communicates something about how one communicant sees herself in relation to another such as on issues of power, control, and intimacy. This process of sequencing responses is inherent in all humans and is neither bad nor good. It serves the purpose of organizing behavioral events and is vital to ongoing relationships. Tendencies to organize interactions can display the specific rules of a culture. For example, if males were dominant decision makers and females predominantly followers, the interpretation of a sequence of events A–D would illustrate this cultural prerequisite. That is, we would judge, and others would confirm, that the interaction begins with A directing B to do something; it would not be concluded that B decided to do something and A simply reiterated the objective of the action after it was first initiated.

Interpretations of the inner workings of arguments further illustrate this point. With a couple who argues, who starts the argument? And, does party A withdraw because party B insults A, or is party B critical because party A withdraws? Who initiates and who reacts—party A or party B? Depending on what patterns these communicants see in their relationship, the reported sequence of events will be different. Both parties may be guilty of distorting reality, and this further complicates the situation. Finally, depending on the cultural orientations of the participants, the beginning, middle, and end may be very different from what we perceive as outside observers or even what each party thinks is occurring. It is clear then that the nature of a relationship is played out in the perceived punctuation of the segments of communication.

The Principle of Symmetrical or Complementary Communication

A final axiom of interpersonal communication that is key in understanding human communication is that communication (in relationships) is either symmetrical or complementary. People take either symmetrical or complementary roles in relationships, and this is evident in their communications (Arnold and Boggs 1995). In the first case (symmetry), communicants tend to mirror each other's behavior. In the second instance (complementary), one party's behavior complements the other's. In the first case, differences between the respondents is minimized; both parties pull toward their common base. In the second type, maximizing differences is important. If we studied the pattern of communication among and across multiple dyadic relationships, we would come to realize that these patterns are decidedly one or the other. The classic examples of complementary communication are the parent-child, boss-employee, and leader-follower dyads. Usually these dyads participate in socially defined ways to depict superior-inferior and primary-secondary roles. Distinctively different are dyads that interact as if both parties were equal. This may be seen in colleague relationships. What is obvious is that communication that depicts these arrangements will generally hold true regardless of the contexts or circumstances. Boss-employee interactions, for example, will reflect superior-inferior status even if the parties interact outside their professional roles.

CONCLUSION

In summary, human communication is indeed complex. The neurological, biochemical processes by which we receive information and the neural activity by which we process the information we receive is fascinating. Additionally, our abilities to utilize communication in patterned ways to initiate, modify, and maintain relationships distinguishes us from all other species. These processes are put forward in this chapter as axioms or principles substantiated by scientific observation. In translating science to pragmatics, we run the risk of overgeneralizing or minimizing details. It is not the intention of this chapter to synthesize all scientific data. Rather, the objective is to discuss key principles that underlie empirical thought from both the biologic and behavioral sciences on the subject of human communication.

CHAPTER 2

The Nature of Therapeutic Communications

Therapeutic communication is an activity which is probably as old as human language. As a matter of fact, one can state, without exaggeration, that whenever a priest, nurse, doctor, or lay person helps another human being, some elements of therapeutic communication are used, regardless of the external situation.

Jurgen Ruesch

CHAPTER OBJECTIVES

- Define functional and dysfunctional interpersonal communication.
- Compare and contrast these modes of communicating.
- Discuss disturbances in perception, processing, and expression.
- Identify therapeutic interviewing skills.
- Differentiate nontherapeutic from therapeutic interviewing skills.
- Describe the interpersonal context of a therapeutic encounter.
- Discuss the advisability of training programs in interpersonal communications for health care providers.
- List guides to nondefensive communication that inevitably lead to functional and therapeutic encounters.
- Complete the personal inventory for nontherapeutic interviewing.

The idea that provider communication can be more or less helpful is not a new idea. The idea that providers create therapeutic effects through communication has been at least partially addressed in all the health care professions. These ideas are often put forth in idealistic terms where meanings of "good" and "bad" are ascribed to various provider-patient encounters. Thus, we determine whether interaction is "therapeutic" or, conversely, "nontherapeutic."

This chapter will discuss several important assumptions of therapeutic communication—some that can be substantiated, others that reflect biases about communication and the nature of the helper-helpee relationship.

THERAPEUTIC COMMUNICATION DEFINED

Therapeutic communication is interpersonal exchange, using verbal and non-verbal messages, that culminates in someone's being helped to overcome stress, anxiety, fear, or other emotional experiences that cause distress. It is also communication that expresses support, provides information and feedback, corrects distortions, and provides hope. If we consider that humans have an inherent need to be heard and understood, we can conclude that any interchange that permits this activity is at some level therapeutic since it provides for a basic human need. Self-expression, for example, is therapeutic; when self-expression provokes acknowledgment and understanding by another person, a tremendously therapeutic event has occurred. The basic need to express oneself and to be heard and understood has been met.

The first and most important assumption is that therapeutic communication is a skill practiced exclusively by health care professionals. This is a narrow application of the phenomena. In actuality, therapeutic communication can be practiced by anyone. Whether informal spontaneous interchanges between friends or purposeful interaction such as between provider and patient, it is assumed that one communicant is more able or ready to respond in a helpful manner and that this occurs over a series of exchanges of messages. It is true that providers care much about the impact of their communication on patients. It is also true that the average person may care and is also capable of being therapeutic. The average person may communicate therapeutically toward others for long periods without realizing it. The recipients may gain much from the dialogue, also without knowing it. Sad feelings may be abated, perceptions corrected, and knowledge gained; these outcomes do not require a "healer" and "healee." Therapeutic encounters are events. It can also be said that therapeutic communication occurs spontaneously. The issue for the provider is to harness this potential and make these naturally occurring encounters occur more frequently.

In summary, therapeutic communication can be practiced by many, not just by providers in very specific circumstances. It can be very spontaneous and occur under ordinary circumstances without much forethought or planning. Understanding this ubiquitous nature of therapeutic communication should provide us with optimism about the human potential as well as the natural helping resources that are available.

What differentiates the provider who practices therapeutic communication and the average person who does the same? There are some distinct differences. First, the provider consciously intends to influence the patient in a therapeutic manner. Second, with this intention, the provider usually has a professional aim in mind; he or she is not using this approach to achieve personal gain. In other circumstances, this is not the case; for example, politicians say helpful things to gain votes and salespersons make people feel good in order to increase sales. Providers have the intention of helping the patient for the patient's sake. The patient's well-being, not the provider's personal gains, are the driving force behind the words used and how they are expressed. A final distinction is that the provider will perceive deficits in the patient's perception, processing, or expression of ideas and attempt to correct these deficits. Providers will focus on ill-expressed thoughts and feelings, breakdowns in expression, and distortions in perception. It is not by chance that deficits in perception, processing, or expression will be addressed. Rather, providers purposefully attempt to improve the communication capabilities of patients (see Table 2–1).

Functional and Dysfunctional Patterns

While some providers will be engaged in restoring patients' abilities to communicate, such as by medications, treatments, or surgical intervention, all providers manage patients' ongoing communication capabilities. In the counseling professions, this responsiveness to communicative behavior is focused in-depth on the form and content of patients' communications. Functional communication is believed to be a sign of health, while dysfunctional patterns of communication are believed to be a sign of disturbance.

Not all individuals are accustomed to expressing thoughts and feelings through expressive language. At a very minimum, persons need capabilities in (1) perceiving appropriately, (2) learning the language and symbolic and metacommunicaton systems that prevail in their community, (3) acquiring and correcting information

---

Table 2–1 Differences in Provider and Layperson Use of Therapeutic Communication

Provider	Lay Person
• conscious intention • professional aim or goal • making people "feel better" is the desired outcome • attempts to correct deficits in others' communications	• spontaneous, sometimes unconscious responses • no particular therapeutic goal behind expression • making people "feel good" may be secondary to achieving another purpose • improving others' capabilities to communicate may not be the intention

in order to maintain an appropriate view of self and the world, (4) integrating experiences into a comprehensive whole and the resolution of contradictions, (5) learning by imitation or experience of the means by which one can achieve desires and influence others, and (6) the ability to sort out and eliminate interferences on the part of internal and external noise including factors in the environment. Depending upon the age, health status, educational, cultural, and socioeconomic characteristics of the individual, a command over these abilities may not be possible. When we say that patients have deficits in these capabilities, we are not only judging their stage of growth and development, we are referring to many other factors that are affecting their communication behavior (see Exhibit 2–1).

Disturbed Communication

Patients may not only be impaired in their communication capabilities, they may exhibit patterns of disturbed communication. When we diagnose disturbance, we are interested in what needs to be restored or rehabilitated. Unlike those individuals whose capabilities have not yet been fully developed, people with disturbed communication, sometimes referred to as dysfunctional communicators, may have regressed in their usual ability to communicate effectively. The reasons for disturbed communication are many, including trauma, poor self-concept, poor health, and retarded growth. Dysfunctional communication is diagnosable through the observations of verbal and nonverbal behavior.

Communication is congruent or incongruent. When one thinks of congruent communication, what is usually understood is that the verbal statement is consistent with behaviors associated with the verbal content. For example, when clients are speaking about the uncertainty of their diagnosis, they demonstrate worry in their tone of voice and physical gestures. They may appear tense or agitated or confused. These nonverbal components are generally consistent with being worried about one's diagnosis. Sometimes clients will exhibit these behaviors but express confidence or denial about the uncertainty of their diagnosis. When this occurs, their communication is incongruent because their verbal message is inconsistent with their nonverbal responses.

Many providers use the spoken message to determine dysfunctional communication. In very basic terms, messages that are too long, too short, or ill-placed indicate that the patient's capacity to communicate effectively is hampered and may be either temporarily or more permanently disturbed. Other providers may focus on a single aspect of the patient's communication, such as the character of the patient's nonverbal responsiveness or the patient's acoustical impact. A patient's nonverbal behavior can depict problems that the patient is having in perceiving and processing information adequately. The acoustic dimensions of the

Exhibit 2–1 Prerequisites to Functional Communication

- perceives appropriately
- learns the prevailing language and symbolic systems
- acquires and corrects information when necessary
- integrates experiences into a comprehensive whole, resolving contradictions when and where they occur
- sorts out and eliminates interference from internal and external environmental "noise"

---

patient's voice, e.g., the intensity of speech, punctuation or emphasis, and speed can depict disturbed states.

What is a healthy voice—can we establish this? We know that people who are under stress speak differently. Actual changes in muscle contraction as well as in the rhythmical patterns of breathing and in the functions of the vocal cords occur when individuals are under stress. Therefore, a healthy voice might be displayed in harmonious tones, smooth transitions, and calm, composed rhythms. But, we might also argue that some people disguise their emotional state and mimic these characteristics to convince others that they are "OK" when in fact they are not functioning up to par. There is a way to differentiate between feigned functional communication and actual healthy communication. First, providers will be able to discern patterns in patient communications. A sense of well-being may be initially expressed, but within minutes the patient's true level of functioning will emerge. Also, observations of inconsistencies in verbal and nonverbal messages is another way to determine dysfunctional communication.

Another way to conceptualize disturbed communication is to take each functional aspect of communication behavior and determine the system that is most defective. Disturbed communication can occur in the realms of perception, evaluation or processing, and expression (see Exhibit 2–2). These systems overlap, and it is extremely important to understand how disturbances are both independently and interdependently manifested. If we take a total-system approach, we will understand that even though these elements can be separated out, they are highly interdependent. That is, a malfunction or disruption in one, for example, in perception, will have implications for the other two functions. A disturbance in perception will most likely have implications for how one processes and evaluates input. This, in turn, may affect expression, at least, the appropriateness of the expression. When, for example, perception is distorted, judgments about input will be faulty. Faulty judgment, in turn, has implications for the appropriateness of expression. Finally, if expression is faulty, then a disruption may occur in further evaluative and perceptive functioning. Thus, problems in any one dimension will

Exhibit 2–2 Disturbed Communication

- disturbance in perception of stimuli/messages
- disturbance in processing stimuli/messages received
- disturbance in expression of messages

---

result in problems in another. The relationship between these systems or channels is complex, and while the principle of interrelationships applies, there is probably more to the interaction than what can be deduced in a causal inference or even from the standpoint of a feedback loop.

We could, for example, say that the patient pulls away from the physician's hand because he or she fears pain or discomfort. The physician is not there to induce pain, so we could call this a distortion of reality. Say that there is a direct link between the perception and meaning assigned and that both these elements, in a linear way, affect expression, which is also "faulty." We know that individuals are affected by both internal and external stimuli; and, what seems illogical to us is very logical to the patient. Former memories of pain come to bear on the patient's current perceptions. A complex array of stimuli impact the patient from a variety of sources, including the data derived from the process of evaluation and expression. If we were to pinpoint the primary system that is disturbed, we would also have to recognize that this is only part of the larger picture.

Disturbed Perception

Disturbances in perception or perception as the primary source of pathology are studied by many professional disciplines. The neurobehavioral, psychosocial, and neurophysiological sciences study the exactitudes of human perception and many of these scientific principles have been alluded to in Chapter 1 of this text. The problems of selective inattention, sensory deprivation, sensory distortion, and the inability to balance between sensory input (from internal and external sources) are examples of problems in perception. The classical example of selective inattention occurs when we ignore significant details of events, perhaps to avoid unpleasant feelings, but in doing so, we negate important details. A former common practice of treating people who experienced hysterical blindness was to shock them, e.g., by slapping them in the face. This jolted the patient's awareness and restored the patient's full vision. It was thought that the blunt directedness of this action forced the patient to reconstitute his line of vision and to respond to a greater number and/ or kind of stimuli. Can you imagine such practice in health care today? What has evolved as current practice is much different from those primitive methods. With chronic cases of selective inattention, the technique of confrontation is preferred.

A provider can awaken the patient to a wider scope of stimuli by observing astutely (nonverbal and verbal communication) and mirroring back or confronting the patient with those facts that he or she has selectively ignored. This does not require the jolt of a slap.

Sensory distortion can occur in other ways akin to selective inattention. Selective inattention refers to the blocking out of stimuli and results in distortions of perception. Certain other behaviors also contribute to perceptual distortion. For example, some people misinterpret others' communications because they apply stereotypic interpretations, or they generally experience things differently. They may even have an intolerance for the ideas or behaviors of others. They may also be unaware of the specific social or cultural context of their interpersonal situations. Sometimes, they are so highly adapted and trained at picking up some stimuli that they fail to see others. These are all examples of selective inattention.

Sensory distortion also occurs because of the idiosyncratic strengths of individuals. Consider the fact, for example, that some people are extremely oblivious to inner cues. Emotional feelings—fear, sadness, anger—may be out of their range of awareness; or physical sensations—pressure, tension, and even pain—are not perceptible. These individuals may, however, be very proficient at perceiving stimuli outside themselves from environmental clues or subtle shifts in the moods and behaviors of others. To some extent, health care providers fit into this latter category. They are very good at perceiving others' needs but much less aware when it comes to sensing their own needs. These introceptively handicapped persons, in the instance of providers, have transformed their natural tendency into a skill and the consequences can be dysfunctional perceptivity.

The extrospectively limited individual perceives mostly internal stimuli, neglecting signals and signs from the external world. To some extent, young children fit this category. They are attuned to internal feelings of hunger, pain, and fear but will misjudge external stimuli. They may purposefully disregard external clues, or because they are ill equipped, they just do not attend to external stimuli. A major role of adults in our society is to protect children from their underdeveloped abilities to perceive and judge external stimuli. Whether or not individuals are strong at picking up internal, or external, clues, the imbalance is important. To help these individuals, we must strengthen the stimulus capacity that is weakest.

Sensory defects is yet another category of perceptual dysfunction and can be of several kinds. The most commonly witnessed sensory defects are those of vision and hearing. They may be congenital and permanent, or temporary, requiring no significant long-term adaptation. Defects in vision will impact expressive behavior. For example, many blind people do not speak with punctuation or intensity. Their speech tends to be bland, due in part to the fact they cannot perceive and therefore react to the nonverbal expressions of the other person. Likewise, disturbances in hearing will affect the development of speech. Other disturbances in sensory awareness include equilibrium and tactile capabilities. These disturbances also impede individuals' perceptions.

Disturbed Processing

Disturbances in processing and evaluation are many, and they include the capacities to cognitively and emotionally deal with stimuli. Decision making and memory are frequently outcomes of the capacity to process and evaluate the perceived stimuli. If we say that someone is having difficulties in decision making, for example, we are suspicious of some deficit in the area of cognitive and emotional processing.

Methods of codification and the ability to assess probabilities are part of the decision-making process. To evaluate by using probabilities ensures individuals of safe and proper actions. When we do not assess events with a notion of probability or when we cannot remember what happened to apply a probability model, we are in danger of evaluating stimuli inadequately. Take, for example, the dieter who chooses to have just one bite of chocolate cake. Having been at the mercy of his or her passion for chocolate cake in the past, this is a dangerous step. One bite can lead to a piece, one piece to a second piece, and so on. If we cannot remember what it was like to be seduced by the chocolate cake, or we cannot assign probabilities to the chance of eating more than we should, our processing of data is defective.

Moods, feelings, and attitudes also influence judgment and decision making. As a matter of fact, these factors have a great deal to do with our decisions. One could, for example, conclude that the reason we fell into the just-have-another-bite situation was that feelings or moods influenced our desires to apply probability theory. Having determined that "good sense" would mean we should avoid even the aroma of chocolate, we short-circuit good sense to get to the pleasure. There is no better way to do this than to default on applying probability principles. Our abilities to make decisions also depend on our ability to scan information that we hold in our memories, to consider this information, to modify our considerations, and to act. The result of acting requires us to make a choice and confine our behavior to that choice. This process can be affected by our abilities to scan, to arrange experiences in an orderly way, and to draw on stored information. Our strengths and abilities in these areas are influenced by many circumstances. Aging has an affect on memory, but it also transforms our abilities to scan for relevant information and establish risks. Some memory disturbances occur when individuals remember experiences but cannot apply what they have experienced and learned to new situations. Each time that they are presented with the problem, they approach it as if they had never experienced it. They carry out the same problem-solving steps that they did when they first encountered the problem. Disturbances in processing information are indeed important, despite the fact that the majority of emphasis is placed on the communicant's abilities to perceive and express.

Disturbed Expression

The overriding function of our ability to express ourselves is the opportunity it affords us to participate in interpersonal relationships. Without the ability to express ourselves, and this involves many aspects that affect our central or peripheral nervous systems, including various motor capabilities, we simply cannot relate to others or get confirmation or acknowledgment of our ideas or actions. In short, we have limited ability to make an impact on others. This condition affects not only our enjoyment of relationships but also our self-concept and self esteem. People who have speech impairments, for example, will exaggerate their associated facial expressions and postural responses. The purpose is to establish enough meaning in their messages to trigger a definitive response from others—a response that they desire. Disturbances of expression can include absent, inhibited, or exaggerated expression. There are also motor defects that can affect our abilities to express ourselves.

Since communication is highly influenced by the interpersonal context we find ourselves in, communicants who display an absence of speech or inhibited or exaggerated expression may be reflecting their perceptions of the interpersonal dynamics in which the encounter occurs. We could say that an adolescent is speechless not because he has a permanent disability but because he is reacting to some stimulus in his interpersonal encounter. Problems of expression, if not biologically caused, usually reflect relationship dynamics, at least the communicant's views of the relationship.

We have all seen patients with defects in expression that are a result of motor impairment. People with nerve lesions, muscular disorders, or other impairments of the peripheral nervous system suffer expressive deficits. This group also includes patients whose expressions are complicated by the involuntary movements of tremors and tics. Essentially, the specific defect alters the character of the person's expression, which is usually permanent, and individuals learn to compensate for the defect. We observe in encounters with these individuals many consequences including: (1) the immediate effect of the defect on speech, (2) the individual's compensatory response to the defect, and (3) the individual's response to his perceptions or anticipation of the reactions others will have in the encounter.

In summary then, disturbances in communication run the gamut of perceptual, processing, and expressive functions. They may be temporary and contextual, or they may reflect a longer standing, motor defect. The exact origin and nature of the problem is important but not always critical to our understanding of how to communicate effectively with these individuals. The most important aspect is that we are able to recognize the systems of communication that exhibit the pathology.

It is not the purpose of this chapter to address at length the medical conditions that affect communication, which are numerous and include specific neurophysiologic and neurochemical deficiencies that are found in a variety of patient populations. They include the variety of language and speech disorders, developmental delays, and specific motor deficits. These conditions are extremely important to the study of disturbed communication, but the exact medical explanations are not a topic for this general review.

Before leaving the topic of disturbed communication, it is important to address the phenomena of dysfunctional communication. While disturbed communication connotes a specific defect, dysfunctional suggests a process that is highly linked to the interpersonal context of relationships. For example, when family therapists describe dysfunctional communication behaviors in family members, they are usually suggesting that patterns of dysfunctional communication are causing family difficulties. Therefore, they attempt to change interpersonal or family dysfunctional communication patterns.

Some theorists have clarified problematic communication by differentiating dysfunctional communication from the functional type. For example, expressive communication that is too much or too little, too early or too late, or tangential (in the wrong place) is said to reflect dysfunction. Dysfunction here not only refers to the explicit communication behavior but to the nature of the encounter as a whole.

Perhaps the most important understanding of dysfunctional communication patterns is found in the historical work of certain theorists' studies of family dynamics (Satir 1974; Watzlawick 1974; Watzlawick, Beavin, and Jackson 1974). Satir (1964), for example, defined explicitly the characteristics of a dysfunctional communicator. According to Satir, dysfunctional communicators overgeneralize; will assume that others share their feelings, thoughts, and perceptions; will assume that their perceptions or evaluations are complete; and that what they perceive or evaluate will not change. These individuals assume there are only two possible alternatives (they tend to dichotomize or think in terms of black or white): that what they attribute to things or people are actually a part of those things or people and that they can get inside the skin of the other person (not only to act as a spokesperson for that person, but also that others can do the same with them).

Individuals who exhibit functional communication, as opposed to dysfunctional, are more likely to use qualification and clarification. These individuals tend to clearly state their case, are ready to clarify or qualify their remarks, and ask for feedback. They are also receptive to feedback when they receive it.

Providers who establish effective communication with patients will not only exhibit functional communication, they will also be model communicators. They exemplify clear communication and also teach patients how to achieve it. To do this, they must spell out the rules for communicating accurately, emphasizing checking out the meanings of messages and correcting invalid assumptions. Providers need to be very clear in their own messages, showing a willingness to repeat, restate, and carefully explain how they reached conclusions. It is hoped that through both the providers' modeling and their capacity to interrupt dysfunctional communication that the patient will be encouraged to move toward more effective communication styles.

Therapeutic communications with patients require many skills and knowledge. Among these are the abilities to engage the patient in therapeutic interviewing, to assist the patient to communicate more effectively, and to avoid the traps of dysfunctional communication.

THERAPEUTIC INTERVIEWING SKILLS

Much has been written about the principles of therapeutic interviewing. In this text, techniques of therapeutic communication and therapeutic interviewing are described in detail in Chapters 4 to 10. The purpose of this discussion of therapeutic interviewing is to lay some general groundwork for the most salient principles.

Therapeutic interviewing has certain objectives. Generally, therapeutic interviewing is established to accomplish one or more of these aims:

- elicit full descriptions from patients of their health care condition and concerns
- create an interpersonally safe place for patients to talk about themselves and be able to explore their problems in detail
- reduce any acute emotional distress associated with the patient's immediate condition
- offer support and reassurance
- establish an expanded list of patients' primary and secondary health care problems
- engage the patient in a problem-solving process that demonstrates the collaborative aspects of the provider-patient relationship

Therapeutic Communications

The specific types of questions and responses that the provider can use are many. With regard to even one therapeutic response, that response can be used again, can be modified, or can be discontinued. For example, the provider can use a question, can re-ask the same question, can refer back to it later, or can even use an inappropriately worded question to open up the patient's expression on an important related topic (see Exhibit 2–3). Therapeutic response modes include but are not limited to:

Exhibit 2–3 Therapeutic Response Modes

- using silence
- offering acceptance
- acknowledging and giving recognition
- offering broad openings
- making and offering observations
- reflection of another's thoughts, feelings, and reactions
- focusing discourse, promoting exploration
- translating thoughts into feelings
- encouraging mutual evaluation or appraisal
- validating the client's perceptions and/or beliefs

- using silence
- offering acceptance
- acknowledging and giving recognition, e.g., verbalizing the unspoken but implied message
- offering broad openings
- making and offering observations and summarizing
- reflecting one's own perception of the patient's thoughts, feelings, and reactions
- focusing the patient, and at other times, prompting exploration
- translating thoughts into feelings and feelings into thoughts
- encouraging evaluation or appraisal
- validating the patient's perceptions and/or beliefs

There are many responses that achieve the overall aim of the therapeutic encounter. In chapters to follow, specific therapeutic response modes are discussed in detail.

Nontherapeutic Communications

Just as there are various recommended responses in therapeutic encounters, there are also those that should be avoided. Exhibit 2–4, a Personal Inventory for Nontherapeutic-Therapeutic Interviewing, is provided so that you can test yourself in this area. Nontherapeutic phrases and gestures are to be avoided because they tend to limit patients' verbal expressions, they cause negative reactions, or they threaten patients. These include the following 14 items:

1. Moralizing—inferring that patients are wrong or not okay. This tends to inhibit expression.

Exhibit 2–4 Personal Inventory for Nontherapeutic Interviewing Skills

	1	2	3	4	5	6	7	8	Total
I. Switches off problem-centered data by talking about:									
• Unrelated focus									
• Incidental material									
II. Maintains superficial discussion by:									
• Avoiding elaboration									
• Switching to unrelated superficial focus; denying significance of the patient's stated problems									
• Asking closed-ended questions									
III. Intervenes personally by:									
• Giving opinion to life situation of patient without exploring									
• Giving unsolicited personal opinion to nonpersonal topic									
• Giving personal information or socializing responses									
• Expressing approval or disapproval									
• Moralizing, belittling, or challenging									
• Seeking agreement from the patient/disagreeing with the patient									
IV. Closes off exploration by									
• Prematurely giving an interpretation									
• Prematurely advising solutions									
• Prematurely giving reassurance									
• Prematurely closing topic									
• Using judgmental stereotypical responses									
• Interruptive responses									
• Excessive probing									

continues

Exhibit 2–4 continued

	1	2	3	4	5	6	7	8	Total

V. *Introduces or follows illogical content by:*

- Changing key words without validating change _____
- Following vague content or referent as if understood _____
- Introducing vague content or referent _____
- Questioning on different topics or levels without awaiting reply _____
- Speaking to question or statement of patient in conflicting ways _____
- Ignoring question of patient _____

Total times problematic verbal patterns were used in each session:

Pattern I. _____
Pattern II. _____
Pattern III. _____
Pattern IV. _____
Pattern V. _____

Use of the Tool: (1) Identify each provider response; (2) Mark it NP = nonproblematic or P = problematic; (3) Total P responses using tool.

2. False reassurance—stating that the patient will be better when he will not. False reassurance can cut off the patient's exploration of his concerns.
3. Closed-ended questions—asking questions that can be answered in one to three words.
4. Summarizing—summarizing may help the patient but also shut the patient down if it is offered too early.
5. Stereotypic responses—using phrases like "that's bad" (meaning "good") to express understanding or attempt to impress patients. The use of stereotypic responses may appear phony and backfire on the provider.
6. Belittling responses—making replies to patients that diminish the significance of their experience is belittling. Saying, to a depressed patient, for example, as he or she reveals the desire to die, "Oh, those are common feelings of people in your position," tends to devalue the individual's experience.
7. Interrupting responses—introducing an unrelated topic breaks the flow of the patient's conversation before he or she can complete thoughts or ideas.
8. Denial of problems—treating patients' concerns in a cavalier manner.
9. Giving approval or disapproval—communicating approval or disapproval explicitly or subtly limits patients' feelings of freedom to say things.
10. Disagreeing—responding like this puts the provider in opposition to the patient. It can make patients defensive about their own ideas and feelings.
11. Advising—advice-giving is not always helpful. Although a great deal of what providers do is to offer patients advice, it can have the effect of making the patient feel incapable of being self-directed.
12. Probing—probing too much may make patients feel like objects.
13. Challenging—challenging is a clear and present danger to the patients' expression. This tends to make patients feel that they have to prove what they say; they generally become defensive.
14. Socializing responses—engaging in chitchat or revealing personal data is nontherapeutic. It generally calls for equal time for the provider to self-disclose. This decreases the patients' time to self-disclose.

These responses are usually nontherapeutic, but not always. There are appropriate ways and times to use advice, probe, and even confront patients. However, for beginning providers, it is helpful to know that most of the responses are problematic, can lead them astray, and result in negative outcomes.

The Context of Therapeutic Encounters

The context of the therapeutic interview is extremely important; this context influences the quality of the patient's communicative capabilities and the interviewing environment.

Patients, as is suggested many places in this text, may exhibit dysfunctional communication. Their dysfunctional communication could be a result of a transient state, e.g., stress, or it may be longstanding, resulting from defects. Frequently exhibited disturbances in perception, processing, and expression are:

- verbalizing too much or too little
- verbalizing inappropriately to the context of the events
- using incomplete sentences or thoughts
- behaving as if they have communicated clearly when they have not
- misperceiving environmental stimuli
- exaggerating certain meanings of a message, ignoring other aspects, or attributing different connotations to an event than what is intended
- overgeneralizing or undergeneralizing and failing to access stored information

Because patients experience difficulties in communicating, part of the role of the provider is to correct for these deficits. This context of therapeutic interview is extremely important; it includes the social and environmental context for the provider's communication with the patient.

The purpose of therapeutic interviewing is to build or maintain a patient-provider relationship and to assess the patient through the patient's disclosure of thoughts and feelings. Because interviews require patients to communicate something personal, and even threatening, the interviewer must establish rapport and trust with the patient. This includes creating a safe place for the patient to disclose. A place that is protected from intrusions and interruptions is important for two reasons. First, a protected environment is likely to make patients feel comfortable. Second, in order to collect data adequately—this includes the multiple levels of patient communication (verbal, nonverbal, and metamessages)—the provider must have a "noise-free" environment.

The data from an interview reflects the context of the interview. It is important to understand how patients communicate based on the context of the interview. We know, for example, that patients react differently to different interviewers. Who you are and what you are like may influence what the patient does or does not tell you. Patients also react to the particular situations in which they are asked questions. They may be rather closemouthed if the atmosphere is threatening or there is little privacy. Patients also react to their most immediate life circumstances, crisis, and symptom status. Finally, patients react to the provider's approach—the specific way in which the provider formulates questions. All successful interviewers take these elements into account.

One's style of interviewing and choice of questions should be influenced by the perceptual, ethnic-cultural, and educational characteristics of the patient. The adage: "Begin where the patient is," is a good one. Basically, we can never push patients further than they can go, nor expect them to adapt to our stylistic peculiarities. It is inappropriate to use complex medical jargon with patients who are incapable of understanding the meaning of even the simplest medical phrase. It is also inappropriate to require patients to endure lengthy interviews of two hours if their anxiety levels or attention spans cannot meet the challenge. Sometimes knowing and using the jargon or language of the specific ethnic or cultural group is likely to increase patients' desires to communicate problems.

Regardless of the circumstances, providers must always demonstrate respect and concern for patients. Showing interest, concern, and understanding indicate that the provider regards the patient as worthy. The affective tone that the provider uses with the patient is extremely important and can make or break the interview no matter how sophisticated the provider is in using techniques.

AVOIDING THE TRAPS OF DYSFUNCTIONAL COMMUNICATION

Avoiding the traps of dysfunctional communication can be accomplished. We need to be able to communicate with others. This seems so straightforward that it is frequently ignored. However, the techniques of effective communications are being taught everywhere, and people, once trained in effective communication, must go back for booster shots. That we can always improve our communications, the business and consulting industry knows well. Billions of dollars are poured into (and are made) helping people communicate with each other.

Training in Interpersonal Communications

Training in interpersonal communications is helpful to health providers because it improves their ability to communicate as well as their ability to help others. The purpose of good interpersonal communication is to help others learn about themselves and make decisions based on this knowledge. Another purpose of good communication is so people can learn about themselves by sharing with others and by monitoring their own words and actions.

One of the biggest entanglements that a provider can experience is the trap of defensive communication. Defensive communication in the provider is generally indicative of a perceived threat and its corresponding feelings of anxiety, fear, and guilt. The consequence of defensive communication is generally that messages will be misunderstood and that communication will reach a standstill. This event in a patient-provider encounter is to be avoided at all costs because a disruption in communication is tantamount to a disruption in care.

Defensive communication tends to be obvious. It has specific elements. The following is a list of behaviors that are generally indicative of a defensive posture:

- labeling
- interrupting
- judging
- using tunnel vision
- advice giving
- preparing rebuttals

While there are many other indicators of defensive communication, these are among the most common. People who are communicating defensively usually use more than one of these responses. So it is not only the specific response that is important, it is the cluster of responses that is used and the impact of this cluster on others. Consider, for example, someone who is reacting very emotionally. They may label or blame, interpret others' behaviors, judge others, and develop rebuttals. When this defensive posture is executed with high intensity, it can be likened to a "machine gun." This machine-gun approach has one result—everybody gets out of the way. No one wants to get caught in the cross fire, so observers are also likely to exit the encounter. The end result is that no one fully understands, and the communicants have a decidedly negative view about the prospects of being heard and understood.

The alternative, nondefensive communication, not only promises that our needs but also those of the other person will be met. It is exceedingly more esthetically pleasing. Nondefensive behaviors observe and report, share information, and engage others in mutual problem-solving processes. They generally produce an increased mutual understanding and encourage communicants to continue their dialogue. The skills of nondefensive communication are taken up again in Chapter 19, Communicating with People in Conflict.

From a diagnostic standpoint, all patient-provider interviews can be judged. Establishing the degree to which one uses nontherapeutic interviewing with a single patient or a group of patients can be determined if one analyzes patient encounters and establishes potential problem areas. Personal inventories help providers establish which, if any, of the common nontherapeutic responses they are using (see Exhibit 2–4). The assumption of this self-inventory is that non-problematic provider responses are those that maintain focus and guide both the provider and the patient's learning; while problematic responses short circuit the therapeutic process.

Assessing one's therapeutic and nontherapeutic communication responses to patients is only the first step. It is, however, an extremely important step since no real change can occur until such an assessment is completed. These assessments can occur formally, for example, through feedback from coursework, supervisors, or peers. Much of this assessment, conducted on a continuous basis, must be carried out through individuals' personal self-assessments. Self-assessments include, but are not limited to, an analysis of encounters that turned out poorly, especially those that produced conflict and tension. Changing communication patterns is not always easy, but if providers believe in the importance of functional and therapeutic communications, they will understand the need for self-examination and continual improvement.

CONCLUSION

Therapeutic communication is not confined to providers; anyone can communicate therapeutically. Providers, however, are more deliberate in their use of therapeutic responses. The therapeutic provider communicates with patients whose communications are potentially dysfunctional. Patients' communications can be dysfunctional for many reasons and have both transitory and permanent causes. As providers, we not only model functional communication, we modify the dysfunctional characteristics of others' communication. Therapeutic interviewing is clearly within the domain of every provider's role. Therapeutic interviewing skills tend to focus the patient and increase learning; nontherapeutic interviewing tends to inhibit communication, especially the processes of feedback, clarification, and qualification. Practicing therapeutic communications requires the provider to conduct ongoing self-assessments in which patient-provider encounters are analyzed on the basis of therapeutic-nontherapeutic dimensions. While formal, peers' and/or superiors' evaluations are critical, providers' personal commitment to conduct self-assessments is critical.

CHAPTER 3

Cultural Differences and Communication

In addressing mental health service delivery: A major problem is found in the continuing reliance on Western European tradition and practices in the treatment of low-income and minority patients. The "Anglo" approach to serving "people of color" has lost its credibility: It is in direct conflict with Hispanic, Asian, American Indian, and Black culture. There is a commonality of harsh experiences that low-income and minority patients encounter as service users.

Frank X. Acosta, Joe Jamamoto, and Leonard A. Evans

CHAPTER OBJECTIVES

- Discuss the inevitability of communicating in a multicultural environment.
- Define culture and cultural differences.
- Describe how cultural affiliation influences the meaning of expressed thought.
- Discuss the concepts of majority and minority groups.
- Discuss the influence of subgrouping on communication.
- Describe the hypothetical continuum: cultural destructiveness to cultural proficiency.
- With at least one other individual, discuss your own cultural programming.
- Acknowledge differences between your cultural programming and that of others.

All people are influenced by cultural programming. This "software" influences our behavior, attitudes, and even when, what, how, and to whom we communicate. Once we recognize what our own cultural programming is, we have the capacity to explore more fully the communications of others.

Communication barriers between health care providers and patients are often of a sociocultural nature. These barriers can be due to differences in culture, language, race or ethnicity, gender, and social class, or they can be due to generational differences between individuals within the same culture. Providers are often most aware of the power of sociocultural diversity when they are confronted with adapting a medical regimen to the patient's unique personal circumstances. In communicating with patients, it is critical that clinicians understand the cultural patterns that influence patients' perceptions of their problems and their acceptance of treatment.

It is hardly ever simple to interact with patients and patients' families when value systems and cultural backgrounds are different. The situation becomes even more complicated when language barriers between providers and patients also exist. Differences in values and the inability to understand the communications of others are important because they can produce social distancing. Social distancing in patient-provider relationships is not conducive to trust and empathy. In these instances the therapeutic relationship is at risk.

Perhaps nowhere is it more crucial to be able to understand and *speak* another's language than in the health-services arena. Whether in an outpatient or inpatient setting and across all levels of illness, the ability to express one's needs and feelings and to know that they have been understood is important. Within health settings, the uncertainty and fear that are naturally occurring responses to an actual or perceived threat of illness and injury are accentuated by the awareness that no matter how hard one tries, the provider may not understand one's expressed thoughts and feelings.

CULTURE AND THE INFLUENCE OF CULTURE ON COMMUNICATION

Definition of Culture

Culture refers to an identifiable integrated pattern of human behavior that includes customs, beliefs, values, behaviors, and communications. Culture can be observed in racial, ethnic, religious, and social groups. Cultural diversity includes group identities reflective of individuals' age, gender, ethnic, and social group differences. Everyone has a cultural identity; more often than not, individuals have several cultural identities. One's cultural heritage can be quite elaborate. Current social affiliations as well as religious and ethnic alliances represent an individual's unique programming.

Cultural Affiliations and the Meaning of Expressed Thoughts

Patients may have many affiliations that influence them. For example, a patient may be a member of the Mormon religion, may also be African-American, may be employed as a public school teacher, and be employed part-time as a tennis instructor. His place of birth may have been Boise, Idaho. This patient's cultural heritage is rich. Predictions about his responses to health care services and communications with providers would best be made with all these facts in mind. Until we know what aspect of his cultural programming are most influential in the context of the interaction, we may not fully understand his communication.

Let us say that this same patient is hospitalized for surgery to correct a deviated nasal septum. On the day of admission, he engages his physician in the following conversation:

Patient: "Play any tennis lately?"

Physician: "I was in a doubles match Saturday!"

Patient: "Oh, how did you do?"

Physician: "James, I need to get you set up here. You remember what I told you in my office."

Patient: "Yes."

Physician: "Good, I'm going to order your pre-op medications. I'll be back later."

Patient: "Okay, Doc—you're the boss, boss!"

From the content of his communication, we would say that James' affiliation with tennis is a dominant aspect of his programming. Still, when we examine this interchange at the metacommunication level we observe that equity is an issue, and deference to the surgeon is an aspect of this interaction. While James attempts to relate to his surgeon as one tennis player to another, his surgeon shifts to a professional doctor-patient relationship. Further, James reinforces the hierarchy by in effect replying: "You're the doctor, I'm the patient, i.e., I'm here to follow your orders (boss)." While the physician may have good intentions about establishing a collaborative physician-patient relationship, the outcome of this transaction may be interpersonal distance: "Let's stay within our roles."

What other possibilities should be considered here? How might James be responding to other aspects of his cultural programming? One possibility is that James is responding to differences in social status as a function of role differences. Another possibility is that he is sensitive to racial differences and is suggesting that African-Americans are considered inferior in the eyes of this surgeon. What enables the provider to better understand James' communication is his choice of words and the intonation of those words. Still, without knowledge of his specific cultural programming, judgments about his responses are at best, tentative. Social distancing displayed in transactions where minority and majority status exist have long been the subject of social scientists. Pinderhughes (1989) discusses the role of power in the dynamics of cross-cultural communication within the clinical setting. It is clear that the character of clinical interactions can be significantly affected by ethnic diversity in both patients and providers (see Exhibit 3–1).

Exhibit 3–1 Principles of Cultural Identity

- All people are influenced by cultural programming; this programming influences not only our behavior and attitudes, but also when, what, how, and to whom we communicate.
- Once we recognize what our cultural programming is, we have the capacity to explore more fully the communication of others.
- It is safe to say that what was "mainstream" culture a decade ago may not be so today.
- The usefulness of describing "mainstream" culture in today's world is questionable.
- To fully understand an individual or family, an individualized assessment of cultural values is advisable.

DEFINITIONS OF MINORITY AND MAJORITY

It is safe to say that what prevailed as mainstream culture in the United States decades ago may not prevail today. In fact, the usefulness of describing majority (mainstream) culture in today's world is questionable.

While our notions of what is and is not mainstream have changed, the concept of a minority group (or subgroup) still has relevance. We know, for example, that Cambodians are a subgroup within the Asian community. In some geographical regions, Cambodians are minorities within a dominant Asian culture. The critical point about minorities or subgroups is that persons from subgroups may not share the values and perceptions of the dominant (majority) culture. Members of minority groups can feel suspicious and fearful of providers where cultural diversity exists. They may view them as powerful; and because they are from another ethnic-racial group, view them as nonempathic. Members of minority groups frequently exhibit, at least initially, suspicion and fear. They may respond as if they are in a subservient position. They may perceive the dominant group as authoritative, powerful, and unsympathetic.

Beliefs about Minority and Majority Groups

Providers frequently harbor attitudes or beliefs about both minority and majority groups with whom they come in contact. There is no question that they sometimes have stereotypic views. For example, Asians are regarded as "stoic"; Latinos are seen as "emotional." Patients can have equally firm views of providers. Caucasian patients may view Caucasian surgeons as supeior, African-American dentists as undereducated and Asian doctors as "unfeeling." These generalizations are inaccurate. The key issue in relationships with patients from different cultures is to focus on effective communication based on respect, understanding, and openness. Providers coming from their own unique value orientations need to communicate effectively with others who do not share the same values, perceptions, and background, and may have made false assumptions about them.

Subgroups Shape Communication

It is understood that communication may differ across cultural groups. It is also true that communication differs across subgroups within a given culture. The following example depicts differences within an ethnic category—Asian culture. In the Vietnamese culture, talking is customary. Silence may be uncomfortable, and unless one party is angry or upset, long silences are unusual. Likewise, in the Filipino culture, talking is enjoyed and silence is uncomfortable. The only time that talking is not approved is when an elder is speaking; then it is a sign of disrespect to talk. These patterns run counter to other Asian groups where silence is considered a sign of wisdom, and speech may be regarded as frivolous.

When health care providers intentionally shape their verbal and nonverbal behavior to be respectful of the patient's background, they are practicing with intentions to be culturally competent. This commitment is a step toward removing cross-cultural barriers.

CULTURAL COMPETENCE—A DEVELOPMENTAL PROCESS

In our multicultural society we are all exposed in varying degrees to diversity. Just how much attention we pay to these differences depends on our values, biases, type of exposure, and the attitudes of our reference groups. If we value individuals as unique in their own right, hold few fixed judgments about a group, have multiple exposures (especially quality exposures) to the differences of others, and our own reference groups value cultural differences, we are more likely to be culturally competent in dealing with others. Within the health care setting, this means a heightened awareness and appreciation for patients' differences in self-disclosing, in interacting in the provider-patient relationship, and in perceptions of illness and risk of disease. Verbal and nonverbal expressive behaviors provide clues about patients' cultural contexts.

Tong and Spicer (1994) describe the basis for frustration between Eastern patients and Western caregivers, noting two distinct characteristics of which Western caregivers are unfamiliar. The first pertains to the fact that the family assumes the major role of decision maker on behalf of the patient. The second relates to the

Eastern belief of silence surrounding the discussion of dying (and impending death), versus Western orientation, which advocates openness and honesty. By gaining a greater understanding of these cultural traditions and practices, we can deliver more culturally competent health care.

As Bilu and Witztum (1994) suggest, patients often hold divergent explanatory models in regard to their symptoms. The universal structure of symbolic healing stresses the importance of provider (therapist)-patient compatibility for therapeutic success. To reach this compatibility, strategic therapists seek to join the patients' explanatory models and employ metaphors and symbols derived from their cultural world. These interventions bring provider and patient closer together despite cultural differences.

To better understand where one is in the process of becoming culturally competent, it is helpful to consider all the possible ways of responding to cultural differences. According to the theory of cultural competence (Cross et al. 1989) it is possible to plot competence on a continuum where cultural destructiveness is at one end and cultural proficiency is at the other. But between these two points on the continuum there are many possibilities. In applying this theory, it is important to keep in mind that individuals are not easily typed and are capable of a variety of responses depending on the context of the situation and the persons involved. Some providers may display cultural competence in some contexts but not in all. Therefore, it is more useful and accurate to think about selected behavioral responses than it is to categorize individuals. Having made this point, we can clarify the various terms used to describe level-of-competence and behavioral responses within complex contexts of interpersonal interaction.

Cultural Destructiveness

At one end of the continuum and representing an extremely negative position is cultural destructiveness (Cross et al. 1989). Attitudes, practices, and communications that are destructive to cultures and, therefore, to the individuals who come from these cultures are represented at this point on the continuum. Individuals and groups of individuals who participate in cultural genocide (targeted at minorities) have been described throughout history. Boarding schools that removed Indian children from their homes, laws that restricted Asians from bringing their spouses to the United States, and the targeted assault on African-Americans by the Ku Klux Klan have been blatant attempts to deny people of color their basic human rights. In the health care arena, services that have denied people of color their natural healers, removed children from their families based on ethnic bias, or purposely risked the well-being of people of color through medical experiments without their knowledge and consent are examples of culturally destructive clinical practices.

Systems can also deny cultural differences by severely curbing individuals' rights to communicate in their native language. Demands that English must be spoken in major institutions (hospitals, clinics, schools, judicial departments) may not deny individuals their basic rights. Still, one could make the case that without choices, and with multiple demands to relinquish one's native language, cultural destructiveness is occurring. Individuals who adhere to this extremely negative position generally believe that there is a majority culture, that the majority culture is superior, and that subcultures are inferior and should be eliminated. Bigotry translates into vast power differences that allow the dominant cultural group to control, exploit, and disenfranchise others. While not many examples are found in the health care system today, it is important to be aware that practices that disenfranchise subgroups could have been implemented and may be historically grounded in policy.

At a much more subtle level, there are aspects of culture that are not obvious but may be prohibited. These include nonverbal communication, body motion, and use of space. When these practices (what is considered to be primary-level culture) are controlled, the unique aspects of the culture erode.

Cultural Incapacity

Not as extreme, but still potentially lethal to a multicultural society, is the position of cultural incapacity (Cross et al. 1989). Cultural incapacity is influenced by beliefs of supremacy of one group but, unlike cultural destructiveness, is not characterized by intentional behaviors to eradicate minority cultures.

Rather than by blatant intentional acts to control minorities, individuals who are practicing from cultural incapacity lack the capacity to be effective due to their paternal and/or maternal posture toward minorities. Their attitudes are frequently fueled by subtle racial biases. The following clinical example describes how cultural incapacity may occur even though the provider is operating with good intentions.

Ramona H., a 24-year-old Latina, unmarried mother came to the dental clinic with her six-year-old son, Alton. Her son needed to be seen for a dental checkup. While she was there, she asked the dental assistant whether she could have her older sons, Javier (10 years old) and Juan (11 years old), seen as well. The dental assistant ushering Alton (of mixed Afro-American and Latino races) to the examining room thought to herself: *Why does this mother keep having babies out of wedlock? She's had so many boyfriends; doesn't she care about these children? She is a typical welfare abuser. They (Juan and Javier) look OK—I'm not going to let her 'use the system.' She'll just have to wait three months for their next regular visit.*

In turn, Ramona may notice the assistant's disapproval and think to herself: "That woman is treating me like dirt! She thinks I'm a bad person. I need to talk to someone else because she won't help me."

The assistant's view that Latinas "use the system" and do not care about their children is a bias that, while not communicated verbally, is communicated nonverbally to this mother and will no doubt cause some conflict between providers and the patient. By maintaining stereotypes, service in this setting will remain unhelpful. At the heart of the problem is a moderate amount of ignorance and unrealistic fear that probably permeates the facility and results in subtle messages that Latinas are not always welcomed and are generally expected to be poor health care investments.

Cultural Blindness

Culturally blind providers also suffer from a lack of information (Cross et al. 1989). Unlike those in the former category, these individuals usually take pride in being unbiased. The problem, however, is that they are blind to their own cultural influences and do not perceive the influence of culture in others' responses. Midpoint on the continuum, these individuals profess that all people are the same and culture or ethnicity make no difference. Providers in this category believe that approaches used to provide health care services to people of the traditionally dominant culture suffice for all groups. In this instance, culture is invalidated by omission, and this problem is often compounded because services are not coordinated. Patients may be left to negotiate service delivery with more than one provider, in a language they may not fully understand. While the service-delivery philosophy is liberal and unbiased, it has the tendency to make services so stereotypical and rigid that they are ineffective for all but the most assimilated subgroups.

An example of this tendency would be the application of family therapy for all groups whose family members have a serious mental illness. Despite this good intention and the fairness that seems to characterize program planners, the model of care reflects a middle-class, nonminority existence. These services and providers ignore differences in views of health and illness and the tendency for some families to keep problems contained and private. To expect some women to express open dissatisfaction toward their husbands in couple's therapy ignores the cultural tenets regarding traditional male-female roles. Culturally blind providers ignore cultural differences and encourage assimilation.

Cultural Precompetence

Unlike individuals who are culturally blind and disregard both the effects of their own and others' cultural heritages, cultural precompetent persons realize the limitations they have in providing culturally sensitive responses (Cross et al. 1989). They also attempt to improve their services to one or more subgroups.

People in this group are growing and moving in their capabilities. They may learn the languages, try culturally sensitive interventions, consult others from the culture, and initiate training for themselves and colleagues. They may recruit minority individuals to serve on boards of directors or to develop an adequate needs assessment. Precompetent providers are clearly committed to delivering quality care through culturally sensitive programs.

Cultural Competence

Toward the positive end of the cultural-competence continuum is cultural competence, which refers to the capacity to accept and respect differences (Cross et al. 1989). This requires continuing self-assessment, careful attention to the dynamics of differences, and continuous expansion of cultural knowledge. A variety of responses are used to adapt health care practices for the specific needs of persons from minority cultures.

Culturally competent providers are highly perceptive. They view minority groups as distinctly different from one another and distinctly separate from traditional majority groups. They understand that within a given minority group there are numerous subgroups, each with important cultural characteristics. Providers in this category seek to hire minority staff who are committed to change and who are capable of negotiating a bicultural perspective. They are concerned that they and their colleagues will become proficient in cross-cultural situations.

Cultural Proficiency

A goal for all providers is to become culturally proficient in a multicultural society. This goal is not easily reached and requires a great deal of self-assessment, knowledge building, and consultation with others. Individuals at this end of the continuum hold cultures in very high esteem. These individuals will seek to research and develop culturally sensitive practices. As such, they will be regarded by others as experts or specialists and they will be called on to restructure health care services (Cross et al. 1989).

At each level in the culturally competent continuum, certain principles can be applied. Movement on the continuum relies on (1) valuing differences, (2) self-assessment, (3) understanding cross-cultural dynamics, (4) building cultural knowledge, and (5) adapting practice to reflect the patient's cultural context.

Wilson (1982) identified 24 attributes, knowledge areas, and skills that are essential to the development of cultural or ethnic competence. These three categories: personal attributes, knowledge, and skills apply to the communication of culturally sensitive health care providers and are outlined on the next page.

Personal Attributes

Personal attributes include:

- personal qualities that reflect a capacity to respond flexibly to a range of possible solutions (openness and nonjudgmental attitudes)
- acceptance of ethnic differences between people
- a willingness to work with clients of different ethnic minority groups
- articulation and clarification of the workers' personal values, stereotypes, and biases about their own and others' ethnicity and social class and ways in which these may accommodate or conflict with the needs of ethnic minority clients
- personal commitment to change bias and racism
- resolution of feelings about one's professional image in a field that has systematically excluded people of color

Knowledge

Knowledge includes:

- knowledge of the culture (history, traditions, values, family systems, artistic expressions) of clients
- knowledge of the impact of class and ethnicity on behavior, attitudes, and values
- knowledge of the help-seeking behaviors of clients
- knowledge of the role of language, speech patterns, and communication styles in ethnically distinct communities
- knowledge of the impact of social-service policies on clients
- knowledge of the resources (agencies, persons, informal helping networks, and research) that can be utilized on behalf of clients and communities across groups
- recognition of the ways that professional values may conflict with, or accommodate, the needs of ethnic minority clients
- knowledge of power relationships within the community, agency, or institution and their impact on ethnic minority clients

Skills

Skills include:

- techniques for learning the cultures of client groups
- abilities to communicate accurate information on behalf of ethnic minority clients and their communities
- abilities to openly discuss racial and ethnic differences and issues and to respond to culturally based cues

- abilities to assess the meaning that ethnicity has for individual clients
- abilities to identify stress arising from the social structure
- techniques of interviewing that are reflective of the worker's understanding of the role of language in the client's culture
- abilities to utilize the concepts of empowerment on behalf of ethnic minority clients and communities
- capabilities of using resources on behalf of clients and their communities
- abilities to recognize and combat racism, racial stereotypes, and myths in individuals and in institutions
- abilities to evaluate new techniques, research, and knowledge as to their validity and applicability in working with ethnic minorities

Cultural competence, skills, and knowledge can be gained through training and experience. Providers must avail themselves of opportunities to build their knowledge and skill. Exposure to the positive aspects of different cultures and even negative experiences in helping relationships will facilitate their learning.

UNDERSTANDING YOUR OWN CULTURAL PROGRAMMING

The culturally competent practitioner has the capacity for cultural self-assessment. This means that providers should be able to assess themselves and develop a sense of their own cultural uniqueness. The premise is that as providers are able to understand how their own culture shapes their life views, beliefs, and communications it will be easier for them to establish how they may need to adapt in interacting effectively with individuals from other cultures. Individuals who are self-aware can anticipate barriers and minimize the negative effects of cross-cultural differences.

To appreciate cultural differences, providers must recognize the influence of their own culture on how they think and act. A purposeful self-examination of cultural influences can lead to a better understanding of the impact of culture on one's own life (Sherover-Marcuse 1987).

Very simple differences can result in major misunderstandings. For example, when anticipating family teaching needs for patients' care at home, the provider must know what "family" and "family involvement" mean to the patient and the family. To the provider, family involvement may be informing the spouse. To the patient, involvement could mean ignoring the spouse and involving the extended family, e.g., the patient's older siblings. Knowing one's own cultural biases can minimize the effects of cross-cultural misunderstanding.

Self-Recognition of Personal Programming

Understanding one's personal cultural programming is best arrived at by questions. Sometimes questions administered in small groups of diverse people have a higher yield. The group discussion tends to stimulate one's own recall and recognition and, at the same time, each member who hears another's self-analysis is learning something about cultural similarities and differences. Exhibit 3–2 provides a list of general questions aimed at stimulating self-recognition of cultural programming.

Many providers do not recognize how their own cultural values have shaped their day-to-day experiences and how day-to-day behaviors have been reinforced by their family, peers, and social affiliations. For those who are still somewhat doubtful of the ability of culture to determine behavior, specific and detailed cultural analysis will reveal just how persuasive culture is. Remember aspects of culture include (1) one's set of values and norms, (2) shared beliefs and attitudes, (3) relationship patterns, (4) communication and language patternsm, and (5) prescribed daily activities, including dress and appearance, food preferences, and time consciousness.

Acknowledging Differences

Taking each one of these more global aspects of culture, it is possible to generate a specific list of the ways in which cultures influence individuals.

That which is accepted in one culture may be considered inappropriate in another. The mainstream Anglo culture, for example, has been said to be characterized by individualism, self-reliance, action, and a sense of control over one's environment. In contrast, Buddhist teachings project a fatalistic view of life. Life is suffering, and suffering is caused by desire. In this context, suffering in pain may

---

Exhibit 3–2 Recognizing Your Cultural Programming

- Identify your cultural heritage by acknowledging your place of birth, current affiliations, and religious and ethnic alliances. For example: are you from the United States or outside the United States, a small town or large city, etc.
- What reactions/curiosities do you have about your own cultural programming?
- Does any aspect of your cultural identity come in conflict with other aspects? For example: Do you see yourself as assertive, but your culture does not support this behavior?
- What is the most influential part of your cultural programming?
- How does your cultural programming affect your communication? For example: Are there things that you would share only with close family members?
- What do you know about the cultural programming of others (patients, peers, etc.)? How can you learn more? Does their communication give you clues about their cultural programming?

be considered to be simply a fact of life rather than a health emergency. Many Asians prescribe to the theory of three possible causes of disease—the physical, the supernatural, and balances (yin-yang). They rely heavily on forms of self-care that include offerings to spirits, dermabrasion, and hot-cold and herbal remedies.

There are 21 Spanish-speaking countries in the world whose people are called Latino. Latinos, however, are not monolithic. In general, Latinos value a present-time orientation, the extended family, the interdependence of family members, differentiation of sex roles, unconditional respect for adults, and deference to authority. Although all Latinos have similar values, there may be a great deal of differences among them. Communication styles among groups differ. Some Latinos are more formal in language and style; South Americans, for example, are said to be more formal than are Latinos from the Caribbean. Characteristics, e.g., immigration status, history, religious affiliation, social makeup, and reasons for migration all play a role in the cultural programming of Latinos. In Latino communities the main barrier to health care is usually economic, but in addition there exists a general distrust of modern medicine. Many Latinos believe in folk medicine and have great faith in their *courandaro*. They feel that the *courandaro* (or neighborhood healer) always knows exactly what is wrong with a patient, while a physician does not. The Latino observes the doctor asking many questions before offering a diagnosis, while the *courandaro* seems to recognize the problem immediately and knows how to deal with it. It is a good idea when working with Latinos to involve the family as much as possible.

Knowing that a patient's culture may judge certain behaviors or interactions more acceptable than others will assist providers in communicating more effectively. Aspects of culture that influence health care encounters are multiple. Values and norms, beliefs and attitudes, relationship patterns, communication and language, and daily activities are influenced by one's culture. Essentially, when aspects of culture are operationalized, the link between culture and patients' responses becomes clear.

In the helping-healing process, awareness of the other's culture and the differences that exist between the patient and provider will enable the provider to anticipate misunderstandings and further sensitize providers in their interactions with patients.

While the first task is to raise one's consciousness, this is not sufficient to establish cultural competence. One must go beyond. This requires acknowledging cultural differences. While people share many common needs and values that are defined within society, cultural differences do exist and will affect the health care system and helping process. And, differences are as important as similarities in establishing an effective health care system. Furthermore, the ability to analyze interactions in which cultural differences exist is an important skill.

Exhibit 3–3 Analyzing Interactions in Which Cultural Differences Exist

Aspects of Culture	Patient's Cultural Reference	Your Cultural Patterns
I. Values and Norms	Formal Bows, embraces, handshakes, kissing	Informal Handshakes
II. Beliefs and Attitudes	Hierarchical destiny predetermined race, class, gender inequality	Egalitarian Determinism Individualized race, gender equality
III. Relationship Patterns	Focus on extended family. Loyalty and responsibility to the family of origin. Relational intimacy less important.	Focus on nuclear family; independence from family is valued. Interpersonal intimacy is desired.
IV. Communication and Language	Implicit, indirect. Emphasis on context of messages.	Explicit, direct communication. Emphasis on content of message.
V. Daily Activities	Religion may control dress. Eat when hungry. Value on promptness, efficiency.	Wide range of dress/style accepted. Eat at a social function. Time is relative. Schedules are changed to accommodate relationships.

Exhibit 3–3 presents each of five previously identified cultural aspects and compares and contrasts a hypothetical patient and provider. Differences in values and norms, beliefs and attitudes, relational patterns, communication and language, as well as usual daily activities illustrate that differences that exist between provider and patient may be significant and may potentially cause opposition and conflict. For example, the value placed upon direct communication (provider) and indirect communication (patient) has the potential to generate conflict, misunderstanding, and mistrust. If cultural and medical practices are not in sync, there is a strong possibility that the patient will leave and not come back.

CONCLUSION

The cultural backgrounds of providers and patients are composed of learned norms, values, customs, and beliefs. If providers are to be as effective as they can be in providing holistic care to patients of culturally diverse backgrounds, their technical expertise must be complemented by knowledge of and respect for the various cultures that they will encounter (Rooda 1992). This is particularly true in situations where providers are from cultural and ethnic backgrounds different from the patients for whom they are caring.

Sound cross-cultural practice begins with a commitment to provide culturally competent care. At the very heart of this commitment must be an awareness and acceptance of culturally different expressive behaviors and an understanding of the dynamics of difference in the patient-provider relationship.

Culturally competent health care providers not only acknowledge cultural differences but also incorporate these differences in planning and implementing care. A culturally competent system of care acknowledges and incorporates—at all levels—the importance of culture, the assessment of cross-cultural relations, vigilance toward the dynamics that result from cultural differences, the expansion of cultural knowledge, and the adaptation of services to meet culturally unique needs. While cultural competence is a concept that can be applied to an entire system of care, it is also a concept useful in assessing one's individual facility in relating in multicultural contexts.

Cultural competence should be viewed as a goal toward which providers can strive. In this regard, becoming culturally competent is a developmental process. We are all at some point on a continuum. Our behaviors and attitudes reflect where we are on the continuum at any one time. It is important for providers to assess their own personal level of cultural competence.

Verbal and nonverbal expressive behaviors are influenced by one's cultural orientation. Above all other circumstances, inattention to obvious and even subtle differences in expressive behavior may serve to alienate patients and their families.

The health care provider must be sensitive to differences in cultural perceptions about the role of the sick, the role of the family in health care, the roles of young and old, the roles of women and men, and even the symbolic importance of foods and diet. Helping the patient comply with health care regimens requires knowledge about these and other cultural values.

A final word of caution is important. While it is imperative for providers to be culturally sensitive, too much attention to differences can inappropriately distance the provider from the patient. Beginning clinicians may be too willing to acknowledge these differences and act accordingly. Accommodating patients, for example, by offering to get someone else to care for them can be problematic. This offer can be interpreted as a lack of acceptance or even rejection. Where language barriers exist, it is important to get assistance, and if the patient openly requests a different provider, then this request should be considered. Cultural differences are inevitable, and diversity training can equip providers in most situations to deal effectively with cultural nuances.

Stumpf and Bass (1992) proposed a combination experiential and content course to help providers become more unbiased in their health care interactions. The model, "Differences + Discomforts = Discoveries," promotes depth of knowledge about underserved groups as well as personal awareness of prejudicial feelings. As a result, students learn techniques to provide less-biased health care to these and other populations.

In practice, respect for diversity is often inadequate and, therefore, the health care needs of many cultural groups are not being met (Roberts 1994). Blackburn (1992) reminds us that caregivers and clients cannot be brought together under the assumption that a harmonious union will occur. Cultural competence does not eliminate all problems, but it does help to reduce cultural conflict in health care.

PART II

Professional Skills in Managing Care—Critical Competencies in Therapeutic Communications

Good communication skills are not acquired by osmosis. Learning good communication skills can be time intensive, but these skills are critical elements in effective provider-patient interactions. Patients do and will react to providers' interpersonal skill deficits. They will not necessarily distinguish between system barriers that make an otherwise compassionate provider appear cold, distant, and uncaring and a provider's level of adeptness. Providers need to take their fund of skills seriously.

If the reader completed the personal inventory on nontherapeutic responses (Chapter 2), some understanding of needs for change has been established. In the chapters that make up this part of the text, important therapeutic response modes are presented. Some of these modes, also referred to as techniques or strategies, are facilitative. For example, showing empathy and establishing trust are ways of communicating warmth and establishing the basis for future change. They are necessary transitions in the patient-caregiver relationship. Other responses, for example, questioning, using silence, self-disclosing, advising, confronting, and the like, are action-oriented response modes. These skills are additive and are usually chosen with a particular aim in mind.

While attention to technique is important, it is equally essential that providers understand that using techniques does not exclusively mean using some form of the traditional clinical interview. Recently, considerable attention has been given to alternative, less formalized, approaches. These approaches include talking (Roter and Hall 1992; Cade 1993), listening to patient stories (Smith and Hoppe 1991; Cole-Kelly 1992), and the conversational interview (Brown 1995) and have appeared in the literature as alternatives to more formalized clinical interviews.

According to Brown (1995), "the conversational interview" is advocated because it is more client focused and is less interpersonally controlling. This alternative, more than the structured interview, is felt to produce an accurate shared understanding of the client's health status. As indicated by Roter and Hall (1992), talk is the main ingredient of health (medical) care. It is the fundamental way in which the provider-patient relationship takes form and the fundamental instrument by which therapeutic goals are achieved. While providers use a number of other tools and tests, talk is what organizes the patients' history, symptoms, and experiences. Several positive changes are advanced and are summarized in seven communication-transforming principles (Roter and Hall 1992).

1. Communication serves patients' needs to tell the story of their illnesses and the provider's need to hear it.
2. Communication should reflect the special expertise and insight that patients have into their physical state and well-being.
3. Communication should respect the relationship between patients' mental states and their physical experiences of illness.
4. Communication should maximize the usefulness of providers' expertise.
5. Communication should acknowledge and attend to emotional content.
6. Communication should respect the principle of reciprocity, in which the fulfillment of expectations is negotiated.
7. Communication should help participants overcome stereotyped roles and expectations so that both patient and provider gain a sense of power and the freedom to change within the encounter.

Interactions between patients and providers vary in structure and intensity. The therapeutic response modes discussed in this section are relevant regardless of the mode in which provider-patient talk occurs.

Chapter 4, The Pervasive Role of Confirmation and Empathy, discusses the importance of a major element in helping relationships. The ability to discern the experience of others and reflect this sensitivity in helping encounters is critical. The process of formulating and delivering effective therapeutic empathic responses is discussed. Another concept, confirmation, which is associated with empathic communication, is presented and discussed.

Chapter 5, Communications That Contribute to Trust and Mistrust of the Providers, addresses the basic role of trust in the process of assessing and helping patients. Without trust in providers, patients will not easily disclose their fears and concerns. Because trust is also critical in promoting change in patients, it is vital to the helping process. Mistrust can derail therapeutic interventions. Trust, once established, can be broken. Understanding conditions under which trust is cultivated and mistrust avoided, arms the provider with capacities to achieve and sustain meaningful in-depth relationships.

In Chapter 6, The Art and Skillful Use of Questions, questions as therapeutic response modes are discussed. One of the most prevalent forms of communication in the health care professions involves the use of questions. In part, this is due to the diagnostic orientation of providers. In short, questions are the primary means by which providers gather data. The format of questions potentiate different responses. Therefore, it is important to understand the types of questions available to us.

Sometimes questions fail to produce in-depth disclosure. Silence is a therapeutic response mode that is examined for its power to establish a comprehensive, in-depth gestalt. Chapter 7, Therapeutic Use of Silence and Pauses, details ways in which this response mode enhances empathy, respect, and understanding. Since silence and pauses can also be used in destructive ways, it is important to understand the power of silence as it is used in helpful and unhelpful ways. Silence also has specific meaning in various cultural contexts. Silence responses may be respectful or punitive; the actual interpretations are dependent on a multitude of interpersonal factors.

In addition to questions and silence, providers can use self-disclosure to facilitate the aims of helping relationships. Chapter 8, The Impact and Limitations of Self-Disclosure, discusses this important nondirective approach. Self-disclosure by providers frequently begets self-disclosure by the patient. This is because provider self-disclosure communicates authenticity, genuineness, and empathy that stimulates, in turn, self-exploration and self-disclosure. The key to provider self-disclosure, as is the case for many other response modes, is appropriateness. Appropriately delivered, self-disclosures will be met with matching responses. Inappropriately offered self-disclosures, such as those that are ill timed, will lead to confusion. Guidelines for the formulation and delivery of self-disclosures are discussed in detail.

Up to this point, the therapeutic response modes addressed are considered to be facilitative and foundational. There is yet another set of response modes that involve being evaluative. In Chapter 9, The Proper Placement of Advisement, the skill of advice-giving is discussed. Providers issue advice on a regular basis; this mode is somewhat reflexive. The provider assesses or diagnoses a problem and follows with a solution. While advice-giving is commonplace, it is a poorly understood phenomena in interpersonal communication. Advice-giving usually contains evaluative and judgmental components. Like other modes, advice-giving works best when a strong relationship has been built through repeated use of facilitative dimensions like warmth, respect, and empathy.

If advice-giving does not potentiate action, other approaches may. Chapter 10, Reflections and Interpretations, examines how these distinctively different strategies produce self-awareness and change. While reflections merely paraphrase patients' expressions, interpretations provide additional information. Interpretations can be mild, moderate or intense; the level of interpretation frequently designates the degree of threat that may result when an interpretation is offered.

The maximum level of demand in health professionals' communications comes from the use of confrontations, orders, and commands. These modes are not comfortable for many providers, especially those who want to facilitate, not dominate the patient's course of action. Were it a perfect world, we could settle for less judgmental, nonevaluative forms of communicating. But the fact of the matter is, it is not a perfect world; these response modes are necessary and cannot be supplanted by facilitative, nondirective approaches. In the final chapter of this section of the text, Chapter 11, The Judicious Use of Confrontations, Orders, and Commands, these approaches are addressed. Providers who utilize these response modes risk being evaluative, judgmental, and conditional. This risk is minimal if these strategies are employed when a strong relational bond exists between patient and provider. The probability of action toward problem resolution is frequently highest when patients are exposed to these strategies. Yet, like many of the other evaluative, judgmental modes, these response modes are most successful when a strong therapeutic alliance has been formed.

In therapeutic relationships, healers must try to understand what the illness means to the patient and create a therapeutic sense of connection in the patient-provider relationship. Several interviewing techniques can enhance such an outcome: Rapport setting, silencing internal talk, accessing unconscious processes, and communicating understanding can help providers enhance their sensitivity to subtle clues on which issues of meaning and connection often depend (Matthews, Sushman, and Brench 1993). Therapeutic response modes are skills, and like all skills, they are to be practiced. Providers will need to exercise patience in the acquisition and perfection of these skills. It may surprise the reader to learn that the ultimate objective is to learn the skill but then to forget it. The mark of a seasoned clinician is knowing the skills but blending the skills with his or her own unique interpersonal style. In large part, it is providers who heal, not the enumerable strategies and skills they have at their disposal.

CHAPTER 4

The Pervasive Role of Confirmation and Empathy

A world with emotions, yet without empathy would be absurd. It would be a world of musicians without hearing . . . without the capacity to empathize with feelings of another, we would be just bodies located physically in space alongside one another—no interhuman connection would exist at all.

L. Agosta

CHAPTER OBJECTIVES

- Distinguish between empathy and sympathy.
- Discuss how empathy is "emotional knowing."
- Discuss how empathy is achieved through active listening.
- Identify how interpersonal confirmation leads to the experience of empathy.
- Discuss two outcomes that cause empathy to be a therapeutic response.
- Identify the steps that providers can use to arrive at an empathic position.
- Discuss several barriers to being empathic with a client or developing the capacity for empathy: discuss client, provider, and environmental barriers.

Empathetic listening is central to modern thought on listening in patient-provider relationships. The intellectual, clinical knowledge of a patient is understood to be insufficient. In order to execute one's role, the provider must know the patient beyond the data immediately available. That is, one cannot truly grasp subtle and complicated feelings and experience except by *emotional knowing*. It is hard to imagine that providers would give care without feeling, at some level, what it must be like to be the patient. And yet many providers seem to disregard the relevance of this experience, or they take empathy for granted. Despite the widespread recognition that it is a vital component in the helping relationship, proportionately little attention is given empathetic listening as a therapeutic response.

It is the purpose of this chapter to define and describe the condition of empathy and the nature of the empathic response. Second, the therapeutic value of empathy will be described, and steps to achieve empathy will be identified. Nonverbal aspects of communication as well as reflective statements and silence will be discussed as they enhance empathic communications in the provider-patient relationship. Finally, common barriers to empathic understanding will be identified, and ways to overcome these barriers will be addressed.

In composing our thoughts on empathy, a computerized library MEDLINE search of the literature revealed 56 citations on the subject in the period 1990–1995. While a few articles addressed the concept as overvalued and that empathy may be impossible to teach, the predominant position was that empathy should be held in high esteem and an unempathic stance may be the result of treatment that is driven by financial concern that overrides the clinical needs of the patient (Book 1991).

DEFINITIONS OF EMPATHY AND EMPATHIC RESPONSE

The word, *empathy*, was originally coined "Einfrehlung" by German psychologist Teodor Lipps who, in 1887, used this term to refer to the experience of losing one's self-awareness and fusing with an object. Today, empathy is described as an objective awareness of and insight into the thoughts, feelings, and behavior of another (including their meaning and significance).

Empathy, or the capacity for "emotional knowing" is a behavioral attribute thought to contribute to the humane qualities of social interaction (Clark 1980). For those who study empathy phenomenologically, empathy is a complex process describing a holistic experience of the patient. It involves a synthesis of human dimensions: conscious and preconscious awareness, subjective and objective views, and closeness but distance from the patient's experience. Physical, psychological, emotional, and cognitive processes—occurring simultaneously—achieve an empathic response.

As indicated, interdisciplinary literature on empathy is vast. Empathy, like creativity, is a complex phenomena not easily measured; rather, an aspect of empathy is observed. According to Davis (1990), empathy is a commonly used but poorly understood concept. It may be confused with related concepts such as sympathy, pity, and identification. Empirical studies of empathy emerged clearly in the middle of the twentieth century because of the influence of Sullivan (1953) and subsequently as a product of the efforts of Carl Rogers (1957; 1961). In recent times, the increased interest in empathy is found to be contextually relevant in a society that suffers from aggression, violence, and conflict. This condition—driving people apart—is believed to be eased proportional to the capacity of individuals to be empathic—a force that reduces interpersonal distance and is believed to create acceptance and altruism.

Perhaps the most significant work on the concept of empathy and its therapeutic value stem from the writings of Carl Rogers in the 1950s. Rogers, in his client-centered approach to counseling, conceptualized empathy as a major factor influencing client (patient) growth and change (Rogers 1957; 1961). Rogers' description of empathy stresses the importance of multiple facets. The empathic way of being with another person, according to Rogers, means entering the private perceptual world of the other and becoming at home in it. Rogers further states that it is a process of being sensitive, moment by moment, to the changing experience of this person, to a multitude of feelings—fear or rage, tenderness or confusion (whatever the person is experiencing). It also means checking with the other person the accuracy of one's sensing and being guided by the replies and responses one receives. Rogers' model and assertions about the influence of empathic understanding stimulated considerable research aimed at measuring empathy and its impact on those seeking counseling. Truax and Carkhuff (1967) designed the first empathy scale, the Truax Accurate Empathy Scale, later revised by Carkhuff (1969).

The measurement of empathy in helper-helpee communications continued to dominate the field of counseling for the next 25 years. Whereas the measures of empathy based on a psychotherapeutic counseling relationship have been challenged for their applicability to health care relationships (nursing and medicine), the importance of empathy and the empathic process remains relevant to all health professionals.

Differences Between Empathy and Sympathy

Perhaps the most confused notion and misunderstood idea is that sympathy is empathy. While sympathy does express feeling "with the patient," it is very different from the expression of empathy, which is the task of mentally putting one in the shoes of another and then verbally conveying to that person that one understands what it must be like to wear those shoes (Rubin, Judd, and Conine 1977). The actions of sympathy include the inclination to think or feel like another, but the crucial difference is that sympathy also includes the display of pity or sadness. People who sympathize are unable to separate their own feelings from those of the other. Empathic responses are not the equivalent of feeling sorry for another person; they involve appreciation for another's thoughts and feelings without displaying feelings of pity and sadness.

Emotional Knowing

With sympathetic responses, that which is usually missing is the emotional-intellectual connection that guides the provider to articulate a reply. Without the ability to fully understand the perceived experiences and feelings of the patient, an attempt to empathize becomes a self-centered exercise of sympathy. Consider the following dialogue between a nurse and a patient who is hospitalized and whose diagnosis is end-stage cancer. The patient has not seen her small children for two or more weeks. The nurse approaches her to assess her depressed mood and establish a relationship.

Nurse: "Hi Mrs. _____. How are you doing today?"

Patient: "Okay—I guess. "

Nurse: "You know I've noticed that you have no pictures of your children in your room."

Patient: "No . . . I don't."

Nurse: "How would you like it if we called your husband and asked him to bring some in?"

Patient: "Well—yes. That would be good!" (*Silence*)

Nurse: "You know, better yet, we could make it possible to have you do a video-tape for them—that way they could actually see you . . . see how you are."

Patient: *Looks at nurse, studying her response.*

Nurse: "What is good about a videotape is that they can keep it forever."

Patient: *Begins to cry.* "I'm sorry . . . I guess I'm just upset."

Nurse: "It's right to feel upset . . . you don't feel that you are going to be around for your children much longer."

Patient: *Nods. Silence.*

Sometimes providers are not ready to deal with the experience and feelings of the patient. They have feelings; yet their attempts to empathize become exercises in sympathy that actually make the patient feel worse. In the dialogue above, the nurse was probably feeling the helplessness that the patient projected in both her state of illness and her emotional response. To recover from her own emotional pain, the nurse responds as if she were trying to make the patient feel better, giving bits of advice on how the patient could establish communications with her children. Believing she had "hit on a good idea," she pursued the idea of videotaping. While videotaping may have been a good idea, what the nurse expressed made the patient feel that the nurse could not handle her feelings nor the tragedy she faced. Thus, the patient apologized for her feelings. Then, in a feeble attempt to make the patient feel better, the nurse follows with a sad commentary: "You don't feel that you are going to be around for your children much longer." While this may be true, it may not be the most salient point for the patient; rather, loneliness and no one to talk to may be. And, while this is a critical issue, the way it is approached tends to be rather cold and distant. Most observers would judge the nurse to be sympathetic. The reader may also judge the interaction as a self-centered gesture on the part of the nurse to find an easy solution, a quick fix. As Stanley L. Olinick (1984) points out, sympathy is rarely a purely altruistic and conflict-free response; rather, it can either serve a defensive or an exploitive function, disguising other feelings that may be inappropriate in the relationship. Frequently, sympathy can mask feelings of relief: "I'm glad I don't have your problem" or feelings of helplessness and powerlessness: "Sorry I can't help you . . . and I don't know who can." Providers may think that their verbal replies do not reveal these conflictual attitudes (*let me help you with this*; *I can't help you*); but, the fact is, providers are rarely able to completely disguise their innermost thoughts and feelings. Unwittingly, providers reveal these attitudes in the choice of their words or nonverbal communication. Merely feeling what the patient is feeling or "suffering with" the patient may not give the provider the objectivity that is needed to fully comprehend the patient's dilemma. In the previous dialogue, the nurse lacked an awareness of herself and her ability to tolerate the patient's expression of pain. This was not immediately revealed in her verbal comments, which appeared accurate but rather, it was more apparent in the direction that her dialogue took—her lack of anticipation of the effects of her statements and her attempts to "fix things." What the patient really wanted was someone to talk to, to listen to her, to be present in her painful situation. When providers establish a high level of empathic responsiveness, feelings of pity and sorrow are irrelevant. Providers are able to sustain a recognition of the patient's pain, maintain separateness, but also prevent unnecessary distancing.

Active Listening and Empathy

An empathic response to patients is facilitated by the process of "active listening." In most descriptions of the process of healing, it is clear that the provider of healing has taken some time and energy to learn about the experience of the sufferer's ailments or difficulties in the process of developing the basis for the plan of care. Further, there has been sufficient data to establish that the troubled and the sufferers have yearned for an interested and concerned listener (Jackson 1992). Fleishman (1989), recognizing the need for persons to have someone to listen with nurturant attentiveness, grouped such yearnings with the need to be seen, known, responded to, confirmed, appreciated, cared for, mirrored, recognized, and identified. He described this need as a yearning for "witnessed significance." Active listening is different from merely hearing and repeating what was heard. Active listening refers to a sensitive, discerning use of the sense of hearing akin to Theodor Reik's (1951, pp. 144, 146–147, 150) "listening with the third ear." Reik, in describing the skill needed by the psychoanalyst, stated that the analyst needed "to learn how one mind speaks to another beyond words and in silence." This process can reveal not only what the sender is saying but what the sender is thinking and feeling.

Empathic listening is a term, claims Jackson (1992), that is a significant feature of modern thought on listening within healing contexts. Characteristics of this process involve the clear intentions of the listener to harken to the sufferer, to hear but also to *know and understand*. And, listening within the Rogerian client-centered framework captures both the active aspect of the healer and the increased sensitivity to the world as the patient sees it. It is the healer's role to assume, in so far as he or she can, the internal frame of reference of the patient. It is the healer's role to perceive the situation as the patient sees it and to perceive the patient as the patient sees himself or herself. In doing so, the healer must lay aside all perceptions from the external frame of reference. This process, an active, not passive activity, places the healer at an advantage in fully understanding the patient.

In summary, active listening is a vehicle for empathy. Active listening increases the probability that the provider will focus his or her full attention on the patient. Without active listening, empathy does not occur. With active listening, providers take in data using all communication channels simultaneously—visual, auditory, and kinesthetic—to fully perceive the patient's needs and concerns. Providers who engage in active listening can be distinguished because they exhibit a variety of behaviors indicative of good listening. These behaviors are listed in Exhibit 4–1.

Active listening requires providers not only to hear, but to listen; not only to see, but to perceive; and not only to touch, but to feel. Sensing without integrating data from these major communication channels falls short of understanding the patient. When it comes to integration, the provider must gather personal strength to see the patient's condition no matter how tragic and painful it may be.

Confirmation and Empathy

There has been a long-standing interest in humanity's basic need to be heard and attended to. These needs have been described by some authors to be as important as needs for personal safety. Security needs, in turn, are thought to be intricately tied to feelings of being attended to and, therefore, valued. Without a sense of being seen and heard, most individuals will not trust their interpersonal environments. This condition has been described in theories of growth and development, in explanations about viable work settings, in concepts of functional-dysfunctional relationships, and even in paradigms that predict conditions of escalating tension and dispute. Those who study the process of conflict resolution and mediation realize that the number-one culprit in creating conflict is the absence of communication in which parties are not really listening and paying attention to the messages of one another. It is the mediator's job to restore communication and set the ground rules that will enhance effective attending and listening behaviors in the disputants. It is presumed that this change will not only prepare the parties to negotiate their interests, but it will also demonstrate parties' willingness to value one another. Disconfirming responses are typical in disputes and are usually what anger parties and make resolution of differences next to impossible. Consider the case of two parties who express through their communications that the views, desires, and concerns of the other are not important. The dangerous

Exhibit 4–1 Behavioral Signs of a Good Listener

> **Eye Contact.** Good eye contact need not mean that the provider is "glued" to the eyes of the patient. Rather, good eye contact may be given in spontaneous glances that express interest and a desire to communicate. Poor eye contact consists of never looking at the patient, of staring at patients constantly and blankly, or of looking away from patients as soon as they look at you.
>
> - **Postural Position.** One's posture includes both body gestures and facial expressions. Good postural positions include sitting or standing with your body facing the patient, while communicating responsive facial expressions. Rigid body posture should be modified with flexible movements toward the patient, again, indicating a desire to be with and attend to the patient. Being preoccupied and in constant movement not related to the patient generally communicates distrust. No facial expressions (stoicism), too much inappropriate smiling, nodding, or frowning also communicate a lack of authenticity.
> - **Verbal Quality.** Good verbal quality is as important as the words that the provider chooses to use. These qualities should include a pleasant, interested intonation. One's speech should be neither too soft nor too loud. It should reflect the context of the contact and any particular feeling state that is expressed by the patient. Speaking harshly to a patient who is crying is obviously inappropriate; still, expressing concern when there is no reason for concern is also disconcerting and bewildering.
> - **Verbal Messages.** Messages to the patient should be worded to reflect the provider's understanding of the patient's experience. This may include choosing culturally relevant terms, the patient's own words for his or her experience, and analogies or paraphrases selected from the patient's description. The provider's interpretation of the patient's message should be clearly separated from the provider's own account of what the patient says or feels.

aspect of this encounter is that these parties interpret the attitudes to mean: *You are not important or valuable.* Such interpretations fuel attitudes of mutual resentment and tend to fix each individual in a position—usually a position antagonistic to that of the other party. Interpersonal "war" results as each party is certain that the other is not to be trusted under any circumstances because no trustworthy person would deny another's views and, in essence, their existence.

In contrast, consider the situation where disputants communicate that they understand that each other's point of view is important (at least to them), but they disagree or have interests that seem to contradict those of the other individual. In this situation the parties acknowledge, up front, that there are other ways to perceive the situation and that the views of one another are equal in importance. These parties acknowledge each other as persons.

Health providers should issue confirmation in their dialogue with patients as if it were a significant healing agent. Confirmation responses have the effect of making the patient feel worthy. Confirmation responses acknowledge the other's unique value as a person.

Northouse and Northouse (1992) identify the following five ways in which confirmation occurs:

1. direct acknowledgment
2. agreement about content
3. supportive responses
4. attempts to clarify messages
5. expression of positive feelings

These responses make a patient feel valued, and although the provider may not agree with everything the patient says or does, these replies demonstrate responsiveness that is necessary in a supportive patient-provider relationship.

Just as there are specific ways in which providers can confirm patients as individuals, there are certain response patterns that deny a patient's worth and tend to make patients feel less valued. Disconfirming responses are generally inappropriate or irrelevant. Not only do they express a lack of empathy, they generally suggest that empathic responses will not be forthcoming. As Northouse and Northouse (1992) suggest, disconfirming responses can be of several kinds. They include:

- irrelevant replies
- interruptive remarks
- tangential comments
- impersonal responses
- incoherent or incongruent replies

Most of these responses ignore or disregard the spoken word as well as the intent of the patient, sometimes not allowing the patient full expression of thoughts and feelings. And, while incoherent or incongruent messages may be confusing to the patient, the indirect effect suggests that the provider is not "in tune" with the patient.

Consider the following dialogue between a provider and a patient who is asking to have a prescription filled:

Patient: "Can you fill this please?"
Provider: "Humm, Pru-Care; George is this thing working now?"
Patient: *Appears confused and concerned; is silent.*
Provider: *Turns to patient:* "We've been having problems with this computer."
Patient: *Looks expectantly as providers talk behind counter for about five minutes.*

Provider to Patient: "It will be about 15 minutes."
Patient: "Will it really be 15 minutes?" (*Noticing that there is no one else waiting*)
Provider: "I say 15 minutes; it might be less. This way patients don't get upset if I give them a high number and it is ready sooner."

Note that the beginning response to this patient was to offer an irrelevant remark. The patient did not get a direct answer—only a remark that ignored her need to know. Although the issue of the computer's being down was relevant to the provider; it was not relevant, at least initially, to the patient. In fact, it really was not until several minutes had passed that the patient's question was answered directly. Notice that the patient even questioned the response—"15 minutes?" not totally convinced that the provider knew how long it would take. The provider made a vague reference to wishing to please patients but implied that he was more interested in preventing patients from getting angry than their needs for reassurance that the prescription could be filled and that this would occur in a timely manner.

The following dialogue between a provider and a patient who is anticipating surgery is yet another example of how patients are commonly disconfirmed in dialogues with providers.

Patient: "You know . . . I'm kinda worried . . . It probably is silly to worry. I guess it's a minor surgery—certainly not a liver transplant or anything. (*Heh heh!*)"
Provider: "There is nothing to worry about—you've got a good surgeon. Before you know it you'll be in the recovery room." (*Irrelevant remark*)
Patient: "Yeah, I guess you're right. It's stupid of me to worry about it (*laughing nervously*)."
Provider: "I'll have the nurse come in and get you ready. In the meantime, try to keep your mind on how you're going to feel when you get out of here." (*Irrelevant remark*)

Here, again, is an illustration of what appears, on one level at least, to be an innocuous conversation. The provider is not critical—in fact, comes across as friendly and somewhat helpful. However, the subtle underlying messages tend to negate the patient's thoughts and feelings. The patient's fear of surgery is minimized to the point that even he feels there is something wrong with him for having those feelings. Through irrelevant and somewhat tangential replies, the provider succeeds in avoiding what is bothering the patient. The message: *your feelings are not important enough to discuss* will probably have a deleterious effect on further attempts by this provider to communicate effectively with the patient.

In short, as Northouse and Northouse (1992) suggest, it is painful if others respond in a disconfirming manner that neglects the receiver's own experience, and it is rewarding or satisfying if others affirm these experiences. Taken in the context of the patient-provider relationship, such responses can make or break the relationship.

THE THERAPEUTIC VALUE OF EMPATHY

When the impact of empathy is put in very simple terms, it can be said that empathy allows the listener to heal. To the extent that providers' communications become the foundation of the relationship, the empathic response is central to more basic issues of trust and self-disclosure. Additionally, in clinical practice, empathy is the skill used by providers to decipher and respond to the thoughts and feelings of the patient in the provider-patient relationship. Empathic understanding and empathic response occur in three phases of every contact: the negotiation phase, the clinical-reasoning phase, and the establishment of therapeutic alliance (Brock and Salinsky 1993). Empathic providers can be trusted. When patients trust providers, they are more likely to disclose important details about their condition, thoughts, and feelings.

Increasing Connectedness

In part, the impact of empathy is achieved through the patients' feelings of connectedness with the provider. Feelings of connectedness are reinforced by confirmation, described earlier as a co-commitant factor in binding the provider and patient together. In Rogers' model of client-centered therapy, empathy, together with unconditional positive regard and congruence, elicits important patient outcomes beyond facilitating the patient-provider relationship. Rogers (1980) stated that through the use of these factors the client (patient) will feel understood and be better able to cope. Rogers' method is said to build patient's self-esteem due to feelings of being cared for, no matter what (Wade and Tauris 1990). The provider's support for the patient, according to Rogers, is eventually adopted by the patient, who thus becomes more self-accepting and better able to cope.

Reducing Alienation

Additionally, according to Rogers, empathic responses reduce patients' feelings of alienation (Rogers 1980). Feelings of alienation can arise in patients for many reasons. Their condition, especially conditions that appear visually distasteful, e.g., scars from severe burns, or those that trigger social judgment such as AIDS, may cause them to be stigmatized. Alienation can be self-imposed as certain patients distance themselves from others either because of their illness, e.g., with schizophrenia, or because of their recovery process, e.g., with grief. Feelings of alienation can provoke loneliness and even separation from reality that have serious implications for people who need treatment and who need to follow medical regimens. People who feel alienated and socially stigmatized may not always pursue early treatment. Feelings of alienation can cause a patient to feel timid about being seen again as well as feelings of incompetence in following medical advice. Empathic responses acknowledge patients and make them feel understood and accepted, thus, directly countering the effects of alienation. In this way, the patient is helped to seek advice, continue treatment, and endure, for the purpose of getting better.

The therapeutic effects of empathy are most notable in the early phase of the provider-patient relationship. As Carkhuff (1969) states, during the early phase of helping, empathy is critical, for without an empathic basis on which to understand the patient's world, there is no foundation for helping. Attempts to help will be perceived as insincere gestures and advice will be felt as irrelevant facts that have little to do with how patients see their world and their difficulties. It is clear to the patient that empathy from the provider is an investment of time and effort. Providers who demonstrate their willingness and their ability to be empathic are perceived as trustworthy. They are perceived as potentially capable of helping and as possessing sufficient interest in the patients' state of well-being to handle the task of caring. Under these conditions, the patient feels secure enough to enter into a relationship with the provider with renewed hope.

The following dialogue between a nursing student and a patient demonstrates how empathic responses can create the leverage needed to move the patient beyond initial dysfunctional responses to the illness.

Provider: "Do you remember me?"
Patient: "I think so."
Provider: "How are you doing today?" (*Sitting down, maintaining eye contact.*)
Patient: "I'm better . . . my leg hurts a lot. It's difficult for me to be in bed all the time."
Provider: "That is very difficult . . . I'm sure. You know, I'm concerned about your pain medication. Is your medication making it (the pain) tolerable?" (*Empathic response*)
Patient: "Well—I want to be fully awake. I don't like to be 'drugged up'—you can't think straight."
Provider: "You have a valid concern. (*Confirmation*) Have you had a past history of bad experiences?"
Patient: "No, not really. Well I've heard what morphine does—the horror stories about being on medications like that."
Provider: "What have you heard?"
Patient: "Oh, of people becoming addicted—being mean and saying things they don't really mean."
Provider: "So you are really concerned that this might happen to you. (*Empathic response*) And, I'm thinking that the pain you have now is more than you need to have."
Patient: "There's the emotional pain too."
Provider: "Yes—would you like to talk about that—the emotional pain?" (*Confir-*

mation)

Patient: "I have a good husband. People—well they say, 'Oh my God, what happened to you.' I hide my leg. I can't take it when they say those things."

Provider: "Are you afraid I might react the same way?"

Patient: "No . . . "

Provider: "You know you've kept the covers over your legs the whole time. Do you think you could show them to me?"

Patient: "Sure—I get upset with other people—I don't like to watch their faces—I feel like a 'circus act.' My legs are three times the normal size from my knees down."

Provider: "Yes, well I can understand that your legs are very painful to you—in more ways than just one." (*Empathic response*)

During this somewhat lengthy discussion, the nursing student was able to establish the meaning that "pain" held for the patient. From the provider's initial assessment, physical pain was the issue. How to get the patient to accept more pain medication was the challenge. Yet, a fuller understanding of the patient's experience of her condition leads the provider into the feelings of shame and disgust that the patient experiences and how this is of equal, if not more important, concern to the patient. The empathic responses of the student become the catalyst for discovery and for gaining insight. It is highly likely that the student will now attend to the patient's world as the patient perceives it, integrating in her plan of care ways in which she can help the patient master the emotional pain associated with her disfiguring medical condition. It is also more likely that the patient will regard the relationship as helpful—not tangential. Under these conditions the patient may be more receptive to taking the advice of her physician and nursing staff.

THE EMPATHIC PROCESS—STEPS TO ARRIVING AT EMPATHY AND THE CAPACITY FOR EMPATHY

It is accurate to say that empathy is established through a series of steps that engage the provider's cognitive and affective capabilities. We are not just empathic when we want to be, and it is not an inherent trait that we are born with. Individuals do have different capacities to be sensitive to others, and some people listen more carefully than do others. Still, it is important to remember that empathy is a skill and is a great deal more complex than simply being sensitive to others' thoughts and feelings in the process of listening well. Later in this chapter, when barriers to empathic communication are addressed, it will be clear that empathy cannot always be easily established, and an otherwise empathic provider may not be consistently empathic in all patient-provider encounters.

The process of establishing empathic communication has been described by various authors, some of whom describe verbal and nonverbal components, others of whom attend to cognitive awareness in the provider. Gladstein (1987, p. 178) identified the various nonverbal behaviors that are usually perceived by the patient as empathic. These are face-to-face positioning with direct eye contact and interest and a receptive appearance conveyed with an absence of defensive postures, e.g., crossed arms and/or legs. Various behavioral indicators of active listening are outlined in Exhibit 4–1.

Ehumann, cited in Sundeen (1994) and Smith (1992), identify steps to be taken in communicating empathically to patients. These recommended procedures attempt to combine cognitive and affective capabilities in providers in order for them to achieve empathy. Ehumann (1971) described the process of empathy as formulated by Katz. The empathic process is summarized here in four basic steps.

Identification

The first condition or step is identification, and is stated as the need for the provider to first comprehend the situation and feelings of the other. This step requires that the provider relax some self-control in order that the other's situation seems real, rather than remote. In the previous example, the provider relinquished her tendency to advise the patient about appropriate dosages of pain medications in order to try to comprehend the patient's view: "Have you had a past history of a bad experience?" This question requires that the provider temporarily refrain from telling the patient what she needs to do. Additionally, it brings the very remote aspects of the patient's experience into better proximity to the provider.

Incorporation

The second step or condition is incorporation. The process of incorporation means that the experience of the patient that is now known to the provider is taken into the self of the provider. Although the experience is recognizable as that of the patient, not of the provider, this step helps bring the patient's reality and its underlying meaning to the provider. In the dialogue between the nursing student and patient, the student commented: "So you really are concerned that this might happen to you." This comment is a verbal indication that the provider has allowed the patient's experience to penetrate the provider's awareness of her condition.

Reverberation

Reverberation is the third step. According to Katz, the provider's past experience interacts with that which is known to the provider from the patient. The student's innermost thoughts, *the patient is afraid of becoming an addict—I know this won't happen, still, the patient feels that it may,* is an example of reverberation. This process of reverberation leads to further understanding of the feelings of the patient.

Detachment

Detachment, the final phase in establishing empathy, refers to the provider's return to his or her own frame of reference. The results of the first three steps culminate with other objective knowledge of the patient, e.g., the patient is ashamed of her disfigurement. This information is then fed back to the patient so that more appropriate steps can be taken in responding to the patient and additional approaches can be identified. The student replies: "Yes, well I can understand that your legs are very painful to you—in more ways than just one." It is important to note that this one fact about the patient's experience is the outcome of empathic understanding. And, this one fact will influence from this point on the approach that the provider will take in addressing the patient's pain.

Smith (1992) identifies six steps in communicating empathically. These guidelines can be useful to providers who are struggling with impediments to their abilities to concentrate. Smith first alerts providers to the need to clear distracting thoughts and priorities from one's agenda. Second, providers must focus on the patient, giving the patient full attention and communicating interest. Third, providers must reflect on both the verbal and nonverbal aspects of the patient's communication. With this as a basis, the provider must then pick out the predominate themes of the patient's experience, e.g., the fear of addiction to pain medications, the patient's desire to be cognitively intact, and the shame she experienced from the disfigurement. The fifth step is conveying to the patient an empathic response, reflecting some of the patient's key words to acknowledge her anguish and anxiety, e.g., "the emotional pain" you are feeling. The sixth and final step, according to Smith, is checking to see if the empathic response was effective. Since the purpose of being empathic is to reduce the patient's burden, e.g., her emotional pain about her legs, it would be important to assess whether the patient did feel better after disclosing her concerns. While the dialogue between the patient and student did not include an appraisal of the results of the conversation, it is easy to suggest what this may have included. The dialogue could have gone like this:

Provider: "I have a much better idea of what you are dealing with. "
Patient: "Yes, I didn't know myself . . . I guess my real 'pain' is about how I look. The physical pain is important too—but not as important."
Provider: "Oh. "
Patient: "I feel better that I finally talked about this. I thought you would think it is silly—guess you don't."
Provider: "I don't."

If the patient were asked directly what was helpful about the dialogue, she might reply: "feeling that the staff understand me better, knowing myself better, realizing that the staff may not think that my feelings are silly."

These guidelines, identified by Katz and Smith, are useful to providers who are attempting to acquire or improve on their empathic responses. Still, the context for empathy is multifaceted. And what will become clear in the discussion that follows is that in the context of health care delivery, empathy and its necessary conditions must be executed in some instances under considerably negative odds.

BARRIERS TO EMPATHY IN THE PROVIDER-PATIENT RELATIONSHIP

As stated previously, empathy engages providers in multidimensional ways: cognitively, affectively, and behaviorally. Demands in the process of communicating empathically cannot always be met. The reasons are multiple and reflect the provider, the patient, and the environment of the delivery system. The following discussion focuses on barriers originating from each of these three sources.

Provider Barriers

Beyond the simple intellectual barriers—not knowing how and why to use empathy—are the personal characteristics of providers that inhibit their abilities to be empathic. These include various cognitive and affective capabilities. Empathy requires passion, more so than does equanimity, so long cherished by providers (especially physicians). Medical students lose some of their empathy as they learn science and detachment, and hospital residents lose the remainder in the burden of overwork and in the isolation of the intensive-care units that modern hospitals have become (Spiro 1992).

Some providers are easily distracted by other pressing concerns. There may be pressures to complete a work assignment, to finish paperwork, or to make it to a meeting. Other distractions of a personal nature, e.g., relationship problems, financial strains, minor health problems, and emotional distress, may contribute to the provider's inability to set aside competing concerns and focus on the patient. Some providers lack the ability to concentrate, which tends to be a trait phenomenon, not a state condition reflective of current stress on the provider.

A second provider barrier is the inability to relax personal self-control sufficiently enough to experience the patient's circumstances. A condition also affected by provider stress is the tendency to regard the patient's condition in terms that are familiar to the provider. Sometimes rigidity narrows the provider's focus to the extent that no new information or new insight is allowed in. When this occurs, provider control works at cross purposes to therapeutic patient encounters.

Although provider control makes the patient encounter appear manageable, the truth is that nothing much is managed except the provider's anxiety. Any assumptions about real management of the patient is illusionary.

Empathy also requires providers to incorporate the patient's experience of forming cognitive associations with what they know. Providers who are unable to concentrate will not be able to complete this process. Those providers who can make the associations but cannot maintain objectivity can participate in reverberation but fail to remain detached and fail to complete the cycle by offering salient observations. Errors of this kind may not only be the result of provider stress but also be the result of bad habit.

A final comment that pertains to provider barriers is the individual's ability to identify and witness the pain and agony of patients. As previously stated early on in this chapter, empathy is an emotional knowing of the patient. The sharing of unpleasant and sometimes painful thoughts and feelings can create an urgency in the provider to do something to block this experience in order to alleviate these feelings. Providers vary in their abilities to witness painful thoughts and feelings, which is due to many factors including personal vulnerability at certain times to certain patients. It is probably not the case that the provider lacks this courage entirely, but that for whatever reasons, one's tolerance waxes and wanes. Obviously, if the provider exhibits a long-standing inability to be in the presence of patient agony, the health care field may not be the career for which he or she is best suited.

Before moving to conditions in the patient that inhibit empathy, some mention of the "burnout syndrome" is appropriate. Burnout, sometimes referred to as the professional stress syndrome, refers to a cluster of behaviors intended to protect the provider from identifying too closely with patients. In those professionals in which burnout has continued unchecked, emotional exhaustion is followed by depersonalization (Maslach 1982). Depersonalization refers to the inability of the provider to experience patients as other than objects. The development of a detached, callous, and even dehumanized response is indicative of depersonalization. Professionals may experience burnout more than once in their career. Sometimes it is accompanied by clinical manifestation of anxiety and depression and even somatic problems like headaches, backaches, or functional disturbances, e.g., in sleep and eating patterns.

Patient Barriers

There are inherent conditions in the patient that may inhibit the level and frequency with which providers can achieve empathic understanding.

Not all patients are open to in-depth exploration of their thoughts and feelings. Some groups of patients regard self-disclosing as a sign of weakness or as a betrayal of relationships with significant others. Patients of this type may not be willing to share their experiences on a more intimate level, even if they could be convinced of its merit. Still other patients may want the provider to understand them but fear disclosure. Disclosure for them raises the likelihood that they may be rejected, and rejection may be more painful than not being fully understood in the first place. Risking exposure is highly unlikely, and the provider may need to accept a rather cursory level of communication with the patient.

Some patients accept being known more fully but lack the ability to communicate in words what it is that they do experience. In these instances, the provider may feel like a "fishing expedition" has begun, but just as soon as the patient and provider have established a common frame of reference with language that suits them both, empathy will occur. Cases wherein providers do not speak the native language of the patient present an even further barrier to achieving empathy.

Unlike the circumstances previously described, patients who desire empathy but have difficulty expressing thoughts and feelings do not regard empathic responses as an infringement on their privacy. With this type of patient it is appropriate to try to establish empathy despite the obvious barriers that difference in verbal faculties and language present.

Environmental Barriers

Some providers will tell you: "It isn't me, it isn't the patient. It's something else that interferes with empathic relationships." That so-called something else usually refers to the physical and psychosocial characteristics of the environment in which the patient and provider find themselves. Active listening, for example, requires the absence of distracting noise. Recounting how a patient's experience fits the provider's knowledge of other patients' experiencing the same trauma requires time in order to piece together facts and observations. Identifying unique aspects of the patient's circumstances requires attention to facts and features not easily derived from patient charts. Providers are "behind the eight-ball" because they frequently practice in environments that are full of distractions where time and individual attention to patients are at a premium. Also, providers practice in stressful settings with patients who are under extraordinary distress. Lack of time and attention to detail further drives them into sometimes haphazardous situations. On rare occasions, unsafe practice environments exist that place increasing demands on providers to take professional risks that they may not be prepared to handle. Although beginning clinicians are least equipped to manage such care complexities, they are often the providers who are thrust into such situations. If the setting itself prohibits the provider in adequately carrying out procedures, there is not only an issue of treating patients appropriately, there is the question of provider satisfaction. Unsafe environments create high levels of tension and, of course, such situations are less likely to yield empathic responses from providers.

Consider the following circumstance in which a patient is experiencing excruciating pain and the environment is not conducive to empathic responses.

The child lies screaming in terror as the clinician proceeds to change dressings covering burns on three-quarters of her body. Noise from patients in the next room, the whirlpool, and providers' communications over the intercom compete with the frightening cries of the young patient. Several other clinicians stand by in silence, appearing numbed to the sounds of the young patient. No one speaks to the patient; they hardly speak to one another.

The barriers to empathic response to this patient are more than those coming from within the providers who are witnessing the patient's agony. They come from the patient's inability to express her fear and also from the circumstances. Debridement of wounds, especially burns, is very difficult to witness. Noise, machines, people trying to communicate, and failure to control the patient's distress all inhibit empathic responsiveness. In actuality, it is these circumstances that present tremendous challenges to providers, and ones they are not likely to forget. Left unexpressed, providers' feelings about this patient-care event may influence them adversely in the future as they are confronted with situations that are agonizing to them and to their patients. The absence of empathy, regardless of its cause, hinders therapeutic outcomes, which is the ultimate goal of patient-provider interactions.

CONCLUSION

It has been said that computed tomographic scans offer no compassion and magnetic resonance imaging has no human face. Only human beings are capable of empathy (Schatz 1995). Empathy is an essential part of our roles as caregivers. Schatz (1995) warns that we must enhance this natural emotion that exists in each of us. The roots of our need for detachment and equanimity go back to Sir William Osler, but the pendulum has swung too far, and the need for retention of millions of data bits overwhelms our souls. Although excessive emotion is destructive and counterproductive, we must not suppress our passion. We must control it (Schatz 1995).

In successful empathic responses, providers are able to "stand inside the patient's shoes," participating in the world of the patient while maintaining sufficient objectivity. Sympathy tends to be a reactive response, turning attention to the provider and away from the patient. If providers share the very feelings and needs of the patient, it is likely that they will be unable to provide any help in meeting these needs.

Empathy is a complex phenomenon that involves cognitive, affective, and communicative components. The process of observing the world of another, feeling what it must be like to be that person, yet maintaining separateness from that world is not a simple process. There are guidelines, steps to be completed that demand attention and concentration abilities. Smith and Hoppe (1991) advocate patient-centered interviewing in order to obtain patients' biopsychosocial stories. This actively involves the patient and ensures that patients' perceptions, needs, and concerns are articulated in the provider (physician)-patient interaction. Evans, Stanley, and Burrows (1993) suggest that the traditional format of interview training and the social ethos of medical training and medical practice result in clinical detachment. Empathy is an important skill that providers need to develop. These authors claim that it helps the provider establish effective communication, which is important for accurate patient diagnosis and patient management. The construct of empathy, however, is complex, incorporating a range of complex emotional and behavioral components not easily taught and not easily evaluated.

In the health care system there are inherent difficulties in achieving empathy. Barriers may come from providers themselves, e.g., their inability to witness difficult patient situations, or they may come from patients who are either unwilling or unable to permit the provider an inside view of their condition. And, finally, barriers are inherent in many health care environments where distractions are commonplace and time and attention to the unique aspects of patients is more a luxury than the standard of practice.

Empathy can be fostered and barriers can be reduced. If providers are willing to use this therapeutic response there are no limits to one's capacity to heal, an outcome set in motion by active listening and the capacity to acknowledge and affirm the unique experience of the patient.

An unempathetic stance in an era of managed care may put us in jeopardy. It may result in treatment that is driven by financial factors that override the clinically driven needs of patients (Book 1991).

CHAPTER 5

Communications That Contribute to Trust and Mistrust of the Providers

It is probably obvious to most of us that trust is a difficult quality to achieve and sustain in these days. As a society, we do not seem to trust our government, our institutions (public or private), our professions, or even, in many instances, our traditions.

Somehow, we must continue to emphasize regaining, sustaining, and fully deserving the unqualified trust of the patients and society we serve.

Christopher C. Fordham III

CHAPTER OBJECTIVES

- Define trust as a therapeutic element in client-provider relationships.
- Differentiate between trust and mistrust in provider-client relationships.
- List at least three phases in the process of trust building in a therapeutic relationship.
- Describe how trust and confirmation are intimately linked.
- Differentiate between confirmation and disconfirmation.
- Describe the confirming-interaction cycle in provider-client relationships.

While barriers do exist in every patient-provider relationship, one that should not be ignored is a lack of trust. Trust is critical, and a trusting relationship needs time to build. And, increased time was shown by Ridsdale, Morgan, and Morris (1992) as a necessary, but not sufficient, condition to promote the greater use of communication techniques by providers.

Critical to the feeling dimension in provider-patient encounters is the phenomena of trust, particularly as it manifests between provider and patient. Mutual trust, despite the length or intensity of the relationship, is felt to be the single most influential factor behind the patient's acceptance of provider opinion and his or her willingness to engage in positive health-related behaviors. Trust, a phenomena alluded to in some cases as *blind trust* in an important factor in any therapeutic encounter. A relationship predicated on trust allows for many things to happen. Patient disclosure is more likely when trust exists, and this disclosure is also more complete if the patient trusts the provider. Trust, then, is important to successful patient assessments. Trust also potentiates change. Patients are more likely to attempt new health-related actions if a climate of trust exists in their relationships with providers. Finally, trust is particularly important to patients with illnesses and/or injuries that make them feel personally vulnerable. Feelings of helplessness, powerlessness, and hopelessness are eased when patients feel that providers can be trusted. At least the unpredictability and uncertainty surrounding their illness and treatment is lessened when providers can be trusted to behave in positive and predictable ways.

DEFINITIONS OF TRUST AND TRUST-BASED RELATIONSHIP

To trust is to rely on the veracity and integrity of another individual. People who trust have confident expectations about the benefits to be derived in relating to others. Trust exists when one individual believes that another individual will behave in ways that are beneficial to the relationship, without controlling or directing either the relationship or the individual (Pearce 1974). Northouse and Northouse (1992) add that trust is defined as an individual's expectation that the communication behaviors of others are reliable.

Levels of Trust

Northouse and Northouse (1992) differentiate between two types of trust—general and specific. According to these authors, general trust is the trust that individuals have of other people in a global sense. People who generally trust others would be categorized as having a high level of general trust. Specific trust, the second type of trust, is the trust an individual has of another person in a specific relationship. People who mistrust a particular provider would be categorized as possessing low specific trust. This distinction is important because individuals can manifest high global trust and low specific trust simultaneously. They may also exhibit low global trust and high specific trust. Trust is not something that is just absent or present. It is a complex phenomena that is manifested differently in interpersonal relationships and can change when an individual is involved in specific relationships, in particular situations. In provider-patient relationships, trust occurs when two conditions are met. First, trust occurs when patients perceive that providers have their best interests in mind, and second, trust occurs when patients perceive that these same providers are capable and competent to help them.

In order for patients to truly trust a provider, both criteria must be met. Consider the contrary. If a patient perceives a certain provider to have his best interests in mind but this provider is judged to lack competence, then the patient may withhold trust. Or, if a patient perceives another provider to be technically competent but noncaring about his interests or concerns, trust is likely to be withheld. Feelings of trust create the belief that events are predictable and that providers are both sincere and competent. It follows that beliefs to the contrary evoke suspicion or mistrust. A list of patient beliefs that contribute to mistrust of providers is contained in Exhibit 5–1.

Trust, Respect, and Genuineness

Trust encompasses respect. All patient-provider encounters, if they are to be therapeutic, must be based on respect and genuineness. Respect means acknowledging the value of patients and accepting their individuality as well as their unique needs and rights. Communications of this type include listening to patients, acknowledging patients' preferences, giving choices where possible, and treating patients with dignity. Genuineness refers to a provider's ability to be open and honest with the patient. Providers who are genuine are congruent in their communications. Their verbal statements are congruent with their verbal and nonverbal communications. Genuineness is often achieved by self-disclosures; providers' self-disclosures can lead to greater closeness with patients. While provider self-disclosure generally encourages greater intimacy, it is a response mode that warrants careful use. Some disclosures can actually create the opposite effect and create distance.

A critical factor affecting patients' trust of providers is the distancing behaviors that communicate disinterest and lack of concern. Providers' nonverbal communications, for example, avoidance of eye contact, lack of expression, physical distancing, and hesitancy to be in a patient's presence for any significant length of time, create feelings of distrust. These behaviors do not send messages about the provider's incompetence; rather, they tell patients that because the provider lacks concern and caring he or she does not have their best interests in mind. While interpretations about providers are not always accurate, the behaviors just cited have indelible effects on patients' assessments of providers. Providers who conduct themselves in this manner will not be convincing in their roles as patient advocates. Neither will they easily persuade patients to alter their health habits.

Trust, like many other aspects of interpersonal relationships, is best viewed on a continuum. That is, patients can exhibit a very high level of trust or a very low

Exhibit 5–1 Patient Beliefs and Attitudes Contributing to Provider Mistrust

---

- "You won't like me, approve of me, etc."
- "You won't be there when I need you."
- "You don't really care about me, my condition, my care."
- "You are more concerned about making money (from tests, procedures, etc.) than being honestly interested in me and my care."
- "To you I am 'a guinea pig,' a burden, unimportant (compared to other patients you see, things you do)."
- "You won't be able to help me or my condition."
- "You may be helpful; but, something will go wrong and I will not get the care I need."
- "You can't possibly know or understand how I feel."

---

level of trust. Somewhere in between are those individuals who exhibit a healthy appropriate level of trust. Beck, Rawlins, and Williams (1988) see the continuum of trust and mistrust including pathological elements; that is, "blind trust" is an example of trusting with insufficient reason. Pathological mistrust is at the opposite end of the continuum. The place wherein a person lies on the continuum is dependent on many factors, including a personality predisposition for trust or distrust, and an environment and/or relationship that evokes trust.

While it is true that trust is "earned," it is also true that some individuals have difficulty trusting under any circumstances. Patients' personal health and social histories will reveal clues about their level of trust and the likelihood that trust will come easily. Patients who have been traumatized as youth, those who have been abused as children or adults, and those who experience cognitive impairment may be particularly cautious or guarded. They are suspicious and need to question the motives and/or the behaviors of providers.

Just as trust is earned, it can also be broken. Nurses who behave in nurturing ways with their patients one day and then the next day, neglect them, show inconsistency. If trust requires consistency, inconsistency will destroy trust. It is difficult for patients to trust providers if they cannot depend upon them. Dentists who promise their patients pain-free extractions and actually cause pain will evoke mistrust. Thus, energy that could or should be directed toward coping with the pain gets confused with the patient's need to assess the provider's true level of caring and trustworthiness.

Sometimes patients will deliberately test the sincerity and trustworthiness of the provider. As long as the provider recognizes this potential and sets appropriate limits, such tests hardly ever result in broken trust.

Trust and Mistrust

Patients who mistrust typically behave differently than those who trust. They communicate with defensiveness. They may be guarded in their speech or be altogether noncommunicative. They may exhibit suspiciousness and caution. In contrast, patients who have healthy levels of trust are open and responsive. They generally communicate hope and faith and are willing to take risks under provider guidance.

The early origins of trust emanate from infancy where individuals learn trust based on what they see, hear, and experience. Beginning feelings of confidence and faith stem from learning that they will receive or have done what is needed. Parents and caregivers perform these functions early on; but, in time, self-confidence results from perceiving that one is self-reliant.

The process that patients go through in becoming confident in their abilities to render self-care parallel this primary experience. That is, trust in providers is felt; and, with it, a growing trust in one's own abilities to get what is needed. Identification with the provider and the helping relationship enables patients to experiment with and become adept at aspects of self-care. Patients who look back on learning self-care measures, e.g., giving themselves intramuscular injection medications, testing their urine, or caring for their colostomy, may comment that they never thought they would be capable of these tasks. Through trust in the provider, patients learn to cope with their limitations, to master skills, and to resolve problems and frustrations related to their health conditions.

Thus, positive outcomes arise from trusting relationships. Trust creates a climate of support. It also produces feelings of comfort and security. Additionally, because it reduces defensive communication, it generally yields more complete and honest disclosures. Because of this, the process of establishing trust is taken very seriously.

THE PROCESS OF ESTABLISHING TRUST

Concerns about trust surface in beginning encounters with patients. Patients' trust in providers usually evolves over time as the patient tests both competence and respectfulness of the provider. The emotional climate of initial encounters may be guarded. Patients may avoid risking self-disclosure until they observe that providers are acting on their behalf.

When we speak of the process of establishing trust, we are referring to the establishment of a good relationship based on mutual trust. Trust specific to a relationship is not arrived at quickly.

The phases of a therapeutic relationship are described in several ways. These phases are usually conceived of in three stages; however, some models contain four or more stages or substages. The model presented here addresses the specific issues of self-disclosure and trust. For a relationship to be therapeutic, respect, honesty, and consistency are critical; but, the essential variable of *trust* and the beliefs congruent with a *trusting relationship* are even more essential to provider-patient interactions.

The Initiation Phase

The first phase is termed the *initiation phase*, also referred to as the introductory or orientation phase. This phase consists of the very first contact between provider and patient. Whether through a telephone conversation or an actual face-to-face encounter, this contact sets the tone and climate for the relationship. The essential importance of this initial contact with respect to trust is that the potential for trust is scrutinized. Patients in this phase are likely to project onto the provider attitudes from former relationships that may have been positive, neutral, or in some cases, negative. The expectations of patients based on previous experience surface and begin to be confirmed or altered. Additionally, providers may have developed preconceptions of the patient, and these impressions are validated and/or revised in this initial phase.

In these initial interactions, it is the provider's obligation to establish a climate that is conducive to trust. This climate includes expressions of respect and caring in a context of genuineness and consistency. These elements, sometimes referred to as a supportive relationship, enhance or foster the possibility that a trusting relationship will result. Any preinteraction expectations that have negative effects on trust must be changed or revised for the patient.

Some providers develop preconceptions of patients that include expectations that the patient cannot be trusted, will be unreliable in following directives, and will lack faith in the treatment plan. The provider's own preconceptions must be tested in this initial phase.

Initial encounters that display understanding and caring for the patient are important because they help to dispel patients' anxieties and fears surrounding their health and any care that they may require. The supportive, nonthreatening aspects of this encounter make it easier for patients to share their fears and concerns. Beliefs that patients have that contribute to mistrust must be countered with factual information or sequential experience. As seen in Exhibit 5–1, examples of beliefs specific to the relationship that may create mistrust, or at least present barriers to trust, are listed. Sometimes these beliefs depict patients' overall global perspectives on relationships. Whether they reflect global or specific attitudes, they are potentially destructive to the therapeutic relationship.

Putting the patient at ease is not only achieved by the general tone or climate of the encounter, it is also achieved by specific communication strategies.

One very common strategy is the use of small talk. This would include comments about finding the clinic or office, about the waiting period before contact is made, or comments about the weather or time of day. Small talk has the potential for putting the patient at ease because it reveals the humanness of the provider—that providers are people and are affected by the same events or conditions that affect patients. Sometimes this small talk includes humor, which also seems to reduce initial tension.

Not all providers are comfortable with small talk. There are some pitfalls in engaging the patient superficially. First, the patient may judge the provider's comments or attempts as phoney. Even more problematic is the patient's interpretation that serious discussions will not occur. For these reasons, small talk is frequently replaced by nonverbal expressions of caring and more direct commentary about how the provider envisions the encounter. Small talk can also be problematic for providers because the shift to more important health issues may be difficult to bridge once this superficial tone has been established.

Trust, then, begins with an initial testing of preconceptions and early attempts to place the patient at ease. These steps are not sufficient, however, either in establishing trust or in completing the initial phase.

Recall that trust is built on the perception that providers are reliable. It follows, then, that an important aspect of creating trust is the task of clarifying the purpose and procedures in a patient encounter. This includes a description of how care is usually rendered and what can be expected at different points in time. While the purpose of contacts is usually clear, the procedure or process to meet the treatment aims is not. For example, patients may understand that the purpose of their visit is a physical exam. The exact steps they must take and when and if they will need X-rays or lab work is not always specified. Additionally, the relationships between these procedures and the original purpose may be unclear. The patient may understand that he is having a follow-up exam but be unclear about how a certain test gives evidence of his recovery.

It is important when communicating the purpose of procedures to give complete information. Partial explanations or incomplete instructions will only serve to increase patients' anxieties. It is always important to give patients sufficient time to ask questions and to obtain enough feedback to put them at ease. Their inability to obtain clarification in a timely manner will serve to be a significant barrier to their trusting providers.

The general perspective that patients have is that providers know everything. If providers do not elevate the patient's knowledge, then providers are suspect. They are judged to be uncaring, to be unable to understand, or worse yet, to be punitive. Any one of these scenarios creates distrust. And, once in place, it is difficult to convince a patient of the contrary. Providers sometimes do "cover their tracks" with explanations that they are too busy or do not have enough time to provide patients with the necessary factual information. These explanations are generally perceived as weak and inadequate excuses. Patients want to be convinced that their worth as individuals is appreciated by providers. And, failure to inform them about the purpose of the contact and procedures that will occur may be tantamount to disrespect.

Statements about the purpose of procedures will provide additional structure to the encounter—structure that gives meaning to the actions that are to follow. Eliciting the patient's willingness to participate, however, is a separate intervention, albeit following naturally as a consequence of the providers' description of the purpose. In many provider-patient contacts, this agreement is taken for granted, i.e., the patient is assumed to accept and be willing to follow the providers' directives. Consider, for example, that patients are generally expected to accept such things as lab work, X-rays, and the taking of vital signs without needing clarification or even without giving their explicit consent. What underlying assumptions operate to suggest that patients have, in fact, agreed? We would say that if patients objected, they could register this objection. However, there is an implied contractual arrangement between provider and patient that is important to understand. Provider and patient roles are, in fact, social roles. Complementary role behavior in most provider-patient interactions consists of the helper (provider) doing something to help the helpee (patient). It is understood that once an encounter has occurred, professional responsibility dictates the performance of role behavior. And, appropriate complementary role behavior includes patients' responsibilities to receive the care that is presented to them by providers who are recognized as clinical and professional experts. Thus, their comfort in asserting their hesitancies will be limited.

Informal contracts are generally replaced with specific mutually agreed-upon plans of action. In health care, these plans are communicated verbally and in writing in the patient's chart. A mutually agreed-upon plan of action is dependent on goals that are clear and fully communicated. The mutuality behind goal formulation, by definition, implies that the care plan is not imposed on the patient. Rather, it is based on collaboration between the patient and the provider.

A level of mutual agreed-upon care planning would seem to be impossible without sufficient trust. First, mutual goal setting requires patient self-disclosure. This level of revelation occurs under conditions of trusting attitudes. Second, for any patient to explicitly agree on a plan of action, they must be convinced of the provider's competence and good will. Thus, it is safe to say that a provider-patient relationship will falter at the point of a mutually agreed-upon plan if trust has not sufficiently been established beforehand.

There are specific problems in communicating about plans of care that do not enlist patients in the decision-making process. While these problems may not reflect a lack of trust, they will affect the level of trust that will emerge in the provider-patient relationship. First, providers may withhold health data or test results because they believe the patient cannot or does not want to deal with the information. Second, providers may move too quickly over plans, leaving the patient with an incomplete understanding. Or, the provider may communicate, but patients are unable to understand the information they receive. This occurs when details are presented in ways in which patients intellectually fail to understand.

Problems of no trust or of inadequate trust in the initial phase have significant implications for the treatment or implementation phase.

The Implementation Phase

Implementation of a course of action whether it is a structure for assessing health or treating disease is ideally grounded in a relationship of mutual trust. During this phase, assuming that trust is in place, the provider and patient are mutually engaged in confronting and working on health problems.

A major role of the provider in the implementation phase is to help a patient cope with and master threats to his or her health. This includes instruction in health-related changes as well as giving feedback from clinical assessments that will help them evaluate the success of the care plan.

As a rule, this phase does not proceed without disruptions and barriers. The first barrier is reluctance. In order to put a plan into action, the patient must accept the authoritative opinions of the provider. If the patient is not convinced of the provider's competence, then forward movement will not occur even if the patient expresses commitment to the treatment goals.

A common problem that also relates to patients' faith in their treatment is that the plan of action may not yield the results that were initially expected and desired. Failed approaches are sometimes interpreted as provider incompetency. Failed plans can also be internalized, and patients may blame themselves for failed attempts. If patients fail to comply and deliberately fail to follow directives, then this cause of personal failure is realistic. However, patient guilt about treatment failures may be irrational much of the time.

Whether the provider's competence or the patient's responsibility is perceived to be at the crux of the problem, failed treatment can severely threaten mutual trust and subsequent therapeutic encounters. It is advisable to discuss the results of interventions fully and completely, pinpointing reasons why these actions fell short of expectations. Providers who are trustworthy are willing to discuss failures and successes. Trust, if damaged, can be restored.

An important supplement to these strategies of building and maintaining trust is the process of assisting patients to manage the impact that illnesses or the threat of illness may have on them. Providers who not only address disease but also the impact of disease will convince patients of their caring and concern.

Since providers do not always address patients' reactions to their illnesses, it is important to explore why this is the case. One explanation is that providers do not recognize this aspect of a patient's experience as germane to their discipline or as important to the patient. Recent research on patients' quality of life criticizes the preoccupation with a "cure" approach. With an emphasis on patients' quality of life comes a commitment to patients' responses to their illnesses and treatment regimens.

Another explanation for providers' neglect of patients' ways of coping with their illnesses and treatments is their inability to confidently deal with this aspect of the patient's experience. While this is a possibility, there is also increasing evidence that providers are being encouraged to deal with patients' coping responses in therapeutic ways and are actually promoting patients' abilities to cope more effectively.

Just as in the initial phase, the implementation phase can produce problems that are unique to the level of intimacy expected of provider and patient. One problem is the provider's inability to appropriately deliver advice and directives. Inappropriate advice-giving or too zealous a confrontation can disturb patients and actually cause them to withdraw. Responding in stereotypic or evaluative ways can also negatively influence patients. Trust, once secured in the initial phase, is at risk. However, the ongoing experience of the patient in relationship to the provider usually encourages patients to explore concerns, disappointments, or conflicts. Patients, at this phase, are not likely to abruptly terminate the relationship even if there have been treatment failures. This is a generality that applies to all patients, though some patients will be more apt to stick it out while others will think nothing of aborting a treatment plan and a provider. Many factors explain patient variability; culture, for example, may shape certain responses to the dilemma of what to do when one is unhappy with the care that is being received.

The Termination Phase

If all goes well, the helping relationship that is initially established will survive the course of an illness. This includes the vicissitudes of treatment where plans are not always successful and barriers to sustained trust have been dealt with. The *termination phase* is that point in time when the therapeutic relationship is closed. Closure ideally occurs because goals have been accomplished and there are no further apparent needs for care. It is the case that many patient-provider relationships, however, end abruptly or before care is no longer necessary. Patients may require referrals, may leave the geographical area, or their health may deteriorate to the point that a different level of care is required.

The primary principle behind a successful termination is ample preparation. This means that providers should discuss termination and discharge issues with the client from the start in the initiation phase.

While the major issue is the appropriateness of the closure, the major task when this issue is resolved is to draw the lines of separation. Officially, termination means no longer being responsible for treatment decisions. It is extremely important that the patient fully understands the conditions of this phase.

Patients, particularly those who have learned to trust and value the provider, may have difficulty relinquishing their emotional ties to the provider. This reluctance should be an important signal to providers to specify and clarify the meaning of ending the relationship.

One difficulty that may occur and is potentially significantly detrimental to patients is the patient's assumption that the provider is still very much in a provider role with them. Sometimes they will execute a referral haphazardously because they know, or at least feel, that they can return to discuss their complaints with their original provider. Because of this, providers must clearly indicate how the patient should proceed if certain symptoms or needs surface. This plan may include returning to the original provider, but if it does not, patients should be given clear directives about the appropriate means of getting the care that they feel they need.

Using final encounters with which to review the care plan and course of treatment, including discussions of successes and failures, will not only provide the patient with perspective but also reaffirm the professional aspects of the relationship.

Problems associated with terminating care include:

- providers' failing to communicate clearly and fully the conditions of closure
- providers' failing to handle the patients' emotional responses to terminating the relationship
- providers' inappropriately continuing relationships despite the advisability of closing treatment

Each one of the several phases of the provider-patient relationship is affected by patient trust in providers. Therapeutic alliances are believed to proceed through these phases. Trust is a factor that can sufficiently affect the speed and quality of progression, and without trust, chances for a therapeutic alliance can be seriously derailed. Progress, whether it includes gathering patient data for a comprehensive assessment or persuading patients to change health-related behaviors, will not be possible.

TRUST AND CONFIRMATION: AN IMPORTANT CONNECTION

As previously indicated, one dimension of trust is patients' observations that providers have their best interests in mind. It was also suggested that without satisfying this element, trust would not occur. Provider competence is only half the picture. A bias toward a patient's best interest is communicated to patients through various behavioral presentations and specific communication gestures. A listing of provider-based global behaviors and specific communications that can evoke trusting responses are found in Exhibit 5–2.

Several of these specific gestures and even global behavioral approaches confirm the patient's value as an individual. Acknowledging the value of patients is a necessary part of conveying concern for their best interests.

However, confirmation is a distinct way of communicating acknowledgment and acceptance, and it plays a unique role in patient-provider communication.

Confirmation Response Modes

As indicated by Northouse and Northouse (1992), confirmation is a relatively unique concept that is receiving added attention in health care. Confirmation refers to specific verbal and nonverbal responses that acknowledge and display acceptance of the patient. Trust is intimately linked with providers' communications that confirm patients.

The origins of the belief that confirmation can be helpful are embedded in existentialism. Buber (1957) believed that all individuals want to be confirmed and accepted for what they are and what they can become. Laing (1967) was also interested in the implications of confirmation but focused on the consequences of disconfirming communications. Laing described the opposite of confirmation to

Exhibit 5–2 Provider Behaviors That Evoke Trust

Global Behaviors	*Specific Communications*
• Honesty • Consistency • Respect and caring, openness and genuineness • Reliability, adequate follow-up and follow-through • Congruence between verbal and nonverbal communication	• Direct acknowledgment, appreciation of patient's uniqueness • Informing about and clarifying expectations • Continued supportive responsiveness • Verbal expressions of positive regard, including respect, warmth, and caring • Active listening • Nonverbal expressions of positive regard—smiling, appropriate eye contact, warmth in tone of voice, and approachable body posture

be those attempts to constrain another, forcing actions with ultimate lack of concern and indifference to the other.

Further understanding of confirmation was also an outcome of studies done by Sieburg (1969) of small group interaction. In analyzing ways of responding and peoples' preferences in interactions, two distinct factors were isolated through factor analysis. One was a set of responses that confirmed the person and that were largely supportive and expressed positive feelings. The other set ignored and/or mistreated the unique contributions of the person. The first factor was labeled confirmation; the second, disconfirmation.

According to Sieburg (1969) confirming responses can validate an individual in three ways. First, confirming responses acknowledge the presence of another and decrease a person's fears of depersonalization. This obvious but extremely important step in patient-provider encounters includes such things as acknowledging the physical presence of the patient and attending directly to what the patient is saying or doing to avoid patients feeling like inanimate objects.

Second, confirming responses validate the individual's own way of experiencing events; thus relieving fears of blame or rejection when those experiences differed from others' perceptions of events. In patient-provider encounters, this component is conveyed in responses that reinforce or support what the patient is saying and in expressions of understanding and reassurance.

Third, confirming responses also reduce feelings of isolation and alienation because they create clear messages of being in relationship with another. In patient-provider encounters, responses that ask for further information and encourage patients' expressions of concern in greater detail not only make patients' thoughts, feelings, and concerns more understandable, they communicate the relational aspects of the contact where mutual understanding is important.

Disconfirming Responses

If confirming responses make persons feel valued and acknowledged as unique individuals, disconfirming responses do the opposite. Disconfirming responses value the person less and may cause the person to devalue himself. In health care, disconfirming responses deny the existence of patients.

Sieburg (1969) identified several examples of disconfirming responses from actual interpersonal interaction. These behaviors included five specific responses. These responses are impervious, interruptive, irrelevant or tangential, impersonal, and incoherent. They are defined below.

1. Impervious responses ignore or disregard the other person's attempt to communicate such as by offering no verbal response to what the other has said.
2. Interruptive responses cut the other person off before a feeling, thought, or idea is fully communicated.

3. Irrelevant or tangential responses react in unrelated ways to what the other person has communicated. These comments may also be tangential if they take the conversation in another direction than the initial focus.
4. Impersonal responses genuinely communicate distance; they may intellectualize or communicate separateness such as by using the third person.
5. Incoherent responses are those that are incomplete or otherwise misunderstandable. They may contain long, rambling explanations. Incongruous responses or acts reveal discrepancies between what one says and what one really means.

Disconfirming responses have in common the ability to discredit the patient. Whether subtly or blatantly delivered, they are damaging to the patient's willingness to trust the provider. For this reason, providers' use of these responses should be avoided and use of confirming responses encouraged.

Confirming-Interaction Cycle

Northouse and Northouse (1992) stress the importance of the fact that confirmation is mutually distributed in the patient-provider relationship, and that providers are also in need of confirmation from patients. It is difficult, for example, to confirm a patient when the patient responds in a disconfirming manner. Additionally, providers who are disconfirming in their approach are likely to get disconfirmed.

There is some evidence that confirmation is a cyclic phenomena. Patients may feel that they are not valued but so may providers. The interaction between patient and provider can either worsen or lessen the feelings of being unimportant or insignificant. Further, providers may treat each other in disconfirming ways and this may affect their feelings about themselves and their abilities to give confirmation to others. While the continuum may be viewed at any point, the idea is that one person will feel disconfirmed or confirmed and respond in turn to another person in a disconfirming or confirming manner.

One would hypothesize that patients who receive confirming responses may feel differently from those who receive disconfirming responses. In all likelihood, patients who are dissatisfied with their care are probably those patients who have been treated in disconfirming ways. Additionally, patients who receive more confirming than disconfirming responses may experience greater confidence in their ability to deal successfully with the demands of their illness or the threat of illness. As indicated earlier, patients who get embroiled in the relational aspects of their care lack energy to cope with their illness. Since their energy is siphoned off, they may also have less energy to participate in self-care measures.

The cycle becomes evident. The provider may be feeling disconfirmed, either unimportant or even disenfranchised from the helping process. This provider enters into a contract with the patient but lacks the emotional energy to affirm and acknowledge the patient. Consequently, the patient—already vulnerable to threats of isolation and alienation—may increase the prospect for disconfirming responses by being argumentative or resistant to the provider. We would expect then that patients' disconfirming responses would make the provider feel more unappreciated and unsuccessful. This chain of responses could be broken by either the patient, an outside person, or a provider, or could continue for a period of time.

Interruption of the cycle requires a realization of the dynamic factors that are involved in producing hurtful feelings. Interacting at the peer level to obtain provider mutual respect can alter the initial sensitivity that providers have. Assessing the chainlike quality in the interaction with the patient is important in the continued assessment of patient-provider interactions. Finally, providers' conscious and deliberate efforts to confirm patients, even if they are still feeling somewhat disconfirmed, potentially relieve the tension between patient and provider and reconstruct encounters to be more confirming.

Confirming interactions build trust. Disconfirming encounters present barriers to trust. Therefore, providers must evaluate their interactions along this dimension as they attempt to secure and maintain a therapeutic alliance with the patient.

CONCLUSION

The purpose of therapeutic patient-provider contacts is not only to obtain information needed to assess patients but also to establish a relationship that serves as the context for a working alliance between the patient and the provider. Provider-patient encounters are effective to the degree to which important data can be obtained and health behaviors negotiated.

Trust is so basic to provider-patient relationships, it is often taken for granted. We know that trust, defined here as confidence in provider competence and perceptions that providers have one's best interests in mind, is critical to therapeutic alliances. Trust in providers helps patients deal with the fears and uncertainties surrounding their care and conditions. Patients are simply unable to do many of the things providers do, and in many ways are forced to depend on providers. Patients need to see professionals as competent and caring individuals. Providers who want to foster trust will seek to build their professional-clinical credibility as well as their reputations to be interpersonally trustworthy.

Patients may have generalized global trust of most things and people or they may be inherently suspicious and guarded. They may also display a range of trust with specific providers and in specific contexts. Sometimes patients are generally trusting individuals but have a specific mistrust of health care providers or health care delivery systems. Patients' reactions to hospitals is a case in point; most patients (and many providers) mistrust what occurs or could occur in hospitals. This mistrust can originate from previous negative or traumatic experience or from a lack of information. Each time a patient encounters a new provider and/or new system, trust must be negotiated, or renegotiated.

The ability to create trust in the patient-provider relationship is dependent on certain generic behaviors as well as specific communication strategies. Provision of information and acknowledging the patient are communications that encourage trust. Overall approaches that demonstrate honesty, genuineness, and caring also contribute to faith in providers. Without the ingredient of trust, the therapeutic alliance will be vacuous.

Providers may argue that there are too many demands on their time to build trust in their relationships with patients. While the building of trust does take time, it is a task that cannot be neglected even in this era of fleeting episodic encounters with patients. It is not that we cannot afford the time to build trust; rather, we cannot afford not to build trust.

CHAPTER 6

The Art and Skillful Use of Questions

What you want to know is not in the answer to your question—but, I'll answer it anyway.

Anonymous Patient (1994)

CHAPTER OBJECTIVES

- Describe different ways in which questions can be used therapeutically.
- Differentiate between the therapeutic use of questions and the nontherapeutic use of questions.
- List ways in which questions can be used with deleterious consequences.
- List and describe three suggested formats for questions.
- Explain how the choice of question format can significantly lessen or increase the client's response burden.

Questions are an important communication mode in the practice of health care. Essentially, the data from which plans for care are derived result from the careful use of questions. Health histories and the majority of the patient's physical assessment are the direct result of the skillful use of questions on the part of the provider. The primary goal of the interview with patients is essentially to elicit information from the patient about his condition. For this process to occur effectively, the provider must have knowledge of, as well as skill and judgment in, the art of questioning. This chapter will review basis principles behind the therapeutic use of questions.

THERAPEUTIC USE OF QUESTIONS

One of the most common modes in human communication involves the use of questions. Questions are customarily the primary tool for health care providers because providers are diagnostically driven and are continually seeking to assess patients. In fact, the provider role is characterized by the privilege, expectation, or habit of asking questions. Providers use several types of questions to obtain, clarify, and specify information about the condition of the patient. According to Nunnolly and Moy (1989), questions allow the provider to follow, focus in depth, and redirect if necessary.

Collecting Information

Perhaps the most basic use of questions is merely to begin the dialogue. Questions provide an invitation to patients to take part in their assessment. In this sense, questions are lead-ins for the patient to begin talking. Information collected from a patient may involve health-history data, e.g., previous diseases, surgeries, hospitalizations, and medications. It will also include sociocultural data dealing with age, income, race, ethnicity, years of education, marital status, and number of dependents. Although this information appears to be straightforward and easily derived, this is not the case. Frequently, patients often do not know or remember specific health-history events. Also, data and information about their sociocultural background are often sensitive topics, and patients are not readily convinced that responding to these questions is a good idea. Some questions may elicit fear, guilt, and embarrassment. For this reason the skillful use of questions may make the difference between incompleteness and completeness and accuracy of data collected. Giving the patient choices about the amount of data and the context in which the data is provided are always important principles to keep in mind.

Clarifying and Specifying

Because patients are not usually able to assemble information in ways that are meaningful to health care providers, a second function of the use of questions is to clarify and specify the information provided by the patient.

For example, when a patient complains of abdominal pain, the clinician wants to know the location, character of, and severity of the pain. This assessment requires assisting the patient to clarify and specify features of his experience of the pain. Is it a dull or sharp pain? A radiating pain or localized pain? Is it low grade or very severe? This data is needed from the patient and requires providers to focus their questions to elicit this data. While exploratory questions are generally useful, a carefully worded question that seeks clarification or specificity of patients' accounts of their experience are critical in this appraisal process.

When patients are having difficulty describing their experience due to immediate distress or language or some other barrier, the provider must thoughtfully sort through those phrases or words that will prompt clarification. Using the patient's own terms or phrases can be quite useful. If patients refer to their pain as "pressure," then providers can seek to clarify this pressure. The provider uses the patient's terms to engage patients in the collaborative effort to define their problem. Because clarification and specification require patients' verbal expression and elaboration, the collaborative nature of this interaction must be preserved.

In conducting a health history, performing a physical exam, or delivering care, it is very important that the provider become specific in the data required. For example, when changing dressings the provider will need to know exactly which techniques are painful and which are less painful. Questions that are focused help to specify the experience and reduce the potential of distress from the procedure. Carefully chosen questions direct the interview or assessment from fruitless to fruitful areas of discussion.

Ruling Out/Ruling In

Just as important as identifying what is occurring with the patient is the situation of ruling out what is not the case. Ruling-out questions may include questions that seek clarity and specificity. They are generally more direct, e.g., "Does the pain extend to your left shoulder?" They also can require the patient to observe a phenomena, compare the experience, and choose a response that fits the choices that the provider has given, e.g., "If I press here, do you feel the pain as sharply as you do now in your left shoulder?"

Some ruling-out questions require patients to recall past experiences and compare them with present experience. For example, the provider may ask: "Does this medication cause you to feel nauseated if you take it before a meal?" And, "Is the nausea you feel different from what you always feel?" In this exchange the provider is seeking to pinpoint and rule out various possibilities. The provider has certain hypotheses about the health event and is collecting data to rule out some possibilities and rule in others.

In summary, while questions seem to have very specific purposes in the clinical interview, they also have a more subtle secondary effect of providing reassurance. Sometimes questions are used in a slow-moving interaction as a filler. An occasional question lets the patient know that the provider is present and is attentive. Using questions not only when the patient needs a lot of silence but also when the patient needs to know that a caring provider is there can be very therapeutic.

NONTHERAPEUTIC USE OF QUESTIONS

Questions are the primary vehicle for therapeutic communication with the patient. While they provide the basis for effective interviewing they can also be misused. Questions can be used therapeutically or nontherapeutically. The following discussion highlights various ways in which questions can be inappropriately positioned in provider-patient interactions.

Interpretative Purposes

There are cases in which questions are posed to make an interpretation. Interpretative questions are not used to collect data; they are used to give information. An example would be: "If you choose not to let your daughter have braces, wouldn't that make you an irresponsible parent?"

The point is that the provider is not interested in whether the parent shares this opinion; she is, however, concerned that the parent know that refusing braces is neglect of the child's health and well-being. While this interaction focuses around a question, no new information is sought. Under the guise of this question the provider delivers an opinion and an interpretation of the parent's behavior. In one sense it is a disguised accusation.

Self-Disclosure Purpose

A second type of question used to give, not request, information is the self-disclosure question. An example would be: "Do you know that your rolling back on the bed (after I got you in position) is making it hard on me?" In this scenario the provider wants to tell the patient not to roll back on the bed. The question is also a telling question. It tells what the provider is experiencing, i.e., difficulty and hardship. Although the question is indirect and may be confusing, the patient gets the point; the provider does not like what occurred.

Advisement Purpose

A third type of question that tells and does not ask is one that gives advice. Consider the following question: "Don't you think that if you take a little juice first that pill will be easier to swallow?" Behind this question is a piece of advice: "It will be easier to take your pill if you drink some juice first." Usually when providers put advice in the form of a question they are attempting to soften their advice and appear less authoritative. They may actually believe that they will have greater success in changing the patient's behavior if this advice is indirect because direct advice is offensive and elicits negative, resistant behavior.

Telling questions, presented as self-disclosures, interpretations, or advisements, are used when direct telling is believed to be undesirable. The provider may perceive directness as too disrespectful. Telling questions tend to be more tactful, more tentative, and sometimes kinder ways of making observations or stating opinions. The major problem, however, is that telling questions can be confusing. It is not always wise to water down a bit of advice when it must be followed. And, the repeated use of telling questions can be distracting and annoying to patients. Some patients mistrust the manipulative quality of this form of communication. Since trust is the cornerstone of effective self-disclosure on the part of the patient, using telling questions carry a risk. A good rule of thumb is to use as few telling questions as possible. Even though one might use them to vary the structure and pace of the dialogue, if questions that honestly gather information are to be believed, questions that tell should be avoided. Interpretation, self-disclosure, and advise are more appropriately delivered directly.

Questions, whether telling or data-gathering questions, can be used defensively. Using questions defensively is also inappropriate. Questions are used defensively to evade the spotlight. Beginning practitioners when confronted with patients who ask direct and personal questions of them often answer a question with a question. Being asked, for example, if they are married may be something the provider finds inappropriate. Furthermore, the process of being asked direct questions by the patient may be disconcerting since it is the provider who should be doing the questioning. The provider responds defensively to evade the spotlight and to avoid the anxiety of the moment.

Indirect questions are often used in place of other stronger response modes. Consider this question used to reflect on the patient's current effect: "You seem angry today. Is this so?" Such a question is less blunt than using the reflective statement, "You're angry." In such cases the provider is seeking information and wants to control the threatening aspects of the question. This type of question simply requests the patient's verbal response; it does not challenge the patient as the reflective statement, "You're angry," seems to.

Deleterious Use of the Direct Question

Perhaps the most frequently misused question format is direct questions. As indicated by Gazda, Childers, and Walters (1982), direct questions may have several deleterious effects on the patient-provider relationship. These authors identify nine undesirable outcomes that may occur if direct questions are misused. The first problem they cite is the creation of a dependent relationship. The use of multiple direct questions can give the effect of provider "take-over"; the respondent learns to expect that essential outcomes only result from this process. The provider-patient hierarchy is quite clear in these interactions as the patient comes to expect positive outcomes from following this direct and authoritative inquiry.

A second deleterious effect and related to the first is that direct questions can put the responsibility for problem solving on the helper. The provider, assuming the role of expert by asking many direct questions, conveys to the patient that a solution is forthcoming. The provider's solution, however, is not always one the patient can use. Although prescriptive actions are appropriate, much more of medical practice is the result of mutual problem solving. Orders on the part of the expert provider make up only a portion of the total treatment plan. Along with this problem is the concurrent result that the patient's involvement in solving the problem is minimized. Responding passively to direct questions prevents patients from actively modifying solutions so that the solutions work for them. Solutions that are not individualized, then, are not really solutions, even though they are assumed to be.

Patients who take a less-active role in formulating solutions are also less likely to accept responsibility for their behavior. Overreliance on experts minimizes patients' tendencies to follow through because they are primed to hold the provider responsible for success or failure of the treatment program. Again, use of direct questions by the provider lessens the willingness of patients to be active participants in designing their care.

Another important deleterious effect of direct questions is the fact that they can produce invalid information. Almost every direct question has within it the preferred answer (Gazda et al. 1982). Consider the following direct questions:

- "Are you ready for your bath?"
- "Would you like help getting out of your chair?"
- "Would you like to be discharged tomorrow morning?"

In every case, the patient can read between the lines; the answers should be affirmative because that is what the provider expects. Most patients want to be agreeable, be approved of, and be liked by providers, and they will try to oblige the provider by listening between the lines and giving the response that they perceive to be desired. The agreement elicited, however, merely reflects the patient's obligatory position; the patient's real thoughts and feelings may not be expressed. Information such as, "I'm not really ready for my bath if it means I'm going to have to change positions," and "I'd like to be discharged tomorrow, but I don't think my family is ready to have me come home yet," may not surface. Thus, the brief responses to the original direct questions would not be entirely accurate, and the provider would initiate activities based on inaccurate or incomplete information.

Finally, two critical attitudinal problems can arise from the misuse of direct questions. The overuse of direct questions by providers can lead to resentment in the patient. Sometimes questions appear to relentlessly probe for hidden motivations; thus causing resentment (Collins 1986). Additionally, relying on direct questions too much can make the provider inattentive to the patient. The first problem relates to the fact that sometimes providers' questions are asked out of curiosity rather than because they are relevant to the situation. Many questions asked at one time seem irrelevant if they are not interspersed with reflective thought.

The following dialogue reveals how useless, probing questions can make the patient resentful:

Provider: "Did you see your doctor this morning?"
Patient: "Not yet."

Provider: "When did he say he'd be here?"
Patient: "He really didn't say."
Provider: "When did he come yesterday?"
Patient: "In the morning."
Provider: "Probably between 10:00 and 11:00 o'clock, right?"
Patient: (*Angry tone of voice*) "Probably; why?"

This series of direct questions can be confusing to patients. It would appear that the provider is interested in the patient's need to see the doctor. However, the specificity and line of questioning suggests that the provider may have other reasons for wanting to know the doctor's schedule. The provider may be concerned about something of which the patient is unaware. Had the provider explained why more exact information was important, the patient would have been less confused. Resentment about the probing may not have occurred. Questions usually carry demands; too many questions increases the demand aspect in the patient-provider interaction. The patient may feel pushed and pulled in ways that are uncomfortable, especially if the line of inquiry lacks warmth, respect, and empathy. This condition generally leads to replies that are hostile and superficial. Sometimes providers ask so many questions because they are responding to internal demands to keep the conversation going or out of discomfort with silence. Providers who have a list of questions to ask are better off allowing silence between what the patient says and what they say. This will also enable the provider to reformulate additional questions in meaningful ways.

The inattentive provider is in serious jeopardy. This provider will rely on direct questions and miss the numerous cues that come from the patient's nonverbal communication. The provider may pay little attention to the person in the patient and be "out of touch" in attempts to understand how and what help is needed. In some respects, the greater the number of direct questions that result in minimal data, the less likely it is that patients will be helped in meaningful ways. This principle is important to remember both in applying questions and in choosing the appropriate format for questions. The reason that many direct questions impose great limitations on the helping process is that they severely curb the quality of listening that occurs. It is listening, not good questions, that enables providers to render compassionate quality care.

Asking "leading" or "loaded" questions is another type to avoid. These questions, usually closed-ended in format, restrict or influence the patient's response because the wording suggests an appropriate answer. Actual data collection is blocked due to the fact that response options are limited. An example might be: "This doesn't hurt, does it?" This type of questioning is usually used because the provider's needs or goals are paramount. The patient may respond out of deference to the provider and give the desired response, i.e., "No-o-o." Still, this answer could be invalid. The patient might deny feeling pain when in fact pain is being experienced. Another possibility is that the patient will minimize the pain by describing the experience as a "little ache," for example. In either case, patients feel trapped and they alter their responses out of deference or even intimidation.

A final type of question that should be avoided is the double-barreled question. This format allows only one answer when really two or more separate questions are asked. An example would be: "Would you like the chair lowered, a glass of water to rinse out your mouth, a magazine while you're waiting?" While this particular double-barreled question seems acceptable, it can be annoying. More than one double-barreled question may anger the patient. These questions are disrespectful because they rush the patient to respond. The patient is seemingly less important than are the answers.

While using questions properly may seem simple, there are many dos and do nots associated with the therapeutic use of questions. Generally, the provider should avoid asking too many questions, especially too many questions in a short time period. Rapid-fire questioning takes the aura of interrogation and may cause the patient to be concerned, to become angry, and even to become withdrawn.

The next section of this chapter focuses on formats for therapeutic questioning and the effects of different types of questions. Question formats allow providers options in meeting data collection objectives. Each type of question requires a certain type of answer. Collecting information, clarifying and specifying, and ruling out/ruling in are the major purposes for using questions. Different question formats perform these functions.

TYPES OF QUESTION FORMATS

When we think of questions that we want to ask the patient, our amount of intent is usually to utilize the most efficient approach to arrive at the maximum information. Patients' potential reactions to questions are important to consider since we are not only interested in the approach that will provide the most information, we must be certain that what we ask and how it is asked will not endanger the positive provider-patient relationship that we are striving to achieve.

Questions can be framed in a variety of ways to elicit information. The following discussion outlines the types of questions available for use.

Closed-Ended Question Format

The most common category of questions is closed, sometimes referred to as convergent, questions (Riccardi and Kurtz 1983). These questions require short, one or two word responses. Usually the responses are simply one word replies, "yes" or "no."

Closed-ended questions have the effect of restricting the patient's range of response. Because of this, the patient is not always assisted to express his or her true concerns, thoughts, or feelings (Hames and Joseph 1986). Because closed questions ask for specific data and provide only limited possibilities for response, the information that is gathered is frequently incomplete.

The following example illustrates this consequence.

Provider: "Are you having much pain?" (*Closed-ended question*)
Patient: "Yes."
Provider: "Is it about the same?" (*Closed-ended question*)
Patient: "I think it's worse."

Observe that the provider's questions call for brief responses from the patient. The patient is not encouraged to describe the pain or give any details concerning his thoughts or reactions. Important information may be missed because the patient does not expand on the information that he provides. In the example cited, the patient may have had important information to share about his tolerance for the pain that he is experiencing. When asked about the degree of his pain he may have expressed concern that it will get worse or that he will not be able to tolerate it if it continues at the same level. Because the patient receives a second closed-ended question asking him to compare this current pain with the pain he was previously experiencing, he may be further distracted from sharing this important information. Although the additional information, comparing the current pain with former pain, is not irrelevant, it may be tangential. And, it has the effect of delaying the patient's disclosure of all data about his experience of pain that is pertinent at the time.

The patient may also feel that there is a chance that the provider will not understand the nature and experience of pain he is having. Asking closed-ended questions when the patient needs to expand on his thoughts can cause him to forget important information.

Closed-ended questions are not always inadvisable, however. When closed-ended questions are asked after patients are permitted to give their own account of their experience, they help to clarify and specify certain essential details. Closed-ended questions, placed judiciously in the conversation, do not hinder communication. Thus, the characteristics of closed-ended questions that can hamper therapeutic communications can actually be invaluable. Let us say, for example, that this same patient is in an emergency situation and that it is difficult for him to verbalize his experience. Vital information must be collected quickly, and closed-ended questions are very useful in cases where, for example, the level and location of pain must be rapidly assessed (Cournoyer 1991).

Open-Ended Question Format

Open (divergent) questions according to Riccardi and Kurtz (1983) are underused in health care. By their very nature they cannot be answered with a single word.

Open-ended questions invite disclosure. "What keeps you from following your diet? taking your pills? calling for an appointment?" are questions that ask the patient to tell more. They are effectively used as lead-ins and ways to gain the patient's perspective on an event, issue, or condition. Open-ended questions not only invite a range of responses, they tend to elicit critical thinking and active participation on the part of the patient (Gazda et al. 1982).

Open-ended questions work very well at the start of an interview. This is because little restriction is placed on the nature of the patient's response. The patient is not only encouraged to provide information but also to establish an open, positive relationship with the provider. Generally, open-ended questions have more of a tendency to convey caring and concern when compared with the closed-ended format.

Consider, for example, the time and individual attention generated in this provider's use of open-ended questions:

Nurse: "Hi, Kristina."

Patient: "Hi."

Nurse: "I'm Dr. Landon's nurse, Julie. He wanted me to speak with you for a few moments before he comes in to talk with you. I understand this may possibly be your fifth surgery."

Patient: "Yeah . . . yeah." (*Nodding head*)

Nurse: "Can you tell me how you're feeling about the possibility of having a fifth surgery?" (*Open lead-in*)

Patient: "Um, I'm getting really frustrated because when they did the reconstruction last September, they told me that was it. I could go to college, play my volleyball, and do whatever I want. Now it's giving out on me (*sounding exasperated*). I don't feel happy at all . . . not that I'd feel happy about my knee giving out. But it's just that when they tell you that you should be OK, and that you'll be a normal young person again, and then you're not allowed to and they can't do anything about it, it's hard. I know I'm gonna be here. I'm gonna probably go to surgery so they can look and see what happened. But, I mean, I can't even walk down a hill because it was giving out on me. I'd have to be carried down the hill, and it was really humiliating, especially when, you know, you've gone through a surgery. After that surgery you're supposed to be fine, and you go through a year of physical therapy. And you're supposed to be fine. And then it gives out; you just don't trust anything anymore."

Nurse: "What has the doctor told you about your problem?" (*Open-ended question*)

Patient: "Oh, well, he . . . well, ya know, he reconstructed the anterior cruciate ligament which, um, I don't know what the problem is right now. Because finally I'm walking on regular land, and I'm walking uphill—it's just the downhill part. He didn't tell me what the possibilities were for the surgery. He didn't tell me if it was, uh, if it was the cartilage, or if the meniscus was torn, or what. So, I don't know. Maybe I could talk to him about that."

Nurse: "Yeah, maybe you could talk to him about that, so you can get a better picture for yourself; so you can have a better understanding of this next surgery. How did you feel about your last surgery?" (*Open-ended question*)

Patient: "That was OK. That was the reconstruction. It was OK because I went in there really hopeful, ya know, because I hadn't played volleyball in four years. I skipped my entire high school career of volleyball. And I figured, not that I'm planning on playing in any big way when I get to college or anything . . . but I want to be able to go outside and play and have a good time. I haven't been able to run, or dance, or swim, or anything. The reconstruction was just a really big hopeful thing for me."

Notice that the nurse started the interview with a brief introduction followed by a broad lead-in. Although the lead-in was not a "what" or "how" phrase, the result was effective. It led to open exploration of how the patient viewed surgery and the prospects of functional recovery. Because the lead-in was broad, the patient was able to elaborate on some feelings and concerns that she had had throughout the past year, giving the provider an overall appraisal and attitude about the patient's condition. A point worth noting here is that the provider could have reflected upon and validated the patient's feelings of frustration and helplessness in order to communicate an empathetic presence, but the open-ended method of inquiry provided the patient maximum freedom to explore the relevant issues. The patient's care then can be individualized. As Northouse and Northouse (1985) point out, open-ended questions allow patients to give unlimited answers. While the patient feels free to express herself, the provider gains essential knowledge on which to build a better understanding of the care that the patient needs. Also, open-ended questions usually evoke more self-exploration by the patient, increasing the probability of collaborative problem solving.

As with closed-ended questions, open-ended questions have limitations. First, because these questions are broad in scope, they result in a certain amount of unpredictability in the direction of the dialogue, and it is frequently the case that some information or facts are omitted. Open-ended questions then are rarely effective if not interspersed with other types of questions that focus patients and direct them along the lines of an in-depth exploration of a specific topic. Sometimes it is very important to limit and focus patients' responses. Patients in crisis or those unable to carry on extended dialogue are examples where open-ended questions may not be the format of choice.

Northouse and Northouse (1985) state that a key feature of the use of open-ended questions is that more time is consumed in the interviewing process. In other words, interviews that use a series of open-ended questions or other broad leads will predictably be more lengthy and time-consuming.

In summary, effective use of open-ended questions requires the following: careful wording of the questions to give some but minimal direction, the provider's conscious effort to actively listen to the patient responses and then willingness and ability to interject when needed to keep the patient focused on the topic. Open-ended questions should never be without structure and direction, even though they invite many possible responses.

Multiple-Choice Question Format

A third question format is the multiple-choice question. Typically, this question offers a number of alternative topics or decision routes, and the patient is expected to choose among the options provided.

Consider the following dialogue between a nurse's aide and a patient:

Nurse: "Good morning, Miss Wilson."
Patient: "Good morning."
Nurse: "Miss Wilson, in what order would you like me to assist you with your morning care? Would you like to brush your teeth, wash up a little, or eat breakfast first?" (*Multiple-choice question format*)
Patient: "I would prefer brushing my teeth first, then eating my breakfast."
Nurse: "OK. Now, the doctor recommended that you walk twice a day for 15 minutes. Do you want to take a nap before you walk or take a shower?" (*Multiple-choice question format*)
Patient: "Let me take a nap because I was not able to sleep last night. Then we can walk."

In view of the dialogue presented, the patient was clearly given a choice, was able to assess the options, and was able to select among them. This process can be extremely helpful to patients who feel as if control has been taken away from them and who feel as if they are mere objects in care-delivery activities. When patients are given the opportunity to choose and prioritize their elements of care, some of the dependence feelings based on these experiences may be lessened.

The multiple-choice format is helpful when the provider is attempting to sort issues and prioritize concerns but needs the patient's cooperation to fully explore these areas. For example, the physician may want to know whether the patient is concerned about postsurgical recovery but also needs to discuss the type of anesthesia and the expected surgical outcomes. The physician can decide independent of patient input what topics will come first or give the patient some choice. It is not that the physician presents a menu of topics from which the patient selects; rather, the patient is informed of all the issues that the physician feels need to be addressed and the patient selects areas in sequential order based on his or her readiness to explore the topics that are presented.

The multiple-choice question format works well with patients who are withdrawn, anxious, depressed, and indecisive. This approach also works well with children and adolescents because it provides security in structure, while at the same time engaging their active participation.

The major drawback of multiple-choice questions is that they are frequently complicated. They can be experienced in much the same way as double-barreled questions where two or more questions are posed at the same time. If patients are not cognitively able to separate, sort, and evaluate options, the result may be frustration. Like double-barreled questions, multiple-choice questions can also cause the patient to feel rushed, resulting in patients getting angry and withdrawing.

CHOICE OF QUESTION FORMAT AND RESPONSE BURDEN

In considering which question format will be best, the clinician will consider a variety of criteria. These include the purpose of the data-collection activity, the essential details about the patient, and the nature of the provider-patient relationship.

Factors about the patient that determine which question format is best includes the patient's present level of distress, the patient's actual and potential responses to the subject matter, and the patient's knowledge and experience. All of these factors significantly affect patients' abilities to communicate verbally and meet the demands of the question-answer task. These elements comprise the response burden. As indicated earlier, types of question formats have certain response burdens. When using a question format, it is always important to consider not only what type of information this format elicits but also the nature of the response burden on the patient.

Open-ended questions allow the patient to verbalize without restriction. They require a minimum amount of sorting and processing. Decisions about what is appropriate or inappropriate are not imposed on the patient. Patients who respond positively to open-ended questions are usually those who need to talk, like to express themselves verbally, and have the energy to engage in extended conversations. They usually have moderate levels of trust and positive attitudes toward providers. Certain other patients are not amenable to data collection with the open-ended format. These patients are those who are less comfortable verbalizing, or they may not have the energy or freedom from symptom distress to engage in lengthy conversations. Even when offered a broad open-ended leading question, e.g., "How are you doing today?" They are likely to be parsimonious in their response: "Not so good," or "OK." While the response burden of open-ended questions, at first glance, seems to be negligible, there are many situations in which open-ended questions tax the patient's ability to respond.

Closed-ended question formats impose a different response burden. With closed-ended questions, responses are brief. Those patients in pain or distress usually respond better to this type of question. However, it is important to understand what is required of the patient. When a provider asks, "Do you feel pain?" several requirements are made of the patient. First, the patient must decode the provider's terms, e.g., pain. Patients must discern what is meant by these terms and why the provider is asking for this information. Additionally, patients must identify their experience as pain or perhaps something else. Patients must be able to focus, decode, and encode their experience and, at the same time, be brief. While not much is required in terms of verbal explanation, more is required in terms of decoding and encoding the communication between the provider and the patient.

Questions worded in the multiple-choice format are like closed-ended questions because they require further data processing and decision-making capabilities on the patient's part. As indicated previously, this format is usually used to pinpoint, i.e., to rule in or rule out different possibilities.

If the provider asks the patient, "Are you having pain here, here, how about here—and, where is the pain worse? here or here?" certain patient skills are needed. As with closed-ended questions, the patient must be able to focus and decode the provider's language and encode his own. However, what is also required with this format is the ability to compare and contrast, cross-referencing different experiences of pain or pressures. For some patients, this requirement is beyond their capability. They may have problems in encoding and decoding and also have problems with comparative analysis. While it would seem that the multiple-choice question mode leads to efficiency in data collection, the provider may get very little accurate data. Language barriers, present distress, and cognitive deficits can all contribute to patients' inabilities to use this question format.

CONCLUSION

As indicated in this chapter, the provider-patient relationship is characterized by the privilege and expectation of asking questions of the patient. The primary therapeutic motive for asking questions is to derive complete and accurate data on which to provide care to patients.

Questions help to open dialogue, direct the interview, command attention in a given area, and clarify. In our society, people experience questions of all types. Many questions seem irrelevant. Still, within the patient-provider relationship, questions are more deliberate than accidental or capricious. Providers are diagnostically oriented and this orientation is based on thoughtful selection of the appropriate context and the appropriate format for questions.

The appropriate use of questions includes gathering data, seeking clarification and qualification, and pinpointing or ruling in or out possible conditions. Question formats—closed, open, or multiple-choice—are options in the provider's exploration of the patient's condition and experience. Different question formats elicit different responses, and it is important to understand the strengths and limitations of each of these formats. In truth, one format alone will not suffice. Rather, providers need to be able to draw on each format discriminately.

Questions are not always used in therapeutic ways. Clearly, they can be misused. And, there are many examples of this. Questions can mask interpretations and advice. In these cases, while questions are used to soften the impact and directness of other response modes, the provider runs the risk of confusing the patient. Direct questions are particularly problematic, since too many ill-placed direct questions can make patients defensive and defeat the essential purposes for which they were designed. Questions should always allow reply without intimidation or defensiveness.

Questions, whether open, closed, or multiple choice in format, are providers' primary means of gathering information. The art of questioning is central to conversing therapeutically with patients.

CHAPTER 7

Therapeutic Use of Silence and Pauses

To learn how one mind speaks to another and in silence; one must listen with "the third ear."

Theodor Reik

CHAPTER OBJECTIVES

- Define silence as a therapeutic response mode.
- Discuss what occurs in the absence of silence.
- List several therapeutic purposes for the use of silence and pauses in the client-provider relationship.
- Analyze the meaning of silence in clients' responses and reactions.
- Describe how one might intervene with defensive silences.
- Identify certain negative effects of silence and pauses.

In some cultures talk is valued, and silence is a deficit in social skills and/or a lack of knowledge. An unwillingness to converse is perceived as an attitude of unfriendliness; silence is interpreted as impolite, unkind, or arrogant (Barbara 1958). Talkativeness, on the other hand, exemplifies intellect and social poise. This is not the case in all cultural groupings, however. For example, among certain Asian groups silence is regarded as a sign of wisdom. People who are talkative are generally perceived as lacking an awareness of the natural order of things.

These mixed orientations to silence influence how comfortable a clinician will be in employing silence as a therapeutic technique. For those providers whose culture values talkativeness, silence may be uncomfortable, and for those who come from cultures that value silence, talkativeness may be uncomfortable and thus, spacing remarks with silent periods is not difficult.

Silence is a type of interaction that can increase both the patient's and the provider's anxiety. The reason for this is not only because of the value that a culture places on talking. There are other reasons. In some groups silent responses are used as punishment. When children are bad, they are told to be "quiet." Adults punish one another by withholding thoughts and feelings. The reasons behind silence are not always clear; and to the extent that an individual's silence is unclear or possibly punitive, these quiet periods can evoke anxiety and increase social distance. For some clinicians the measure of a successful interview is the extent to which silence is kept at a minimum. As with all therapeutic responses, silence can be overused. This chapter emphasizes the need to become comfortable with silences, to understand their meaning when it is the patient who is silent and to draw on them in the therapeutic interview to enhance the productivity of patient-provider contacts.

DEFINITIONS OF SILENCE

Silence is the absence of speech. According to Hein (1980), it is that period in the therapeutic relationship during which the provider waits, without interruption for the patient to begin or resume speaking. Further, when used therapeutically, silence can be interspersed with encouragements, e.g., "humm" or "uh-huh" since these sounds do not interrupt the patient (Norton and Miller 1986).

In actuality, there are two types of silence in the therapeutic relationship. The first is when the patient stops speaking and there is absence of speech before the provider starts speaking, or when the provider stops speaking and there is absence of speech before the patient speaks. The implicit understanding behind conversation is that patient and provider verbalize in the pattern of first one, then the other. This assumption underlies our understanding of when there is silence. A second type of silence refers to that absence of speech that occurs when either patient or provider stops speaking and then the same person resumes speaking.

In either case, the silent space may be long or very short, such as in a pause (see Exhibit 7–1). A pause is said to be a natural rest in the melody of speech; whereas silence is longer. Usually absence of speech beyond three to four seconds is considered a silent period, not just a brief interruption in the course of conversation.

Another way to perceive silence is as an interpersonal space. The psychosocial space between two individuals is referred to as interpersonal space, which continually changes for the duration of the dialogue. This space can be expanded or reduced depending on either or both individuals. Applying this principle to one's daily experience, it should be obvious that increases or decreases in silent periods do occur and reflect the nature of our moods and the characteristics of our relationships. Experimenting with the effects of changing the length of silences enables us to measure the different ways in which we relate to others. Changes, even small ones, in how interpersonal space is used can make a difference in the quality of our interactions.

Exhibit 7–1 Summation of Basic Principles Underlying Silence as a Response Mode

---

- There is a relationship between interviewer and respondent use of silence; the more silent the interviewer, the more silent the respondent.
- The speech-silence behavior of any given individual in the context of an interview is highly consistent despite large individual differences in the characteristics of interviewers.
- Unfilled pausing time (silences) are associated with superior, more concise and less problematic expressions; filled pauses, e.g., with the use of "uh huh," "er," and "um" are associated with inferior achievement, e.g., long-windedness.
- In some cultures, silence denotes wisdom; while in others, silence may be viewed as a sign of insecurity and dullness.

The following interaction illustrates the impact these changes can have on personal distancing in this physician's first visit with a new patient.

Physician: "What we should do is take a blood test, increase your Theophylline. Also, I think we should add . . . "

Patient: (*forcefully*) "I don't want to have the blood test."

Physician: "You're not going to get significant results if your dose is not at therapeutic level." (*Silence*)

Patient: "I go to an allergist. He told me what I need to do. I just want an antibiotic for my bronchitis. (*Pause*) I don't think a blood test is necessary!"

Physician: (*Silence*)

Patient: "You think I should increase my medicine? And, I should probably increase my inhaler, right?"

Physician: "Yes, that's right. (*Pause*) And, if you're not feeling better in a week, come back and see me."

Patient: "OK."

In this case, silence by the provider shifted the apparent "power-struggle" in this relationship. The patient was openly resisting the clinician's advice, even the idea of doing much more than getting an antibiotic was out of the question. This provider, through the use of silence, moved the patient from a position of resistance to one of considering the physician's advice. Although the physician did not persuade the patient to take the blood test, agreement about increasing the patient's routine medications was established. There may be other reasons why the patient refused a blood test (other than unnecessarily increasing medical costs). These reasons could reflect noncompliance on routine medications, which would be apparent with the blood test. In this case, the patient would not risk discovery. There are other less directive approaches the physician could have used; still, the use of silence seemed to reduce the patient's blatant refusal to follow this physician's orders.

IN THE ABSENCE OF SILENCE

To understand silence, it is important to address what occurs during silence. There are three basic aspects that are worthy of attention. These events are: (1) interresponse time, (2) the interruption response, and (3) the overtalk response.

Interresponse Times

Interresponse time refers to the number of seconds or minutes in a silence period. A typical social conversation contains many interresponse times that are less than a second long. This feature of conversation, many short silences, tends to characterize social interaction. It would be peculiar to engage in longer silences when speaking with casual acquaintances. However, there are some cultures that abide by longer response times. This and the slowness of their speech are typical. For example, inhabitants of Maine, the Appalachians, and parts of the South and Southwest may speak slower and use interresponse times that are over a second in length. Groups such as these can be contrasted with residents of New York; these individuals may exhibit fast-paced speech. Their "crowded" speech contains many examples of interresponse times that are much less than a second. These distinct tendencies become even more obvious when situational or environmental situations influence them. For example, the city dweller on a camping vacation in the mountains or on a sailing excursion may feel out of sorts. In turn, those slower speaking individuals may find it very irritating to stand in line at Kennedy Airport or hail a cab on Fifth Avenue (New York).

Patients' conditions can be reflected in the speed of their speech and their tendency to use short or long durations between phrases. For example, patients who are suffering pain, fatigue, or lethargy or who are depressed will tend to exhibit longer interresponse times. The elderly usually require added time to assemble their ideas due to slower physical and mental processes as do people with limited intellectual ability or developmental delays. Patients who are anxious, excitable, agitated, or manic will exhibit more rapid speech that allows for fewer interruptions.

Interresponse times of three or four seconds or more are more than brief pauses between expressed ideas. They are unique and are frequently used as space to think something new over or to think about what was previously expressed. These times are distinctive and do not resemble pauses wherein little thinking and feeling is occurring. In a fast-paced conversation, however, two-second interresponse times may be enough to provide additional thinking and feeling experiences and thus are not merely pauses. In a helping relationship or therapeutic dialogue, silences can last up to ten seconds. Also, a change in dialogue where one or two seconds of silence are added, may communicate permission to think and feel about what is being expressed, and can allow patients to regroup thoughts or develop a new slant on the feelings they have expressed.

One study of physicians and adult clients revealed that the use of silence (reaction-time latency) between speakers contributed to patients' satisfaction (Rowland-Morin and Carroll 1990). Patients were more satisfied not only when silence occurred in interviews but also when physicians utilized words that the patient used and interrupted with reflections.

Interruptions

Just as adding a mere two seconds to silence can provide patients interpersonal space, taking from the silent pattern one or two seconds can create a feeling of being crowded or rushed.

Consider the following dialogue and the effect of changing interresponse time in periods of silence. This is a dialogue between a nurse and a patient where the patient is describing his headaches.

Nurse: "Did the medication help you?"
Patient: "Yup—but it was hard . . . "
Nurse: "Do you have any ideas about what you can do?" (*Interruption*)
Patient: (*Looking at nurse*) "No—I feel frustrated!"
Nurse: (*Silence, four seconds*).
Patient: "I really don't know what I'm going to do about this stuff the doctor gave me. If I take it, I'm worthless as far as working goes and actually everything else, and so I just get further and further behind. If I don't take it, I can't see straight and I don't get much more done. God, I feel frustrated!"
Nurse: "Yes . . . " (*Silence, two seconds*)
Patient: "Actually, I wonder what would happen if I only took half the pill? Maybe I'll run that by the doctor and see what he thinks. Or, I could call him and see if there is anything else he could give me."

Notice that in the beginning of this conversation the nurse crowded the patient, even interrupted him in midthought. By being given extended interpersonal space, the patient was able to gather his thoughts and decrease his frustration by coming up with a plan. He constructed two potential solutions to the dilemma he was facing. By altering the interresponse time between statements, the nurse was able to alter feelings of pressure generated from the frustration and create a climate for problem solving.

Interruptions have a significant impact on conversation. Interruptions are disruptions of another individual's speech and generally have the impact of cutting short the expression of the person's ideas. Interruptions can occur in the middle of a statement or in the brief lull that occurs between expressed thoughts and feelings. The circumstance in which both parties begin speaking simultaneously is called overtalk.

Overtalk

Conversation can be filled with interruptions. If this is the case, overtalk is usually a significant impasse in the productive expressions of both individuals. There are specific circumstances wherein most people will engage in overtalk. For example, when either or both parties are feeling threatened, overtalk may be a defense against any distress they may be experiencing. Overtalk essentially communicates the message: *Cease* or *stop this*; yet, what actually occurs is an escalation of comments, usually accusations.

Some people habitually interrupt. This style of communicating influences the way these people work with others and the way others feel about them. These individuals tend to feel perpetually threatened. Because they crowd out others in their communication, they are prone to fear rejection. In addition to being associated with anxiety, interruptions can also reflect boredom, the need to dominate others, reactions to redundancy, or reactions to freshly stimulated thoughts and feelings. In this way, the person is communicating: *don't finish, listen to me*! Or the message may be: *I can guess what you are going to say—let me say it*. Conversations with many interruptions and a good deal of overtalk are filled with incomplete messages. If one individual does not back off for three or four seconds, overtalk fills the space and significant interpersonal crowding sets in.

In sum, overtalk and interruptions are important events that can occur at the interresponse boundary when there is no silence. Overtalk and interruptions crowd conversation. Silence allows for thoughtful reflection and the development of insight, which is the primary objective in provider-patient relationships. Hence, silence in helping relationships can extend to ten seconds or even longer. Crowding can actually reduce the tendency for patients to disclose. With crowding, patients will experience being misunderstood, frustrated, and dissatisfied. While the precise reason may seem to be a mystery at the time of the interview, it has a significant connection to the individual's inherent need to be heard and understood, a desire acutely felt in patient-provider encounters. If patients are crowded, they anticipate that their needs for understanding will certainly go unmet.

A final point is that, like all other response modes, there is a tendency to respond with silence, interruptions, or overtalk. Providers can elicit these responses by initiating them. Additionally, they can mirror them back to the patient almost unconsciously, matching the pace and character of the patient's overtalk or interruptions. The results are two frustrated and dissatisfied individuals. In the event that this happens, the primary corrective measure is the provider's conscious and deliberate use of silence to alter the nature of the exchange. Providers can use silence to slow down the pace and change any tendency to interrupt and overtalk.

THERAPEUTIC PURPOSES OF SILENCE IN THE PROVIDER-PATIENT RELATIONSHIP

There are several important purposes for using silence in therapeutic dialogues with patients. These include (1) providing space for assessing and analyzing the patient's condition and (2) communicating empathy. However, the primary purpose in providing interpersonal space is to encourage patients to take the initiative to communicate their experiences verbally.

Encouraging Patients To Speak

As previously indicated, silence can cause patients to speak, especially if the provider shows interest and expectation. This kind of silence indicates to patients that the provider expects them to speak—initiate the topic that they feel is most pressing or more important than the one being discussed. Silent interludes give patients the opportunity to collect and organize their thoughts and think through what they want to say next. Using silence can also reduce the pace of the interview, creating more interpersonal space in the encounter. This strategy can cause the patient to delve more deeply, weigh a decision, or consider alternative actions.

These therapeutic effects of silence were demonstrated in the dialogue between the nurse and patient described earlier. By providing the patient with silent interludes, the nurse provoked the patient to delve more deeply into his dilemma; as a result, he generated a new course of action. By not asking pointless questions, the provider gave the patient room to be spontaneous and to move from simple to more complex analyses of his dilemma. Rather than remaining confused and upset about the medication he was prescribed, he decided to call his doctor and request an altered dose or a new drug with the same effects. While the nurse could have cut short this decision process by merely advising the patient what to do, the real value of this interchange was that the patient came to his own decision, and this process emphasized both his responsibility to communicate with his physician and his right to receive more appropriate care.

Communicating Empathy

Silent periods have been noted for their ability to touch emotions (Martyres 1995). Emotions are experiential and complex, having origins in personal history. Words that are used to described emotions are generally inadequate and simplistic. According to Martyres (1995), silence is a useful experiential medium in which to identify and work with emotions. It is important to recognize what is being communicated by silence during each silent period.

Communicating empathy in a therapeutic interview is facilitated with the use of silence. Silence conveys active listening. To successfully achieve active listening, the provider must display interest. As active listening, silence represents that providers have a willingness to hear what patients have to say—to enter the world of the patient and understand it more fully. It conveys an interest in the patient's well-being beyond that demonstrated by specific gestures that "do" something. The power in silence is that it provides an unhurried atmosphere in which patients can reflect on their experiences in the presence of their provider. Providers in their own hurried states are usually perceived as incapable of full understanding. When they relinquish their distractions and focus in silence on the patient they are conveying not only the willingness to understand the patient but also the capability to do so. While it would appear that the provider is doing nothing in these moments of silence, in actuality much is going on. During these interludes the provider is observing what patients do, hearing what patients say and how they say it, feeling how patients feel, and sensing what patients have not said but may want to say. Silence often communicates caring when words are superfluous.

Assessment of Patient Condition

In addition to encouraging patients to verbalize and in addition to conveying empathetic understanding, silent interludes are critical to the process of fully assessing patients. This idea goes beyond the obvious point that to obtain clinical data providers will lapse into silent periods as they listen for chest sounds, palpate a pulse, or examine a severe overbite. During silences providers have opportunities to observe verbal and nonverbal behaviors. They also have opportunities to look for incongruencies, in how patients feel about their condition or the prescribed plan of care. To be aware of incongruencies, providers must understand the full range of nonverbal expression of effect: fear, anxiety, hostility, sadness, depression, relief, happiness, and excitement. Because silences provide open-ended opportunities to observe, clinicians may need to organize their points of focus, e.g., to use verbal and nonverbal messages of thoughts and feelings, pick up subtle attitudes and underlying beliefs, to observe patients' own reactions to their disclosures, and to construct a composite picture of the patient's experience as witnessed by the clinician. This process then tends to further convey understanding on the part of clinicians as well as their ability to be helpful.

Thoughtful Self-Reflection

A final purpose of silence is the provision for thoughtful self-reflection on the part of the provider. The opportunity to observe oneself in therapeutic encounters is not something that is familiar to clinicians. The provider generally stays focused on the patient. But when the provider is distracted, the need to eliminate distractions and properly refocus on the patient is important. When providers observe themselves in the context of their encounters with patients, they will learn that a great deal is happening between them and their patients, some of which they will not immediately understand. The following data can be retrieved by simply reflecting on one's own thoughts and feelings in the silent periods of a therapeutic interview.

- How am I feeling about what the patient is saying?
- How am I reacting to the manner in which the patient is communicating?
- How is the context of this interview affecting me and what I do and do not say?
- What am I trying to achieve and how well is it working?
- What do I want to communicate above all else?

Just as silence gives patients the opportunity to think through a point or to consider introducing a topic, providers are given the same opportunity to collect and reassemble their thoughts. In actuality, silent periods provide both providers and patients important time-outs that serve the therapeutic aims of the interview.

ANALYSIS OF SILENCE IN PATIENTS' RESPONSES

Sometimes patients are silent, but this silence does not seem to serve the patient therapeutically. The answer as to why the patient is silent is usually a very complex one. When it is not complex, providers may assign significance inappropriately to these periods of silence. Patients who respond with silence are not easily understood. Sometimes this is a matter of cultural differences. Davidhizar and Giger (1994) suggest that a number of problems may arise when silence occurs in an interpersonal situation. Among these problems is the different meanings that silence may have from culture to culture. Sometimes patients refuse to talk, and while these cases are not as common as lapses into silence, they are extremely important to understand. There are three reasons why patients may refuse to talk, including: (1) defensiveness against perceived threats, (2) provocation—to get the provider to seek them out, or (3) underlying hostility and resistance.

Defensive Silences

The defensive use of silence demonstrates patients' beliefs that if they are silent and withhold thoughts and feelings, they will not be hurt. Patients who harbor such ideas have usually had repeated exposures to being insulted or assaulted when they expressed themselves. Their families may have simply shunned expressions of different thoughts or ideas, or significant mental and physical abuse could have occurred when the patient spoke up or spoke out. In any case, the patient developed a patterned response to withdraw and/or to remain silent under certain circumstances. Over time this defensive reaction may have even become unconscious. Therefore, it is possible that the patient is not aware that his silent episodes are a reflexive reaction to his perception of a real or anticipated threat.

A second dynamic behind patients' refusal to speak could be their desire to be sought out to receive special treatment. This silence may be conveyed as provocation, e.g., *there is something I can do to make you respond in a special way to me as a patient.* In this way, the patient not only nonassertively tests the provider's desires to be helpful but also tests the provider's generalized attitudes toward him. Providers may notice that the patient withholds thoughts and feelings, bates the provider with clues, and reinforces the provider when given added time and attention. These behaviors are manipulative and tend to engender anger, hostility, and resentment in providers. And, while the original intent of the patient was to secure a helping relationship, the outcome is the opposite—the patient has provoked the provider who avoids responses rather than engages responses that the patient needs and desires.

A third and final explanation for silence is feelings of hostility, anger, and resentment that are harbored by the patient. Patients who exhibit silence out of hostility, anger, or resentment communicate these feelings but act as if they do not. These silences are usually cold, rejecting, punishing kinds of silence. Silences of this kind are frequently used in social relationships, for example, to communicate anger when one's partner is late or has forgotten an important occasion such as an anniversary. This example demonstrates how silences can carry a wide array of meanings and are not always clear. In fact, some individuals will use the ambiguity surrounding silence as a punishment, i.e., *You think you know why I am quiet, but I know you don't know for sure. You will have to suffer with uncertainty until I decide to tell you why I won't speak to you.* Many providers assume that patients will not exhibit these patterns in their interviews with providers. There are, however, many reasons why patients may in fact communicate their hostility through silence. First, providers are regarded as authority figures and patients may be patterned to be passive-aggressive in the context of dominant-submissive relationships. Second, patients may fear reprisal if they communicate their anger directly. They may fear or fantasize dire consequences. And third, whatever irritation or upset they experience may be perceived as insignificant in the context of the larger picture. That is, patients may recognize their distress and deliberately minimize it because there are so many other issues of equal or greater importance to them. Nonetheless, the result is the same. The patient contains his feelings and lapses into silence. Still angry, he extends his silence to communicate passivity, feigning the desire to be cooperative and compliant.

Intervening with Defensive Silences

It is important to understand that the negative use of silence by patients is not easily discussed. In fact, one's first take should always be understanding silence at face value and extending to patients the opportunity to respond at their own rate. When silence, however, proves to inhibit disclosures that are necessary, patients need to be helped to open up and get past their destructive use of silence.

There are important steps in dealing with negative, defensive silence in patients. Initially, the provider should demonstrate acceptance of the patient's silence. Providers should listen beyond the silence, reflecting and attending to the patient. This behavior will demonstrate acceptance. Second, providers should note the context of the silence and if there is a trend. Does the patient lapse into silence about certain topics? Approach these topics with respect. If patients lapse into silences, they are generally more sensitive about these topics. If patients' silences are interrupted, they may become more defensive and be increasingly anxious. The provider runs the risk of permanently cutting short the patients' disclosures. When asking for verbal replies it is advisable to begin with neutral themes or superficial material with which the patient feels more comfortable. Providers should also consider silences as symptomatic of something else. A gentle lead, e.g., "I'm trying to understand what's on your mind . . . but, I'm having difficulty knowing exactly what's bothering you," or "I am interested in helping you through this . . . " is helpful. Exploring the meaning behind patient silences is important. This is done most effectively with a simple suggestion that their silence is a sign that something else is bothering them and that if they share it, they may be able to cope more effectively with it. Chances are, the patient is experiencing some degree of approach-avoidance conflict and needs only the suggestion of positive results to tip the scale toward disclosure. Patients will frequently experience feeling uncomfortable if they do not talk, yet uncomfortable if they do. Exploring the conflict or suggesting resolution will enable the patient to feel the provider's support.

NEGATIVE EFFECTS OF USING SILENCE

Silence is not always a helpful technique in patient-provider interactions. It is often difficult to apply in a manner that will achieve maximum benefit and minimize the chance of sending the wrong message (e.g., aloofness, uncaring, coldness) or otherwise being counterproductive. These effects stem from the fact that silence can extend beyond the point of usefulness, thoughts tend to drift, and the focus of the interview can be lost (Collins 1977). When this occurs, the silence becomes uncomfortable and may provoke anxiety in both the provider and the patient.

Mixed messages about the provider's tolerance of silence can also defeat the therapeutic effects of silence. The ambiguous message, *I accept your need to be quiet but at the same time don't like the stillness in the room*, gives two conflicting messages. This situation also results in an environment where it is difficult to self-disclose. In this case, silence is no longer beneficial.

Providers have been described as needing to fill every void in conversation with verbiage. Usually this is attributed to personal embarrassment, self-consciousness, or anxiety. When providers have difficulty dealing with silence they can inadvertently punish the patient while remaining mostly silent. Punishment can be delivered by insincere or sarcastic responses or simple gestures that suggest in subtle ways: *If you have nothing to say (ask, talk about) then I'll just leave*. A potential therapeutic encounter becomes useless when the provider's needs take precedence over those of the patient.

The opposite situation, where the provider feels more comfortable with silence and the patient's natural mode is to be talkative, can elicit similar outcomes. Essentially the patient will experience little direction from the provider. The patient's need for a response and feedback is thwarted, again because the provider's needs take precedence. Usually when patients do not receive the feedback they need, they will begin to repeat themselves in a second or even third attempt to get a response. With patients who are distrustful, silence of any length can evoke anxiety. It is as if the patient needs direct and continuous feedback in order to assess the provider. Providers' silences can be interpreted as manipulation, assertiveness, or domination. Also, too much silence from the provider tends to put pressure on the patient to speak. The provider's silence can convey that a response is wanted, but the patient may feel uncertain about how to respond. Also, if patients perceive the silence as a form of manipulation, they may retaliate by withholding the information that they believe the provider wants. Generally, an interaction filled with too many pauses or silent periods will result in feelings that the purpose of the conversation is unclear and unfocused.

The tendency to respond in kind can also present problems in the therapeutic interview. In this case, the provider's silence can even become a game where the patient offers little, waits to hear from the provider, or simply plays "who can hold out the longest." Communication becomes a game, and the therapeutic benefits of silence are lost.

While effective silence is useful to collect thoughts and determine what should be conveyed next; confused, uncomfortable, or resistive silences are seen as unconstructive and should be remedied with corrective measures. An example of confused silence is displayed in this interaction between a provider (counselor) and a patient:

Provider: "Do you think your wife truly supports your decision (to return to school to get a degree)?"

Patient: *Says nothing for approximately six seconds.*
Provider: "You look confused. Did you understand my question?"
Patient: "I don't know what decision you're talking about."

Had the provider not tracked the fact that the patient had not answered or that the patient looked confused, clarification may not have occurred. One instance of confused interaction can take a tremendous toll on the provider's relationship with the patient. And patients may perceive too long a silence as disinterest or noncaring. Corrective measures help to emphasize the fact that the interview is purposeful and that providers are sincere in their attempts to understand patients.

In summary then, silences can elicit therapeutic gains; however, they can also be detrimental in the course of interaction. It is important to distinguish and evaluate their impact so that any corrective measures can be taken before long range negative effects occur.

CONCLUSION

Virtually all interpersonal relationships depend on verbal communication. In truth, in contemporary Western society conversation is highly prized. We are often judged by how often and to what degree we engage in conversation. Being socially acceptable is, in part, related to our ability to relate verbally to others. The verbal form of communication is believed to be preferable, at least for some groups. This is not the case for individuals from other cultural groups.

While the absence of verbal communication implies silence, silence does not imply an absence of communication. It may sound paradoxical, but silence is a form of communicating where meanings are shared nonverbally.

Therapeutic silence occurs when providers deliberately use silence to facilitate patient exploration of problems. The provider conveys understanding or at least a desire to understand the experience of the patient. Silence in itself tends to encourage patients to verbalize if it is an interested, expectant silence.

The major barrier of providers' therapeutic use of silence is their assumption that nothing significant is occurring in these periods. They may judge that their time is being wasted, become bored, and let their attention wander. If providers are able to observe themselves and their patients in these periods of silence, they will learn that a great deal happens in these moments. Listening beyond the surface of the spoken word is facilitated by silent interludes.

Either party can modify the amount and length of silence in an interaction. The giving of silence will eventually result in the giving of silence in return. Silence responses can contribute to the experience of being "known" by the provider, since silence responses are also part of the response referred to as empathy. Short interresponse times may lead patients to feeling less understood. Sudden changes toward very long silence periods, however, may cause distraction and complicate the process of effective communication. If the provider uses too long a period of silence, the patient may become distracted. Silence and the length of silences thus have to be thoughtfully brought into the interaction to avoid confusing the patient.

Repeated crowding in an interaction can also cause a chain reaction when crowding is returned. The chain reaction where crowding begets crowding, silence begets silence, is referred to as response matching. Providers can slow down crowded communication by intentionally giving a series of medium-length silence responses.

Overall, it behooves the provider to be aware of both the positive and negative effects of silences in interviews. Effective interviewing requires skillful application of pauses and silences where thoughtful observation of the patient directs the pace and depth of the interaction.

The essence of being present with the patient is often thought of as a prime feature of silence. As Pettigrew (1990) explains, the providers' presence can lessen negative effects of suffering as one comes alongside and enters that suffering by listening and becoming available in a way that involves self-giving, as the provider chooses to wait with a person who is in turmoil and wrestling with thoughts and feelings somewhat invisible to the provider.

CHAPTER 8

The Impact and Limitations of Self-Disclosure

One of the most meaningful interactions (with physicians) I had was when the physician cried and said, "I don't know what else I can do."

And what is as important as knowledge? asked the mind. Caring and seeing with the heart, answered the soul.

Anonymous

CHAPTER OBJECTIVES

- Define self-disclosure as a therapeutic response mode.
- Describe how self-disclosure may be different by intent and level.
- Describe several therapeutic effects of self-disclosure.
- Identify several types of provider nontherapeutic self-disclosures.
- Describe how to manage requests for self-disclosure from clients and when it is appropriate to do so.

It is clear that in any human interaction one is always disclosing aspects of oneself to some degree. In this sense, self-disclosure is unavoidable. Nonetheless, deliberate self-disclosure to facilitate therapeutic aims is a somewhat foreign idea. Although self-disclosure was once judged to be inappropriate, it is now viewed as acceptable and, in some cases, an important adjunct to traditional interviewing styles.

While self-disclosure by providers can facilitate therapeutic aims, they can also be problematic. The issue is one of anticipating the potential impact and judiciously using self-disclosures. The amount and timing of self-disclosures become particularly critical in judging their appropriateness in the therapeutic relationship.

The purpose of this chapter is to present self-disclosures as aids to therapeutic communication with patients. However, before touching on the subject of the deliberate use of self-disclosure in the patient-provider relationship, it is important to describe the nature of self-disclosure, present arguments for and against this response mode, and identify types of nontherapeutic as well as therapeutic disclosures.

DEFINITIONS OF SELF-DISCLOSURE

Self-disclosure is defined as instances of openly sharing personal information about oneself, including experiences, attitudes, and feelings (Evans et al. 1989). In general terms, all statements beginning with the pronoun *I* could be labeled self-disclosures. "I" statements, however, are also used to introduce other motives—advising, interpreting, and expressing opinion. In these situations, while self-disclosure is purported, the primary impact of the message is some other purpose. Consider, for example, this statement: "I think you should try another solution." This statement begins with "I." It also discloses what the sender is thinking. Still, the major intent is not to share personal data about oneself but to influence the receiver's behavior. This is an example of advisement.

Because "I" statements also introduce advisement, interpretation, and the expression of opinion, it is not enough to say that all "I" statements are primarily self-disclosing. A distinction should be made between statements made with self-reference and those that are clearly self-disclosures. Self-reference statements refer to I or me but disclose little personal data about the sender.

Self-disclosure, then, is when an individual reveals nonobvious aspects of the self, e.g., thoughts, feelings, attitudes, or experiences, through a distinct and meaningful self-reference. While "I feel upset with my care in the hospital" is a self-disclosure, "I think you need to close the curtain" is not.

Conceptualizing Self-Disclosure

Self-disclosures may be delivered in very intimate circumstances or be made to many people. Self-disclosures, for example, "I like you," made in the context of a one-to-one relationship are very different from public disclosures. Public disclosures, for example, "I'm a registered Democrat" or "I have a BA degree in Biology," made to many persons at the same time are usually more superficial. Although they also reveal the nonobvious, they present much less threat of exposure than do one-on-one self-disclosures.

Self-disclosures can also be conceptualized in terms of the content of the disclosure. Content in disclosures may vary. In social situations, this content may be personal attitudes or the type of work one does. Other disclosures, say, about one's personality, religious beliefs, and perceived body image are likely to be offered in more intimate situations or when a certain level of trust has been established and a desire for a relationship has been expressed. It is important that providers are aware of this fact so that they can be sensitive to what hesitancies patients may have.

Finally, self-disclosures can be categorized as here-and-now, present-experi-ence disclosures or historical disclosures that refer to the past. Consider, for ex-ample, the remark, "You make me feel comfortable." This statement refers to the sender's immediate experience. Statements such as "That reminds me of how I felt before my surgery" refer to past feelings. This distinction is important in judging a patient's level of trust. Usually statements made about here-and-now experiences are more threatening than those made about past experiences. When patients feel free to disclose a concern, fear, or impression about their current relationships with providers it is usually indicative of moderate to high levels of trust.

Intent and Level of Self-Disclosures

There is still another way of classifying self-disclosures that addresses the in-tent and level of intimacy of the statements. The following types of disclosures will be described in this section: (1) metadisclosures, (2) promiscuous disclosures, (3) disclosures in the service of aggression or manipulation, and (4) competitive disclosures.

The first type of disclosure is a metadisclosure. Typically, metadisclosures are disclosures about a disclosure. For example, "I lied to you because I wanted you to think I was better than I am" is a metadisclosure. These disclosures reveal some-thing about a previous self-disclosing situation. Metadisclosures are useful in helping relationships refocus on the difficulties of understanding the patient. For example, "I'm having trouble understanding what you are saying about your breathing—let me ask some questions" comments on the character of the commu-nication and improves the potential for clear communication. These statements are also referred to as "process" disclosures because they focus more on the process of communication versus the content of the dialogue.

Promiscuous or irresponsible disclosures are made without any real regard for the receiver. In the patient-provider relationship they are forbidden. If a patient is describing, for example, his difficulty maintaining an erection, statements such as "Getting an erection has never been a problem for me" would be irresponsible. Essentially, the person fails to take into account the impact of the disclosure on the patient. This statement goes beyond the current frame of reference of the patient and increases distrust in the provider who appears more concerned with himself than the patient.

Disclosures in the service of other feelings—aggression and anger—are com-mon in social interactions. They are frequently used to punctuate the negative judgment the sender has made. Consider, "You're always cheating on your diet, so how do you think I can help you if you keep doing this? (*angry tone*) No other patients of mine are as difficult as you." Angry disclosures of this kind express aggression. The underlying intent may not be to inflict disgrace or distress, though that generally is the outcome. Providers' frustrations are unleashed on the patient not only in unhelpful ways but in ways that are hurtful.

Disclosures can also be made to persuade or manipulate. Persuasion and manipulation are also used in instances where the receiver is viewed as resistant or recalcitrant. "Come on now, you can tell me whether you took your medication. I can find out anyway" is manipulative. This disclosure is used strategically to get patients to disclose when they may not want to. This type of disclosure not only manipulates, i.e., "I'll find out anyway if you don't tell me," it feigns a level of intimacy that's not there. "You can tell me" suggests a level of trust and intimacy that just is not present between the provider and patient. If it were, the patient would be telling the provider the details without needing to be manipulated.

Competitive disclosures are also frequently used in social situations. The primary purpose is to gain attention from others. Statements like "Guess what, I'm so cool I just got asked to be the group's representative" could evoke a competitive counter, e.g., "I've been the representative for three years already. They want me to be the chair because they like how I handle the budget." The aim is to take the floor from the first person, making oneself more significant.

In provider-patient dialogue, competitive disclosures can occur even though they are clearly disruptive. Consider the following dialogue:

Patient: "I wonder when I'm going to see my doctor. Is he here yet? I think he forgot me today. He's usually here by now. I don't think I can go a whole day without talking to him."

Provider: "That's nothing. I'm going a whole week without talking to my husband. He is on a business trip, and I can't reach him by phone because of the time difference. If I don't get some help with the kids—the babysitter is sick—I don't know how I'm going to work these two 12-hour shifts coming up." (*Competitive self-disclosure*)

Clearly, the provider's motive in self-disclosing is not patient centered. She is more focused on her own problems than on the concerns of the patient. In this dialogue, she is jockeying for priority—*You think you have problems reaching someone important to you, wait until you hear this!* In some ways there is no room for the existence of the real patient; the provider's needs are taking precedence.

THE THERAPEUTIC EFFECTS OF SELF-DISCLOSURE

Self-disclosure on the part of the patient is, without a doubt, essential and most often therapeutic. Without patient disclosures, providers cannot conduct valid assessments. Patient self-disclosures also are healing in that they create the potential for being understood, and every patient has a basic need to be attended to and understood.

There is, however, therapeutic value from the provider's self-disclosing personal data. Perhaps the most significant work that contributes to the body of knowledge about the therapeutic aspects of self-disclosure is that of Jourard (1971). Jourard expressed the view that self-disclosure encourages self-disclosure and that open-disclosure statements are most effective in conditioning the subject's (patient's) self-references in a face-to-face interview. Since Jourard's initial work, open-disclosures in the interview setting have been found to be effective in increasing the rate of emission of both positive and negative self-references. Provider self-disclosures, however, must meet certain criteria. First, they must be true statements. Second, they are subjectively perceived statements about the self. And third, they are intentionally revealed to the patient with a therapeutic aim in mind.

Review the dialogue between this provider and patient:

Patient: "I'm worried about my tests. What if they come back 'bad'?" (*Self-disclosure*)

Physician: "We won't really know until next week."

Patient: "I have problems enough without . . . you know, I don't think I could get through another surgery after all I've been through." (*Self-disclosure*)

Physician: "You have been through a lot and I know it wouldn't be easy."

Patient: *Begins to cry.*

Physician: "You know, when I think back on how you have 'held your own'—gone through these last two years, I feel a deep respect and admiration for you." (*Self-disclosure*)

Patient: (*Smiling and tearful*) "I didn't know that."

Physician: "Yes. I care. I'm in this for the duration." (*Self-disclosure*)

Patient: "Then I'll get the courage from somewhere—can't let you down (*jokingly*)."

This self-disclosure has a very strong therapeutic value. The physician shares some intimate details about his reflections and feelings about the patient. And, the disclosures began at a superficial level and became deeper. The conversation culminates with the provider and patient sharing attitudes about the here-and-now context of their relationship. The provider evokes self-disclosure by making personal disclosures. These statements stimulated the patient to express the innermost thoughts and feelings that influence the patient's outlook about forthcoming treatment. The nature of these disclosures suggest that there is a context for mutual trust in this relationship.

There is a tendency for communication to be expressed in symmetry, responses of one kind are likely to evoke similar responses. This tendency for one person to open up on a subject and the other to follow suit is called response matching. Response matching means that if providers self-disclose, they are likely to evoke self-disclosure in the patient. When the patient is reinforced or encouraged to continue to talk about a subject in a meaningful way, then the provider's self-disclosure has facilitated the therapeutic goals of the relationship. Thus, social penetration—increasing depth and breadth in disclosures—increases over time. In this way, provider self-disclosure is used to elicit more data and engage the patient in mutual problem solving. The principle of response matching in the use of self-disclosure is the primary justification for using self-disclosure in the provider-patient relationship.

There are other therapeutic effects of self-disclosure. These effects arise from the patient's realization of the humanity of the provider. Four effects, (1) the sense of being understood, (2) the enhancement of trust, (3) decreased loneliness, and (4) decreased role distancing, will be elaborated on.

The Sense of Being Understood

The therapeutic value of being understood was first documented in the literature by Jourard (1971), who stressed disclosure as a means of understanding the self and the world as another experiences it. One of the major tensions in the provider-patient relationship is the uncertainty about whether the patient will be understood fully enough to execute the best possible intervention. When the provider self-discloses pertinent personal data, the patient gains reassurance that the

- provider listens carefully
- provider is processing the patient's experience
- provider is empathetic
- provider understands, at the human level, what this illness or injury and its prognosis means to the patient

Patients whose providers offer brief but well-timed disclosures are more likely to feel that the provider really understands. Whereas those patients whose providers never disclose and assume a neutral position are likely to view the provider as impenetrable and therefore impervious to the contextual aspects of worrying and suffering that are important to patients and that affect their quality of life.

The Enhancement of Trust

When the patient perceives that the provider more fully understands the context of his experiences, the patient is likely to feel that he can trust the provider. Trust in the patient-provider relationship has two elements, (1) the patient perceives the provider as knowledgeable and competent, and (2) the patient perceives that the provider has his best interests in mind.

The presence of one element and the absence of another is not sufficient to create a sense of trust and confidence in the patient-provider relationship. Rather, it is these two elements operating simultaneously that build trust. Trustworthiness of the provider is assessed frequently at the beginning of the relationship since the patient is in the initial stages of deciding whether his care and treatment can be adequately provided by the clinician he chose or to whom he was assigned.

Decreased Loneliness

Provider self-disclosure can reduce feelings of loneliness in the patient as it alters the level of intimacy in the relationship.

The provider's self disclosure confirms that the patient is not all alone in the process of combating illness. The provider's self-disclosure clearly communicates presence, i.e., *I am present not only as a provider but at the human level.* To some extent, decreased loneliness occurs as patients realize that they are not so different from other people, in this case, the provider. The provider's disclosure communicates shared experience, and this works directly to alter the personal isolation that the patient encounters. Interestingly enough, the provider's disclosure may increase the attractiveness of the provider. Clinicians have observed that self-disclosure induces liking. Perceived as a reward, the patient feels singled out in a special way to hear the provider's (usually) unexpressed thoughts and feelings.

Liking and self-disclosure are positively associated. When asked to selectively disclose to several clinicians, the patient will disclose more intimate data to those for whom he has a greater liking. Also, at the end of a period of mutual self-disclosure, patients will indicate a greater liking for those with whom they have exchanged more intimate disclosures. The patient who views the provider as someone with whom intimacy is possible will most often apprise the relationship as desirable and be less likely to avoid and more likely to approach the provider. The provider's sense of appeal is a subtle but important factor in many issues concerned with treatment, including the willingness of the patient to be treated by the provider, patient comfort in disclosing intimate details to the provider, and patient compliance with the treatment program prescribed by the clinician.

Decreased Role Distance

A fourth and final therapeutic outcome in the provider's use of self-disclosure is that role distance is decreased when providers disclose. This outcome has the indirect affect of modifying the patient's dependency on the provider and maximizing the likelihood that mutual collaborative problem solving will occur.

When the provider uses self-disclosures for the expressed purpose of their therapeutic outcome, certain steps will ensure success. First, the provider should listen carefully to the verbal and nonverbal aspects of the patient's communication. Second, the provider should, while focusing on the patient, express an empathetic response. Third, the provider should reveal a similar personal experience thereby increasing the impact of the empathetic reflection. And, following the disclosure, the provider should evaluate the relevance of both the empathic response and the self-disclosure. These steps will result in patients who feel more understood and encouraged to expand on their own experiences.

TYPES OF NONTHERAPEUTIC SELF-DISCLOSURE

Just as there are therapeutic outcomes with self-disclosures, there is also the potential for disclosures to have nontherapeutic results. Thus, there are dangers in using self-disclosure, and providers must be fully aware of these potential drawbacks.

Decreasing Understanding

There are at least three key difficulties that can arise. First, the provider may express thoughts and feelings, but these will not be within the patient's current frame of reference. This is a common error. In an attempt to make the patient feel better, the statement actually could make the patient feel worse.

Patient: "I've put on a lot of weight—can't seem to get it off."
Physician: "I've lost 20 pounds this year myself. Couldn't feel better." (*Self-disclosure*)

The topic is weight gain and the difficulties of losing weight. The provider reveals success. It is obvious that the provider is not at the same place as the patient with this problem, and this might be disconcerting to the patient. The result is more social distance and decreased feelings of being helped. A point worth stressing here is that the provider should avoid disclosing more effective sides of the story when confronted with a patient who is struggling and not succeeding with a health problem. Evans et al. (1989) notes that provider disclosures should relate to patient disclosures in order to keep the focus on the patient's specific and immediate problem. In this way, distraction from the patient is minimized.

Role Reversal

A second major nontherapeutic consequence is that as the provider uses self-disclosure, the patient and provider switch roles. The provider, formerly the advisor and helper, becomes the helpee. There are circumstances under which patients would benefit from this role reversal; namely, it gets them off the hook. They do not have to reveal aspects about themselves or collaborate on their own treatment program. The following dialogue describes this process as the provider is trying to encourage a resistant patient to follow a low-fat diet.

Provider: "There are reasons that the doctor wants you to keep your diet low in fat."

Patient: "I know—but I like salami, chopped liver, fries—a meal is not a meal without bread and butter."

Provider: "I can understand, Mr. S____, that it is hard for you. I've had to eliminate nearly all fat from my diet, and it is difficult to turn my back on things I like so much." (*Self-disclosure*)

Patient: "What foods have you turned your back on?"

Provider: "Ice cream (my favorite), butter, cheeses, sausage . . . " (*Self-disclosure*)

Patient: "It probably wouldn't hurt you to have an occasional piece of cheese or an ice cream cone."

Provider: "If I start cheating I seem to have no control." (*Self-disclosure*)

Patient: "Maybe what you can do is check into some of those low-fat ice creams or yogurt—my wife eats a lot of yogurt."

In this scenario, the patient has distracted the provider from the purpose of exploring his own diet restrictions. He has gotten the provider to talk about her own difficulties. And, he is even beginning to give her advice about her problems of coping with diet restrictions. Role reversal is evidenced by the fact that (1) the focus switched to the provider's problem, (2) the patient assumes a helping role, and (3) the provider replies to the remarks in a complementary fashion, reinforcing the reversal of roles.

There is more than one possibility to explain why this occurred. First, the patient may have felt that the provider's questions were too intrusive and wanted to avoid disclosing. Second, the patient does not want to change his eating patterns and simply wants to stop the provider from "pushing" him. A third possibility is that the patient does want to comply but is unwilling to work with this provider on the problem.

Also, there are various reasons why the provider failed to remain a helper in this dialogue. First, the provider may not have anticipated the negative consequences of a self-disclosure with this patient. The provider may even be unaware of the patient's motives to take the focus off himself. Second, the provider may have perceived the resistance in the patient and decided that expanding on her own disclosures would increase the patient's trust. Finally, the provider may have some strong feelings about her own problems with compliance and was unaware of these. The patient's questions may have elicited attitudes that she needs to discuss with her own physician, i.e., the patient has uncovered the provider's problem. The surprise element for the provider—*Gee, I thought I accepted my restrictions* and the realization that this is not the case may further distract her in refocusing on the patient's problem. The provider may not be fully cognizant of the role reversal because she is caught up in thoughts about her own problem.

Role reversal is reversible. That is, providers can regain their professionalism in these cases. The question is more of when the provider will "catch on" and how the provider will react to the manipulative quality of the patient's interaction.

CRITERIA TO JUDGE THE BENEFITS OF SELF-DISCLOSURE

Because provider self-disclosure is both beneficial and problematic, clinicians have developed criteria to evaluate its usefulness. Auvil and Silver (1984), for example, have identified four guidelines for judging the merits of a disclosure. First, will the disclosure enhance the patient's *cooperation*, which is necessary to the therapeutic alliance? Second, will the disclosure assist the patient in *learning* about himself, to set short- or long-term goals or deal more effectively with his problems? Third, will the disclosure assist the patient to *express* formerly withheld feelings and concerns that are important for emotional support? And, fourth, will the disclosure provide the patient with *support* or reinforcement for important changes or goals he must act upon?

Finally, one rule of thumb to keep in mind in employing self-disclosures therapeutically is that self-disclosure should be tied to a goal or aim. If the provider does not have a patient-centered objective for using a personal self-disclosure, then it probably should not be used. If providers are not patient centered in their use of disclosures, they are probably acting on other motives, including getting their own needs met. Meeting your own needs rather than the patient's is in most cases nontherapeutic.

DEFLECTING REQUESTS FOR SELF-DISCLOSURE

There are times when providers are asked to disclose personal data about themselves. There are other times when providers feel that they must self-disclose because it would not be humane or even courteous if they did not. The following discussion addresses ways to avoid self-disclosing when it is not appropriate or when one is uncertain of the potential therapeutic value. Therapeutic self-disclosures require cognitive awareness of the dynamics of the interaction and the ability to predict outcomes. When these elements do not exist for the provider, self-disclosures may become very uncomfortable and unwieldy. In many cases, lack of clarity about interventions and interactions on the part of the provider will stimulate the patient to request a self-disclosure.

Take, for example, this dialogue between a medical student and patient:

Student: "Mr. J____, I'm here to gather some information about the symptoms you're feeling right now."

Patient: "Who are you?"
Student: "I'm a medical student. I work with Dr. S____."
Patient: "How long have you been in school?"
Student: (*Feeling somewhat uncomfortable*) "Several years."
Patient: "Am I your first patient?"
Student: "No, I've seen many patients."

Clearly the patient is asking for personal data from the medical student because he is not sure that the student knows what he is doing. The patient is sizing up the student and asks several questions to ascertain whether the student is competent enough to assume any part of his care.

Self-disclosures on the part of the provider can be uncomfortable. When such disclosures are requested by the patient they are not readily linked to a patient-centered objective, though it appears that by responding to the request the provider is meeting the patient's need. The need for the information is obscure, and the provider does not know exactly why the information is desired and how the information will be put to use. Additionally, there is the threat that what the provider discloses may lead the patient to reject the provider. Being approved of or disapproved of on the basis of education and experience is a threat that probably underlies this student's feelings of discomfort. While the provider may not be rejected, the threat or anticipation that rejection could occur makes the provider more self-conscious and hesitant. All self-disclosures have the impact of exposing vulnerabilities. And no one, patients and providers alike, is comfortable with feeling vulnerable.

There are cases when self-disclosures should be deflected. These cases are determined on the basis of certain criteria that will help the provider know how to respond.

Absence of Patient-Centered Rationale

Does the provider's self-disclosure have a patient-centered rationale? Sometimes complying with the request to self-disclose will benefit the patient directly or indirectly. Indirect benefits may include (1) balancing the dialogue, (2) giving the patient an opportunity to relax—a break from the intensity of the interview, and (3) communicating the humanity of the provider so the patient will feel more comfortable in disclosing around a selected topic.

Benefits that occur directly as a result of provider self-disclosure include those identified earlier; i.e., the patient derives a sense of being understood, trust in the provider is enhanced, the patient experiences a decrease in feelings of loneliness, and role distance (between provider and patient) is reduced. If an invited self-disclosure does not seem to address one or more of these aims, then chances are that it did not serve a useful purpose. Under these circumstances, the provider may choose to deflect the request.

Highly Personal Requests

There is still another instance in which the provider will deflect a request for self-disclosure. When a request is too personal and causes discomfort, the request should be denied. Examples of these requests vary, but are typically questions about the provider's age, religion, marital status, residence, and/or financial standing. Sometimes these requests are even more personal and include questions about sexual preferences, dating patterns, and personal life events affecting the provider and/or the provider's significant others. The questions may be innocuous or intrusive. "Are you married?" seems innocuous. "Do you and your wife fight a lot? Who wins—you or her?" is a good deal more intrusive. In any case, the provider deems it inappropriate to answer.

Although the provider may choose to answer and answer honestly, there are other options. If the provider feels uncomfortable with a request, then a statement to the effect, "I'm not really comfortable answering those kinds of questions" is appropriate. It is not required that the provider give an explanation, but explanations such as, "I don't discuss my personal life with my patients" helps to clarify the provider's response. With these remarks the provider is setting limits on the discourse and also communicating the parameters of the therapeutic relationship. Frequently, the patient means nothing behind the question and may have resorted to social chitchat because nothing else seemed to surface as important. Nonetheless, the provider still may be uncomfortable in sharing this personal information.

Guidelines in Deflecting Requests for Self-Disclosure

Auvil and Silver (1984) identify five further ways to circumvent a situation where providers' self-disclosure, at the patient's request, may be problematic. These include (1) expressing benign curiosity, (2) redirecting or refocusing the patient, (3) interpreting the patient's request, (4) clarifying the meaning behind the request, and (5) offering feedback along with limit-setting.

Provided one can be sincere about it, the easiest and most nonthreatening response is benign curiosity. The patient requests personal data and the provider responds with, "I'm wondering why you are asking me this." This reply may call for further disclosure from the patient that gives important feedback about the relationship, e.g., "I didn't think you understood about my holding things back from my wife."

Redirecting or refocusing the patient is a technique to bring the patient back to the original topic that preceded the patient's request. This is done in a manner that indicates that the provider may not have heard the patient's request. It does not negate the fact that the patient did make a request; it simply reestablishes priorities in the therapeutic discourse. The following example indicates how this is achieved in a relatively nonaggressive style.

Provider: "So tell me how this feels when I press here."
Patient: "It hurts but not as bad as it did yesterday."
Provider: "How about here?"
Patient: "Nothing—has anyone ever told you that you have pretty eyes?"
Provider: "What about here, feel anything when I press harder?" (*Deflected request for self-disclosure*)
Patient: "Yeah, that hurts."

The provider deflects the patient's request by responding as if she did not hear him. This was not done critically or angrily; the provider simply redirects the patient to follow her line of questioning.

Interpreting why the patient is asking for personal data requires a great deal more knowledge and skill. It is appropriate but less frequently used, especially by neophyte clinicians, because it calls for judgments that the provider may not be able to make.

Consider the following exchange:

Patient: "Are you married? Do you have kids?"
Provider: "Knowing something more about me as a person makes you a little more comfortable with me, doesn't it?" (*Deflected request for self-disclosure*)

This type of response requires patients to examine the context of the relationship and their inability or unwillingness to move forward. If patients are not capable of such insight, the interpretation usually loses its impact even though it may successfully deflect the patient's request.

Clarifying the patient's request is a less-presumptuous strategy. For example, "You asked me if I were married, had kids—I wonder what concerns or uncertainties you might have about me." The provider expresses acceptance and positive regard for the patient's desire to know but seeks clarity about why the information is important.

Finally, responding with feedback deflects patients' requests for self-disclosure. Some patients will come across as offensive and insensitive and may even be aggressive. For example: "What do you like, Doc—blondes, brunettes; big ones, small ones, huh?" Sometimes patients need concrete feedback about their manner. The provider should feel that it is appropriate to instruct patients about the effect of their behavior not only on the provider but also on others.

CONCLUSION

In the most general sense, all communication discloses something about the speaker. Even nonverbal gestures disclose something personal. Still, when statements are made that reveal the nonobvious—a thought, feeling, attitude, or experience—and a distinct self-reference is made, the communication is more deliberately self-disclosing. The use of self-disclosure facilitates open communication that is critical in the establishment of a therapeutic alliance with the patient. When used effectively, self-disclosure can convey empathy, promoting a deeper closeness between provider and patient.

There are various reasons for self-disclosure to be problematic. Essentially, disclosures that miss the target can alienate the patient because the expression would fall outside the patient's frame of reference. Interrupting the flow of the patient's own disclosures can also occur. Role reversal is still another hazard in the deliberate use of self-disclosure. However, there are some very therapeutic outcomes that can occur with self-disclosure that are not a product of other response modes. Trust and the feeling of being understood can be achieved with other response modes to some extent; however, less loneliness and decreased role distancing are outcomes relatively unique to this therapeutic response mode.

Self-disclosure is difficult and it may not be the provider's first choice. Self-disclosure by the provider takes courage and exposes one's vulnerability. Providers are not immune to the fear of rejection or disapproval that comes from disclosure. For these reasons, deliberate use of self-disclosure is a therapeutic response mode that should be addressed with caution. And, if providers find themselves self-disclosing without having a patient-centered rationale for the disclosure, the likelihood is that the provider is not in a therapeutic position to significantly help the patient.

Although self-disclosure is used in social relationships, its application to therapeutic relationships with patients is still another matter. Provider self-disclosure is a skill that needs to be thoughtfully executed and evaluated.

CHAPTER 9

The Proper Placement of Advisement

We live in a society where most of our responses are shaped, in some way, by the (expressed) opinions of at least one other person (or group).

Gwen van Servellen

CHAPTER OBJECTIVES

- Define advisement as a therapeutic response mode.
- Describe several misuses of advisement and opinion giving.
- List several helpful principles in using advisement with clients.
- Describe some problematic client responses to advisement.
- List guidelines that enhance acceptance of advice.

Advice columns, e.g., "Ann Landers" and "Dear Abby," and to some extent national syndicated television shows, e.g., *Geraldo, Ricki Lake, Sally Jessey Raphael, Donahue, Jenny Jones, Montel Williams,* and, of course, *Oprah Winfrey*, serve a common function in our society. They perform the activity of helping their audiences choose the better course of action. Sometimes their advice is direct, stating the proper way of responding to a problem. An alternative approach for helping is throwing the audience into situational dilemmas and creating a form of "group think," i.e., the audience is encouraged to solve the problem of the various panel members who describe idiosyncratic elements that make thoughtful deliberation necessary and "quick advice" irrelevant. Both the advice columns and the television shows address two aspects of the problem; first, *how* one should think when confronted with the situation, and second, *what* conclusions one should come to at the end of the process. In short, what we have in these public-media events is mass instruction in problem solving. Along the way, we may even learn something new about such dilemmas as whom you should invite to your wedding, how to deal with a boyfriend/girlfriend who is cheating on you, how to deal with troubled friendships, how to cope with overbearing parents, how to raise a teen-

147

ager, what to do when a roommate does not pay the rent, and how to confront men/ women who will not commit.

In our society people both seek advice and express it. They also like to challenge advice, particularly if the directive is not clearly something that *must* be followed. Generally, advisement situations generate a great deal of discussion because by disclosing opinions one invites open dialogue about what one should do and how it should be done.

In this chapter, the differences between opinion giving and advisement will be described. The misuse of both advisement and opinion giving will be discussed as they interfere with mutual problem solving in the patient-provider relationship. Finally, principles behind the therapeutic use of advisement will be identified and specific guidelines will be presented. An indirect, open style of advice giving makes the patient less resistant and suspicious of the provider. It also increases the chances for patients' thoughtful exploration of their own dilemmas.

DEFINITIONS OF ADVISEMENT

Advisement is one of the least studied therapeutic response modes. This is surprising when one considers the ubiquity of advice giving in our society. Advisement is the act of disclosing what one thinks or feels about another's experience, namely, what you think they should or should not feel, think, or do. It is unilateral in that most of the data and assessment of facts come from the provider.

In its broadest sense, it refers to the listener's use of suggestions, directives, instructions, or commands. Its aim is to effect change in the patient's behavior, attitude, and/or emotional response.

Intensity of Advisement

There are two kinds of advisement. Low-intensity advisement is the process of giving information, opinions, and recommendations and the patient has maximum control over the ultimate course of action. This form of advisement is very nondirective. High-intensity advisement, on the other hand, is a powerful suggestion, frequently worded as a command. Patients essentially abdicate their control over their decisions. This latter type of advisement is taken up again in Chapter 11 where the use of commands, directives, and orders are discussed.

Advisement differs from the act of giving information and expressing opinions. Essentially, giving information and expressing opinions are preferable because they more likely result in mutual problem solving. Advisement is more forceful and linear. It does not give the patient decision-making power and is usually not respectful of the patient's thoughts and preferences. Expressing opinions and offering information, on the other hand, shows respect for patients' views and engages patients in at least part of the decision-making process. These modes are usually absent of manipulation and disrespect that sometimes characterize advisement.

Patient Responses to Advisement

Patients' responses to advice often depend on whether the advice was sought. Bertakis, Roter, and Putnam (1991) found that patients were less satisfied in health care encounters when providers (physicians) dominated the interview by excessive talking, such as giving too much advice, or when the emotional tone was provider (physician) dominated. Usually, when patients ask for advice, they are open to hearing and modifying the information to fit their individual circumstances. Accepting advice may also be a function of cultural orientation. In some cultures, individualism is stressed and individual rights are valued above all else. Individuals with this orientation may be less inclined to accept advice than are those individuals whose culture stresses conformity.

Advisement, and to a lesser extent, opinion giving, can be misused. Essentially, when providers are telling patients what they should think, how they should feel, or how they should behave, they are implying that they (the providers) know what is best. This position tends to prevent patients from struggling with and thinking through their own problems. Providers can use advice not solely to assist patients. Advisement can be used for ulterior motives such as to avoid uncomfortable patient-provider situations. Some patient decisions are very difficult, and sometimes providers use advisement to avoid uncomfortable silence and to avoid focusing on difficult or painful thoughts and feelings that the patient situation evokes. Perhaps the most common misuse of advisement is to solve a problem quickly. And, in this case, the provider may be given too much credit for the resolution of the problem. Using advice in this way tends to discount the idiosyncratic explanations as to why some suggestions just do not work. And in some instances, it is these factors that account for the way in which patients themselves have not instituted an effective change. It is as much the provider's task to assess why something may not work as it is to offer medically sound advice.

Providers' own responses to patients' needs for and reactions to advice are critical. Patients who openly ask for advice but are denied will feel cheated because sometimes they feel they need quick answers. Patients and providers alike may react to the uncertainty involving a course of action. The ambiguity that exists can be uncomfortable and disconcerting. Although a clear answer may not be forthcoming, some reassurance by the provider that an answer (viewed by the patient as a solution) is at hand is helpful. A provider's reaction to a patient's accepting or rejecting the advice given is a reflection of the provider's personal need for control. Because of this, providers who explore their reactions to needy and/or recalcitrant patient responses will be better equipped to deal with the entire range of patient-provider interactions in which advice becomes an issue.

THE MISUSE OF ADVISEMENT AND OPINION GIVING

Studies seem to suggest that advisement, while common, is problematic in the therapeutic relationship. In fact, within the Rogerian client-centered framework, advice is discouraged for four reasons.

1. It is comparatively poor in generating rapport and unconditional positive regard.
2. It can produce more-guarded responses in patients.
3. It may encourage dependency and diminish learning.
4. It tends to increase overt resistance in the patient.

Taking Control from the Patient

Consider the following dialogue between a provider and a young adult patient who is being seen in the clinic for an injury to her arm:

Physician: "So how did you hurt your arm?"
Patient: "I fell while I was snowboarding. It didn't hurt too much at first, but about an hour later, it started to swell and throb."
Physician: (*Silence.*) "Well, my children are not allowed to snowboard for that very reason. I have three rules: no snowboarding, no skateboarding, and no rollerblading." (*Advisement-indirect*)
Patient: (*Silence.*) Oh . . . well, I've been snowboarding for three years and snowskiing for ten years and this is the first time I've gotten hurt."
Physician: "Well, you have just been very lucky, young lady!"

The physician in this scenario approached the patient parentally, suggesting that she was a "bad" girl and "look what happened." His advice—follow my rules—was posed indirectly through a self-disclosure. The effect on the patient was problematic because she judged the self-disclosure irrelevant. The patient already felt bad and the physician's comments made her feel worse. His parental tone was annoying to the patient evidenced by her later statement, "I have my own parents and I don't need his opinion." Further, the physician's comment, "You've been very lucky!" was taken as indirect advice, i.e., "You shouldn't snowboard anymore." Resistance was generated, though not verbalized. The patient felt that her snowboarding was none of this doctor's business. *I came to have my arm x-rayed and set, that's all*! Additionally, the physician's prolonged silence conveyed his disapproval of her activities. And, in the patient's later words, "It made me feel uncomfortable and like a child. It would have been nice if he could have made me feel a little better, since I already felt bad because of my throbbing arm!"

This patient's experience caused her to request a change in doctors. The patient saw absolutely no benefit in continuing with this physician since she did not feel supported, did not learn anything new, could not express her feelings freely without feeling judged, and felt no desire to cooperate. Had the physician listened to his patient, kept his opinions to himself, and tried to make the patient feel better, the outcome may have been much different.

By giving direct advice, even disguised, providers take away from patients the responsibility that is rightfully theirs. This keeps patients in a state of immature dependence on the judgment and guidance of the provider. By giving the patient information, *offering an opinion*, the provider is supplying patients with data from which they can later formulate their own decisions and actions.

Altering Negative Effects of Advisement

Consider how the previous dialogue could be altered to achieve a therapeutic aim. Assume that the physician is not only a competent provider but deeply cares about the health of his patients. What could he have done? First, he could have explained that he has treated many of these injuries and that this was like the others he has treated. He could also ask his patient to describe how it happened, expressing interest in the trauma aspect of the accident. Actively listening to the patient describe how the event was a shock and what put her at risk would make two points. First, even though we are pretty certain that we will not be injured, it does happen. Second, reliving the movements she did or did not take that culminated in the injury would have provided her with information about how to prevent future injuries. Data such as, "There is one chance out of 25 for this injury to occur" would encourage his patient to consider the odds that it will happen again. The overall purpose of advisement is to alter behavior. Subtle and indirect advice can be more effective than straight-on directives. Phrased in this dialogue as a self-disclosure, the advice is indirect but not very subtle.

Unlike advisement, expressing opinions establishes equal opportunity and mutual respect between the patient and the provider. Expressing opinions is assertively interactional. That is, provider opinions are offered as additional information for the patient's decision-making process. Consider, for example, the feelings that these statements evoke: "It's my opinion . . . " and "Based on what I've read (heard, seen), I would say that this course of action is better." Expressing opinions is not making the decision for the patient, it is simply giving the patient the benefit of the provider's knowledge. In contrast, giving advice is a unilateral process of solving problems or making decisions for another (Hanes and Joseph 1986).

PRINCIPLES BEHIND THE THERAPEUTIC USE OF ADVISEMENT

In some ways, presenting patients with information about their condition is the provider's duty and neglecting to do so would be very poor practice. The balance that must be achieved is to provide information and opinions without negating the patients' rights to express their own opinions and to ask for further data on which to base what they think is the best course of action.

Less-Direct Advice

The first basic principle in using advisement is that for many patients the less direct the advice, the less likely it is that resistance will occur. To hold to this principle, providers must have an open style—a willingness to have their advice rejected. Advice that must be followed is not advice but rather a command or directive, and when the advice must be adhered to, providers must clearly say so.

Many patients are sensitive to advice even though they have come to providers for help. At its worst, advice communicates that the receiver is incapable of self-direction, which can be humiliating and belittling. Many people have received advice that was not helpful or received directives in an unhelpful manner. Just the words, "You should . . . " may be the first and only things the patient hears before tuning out and turning off. Some individuals have been subjected to critical parental figures and are not able to set their reactions aside when providers begin to advise with parental inflections. Such individuals may also be unable to accept advice from anyone because authority figures have not proven themselves to be trustworthy.

A useful way to present advice to persons who are suspicious of advice giving is to present the advice in ways that do not resemble advice. Suggesting an "alternative" or "a possibility" lessens the emphatic context of the idea. Presenting ideas as hypothetical is also a way to soften the harshness of advice. The following phrases, juxtaposed on an idea, can soften the impact of direct advice:

- "Do you think this idea will help in your situation?"
- "What do you think about these recommendations?"
- "How do you think this suggestion will fit your lifestyle?"
- "Can you adapt any of these ideas to your situation?"

Providing Rationale

Another method for giving advice indirectly is to credit it to experience, another source, or another authority. This is called providing a rationale. For example, "Patients who followed this treatment for two years experienced better results," or "According to research on the effects of the long-term use of sleeping medication . . . " In these cases, the provider can appear to be unbiased while at the same time appear to identify with the patient's dilemma. Together they come to a joint decision, though in actuality, it was the provider who swayed the patient to select a specific course of action.

Decrease Confusion

Other response modes used with advice giving create confusion. One example illustrated in the dialogue between the physician and his patient who suffered a snowboarding injury was self-disclosure used with advice giving. Obviously, the patient was as concerned about the response that the provider gave as about the response that was not given. Still another instance is when questions are used with advice giving. Imagine this same patient being asked: "Don't you think that if you continue to snowboard you will suffer an even more serious injury?" This leading question clearly is not one to be answered simply "yes" or "no." The implication is that any patient in his or her right mind would understand this fact, i.e., "What's wrong with you that you don't see this?" Advisement can inhibit the exploration of a problem.

Recognize Problematic Patient Responses

Inhibition of further exploration can take many forms. In the earlier scenario between physician and patient, the advice given was ignored and the patient responded with silence. Some typical patient responses to advisement include (1) placating, (2) changing the subject, (3) ignoring the advice, (4) reacting with silence, and (5) passively agreeing with the advice.

Placating is a response that is frequently given by patients. The classic exchange, "You should . . . " and "Yes, I probably should . . . " establishes that the patient has heard the advice but has little intention of taking the advice. Rather, the desire is to cause the provider to back off, suggesting that the advice is unwanted.

Patients can change the subject or transition to the next topic as if the advice is "a done deal." The underlying message is, "Let's go on to something else."

Consider the following comments of a patient who is receiving prenatal care in a community clinic:

Nurse Practitioner (NP): "You have been taking care of yourself, right?"
Patient: "Yes."
NP: "I hope so. You need to eat properly, because if you don't it can cause great harm to your baby." (*Advisement*)
Patient: (*Silence. Feeling humiliated and small.*) "When do I have to come back again?" (*Change of subject*)

The patient was not allowed enough time to seriously answer the question asked of her. Additionally, the advice was levied as a "warning," making the patient feel guilty and inferior. The patient never really got a chance to explain how well she was caring for herself since the nurse practitioner answered the questions herself. Had the nurse's nonverbal behavior displayed interest, the patient may have fought for a chance to discuss the topic. In her own judgment, the patient describes this nurse as a noncaring, bossy individual who thinks that she knows it all. There was no talking to her—one might as well change the subject, and by transitioning to the next subject or changing the topic the patient avoids a discussion of the advice.

Ignoring the provider's advice with open defiance is yet another potential patient response. Sometimes patients can argue just as convincingly against an action as the provider can argue for this action. What results is a battle of wits over who is more right. In some instances, the patient may even seek this advice before ignoring it. The provider offers the advice, then is puzzled, maybe even angered, by the fact that the patient does not follow it. The natural counter is, "Why do you even ask my advice if you're not going to take it?!"

Silence and unelaborated passive agreement are still other responses patients may give to direct advice. Silence occurs when the provider suggests a course of action, i.e., "You should . . . " and gets no answer. Unelaborated passive agreement occurs in circumstances where the provider suggests a course of action, i.e., "You should . . . " and gets a curt response, "Uh huh."

Guidelines That Enhance Acceptance of Advice

Whether expressing opinions or giving advice, there are specific guidelines that more likely ensure success. An important principle is to ask the patient (or patient's family) if they want to hear your ideas or points of view with statements such as, "I have cared for other patients with this illness and have read a great deal on the subject. I could provide a summary if you would like to hear it." If the patient's nonverbal response is avoidance or if the patient argues with your views, it is best to drop the discussion and reestablish the patient's frame of reference before continuing.

Advice That Is Tentative

Advice that is tentative is more likely to be accepted. If the provider avoids being dogmatic and makes allowances for the uniqueness of the individual patient, the advice will be more palatable. Questions such as, "What do you think about the suggestions I've given you?" also discourage the provider from being too presumptuous about the patient's readiness to accept the advice. It is always good practice to adapt one's advice to both the situation and the patient. If the patient is an individual who rarely appreciates advice, it may be better to cushion the advice with a story, a self-disclosure, or a link with another source. Additionally, it is important to stay close to the patient's own language, cultural viewpoint, or age-related jargon. This not only enables providers to further individualize their advice, it decreases the distance that may be felt between the provider and the patient. In the case of young adults or adolescents, it is particularly useful to frame advice in terms that are important to them, because this group is particularly sensitive to criticism and feelings of being put down by adults. After all, if the patient's dilemma was simple, then the solution could be straightforward. By helping patients save face, the provider minimizes threats to the patient's self-esteem and increases the likelihood that the patient will accept the advice or opinions that are offered. Advice can be perceived as control, and if this occurs, the patient will react negatively to the advice.

Assessing Patient Readiness

Before offering advice or information or rendering opinions, the provider will need to assess the readiness of the patient. Carkhuff and Rordan (1987) describe a model for determining patient readiness. Essentially, the patient may be at any one of the following five sequential stages: uncertainty and confusion, awareness, understanding, constructive action, or learning.

At Stage 1 (uncertainty and confusion), the patient has not yet realized the problem or the magnitude of its effects. Facts and feelings about the situation may be diffuse but still upsetting. Shocked, in denial, or otherwise overwhelmed, the patient is not ready to explore either the problem or the potential solutions. Attempting to give the patient advice at this stage would be useless.

However, in Stage 2, awareness, patients are more prone to identify a problem and examine the effects that the problem has on their lives. Advice giving at this stage is also futile. The patient is still attempting to sort through the various thoughts and feelings that have been evoked by the problem. It is at this point that the provider can close in on the problem. It is appropriate to discuss how the problem came about and what the potential consequences are. While the need for intervention can be discussed, the provider should refrain from discussing specific solutions.

Increasingly, the patient is developing, in Stage 3, a realization and an understanding of the problem. At this point, patients are ready to receive information about solutions. This may be communicated in a variety of forms—as information, as professional opinions, and/or as more direct forms of advice.

When patients have reviewed the wisdom and meaning of the options, providers can provide them assistance in selecting a course of action in Stage 4. This stage is met with constructive intervention and can be supplemented by evaluating the actions taken. In this way, patients' knowledge increases significantly in depth as well as in breadth.

Including one's rationale behind the particular piece of advice establishes a guide for patients to judge the wisdom of the advice. Again, it turns the final decision back to the patient. Sometimes, in Stage 5, patients will learn more from the provider's discussion of the rationale than they could ever learn with simple statements of advice.

When all is said and done, however, providers must be ready to be wrong about their advice. Also, their opinions may not always agree with the patient's feelings at the time. And, premature closure of a topic with the offer of advice can be as problematic as no closure at all.

CONCLUSION

In offering advice or opinions, providers must be aware that the process can diminish a patient's responsibility for decision making. This responsibility is rightfully his, and keeping the patient in a state of immature dependence on the judgment and guidance of providers minimizes patients' abilities to formulate their own actions. Strong advice does not afford patients the opportunities to sort through their own thoughts and arrive at their own decisions.

Providers may find it difficult to let patients make their own choices. They may be especially inclined to put their expertise to work while infantilizing the patient. Remembering that each patient requires a unique solution to his or her problems enables the provider to forestall the enthusiasm for a "quick fix."

With regard to very tough decisions and courses of action, providers must remember that the lack of advice is just as bad as bad or poorly communicated advice. Uncertainty and indecision are uncomfortable for patients, and patients will not be able to tolerate this condition for long. Accompanying patients (and patients' families) in the journey to arrive at the best possible course of action requires providers not to be timid about their professional opinions.

CHAPTER 10

Reflections and Interpretations

On the nature of interpretations: " An idea under the idea, or a feeling beneath the feeling, can be assisted to emerge, and the process becomes more than an intellectual exercise; it produces an actual shift."

E. F. Hammer

CHAPTER OBJECTIVES

- Define reflections as a therapeutic response mode.
- Describe how reflections can be therapeutically applied in provider communications with clients.
- Describe ways in which reflections differ by content, intensity, and length.
- Define interpretations.
- Differentiate reflections from interpretations.
- Discuss how reflections and interpretations differ from other therapeutic response modes.
- List several guidelines in using reflections.
- Identify the inappropriate ways in which interpretations are used in social contexts as well as their appropriate use in therapeutic encounters.
- List several guidelines in the therapeutic use of interpretations.

In studies of patient responses, certain patient responses have been linked qualitatively to provider behaviors. A good deal of attention has been directed to which provider behaviors elicit negative or defensive responses and which provider behaviors elicit positive reactions. While the contribution of the provider's personality and experience as well as the patient's characteristics are not to be minimized, a good deal more weight is given to the momentary changes in the provider-patient dialogue. Surely, the content of the provider's remarks, the participation of the provider as a listener, and the provider's role with the patient do make a difference in patient responses. Certain response modes are known to make a difference in the kind and quality of patient response. By comparing the different effects of reflection and interpretation, we can illustrate the principle that provider responses make a substantial contribution in shaping the patient's self-disclosure and attitudes about the helping process.

This chapter will describe each response mode—reflection and interpretation—in detail. Comparisons will be drawn between these therapeutic responses. The strengths and limitations of each will also be identified, and guidelines for their use will be specified.

There are many determinants affecting the disclosure and attitudes of patients. Evidence, however, that the nature of the provider's comments affect both the patient's attitude toward the provider and the particular way the patient speaks will be stressed.

DEFINITIONS OF REFLECTION

While reflection can simply be a restatement or paraphrasing of what the patient has communicated, in the classical sense, reflection is more than this (Bernstein and Bernstein 1985). Hill and Gormally (1977) stated that while reflection includes a repeating of the patient's statement, it must also contain references to stated or implied feelings. Reflections can stem from patients' current or previous statements, nonverbal behavior, reference to the context of the interaction, and even the provider's knowledge of the patient's total situation. Reflections may be phrased tentatively or as affirmative statements. Quite frequently they are stated as observations, e.g., "As you are talking about your surgery, I hear some uncertainty in your voice."

Reflection, then, is a response by providers that redirects the patients' ideas, feelings, and/or the content of their message. While reflections may include paraphrases and restatements, they usually display more depth. Paraphrasing what the patient said is simply choosing parts of the verbal message and stating these ideas again, usually without extrapolating a primary idea. Restatement involves reiterating almost word for word what the patient has said. In cases of paraphrasing and restatement, no reference is made to the patients' underlying meaning or attitudes or the nonverbal aspects that give clues to patients' in-depth thoughts and feelings.

Consider the following example. The patient is describing a concern about the anesthesia that will be used in surgery.

Patient: "I still don't know. What if I get real sick from it? They don't really know if they'll be able to use a general anesthesia."
Provider: "They don't know if they'll be able to use a general." (*Restatement*)
Patient: "That's what they said."

Provider: "So, let me see; you don't know yourself what they'll use or whether they will use a general?" (*Paraphrasing*)

Patient: "Yeah—it makes me nervous. My mother never could have a general."

Provider: "So as I'm listening to you—I sense that this is very much on your mind—what anesthesia they'll use—and I hear that you are afraid you'll get sick if they do give you a general anesthesia." (*Reflection*)

Patient: "Yeah—maybe I worry too much, but I do want to know ahead of time. I don't want a general because I'm afraid of reacting like my Mom did. Maybe I won't, but it still scares me."

Provider: "Yes, I understand why you are worried."

This series of statements by the provider illustrates the use of restatement, paraphrasing, and finally, reflection. Notice that the reflective remark makes reference to a stated or implied feeling, fear, while both the restatement and paraphrasing did not. Also notice that the reflective response elicited a discussion of depth, while the paraphrasing and restatement allowed the patient to stay with the theme on a superficial level.

Reflections, then, are not only statements by the provider that summarize what the patient has said, they state what the provider thinks are the patient's feelings about the topic being explored. The provider may reflect the early, middle, or the later aspects of what the patient has said, or some part of all phases of the patient's disclosure. Reflection tends to focus the patient at a more in-depth level and at the same time discloses the providers' empathy. Reflection, then, is a demonstration on the part of the provider that he or she understands the patient. Restatement, while similar to reflection, deals more exclusively with the content and words that the patient uses. Reflection deals more with the feeling dimension of what the patient has said.

While it would seem that reflection is an easy response mode to implement, this is not the case. Reflection is a specialized response unfamiliar in the context of everyday conversation. Social situations elicit response matching and the detached, objective role that reflection conveys is not anticipated in the give-and-take of social discourse. In fact, for this reason, providers may feel somewhat artificial and clumsy when they first use it. Reflection is usually more difficult to master than is the therapeutic use of questions and silence because it is not often used in everyday conversations and is a less-familiar response.

THERAPEUTIC USES OF REFLECTION

While reflection is an unfamiliar response in social conversations, its use in therapeutic discourse has a substantial history, particularly in psychotherapy. The term *reflection of feelings* became a well-known aspect of a counselor's approach to people in distress.

Over the last 25 years, since the advent of Rogerian client-centered therapy (Rogers 1951), reflection has slowly infiltrated the American, European, and Asian professional cultures. Reflective techniques are now used by a wide variety of providers who must demonstrate understanding of their client's feelings and experience. The reflective response is excellent in capturing the emotional meaning of the discloser's expressed message and is often used to show the patient that the provider is not only listening but also understands his or her feelings. The desired impact then is to give the patient the experience of being known. This is achieved by slowing down the interaction, thus giving the patient more time to think out and clarify what was said (Beck, Rawlins, and Williams 1988). Instead of describing a thought and moving on to the next subject, reflection replays the theme, sometimes doubling the time given to exploring the thought (Goodman and Esterly 1988).

Reducing Isolation and Loneliness

In the context of confronting an injury or illness, the patient sometimes has acute feelings of being alone. Reflective statements, when communicated empathetically, can give patients the experience of being escorted through the process of dealing with the burden of their injuries or illnesses. As Rogers (1951) so aptly explained, accurate reflections serve as a companion as the client (patient) explores (sometimes) frightening feelings. It is assumed that sustained experiences of being known provides patients the safety, courage, and company they need to confront the stress of the illnesses that they face.

Reducing the experience of isolation and loneliness is something that providers can do with skillfully placed reflections. The following dialogue is between a student nurse and a patient diagnosed with leukemia. Chemotherapy has caused the patient's white-blood-cell count to drop, which necessitates the patient's transfer to protective isolation.

Student Nurse (SN): "O.K., Mrs. R____, it is time to move to the other room. Are you ready?"

Patient: "Yes, I am (*not smiling, looks worried*)."

SN: "You seem quiet right now. (*Reflection*) Are you feeling OK?"

Patient: "It is just that Mrs. K____ (her roommate) thinks that I am moving to another room because I don't want to be around her. I've tried to explain, but she doesn't understand."

SN: "Would you like me to get an interpreter to explain it to her? One of the nurses speaks Korean."

Patient: "Yes, I would appreciate that so much!" (*Smiling, then quiet and looking worried again while fighting back tears.*)

SN: "It seems like you are unhappy about something else." (*Reflection*)

Patient: "I just don't want to go to isolation again. It is so quiet in a room by yourself. Well, as least I can play my music louder." (*Smiling, half-heartedly, then looking away.*)

SN: "It seems to me that you are afraid of being lonely in isolation." (*Reflection*)

Patient: "Yes, I was so lonely last time. The day just drags on and on."

SN: "Going to isolation must make you feel even more alone since your family is so far away." (*Reflection*)

Patient: "Yes. Until now, it has been OK that my husband and kids couldn't visit me because I could go in and out of my room as I pleased."

SN: "You sound very sad." (*Reflection*)

Patient: "Yes, that is exactly it." (*She begins to cry.*)

The student nurse stayed with this patient for a few minutes talking about ways in which she could feel less isolated. Subsequently, the patient called her husband.

In this interaction the student listened empathetically to the patient, observing that the half-hearted smiles could be cues to some distress. Not knowing exactly what was bothering the patient, the nurse used reflection to help both herself and the patient identify the problem and explore the patient's feelings. The patient's self-disclosure actually decreased her sense of isolation and feelings of loneliness.

Promoting Positive Self-Worth

As summarized by Bradley and Edinberg (1990), reflection is employed therapeutically to achieve several outcomes. Reflections can impart powerful covert messages of positive self-worth. They obtain feeling responses from the patient. They deepen the patient's feeling state, thus making feelings and attitudes more accessible. Reflections also facilitate communication to continue beyond the point where it might have been stopped. Because reflections highlight feelings as well as content, they increase patients' awareness of feelings through a greater sensitivity to what and how thoughts are communicated. Bernstein and Bernstein (1985) suggest that by re-presenting the patient's message, reflections provide patients with new insight. Thus, reflections mirror back to the patient important thoughts and feelings that are made more apparent because of the extended attention they receive.

Reflection has become such an integral part of the helping process that the issue is not whether they are useful, but rather, the issue is the best way in which to teach this therapeutic response. A reflection used mechanically in the absence of empathy, however, loses its impact.

KINDS OF REFLECTIONS

As with most other response modes, reflections differ qualitatively from one another.

Ways Reflections Differ—Content

One way in which reflections differ is in the selected content that the provider chooses to paraphrase. From the whole range of material stated by the patient, the provider will select and paraphrase what the patient has said. Since providers will condense what the patient has said, exactly what providers use in their reflections may vary. In some instances, they may focus on the feeling aspects of the patient's communication. In other cases, they may paraphrase the words that the patient used with only minimal reference to feelings.

Ways Reflections Differ—Intensity

Another way in which reflections differ is by level or depth. Reflections can be graded as light, medium, or heavy, according to their intensity and the insight expected from the provider. Heavy reflections come with high demands, and like interpretations, might be resisted. Generally, the difficulty is that the provider is reflecting that which is obvious to them but it may be outside the patient's awareness. Providers might, for example, label the distress that they hear in the patient's tone of voice and refer to it as anger or rage. These labels may be too threatening to the patient, especially if these are feelings that have never been acceptable. The patient's predictable response in this situation is to quickly deny or challenge the validity of the reflection. Other patient reactions may include their blocking exploration, ignoring the provider's statements, or attempting to clarify the provider's observations, e.g., "Why? Do I really sound angry?" The response of the provider should then be to use less-threatening labels, e.g., "upset" instead of "angry" and "uncertain" instead of "anxious." Backing off allows patients to lower their resistance and explore more comfortably the feeling dimension behind their statements.

Medium-level reflections are less offensive than are heavy reflections. Still, the patient may not understand why the provider's summary includes the labels that are used. Patients will not openly resist medium-level statements and will generally allow the provider to help them see the connection between their verbalization and the provider's impressions. With a little explanation or a passage of time, the patient will usually become open to the connections that are presented.

Consider, for example, the following dialogue:

Patient: "If you want to know the truth, I'd rather you take it (tumor) out right here. It's got to be done. Take this thing out."
Provider: "You want me to take it out here—now? We'll do it. Finding the lump must have been a real shock to you." (*Reflection*)
Patient: "Good." (*Falls into silence expecting the procedure to be carried out, makes no reference to feeling shocked.*)

At a return visit to the surgeon's office, the patient offers:

Patient: "This was the shock of my life—I couldn't believe it when I found it. I just wanted to get it out of my body."
Provider: "Yes. . . . (*empathizing with patient*) You caught it pretty early."

The reflection accomplished two things: It acknowledged the patient's request, and it identified the more covert experience of the patient (shock and disbelief about having discovered the tumor).

The reflection re-presents the patient's experience without much addition or subtraction from the verbal and nonverbal aspects of the communication. Feelings were addressed without adding too much new data. The provider was able to demonstrate empathy. While the patient did not initially address the shock that she felt, this aspect of the diagnosis was something the patient addressed after surgery. All in all, the patient was reassured by the provider that what was said made sense and was understood at a deeper level.

Light reflections are rarely resisted by the patient. Essentially, they are comments that the patient may have made, usually just before the provider's statement. They frequently come across as "mind-reading" comments. Essentially, the provider puts things together for the patient, sometimes just before the patient is about to reflect these same thoughts. The difference may be that the provider chooses more cryptic expressions. The key to light reflections is that they rarely interrupt the flow of the interaction, and the patient almost always responds in ways that validate the content of the reflection. The patient might reply, "Yeah" or "That's right," and then go right on with remarks that further explore these ideas.

Short and Long Reflections

In addition to the specific content of a reflection and the level of intensity, reflections also differ in how much is re-presented to the patient. Shorter reflections, e.g., a few words, are generally considered better than those that express several thoughts simultaneously. If the provider has been listening carefully, summarizing the patient's communication in a few words is not difficult. The problem arises when the provider fails to respond and allows the patient to roam aimlessly from thought to thought and topic to topic. At this point, providers probably have lost the essence of the discussion and will need to prioritize, using their own frame of reference. To the extent that this frame of reference does not re-present the patient's, the intervention will fail to stimulate awareness and communicate empathy. Capturing the patient's remarks in a few words also presents less demand on the patient. As a receiver, many thoughts and ideas are confusing, need sorting, and are sometimes difficult to decode, so short reflections tend to preserve the steady flow of patient problem solving.

The therapeutic purposes of reflection are many. They help patients examine their plight, feelings, and attitudes toward their health problems. They invite the patient to explore, in a gentle nondirective manner, their experience. Communicated with warmth and openness, they provide empathy. Sometimes reflections act to reinforce or reward selective patient responses. In other words, as the provider selects from the patient's statements, the attention paid tends to reinforce that which is restated and increases the potential for exploration in this area. Reflection has also been noted to produce relaxation, which may come from the patient's realization that he or she has been heard. Uncertainty about being heard and understood can be lessened through reflective statements. Finally, reflections can be used to clarify the patient's experience so that the provider has a better idea of what is important to the patient.

REFLECTIONS AND INTERPRETATIONS

Reflections Differ from Interpretations

To fully understand reflections, it is important to differentiate them from interpretations. Generally, the differences between these responses are not always clear.

When the patient communicates something to the provider, the provider can use either a reflection or an interpretation to better understand the patient's experience. If the provider fits the message into some language that fairly accurately portrays what the patient said, the provider is using a *reflection*. If the provider, however, associates what the patient has said with some theory or data about the patient's past experience of life events, then the provider is using an *interpretation*. That is, if providers give patients their understanding of patient remarks using the patient's point of view, they are more likely using reflective therapeutic responses. If, however, providers attempt to understand patients' remarks through a theory or through the providers' experience, they are more likely using interpretative therapeutic responses. The intent of the reflection is to give the experience of being understood from their point of view or frame of reference. The intention of the interpretation is to convey an understanding of the patient greater than the patient's own understanding of himself.

In very simple terms, reflections are simply to let the person disclosing know that he or she has been heard. Reflections are given frequently throughout a single interaction with a patient. In contrast, interpretations are offered much less frequently and only after a great deal of data has been gathered, e.g., at the end of an interview and well into the relationship.

For example, the provider might say, "When first I saw you, you were having difficulty even considering your diagnosis. Now you're saying, 'Why did this have to happen to *me*? *now*?' I know this is all very upsetting. This distress will pass—what you're going through is the whole adaptation process. At some time in the future your distress may lessen and you'll come to some level of acceptance" (*interpretation*).

This interpretative response accomplishes two goals. First, it links the patient's past and present experience in some meaningful way, i.e., that disbelief and current distress are related to one another and both are part of the patient's lived experience of the illness. Second, this reflection reports on a theory of adaptation to illness where responses occur in predictable sequence. Reflections, however, do not intend to link past and present or give patients a window to a theoretical explanation of their experience.

While reflections do not provide the extra data and insight that interpretations do, they may still provide new information. Reflections allow patients to concentrate, a second time, on material that they have shared. This process is likely to generate new thoughts and even new insights in the patient. Reflection promotes exploration that generally is not available to patients if they were considering their circumstances alone, in isolation from a helping person. Reflections also provide new data because it is impossible to re-present material exactly as it was presented. And, even minor or subtle changes can stimulate new thoughts on the part of the patient.

Definitions of Interpretation

A good interpretation, or one placed at the right moment, can significantly increase both patients' faith in the provider and patients' insights into their own experiences. Essentially, the purpose is to allow patients to see beyond the surface of their thoughts, feelings, and behavior.

Interpretations are the explicit statements of providers that give meaning to a segment of patients' feelings or behavior. There are essentially two types of interpretation; one links past and present events, and the other links theoretical significance with patients' experience.

In either case, these interpretations are speculations at best. The linking of past and present events, e.g., about a childhood situation and a current event, assumes that there is some cause-and-effect relationship that justifies the association between these two points in time. Both the past and current experience should have been discussed in the patient-provider relationship. Assumptions about a probable experience are highly speculative and not easily verified. Such interpretations are made on shaky grounds because at least one-half of the speculation is completely out of the patient's awareness.

The second type of interpretation, introjecting a theoretical premise, requires both a reformulation of the statements of the patient and the application of a concept or principle. For example, a young mother who is describing a problem with her infant would be assisted by understanding the theoretical explanation for the reasons behind her infant's behavior. This particular theory of growth and development may not be familiar to the young mother. For the theoretical interpretation to really be of value, though, the provider must assess what this mother already knows about stages of infant development.

The major way in which interpretations depart from either restatements or reflections is in the depth of understanding these responses evoke. Interpretations take patients further along in understanding than do either restatements or reflections. Interpretations actually offer explanations, reflections simply mirror back words and implied feelings. Whereas reflection can be applied early in the helping relationship, interpretations require the collection and analysis of a good deal of material. Interpretations are offered much later in the relationship. In fact, if interpretations are given too early, it appears that the provider is jumping to conclusions, stereotyping the patient, or simply projecting personal bias. Interpretations are more successful when they are preceded by one or more restatements.

Reflections and Interpretations Differ from Other Response Modes

Therapeutic response modes, e.g., the use of silence, questions, and self-disclosure, differ from each other in terms of the direction in which they lead the patient and in the amount of work that the patient will be required to do.

That is, the person who does most of the talking, thinking, and feeling may be different depending on the response mode used. Response modes can evoke patient- or provider-driven interaction. When providers are interested in getting patients to explore their problems, reflections are recommended. Providers who are exploring patients' problems from the provider vantage point will use more questions and fewer reflections. Directive statements, e.g., interpretations and closed-ended questions, tend to be followed by talking about symptoms and problems and by less reference to the meanings or feelings behind those symptoms or problems. It is believed that reflections generate less resistance from patients than do direct questions and interpretations because they are less offensive and, therefore, cause less defensiveness on the part of the patient.

Reflections do not attempt to understand patients better than patients understand themselves. Unlike interpretations, reflections do not add much to what is told by the patient nor do they fit the experience into some theory or explanation of cause and effect. Reflections are also less likely than advisement to communicate provider values. Less directive than questions, reflections tend to let the patient chart the direction that learning and insight will take.

GUIDELINES IN THE USE OF REFLECTION

If there is one single principle that applies to using therapeutic response modes, it is that of moderation. Moving too quickly and too deeply into the patient's experience is ill advised. Not only from their obvious intrusive nature, ill-spaced, ill-timed reflection and interpretation can undermine the provider's attempts to obtain data and establish a collaborative helping relationship. How to phrase reflections and how and when to use interpretations are important issues.

Goals for Using Reflection

When the provider uses reflections, the goal is to convey empathy and, at the same time, promote problem exploration. In order to achieve this balance, several guides are useful. One way to approach reflection is to shift attention from the content of the patient's message to the feelings the patient must have, then silently reflect on how the feeling is associated with the content. The provider can then reflect back the essential thoughts and feelings that have come to mind. Rogers (1951) points out that the provider's tone of voice is critical. Reflections without empathy appear as declarations that have a somewhat judgmental tone. Reflections should be kept light. These are reflections that simply let patients know you have heard and are following their line of thinking. The provider should avoid interrupting in order to offer a reflection; pauses can occur that allow some space between the last remarks of the patient and the reflection of the provider. In choosing a paraphrase, the provider should stay within the patient's frame of reference, inserting little, if any, new material. Keep the reflections centered on the here and now of what is communicated. Historical reflections border on interruptive remarks and are not easy for the patient to relate to.

Forming a Reflection

Providers are not always confident about their reflective remarks. Beginners frequently worry about sounding phony. It is true that providers who concentrate too much on a few key words will miss the patient's message altogether. Inflection at the end of a speculation communicates the provider's uncertainty about the importance of what has been said and/or the understanding that the provider has of the patients' remarks. Reflections that are worded as statements, e.g., as observations, communicate confidence and generally encourage patients to focus on their own experience rather than on the provider. Dutiful reflections—offering a reflection because one feels it is time to or one should—are rarely effective. The provider who uses this type of reflection lacks the empathetic character needed to make the patient feel the presence of a sensitive provider.

Countering the Awkward Aspects of Reflections

Reflections are not always easy to make. There are several common difficulties in learning to give effective reflections. Self-consciousness, awkwardness, inability to capture the patient's words in vivid remarks, and confusion about what aspect of a long message should be reflected are difficulties the provider may experience.

These difficulties can be managed by employing a number of actions that enhance reflections. Long interresponse times before reflecting allow the provider to sort and examine carefully the patient's remarks. Silently reflecting on what the patient has said, using one's imagination to tap into the patient's experience, is also useful. Repeating key words or using metaphors may capture the patient's experience, as will introjecting a disclosure before a reflection when the message is confused.

The most common beginner's problem is a tendency to add too much or to omit important content when re-presenting the patient's experience. Sometimes this results in serious distortion or exaggeration, thus softening or watering down aspects of the patient's remarks. If the provider is a beginner, it is important not to sound too mechanical. If this happens, reflections are presented stiffly and sound strained. Voicing reflections under one's breath is helpful, but it is also important to recognize that one may need to use 50 to 100 reflections before feeling authentic when using this response mode.

Usually, in the beginning, one feels like an echo. There does not seem to be time to think through what one is going to paraphrase. Silence response modes or pauses, however, can stimulate creative associations and evoke metaphors. Statements like, "You feel you're on slippery ice" (fear) or "You must feel like you're in a corner and can't get out" (helplessness) are vivid images that help capture the essence of the patient's story.

When the patient talks too quickly or too long without giving the provider an opportunity to introject a comment, reflection is difficult. Sometimes the patient has presented confusing or even contradictory messages, and precise interpretations are not always possible. Reflecting the most useful parts of a complex disclosure is a skill that develops over time. One strategy is to reflect silently, assess the most important aspect of the message, and reflect it back verbally to the patient. If the patient communicates contradictory or confusing material, it is advisable to reflect the contradiction. For example, "I've heard you express good and bad things about this change; on the one hand . . . but . . . " If the confusion is complicated, the provider may offer, "It's hard to really know how you're feeling about this change." Remember, the patient may not be confused at all; it may be that the provider's ability to track and comprehend all that the patient has said is limited. In this case, it is better to disclose one's inability to comprehend the patient's feelings.

Avoiding Overuse of Reflections

Reflections can be used too frequently or indiscriminately. When this occurs, the provider may appear disinterested. Collins (1977) suggests that "parroting" can appear as mimicry and can make reflection and other nondirective techniques seem ludicrous. Consider the following dialogue between a person in pain and a medical student.

Patient: "I have pain in my shoulder."
Provider: (*Scanning patient chart*) "You have pain?" (*Restatement*)
Patient: "Yes, right here—my left side—it hurts a lot."
Provider: "Your left side is really painful—it concerns you?" (*still thumbing through chart*) (*Reflection*)
Patient: "I told you twice—my side hurts. Aren't you going to look?"

Understandingly, the patient is getting agitated with the provider. This overuse of the reflective technique actually worsens the inattention that the patient experiences. Notice that one therapeutic benefit of reflection is establishing empathic understanding, yet this use of restatement and reflection, which is ill-spaced, actually communicates the opposite.

INTERPRETATIONS USED IN SOCIAL AND THERAPEUTIC CONTEXTS

Interpretations go beyond patients' surface messages and into the less-obvious meanings and motivations behind remarks. Because they deal with less-obvious material, they are subject to error.

In Social Contexts

In social situations or social relationships, interpretations are received negatively. There is no justifiable reason to support interpretations in these interactions. Frequently, they make the receiver feel vulnerable and the sender feel superior. All providers who are trained in interpreting patients' remarks should be extremely careful to avoid slipping into this mode outside the therapeutic relationship. In truth, the provider may get into very complicated situations and come across as arrogant.

Consider, for example, the provider who meets an eligible dating partner, and after learning something about the young lady, offers this explanation about her hesitancy in accepting a date. "From what you've told me, you've been burned badly. Many girls I know carry around excess baggage. You probably struggle with problems of intimacy coming from your early childhood years." These interpretative remarks are interesting and might even be accurate. However, the balance in this social relationship has shifted. The young woman is left to believe that she has major problems—some she did not even know about. Her reaction may be to hesitate further—why would she consider getting to know someone who makes such giant leaps with just a little knowledge of her. She may feel badly about the labels that have been thrust on her.

Because interpretations violate the norms of social relationships, they are not comfortably employed in therapeutic relationships. And the way interpretation is misused in social relations can color provider attitudes in using interpretations in helping situations. In addition, providers may hesitate to use therapeutic interpretations because they are concerned about the response matching tendency in the patient. That is, provider interpretations may be matched with the patient's interpretation of the provider. In reality, this type of "turnabout is fair play" rarely occurs, though providers do worry about the possibility.

Therapeutic Uses of Interpretation

Interpretations, however, are response modes that *can* provide comfort to the patient. Interpretations can be experienced both as providing new information and providing new order to old information. A sound interpretation by the provider can increase the faith and confidence of the patient in the provider. Fisch (1994) believes that for interpretation to be "experience near," there must be a consistent focus on the patient's self-experience. Thus, interpretation has the potential to decrease patient anxiety and increase feelings of security.

Consider the following dialogue between provider and patient. The patient is in much distress over the physician's refusal to discharge him early from the hospital. The nurse caring for this patient has observed his course in the hospital and has read his chart describing his past history and multiple hospitalizations related to his chronic illness. The nurse says, "You're upset you can't go home earlier—I understand that. I think you're also reacting to the long struggle you've had with repeated hospitalizations. You may be more angry with your illness than with any of us. We are safe targets for this frustration. This happens a lot." Note here how the past is drawn into the present and how the nurse suggests that the health care team, not his illness, is the target for his stored-up frustration and futility. The patient learns that his reactions are not random and disconnected but form a continuity that reveals a problem over time and, in this case, is related to his adaptation to a chronic illness.

In this way, interpretations can translate a set of apparently unrelated or surface-related events into a coherent whole. This process in turn creates a more meaningful understanding for patients and deepens their awareness of what is happening to them. Said differently, the need for receiving interpretations is a need for creating new meaning from a series of events that evoke helplessness. Even minor interpretations can be perceived as helpful by someone who is struggling to make sense of undesirable or unmanageable situations.

The use of interpretative remarks in helping relationships has not always been judged helpful or advisable. In fact, there are some psychotherapeutic schools of thought that view interpretations as irrelevant and dangerous. Cognitive behavioral therapists, for example, generally regard theoretical interpretations as, at best, chancy, and interpretations linking past and present as unimportant to the process of facilitating change. What is important is what is manifested here and now. The reasons that the past relates to the present are not critical to achieving change. Some clinicians view provider interpretations as mere projections of the provider's own conflicts or dilemmas. If interpretation is putting on the patient what is truly only relevant to oneself, then providers are making gross errors in their assessment and treatment of patients.

A more moderate view suggests that interpretations can be therapeutic, and since no single therapeutic response will do in all situations, it is better to have more options. Thus, interpretations are suitable options if utilized properly. Still other clinicians caution that interpretations should be offered only when the patient has established a connection and is about to expand his or her insight in a particular area. Research indicates that interpretations that are much more removed from the patient's awareness are more likely to be resisted. Thus denial, blocking, and inattention on the part of the patient are important clues that the patient's readiness to hear and deal with the implications of the interpretation is not what it should be. The patient should be able to listen to, ponder, and ultimately understand the interpretation if it is to be successful. The patient's readiness to receive an interpretation is felt by some to be more important than the accuracy of the interpretation.

It is possible to plot reflection and interpretation on the same continuum with the expectation that as the provider moves from simple reflections to restating material not immediately within the patient's awareness, the depth of interpretive responses increases. That is, reflection begins with a restatement of remarks. When comments are made to link previously unrelated statements, the provider is moving into the domain of interpretation. Reformulating behavior and feelings in a way not previously recognized by the patient are mild- to moderate-level interpretations. Speculation about past events, e.g., childhood experiences in relation to current feelings, or hypothesizing about influences removed from the patient's current awareness represent more in-depth interpretative remarks.

GUIDELINES FOR THE THERAPEUTIC USE OF INTERPRETATIONS

Patient exploration of situations, dilemmas, or problems must be preserved. Principles for the effective use of interpretative remarks stem from this idea. The basic outcome, to enhance patients' sense of control over the situation and to allow them to grow in knowledge surrounding the condition, directs the choice and placement of interpretations.

Placing Interpretations after Reflections

Interpretations placed after reflections tend to make problem exploration go smoothly. Also, interpretations that start out simple and build on increased perceptions of the situation are likely to be less obtrusive.

Validating Interpretations

Interpretations should be evaluated. Validation can include comments such as, "Can you see the connection I described?" or "How does this idea fit with your thinking about this situation?" Delivering a few interpretative remarks with adequate evaluative follow-up generally permits more self-exploration than does direct unsubstantiated interpretations. Interpretation, though, can lead to the abandonment of self-exploration with the result of silence, denial, or blocking. Usually, interpretations made tentatively are less likely to cause patient anxiety and therefore preserve the flow of patient self-disclosure. While an interpretation may be true, there may be several others that are also true. One's interpretation may be true but not salient. For this reason, evaluative comments are needed to enable the provider to put interpretative remarks in perspective.

A common problem when making interpretations is the juxtaposing of one theory with every instance. Using one principle to explain all behaviors within and across groups of individuals is a faulty application of interpretations. No theory exists that adequately and accurately explains a single behavior across individuals. Interpretations using theory, then, are always tentative.

To summarize, effective interpretations can be made by even the beginning practitioner. Adequate observation of the patient and a theoretical basis on which to draw one's conclusions is essential, however. The delivery of an interpretation will meet with more success if it is communicated as a tentative suggestion, inviting the patient to collaborate in validating the ideas. Sometimes self-disclosure, e.g., "I'm wondering how your frustration about your discharge is related to the total experience of your illness," presents the interpretation in a mild, nonobtrusive fashion. Or, a question in the service of interpretation can be delivered more palatably, e.g., "Do you see a connection between your frustration with discharge and the experience of your illness in general?"

Using Interpretations Sparingly

Interpretations should be used sparingly. Because accurate interpretations require thoughtful reflection by the provider, the ability to deliver several interpretations in a single discourse is not the point. In fact, patients who are encouraged to stay on this intellectual plane may miss the feelings associated with their disclosures.

CONCLUSION

Reflections and interpretations are two additional therapeutic response modes. While they are similar to some degree, they are also very different. Interpretations move the patient to a deeper exploration of experiences because they mirror the patient behaviors and feelings that may not be within the patient's immediate awareness. Because of this, they are also more open to error. Reflections, however, are tied closely to the patient's current experience, and they paraphrase the words and feelings of the patient that are reflected in the patient's story. When empathically expressed, reflections disclose that the provider is present, listening, and respectful of the patient's need to direct the focus. Reflections acknowledge the patient's right to have opinions, to make decisions, and to think for oneself. With reflections, patients are doing most of the thinking and feeling. Interpretations can elicit deeper understanding and even reduce anxiety in patients by explaining what is felt to be confusing or out of control. The major drawback of interpretations over reflections is that the latter can be more provider-driven and therefore, less patient-centered. In the case of interpretations, providers are doing most of the thinking.

Guidelines in using both response modes include phrasing them properly, using them sparingly, and presenting them in ways that are least offensive to the patient.

Timing is important, particularly with interpretations, so that the revelation is accepted or, at the very least, provides useful material for discussion. Interpretations should never be presented as accusations or moral judgments but rather as supportive remarks offered as tentative explanations. Finally, whereas reflections can be made early in the provider-patient relationship, interpretations are best reserved for a period when provider-patient rapport has been secured.

While reflections express the patient's experience from the patient's frame of reference, interpretations tend to express the patient's experience from the provider's frame of reference.

CHAPTER 11

The Judicious Use of Confrontations, Orders, and Commands

Confrontation without a solid relationship created through the communication of empathy, respect, warmth, and genuineness rarely is helpful.

G. M. Gazda, W. C. Childers, and R. P. Walters

CHAPTER OBJECTIVES

- Define confrontation.
- Differentiate between levels of confrontation.
- Identify problems that may occur when confrontation is too intense.
- Differentiate between factual and experiential confrontation.
- Describe how one would regulate the intensity of confrontations.
- Differentiate commands and orders from confrontations.
- Identify ways of assessing compliance to commands, orders, and directives.
- Describe appropriate ways of summarizing directives to clients.

Up to this point, the therapeutic response modes that have been presented are largely facilitative. Showing empathy, confirming the value and worth of the patient, and establishing trust contribute to genuineness and unconditional positive regard in patient-provider encounters. Additionally, the use of questions, advisement, reflections, and interpretations can be rather gentle techniques to prompt patients to cooperate in their health assessments and care planning. These approaches are all relatively nonjudgmental. It is, however, appropriate in selected instances to show judgment and to participate conditionally. Providers must draw on their expertise and experience, and sometimes this requires being more forceful in their approach. In this chapter, the use of confrontation, orders, and commands will be discussed. It is through the use of supportive communications—empathy and unconditional acceptance—that providers gain authority. The use of more directive approaches can be successfully incorporated when this authority has been established. Confrontations, orders, and commands involve being judgmental and evaluative. These responses are employed to ensure action—to cause a reaction to occur that has either been avoided or is so necessary that the avoidance of action has serious consequences.

In one respect, confrontations, orders, and commands involve the sequential escalation of provider power. Confrontations are more indirect, orders clearly state one or more recommendations, and commands demand a specific response (avoidance of which would involve undesirable consequences). In actuality, these responses are often used together. That is, orders or commands are often given in an encounter where confrontation has occurred.

Confrontations, orders, and commands have an important role in health care. Not all patients are willing or able to participate effectively in their care. For many, maintaining wellness is not forthcoming without having providers who communicate clearly and forcefully what course should be taken.

CONFRONTATIONS: DEFINITIONS, LEVELS, TYPES

Definitions of Confrontation

Confrontation is the deliberate use of statements or questions to point out to another individual certain discrepancies. These discrepancies may be (1) differences between what persons say and what they do, (2) differences across several elements of communication or statements made, and (3) differences between what individuals should do and what they are actually doing.

The value of confrontation is that it offers alternative views about what is really going on. Assuming that patients are truly interested in the provider's point of view, feedback about discrepant behavior can be informative and can actually contribute to patient insight. When this feedback comes from a health care provider, it is generally presumed that the observations are valid and have some bearing on the patient's well-being. In some cases, the providers' observations may be more complete than the patient's. Confrontations that increase patients' knowledge or self-awareness stem from providers' extensive experience and high level of expertise.

Levels of Confrontation

Confrontations may be more or less intense. And, like interpretations, they may be more or less threatening. *Low-level confrontations* are mild and consequently arouse low levels of emotional response. Consider this dialogue between patient and physician; the physician is speaking to the patient about the necessity of a low-fat diet:

Physician: "OK, Janice, now I know you like fast foods, but, if I catch you at a fast-food restaurant I'm going to get upset (*smiling*)."

This confrontation delivers a message, i.e., despite an urge for fast foods, the patient must avoid them. This confrontation is low level because it is offered in a friendly, almost ambiguous manner. It is also delivered in a jovial fashion. It may arouse feelings in the patient, but it does not really pose a threat. While the patient may make use of this feedback, the informality may dilute the professional rationale behind the recommendation. Therefore, this confrontation may be too weak.

Confrontations that are moderately intense but are not so direct as to cause damage to the patient-provider relationship are *middle-level confrontations*. Consider the following dialogue between the patient described above and her physician:

Physician: "Janice, I know you like fast foods, but, if you continue to overindulge, you will not feel well and your health is not going to improve."

There is nothing ambiguous about this confrontation. The threat is clearly described as a maladaptive eating pattern. This confrontation is more intense and the need to comply is clearly articulated.

There are also instances in which confrontations are too strong. Typically, these *high-level confrontations* arouse intense feelings and can be perceived as very threatening. Consider this third adaptation of the same patient-provider encounter:

Physician: "Janice, I know you enjoy fast foods, but you've got to cut them out of your diet. I can't continue to treat you if you self-indulge like this."

This confrontation reproves the patient. It may make the patient feel inadequate, "bad," and unwanted. It does not elicit constructive problem solving nor does it empower the patient to correct her unhealthy eating patterns. The purpose of the confrontation is lost in the idea that the provider may decide to release the patient. As such, the threat is actually the loss of a provider, not the loss of health. This confrontation is very threatening and is likely to arouse very strong negative emotions, which can be a problem.

Gazda, Childers, and Walters (1982, p. 143) address the problems of strong confrontations. They state that if confrontations are too strong, five undesirable outcomes may occur.

1. The patient may respond defensively, with explanations and rationale, building a wall against the provider's influence.
2. The patient may be driven away.

3. The patient may become angry and go on the attack.
4. The patient may pretend to accept the advice but actually ignore it.
5. The patient may feel helpless and become inappropriately dependent on the provider.

Any one of these negative outcomes reduces the probability that further communication between provider and patient will be constructive.

If the confrontation is too weak, however, the outcomes can be equally undesirable. There are three undesirable outcomes as a result of confrontations that are too weak.

1. The patient loses respect for the provider. Otherwise, the patient may assume that the providers do not really believe in what they are talking about or that they lack the courage to be forceful about their judgments.
2. The confrontation has no effect whatsoever. The patient neither notices nor pays attention to the providers' statements.
3. The confrontation is so feeble that it has the potential for not changing, but rather, reinforcing, the original discrepant behavior. The impression given to the patient is that the discrepant behavior is really OK, i.e., "You shouldn't eat fast foods—but, it's OK if you do."

In the example of the physician who confronts the patient about habitual destructive eating patterns, we note that the first example (low intensity) resulted in the patient's feeling confused about the convictions of the provider. The high-intensity confrontation, however, runs the risk of causing a defensive response that ranges from inappropriately high levels of dependency to the avoidance of the provider.

In summary, the intensity of any confrontation should be strong enough to elicit action but not so strong that it immobilizes the patient by presenting overwhelming consequences that make the patient feel bad or inadequate. To achieve this aim, it is important to regulate the intensity of the confrontation. In accordance with patients' reactions, confrontations can begin as gentle statements and progress in intensity if patients show resistance to change or action.

Types of Confrontation: Experiential or Factual

Confrontations can also be described as either experiential or factual. That is, providers can speak from their firsthand experience of patients' behavior, or they can present data of a factual nature that will impose reality on the patient. For example, if providers state that the patient is trying to avoid fast foods but is not able to, the confrontation is experiential. That is, the provider has observed firsthand two events that are discrepant: (1) the patient's attempt to avoid fast foods, and (2) the patient's inability to be successful. If the provider, however, states, "Janice, if you continue to eat fast foods the way you are, your liver tests will not improve significantly," then the provider presents clinical judgments that are substantiated by factual data. This confrontation is a factual confrontation because it addresses the patient's behavior and factual data related to the eating pattern.

Confrontations, as has been explained, present discrepancies. They may be more or less intense and more or less threatening. They may reflect the provider's direct observations of the patient and/or draw from the provider's expertise and knowledge in the field. For any confrontation to facilitate change in the patient, the dimensions of trust and empathy are critical. High levels of trust and empathetic responsiveness in the patient-provider relationship are prerequisite to effective confrontations. To increase the probability that a confrontation will be both accurate and helpful, the provider must understand the patient.

Easing into Confrontations and Regulating Intensity

The procedures of easing into confrontations and regulating intensity have been described in the literature in some detail. The following six steps seem to follow logically and ensure that confrontations occur when the patient-provider relationship itself is substantially strong enough to permit the provider to confront the patient.

1. The provider establishes a good relationship built on trust and caring.
2. The provider uses statements that indicate empathy, positive regard, respect, warmth, and genuineness.
3. The provider approaches health behaviors in general, laying a foundation for addressing this patient's particular responses.
4. The provider uses some expressions of tolerance of the negative behavior so as not to appear overly critical and accusatory.
5. The provider clearly states any discrepancies and aspects of the patient's behavior needing change.
6. The provider establishes his or her own role and commitment to helping the patient make any necessary changes.

Returning then to our scenario between the physician and the patient who is overindulging in fast foods, and therefore placing her health at risk, the following process exemplifies how to prepare the patient to receive the confrontation.

The physician first empathizes with the patient about how difficult it is to resist fast foods and even supports the patient in having made some attempts in this direction. To communicate further respect and appreciation, the physician may ask the patient how she sees the problem and what solutions she would propose. Before zeroing in on this patient's difficulty, the physician speaks generally about other patients' difficulties and/or what she has learned through her professional experience and through reading about this problem. At this point, expressions of tolerance, if not previously expressed, may be given, e.g., "I know, it's tough," or "The most difficult thing is to resist those 'Golden Arches.'" Finally, the physician states clearly and succinctly, "Eating fast foods is going to prevent you from reaching full recovery. You're going to need to change this pattern—I don't expect you to do it without help. But we are definitely going to get very serious about this so we can get you better."

In most cases, this process is sufficient to both gain the patient's attention and increase his or her desire to make changes. If the provider determines that what is really called for is a great deal more forcefulness, there are five specific ways in which this confrontation could be strengthened.

1. The more personal the reference is, the more direct the confrontation. By making it clear that it is the patient's behavior, and nothing else, that is the issue, the confrontation becomes decidedly more direct.

2. The more concrete the examples are, the more difficult it is to challenge the accuracy of a confrontation. For example, the physician could remind the patient that she is becoming more noncompliant than she was six months ago.

3. The more recent the events are, the more powerful the examples. Behaviors that occurred in the past are less threatening even if they reflected poor judgment on the patient's part. The physician could remark, "In the last month you've shown me you cannot go a week without going off your diet."

4. The more behaviors, not just words, are dealt with, the more pressure can be applied because behaviors are not easily dismissed or invalidated. Thus, the physician's reference to specific examples of going off her diet cannot be argued.

5. The more using what the patient has said or done earlier to contradict what she is saying or doing now, the more a confrontation is strengthened. The physician may comment, "The last time you were in this office you said you would stay on your diet, yet you tell me you didn't."

Considering that providers can either strengthen or weaken confrontations, and that they can even do both within a single encounter, it is important to consider general instances in which confrontations are appropriately intense.

Most patients will respond to simple first-level confrontations; however, there are instances that require more direct approaches. When patients are asked to make changes, these changes are not always easy to implement. Some changes involve altering rather deep-seated patterns, and patients are not easily convinced that the change is worth it.

In the following dialogue, the nurse practitioner is trying to persuade an elderly patient to adhere to a low-fat diet. The patient is recovering from hepatitis that was incurred as a result of a blood transfusion at the time he was hospitalized for hip surgery. Mr. O____ was hospitalized but has been discharged and is receiving follow-up care and instruction because his liver damage was significant and recovery has been slow.

Nurse Practitioner (NP): "Mr. O____, I've looked at your test results, it looks like you're going to have to stay on your low-fat diet for a while more."

Patient: "But, I love chopped liver, poor-boy sandwiches, pizza . . . "

NP: "I know it's hard being on a restricted diet—have you ever been on a restricted diet before?"

Patient: "A low-salt diet . . . "

NP: "And did you stick to it?"

Patient: "Mostly . . . yes. I had a stroke."

NP: "So you stuck with it because you were afraid something bad would happen to you?"

Patient: "Uh huh."

NP: "Do you know why you are being kept on a restricted diet?"

Patient: "No—not really, no."

NP: "The liver and gall bladder are involved in digesting fat. Your liver was traumatized because of your hepatitis. It cannot work as well as it should. So, we need you to keep fat out of your diet so we can give your liver a chance to heal. Right now, your liver needs a rest."

Patient: "But I've been on it (the diet) a long time—how long will it last?"

NP: "It takes a long time for the liver to heal—especially when you are older."

Patient: "But I love corned beef and cabbage, a beer before dinner, and . . . "

NP: "I know, but, for now, you really need to stick with your diet. I'll get you a copy of the revised food list. Later we can be a little more lenient; but for now the thing you need to do is stick to it."

Patient: "Livers are pretty slow to heal, huh?"

NP: "Yes, I can't really release you from the restrictions until your tests are better."

Patient: "Sure I can't have just a little chopped liver?"

NP: "No, I'm afraid not. It's not going to be this bad forever. Try to think ahead to when your liver is healthy."

In this scenario, the patient expressed how difficult it was to abide by the medical orders. Chances are, he was cheating on his diet but not enough to feel the effects. At first, low-level confrontation strategies were used. Then the nurse practitioner intensified his confrontative responses in several ways. His presenting factual information that had specific meaning to the patient was an example of confronting with expert knowledge. His not giving in but repeating and more emphatically stating the need to remain on the diet gave the patient very clear messages. Also, his applying authoritative leverage by suggesting to the patient that he was under orders, gave the patient the absolute impression that under no circumstances was this order to be changed, at least not at this time.

Health care providers are particularly committed to promoting and maintaining health. If they observe that patients are doing things that run counter to these values, they are likely to intensify their actions and their confrontations as well. Patients who resist necessary health-promotion or disease-management recommendations generally require strong confrontational approaches. Additionally, patients who are deliberately self-destructive need more intense confrontations.

ORDERS AND COMMANDS AS EXPLICIT DIRECTIVES

Confrontations are frequently associated with two additional therapeutic response modes—orders and commands. Orders do not refer exclusively to written orders that are typically found in the patient's chart. Rather, what is meant by orders (and commands) is the provider's action to elicit change by insistence. When a patient must adhere to a course of action, providers should issue an order if it is within their authority to do so. Orders and commands are used to increase the probability that a certain action will occur. They are delivered with authority and often require immediate response. In many respects, giving orders or commands is simply directing patients about what you want them to do.

There is yet another important element—the demand aspect of the directive—that separates commands from simple directives. In the scenario between the nurse practitioner and the hepatitis patient, the provider gave directives, e.g., "for now, you really need to stick with your diet," and "I can't really release you from the restrictions until your tests are better." These directives were clear and firm. They were, in fact, statements of the medical order, and stating that the patient *must* stick to his diet expressed a demand quality. Phrased differently, it would have been a directive but not a command. For example, the nurse practitioner's statement, "I've looked at your test results, and it looks like you're going to have to stay on your low-fat diet for a while more," comes across as a directive but the tone is less insistent. While it is clearly a directive, it is not expressed as a strong command.

Differentiating Orders and Commands from Confrontation and Advice

Orders and commands in health care differ from confrontations and from advice giving. Also, orders differ from commands—both need to be followed—but commands denote the critical and immediate necessity for the action or change.

It is the provider's responsibility to see that every order is understood. Thus, in our scenario, the nurse practitioner spent time giving the patient information about liver damage and the healing process, as well as data about his specific condition—his liver-function tests did not warrant the relaxing of restrictions. In order not to confuse the issue, the nurse practitioner was clear and succinct in his presentation of facts and imperatives. This is a requirement of issuing orders; that is, procedures or steps to be taken should be worded simply. When orders are very complicated, requiring many steps, and/or when the patient's memory and concentration are impaired, orders should be followed with written instructions.

Pharmacists and nutritionists are particularly aware of the need to specify orders in writing. Usually there are so many important details that these orders should be written. Consider what would seem to be a very simple instruction about a patient's medication.

- "The doctor wants you to take these medications two times a day."
- "Take two capsules of this medicine and one pill each time."
- "Take these medications after your meals—in the morning after breakfast, at night after dinner."
- "This medication should be taken within an hour after eating."
- "Continue taking these medications until they are gone—7 days for this medication, 14 days for the second medication."
- "While you are on this medication, you should drink ample amounts of water —eight glasses a day."
- "Also, you should avoid alcohol while taking these medications."
- "If you have excessive nausea or drowsiness while taking these medications within the first day or so, you should call and speak to your physician."

It is obvious that this information is more than good advice. Embedded in these instructions are orders.

As with advisement, an order is always more acceptable to a patient when the provider has established a relationship and uses the language and knowledge of the patient. Providers should accompany orders with ample explanation and time for the patient to respond and ask questions. When possible, orders should be linked with the patient's own goals, for example, to be able to eat certain foods again.

In the scenario between the nurse practitioner and the patient, the nurse practitioner was not certain that the patient knew enough about his condition or treatment to understand the medical order. And, the patient responded as if he were confused or puzzled. It was important for the nurse practitioner to notice the patient's verbal and nonverbal responses, since both gave clues about the patient's readiness to hear, accept, and implement changes. While head nodding or the patient's reiteration of the directive are good signs, blank stares, confused expressions, and repeated questioning about the necessity of the order are not. Such signs suggest that the patient will have difficulty following the orders. The provider must ascertain both the patient's intentions to comply and the reasons why he may be reluctant. In some cases, orders can be revised to incorporate the specific preferences of patients. However, in most cases, orders are to be followed precisely as they are given. And, even though the provider may want to relax the order, e.g., in the scenario between the nurse practitioner and patient, orders generally cannot be altered.

Responsibility for Assessing Compliance

Once an order is issued, members of the health team are obliged to evaluate the patient's level of compliance. When a patient is found to be noncompliant, the provider's response is important in further modifying the patient's behavior. In our scenario, the nurse practitioner did not assess the patient's level of compliance. It is also possible that the nurse practitioner did not want to arouse the patient's defensiveness by suggesting that he was noncompliant. Assessing noncompliance, however, is extremely important for several reasons. When noncompliance or partial compliance has occurred, the original order may need to be extended. The original order may also need to be altered since the approach did not work, in which case patients' explanations can give clues about how the approach can be changed to fit their unique needs or preferences. Finally, in the case of ongoing disease management, a patient's response to one aspect of treatment may provide implications for future intentions to comply.

Generally, it is advisable to absorb the blame for patient noncompliance if it is appropriate. For example, in our scenario, the nurse practitioner replied that he would get the patient a copy of the revised diet outline. If the patient does not follow a particular directive or medical order, it is generally because something was lacking in the approach. This does not mean that the provider should totally excuse the patient for noncompliance. Providers always need to be clear and firm about their directives and orders and the consequences of noncompliance; however, sometimes providers elicit renewed efforts by avoiding critical or punitive responses (see Exhibit 11–1).

Commands Differ from Orders and Directives

Sometimes commands fit into the category of needing to be done correctly and immediately. These directives, like orders, are phrased as necessities, but the seriousness of the context is usually more apparent. Directives that command not only convey that a behavior is mandatory, they imply immediacy.

"Take this medication now" is a command. The behavior is mandatory and the immediacy of the action is clear. While some providers may be uncomfortable

Exhibit 11–1 Assessing and Responding to Patient Noncompliance

---

- "What do you remember about (specific action or change directive)?"
- "How are you doing with (specific action or behavior change)?"
- "Are there things that keep you from (specific action or behavior change)?" "What are they?"
- "Looking back at it, what do you think helped you do it or kept you from doing it?"
- "What did you think you should do instead?"
- "What happened when you did it?" "What happened when you didn't, or did it only partially?"
- "Given the same situation again, what would you do?"

---

with commands, the skill of issuing both orders and commands is a necessary addition to their less-demanding response modes.

In issuing orders or commands, which should be communicated clearly and simply, it is extremely important that the patient not only understand the proposed behavior but also that these orders or commands are not mistaken for advice or extraneous information. Unlike advice, orders and commands must be followed. Because there is much at stake in noncompliance, verbal orders are best complemented by written instructions. In cases of orders and commands, the inference that the patient has a choice to not comply or to comply only partially must be avoided. Also, the patient must understand that noncompliance or partial compliance cannot be dismissed or excused.

Orders and commands must not be received as advice. Discussing difficulties that the patient may have in complying with an order can sometimes be perceived as a choice not to comply. In our scenario, the patient wanted to negotiate a relaxation of the diet restrictions—"sure I can't have just a little chopped liver?" The responsibility lies with health care providers to reaffirm the seriousness of these directives.

Summarizing Directives for Patients

Closing discussions with patients when confrontations, orders, and commands have occurred is sometimes complicated. Essentially, the provider must assess not only what has and has not been understood but also how it has been understood. Usually, to assess the patient's response the provider will summarize the important points of the discussion, including any directives given. Some providers will prompt the patient with a gentle command, "Tell me what you heard and what you plan to do," to assemble all the essential facts of the discussion. Asking patients to assemble the points they remember is a good way to assess the level of shared meaning that exists between provider and patient as well as any misconceptions patients may have about what the provider said.

It is advisable for providers to alert patients in advance about the closure of the interaction. This notification may prompt patients to clarify points about which they are uncertain. They should understand that if they were not clear about a directive or were feeling that they could not comply, they have a limited opportunity to pursue the issues. Most providers announce their impending departure by rising from their seated position or moving toward the door if they have been standing.

In all cases, it is important to summarize the exchange in a positive manner. If the patient has displayed resistance, has argued about the directives, or has even accused the provider of not being realistic, these points of departure are well left alone. What providers should focus on is the shared understanding, consensus, and plans that have come from the discussion. Additionally, providers may make particular notice of gains or progress made in previous attempts to comply with medical directives. The emphasis on the positive outcomes of the interchange help to reinforce the patient's willingness to leave the side of the provider and implement the orders as they were meant to be followed. It is not entirely clear why ending on a positive note typically improves compliance. It is possible that it induces self-confidence in the patient, reinforces the collaborative aspect of the patient-provider relationship, and reminds the patient that recognition and attention will result when he or she complies with provider directives.

CONCLUSION

Assisting patients to achieve health and manage disease requires action strategies unlike facilitative approaches such as empathy, trust, respect, and warmth. While many times providers will avoid acting on their judgments of patients, there are specific instances in which it is appropriate to make more deliberate and assertive efforts to convince patients to change or take on a new behavioral approach to their problems. Providers must reveal and act on their confident command of clinical knowledge.

It is widely understood that the action potential of confrontations, orders, and commands are best delivered when providers have earned the right to use these techniques. Confrontations, for example, can be quite punitive and harmful. Confrontation, a key action-oriented therapeutic response, however, can be extremely helpful when patients have learned ahead of time that the provider is concerned for their welfare and cares enough to risk the relationship (by potentially arousing negative feelings).

Confrontations deal openly with patients' displayed discrepant behaviors or with discrepancies between what patients should do and what they are actually doing. Confrontations can be mild or very threatening. The most threatening type of confrontation is the one that deals with the present and is accusatory. Patients usually respond defensively to these high-level confrontations, so it is important to assess the need and wisdom of using confrontations of this type. In actuality, a provider has many options in any given encounter that begin with a mild, low-level confrontation and proceed with more direct, intense confrontations.

Although orders and commands are frequently used along with confrontation, they are actually separate strategies to promote change. Both orders and commands are directives; however, commands are usually issued more forcefully and require immediate response. Situations requiring rapid response are best treated with commands.

Confrontations, orders, and commands are frequently preferred over advice and opinions. Advice can lack strength and influence while confrontations, orders, and commands, even mildly phrased, do not. Patients who are at risk for ignoring advice and instruction require strongly stated imperatives. While confrontations, orders, and commands increase self-awareness and promote change, their distinct contribution is that they stress the importance of provider input, punctuating the necessity to listen and comply with providers' directives.

PART III

Communications To Assure Comprehensive and Continuous Patient-Centered Care under Difficult Circumstances

Most people would agree that communication is difficult. Under the best of circumstances, we can get poor results. Individuals can fail to send messages in ways that they can be understood. What is said is not always perceived and processed in the manner that we intended. By definition, human communication can be problematic.

What if we upped the ante, so to speak, and tried to communicate in already difficult interpersonal circumstances. Would we need to quadruple our skills and knowledge? Most likely, because to communicate effectively in these instances we have to know a considerable amount about the specific so-called difficulty. In health care, we are confronted time and time again with difficult circumstances— circumstances that are intense and emotion-laden, circumstances with a high risk for not turning out well, circumstances in which patients successfully resist our good judgment and good care.

In this section of the text, specific attention is drawn to communicating with patients and others under difficult circumstances. Difficult circumstances means that we communicate under conditions of conflict and crisis. It also means that we communicate with patients who display significantly negative or resistive behavioral patterns. What is difficult for one provider may be elementary to another, so the situations chosen for discussion in this section of the text may or may not be challenging to most providers but at least for the beginning clinician, they should be. Barriers to communication in these situations have been amply described in the literature.

In Chapter 12, Communicating with Patients in Crisis, the deficits in communication that individuals in crisis typically exhibit are detailed. Patients' subsequent reactions to the stimulus and crisis events are discussed. Finally, guidelines for communicating effectively with individuals in crisis are presented.

Providers who are engaged in the management of chronic-disease and life-threatening illness must know a great deal about patients' actual and potential responses to illness. Managing care includes managing responses to illness (and treatment). We are to be both healers of disease and healers of maladaptive coping responses. In Chapter 13, Communicating with Patients with Chronic and/or Life-Threatening Illness, the concepts and principles of communicating with patients take on particular specificity. Knowing what patients may be experiencing at a certain phase is important in establishing how to respond therapeutically. Knowing how the threat of patient noncompliance factors into disease management is yet another dimension of communicating with these patients.

Communicating with patients who display emotion, specifically when the display is negative, can be moderately to extremely difficult for most providers. In the final chapter of this section, Communicating Effectively with Patients Displaying Significant Negative or Resistive Coping Responses (Chapter 14), the emotional situation is not so much the challenge. The specific behavioral response is the challenge. If we asked a thousand health care providers which specific patient behaviors caused them problems or created substantially negative effects, we might develop a significant level of consensus. The difficult patient behaviors discussed in this chapter have also been addressed elsewhere in the literature. The accusatory, complaining, demanding, aggressive, and self-pitying presentations usually aroused emotions in providers. These emotions are soon followed by defensive and/or aggressive reactions—reactions that unfortunately aggravate a pre-existing bad situation. Understanding these patient behaviors, their underlying causes, and what providers can do to avoid interpersonal traps are essential to communicating effectively with patients.

In summary, Part III of this text addresses communication skills at a somewhat higher, advanced level. This is not to say that the basis generic skills presented in Part II are not useful. Rather, generic skills must be added to. Experiences with actual patients in the context of health and illness provide depth and wisdom for our communicating effectively as health professionals.

CHAPTER 12

Communicating with Patients in Crisis

Crisis may be considered an acute variant of stress that is so severe that the individual or group (family) reaches a state of disorganization in which ability to function deteriorates . . . crisis, which is a temporary state, can be a source of renewed strength when successfully negotiated.

Ellen H. Janosik

CHAPTER OBJECTIVES

- Define crisis response.
- Describe both individuals in crisis and groups in crisis.
- Describe typical dysfunctional aspects of communication in times of crisis.
- Discuss the relevance of stress and adaptation to crisis responses.
- Distinguish between adaptive and maladaptive coping responses.
- Discuss stressors, coping resources, and stress resistance resources.
- Differentiate between situational and developmental crises.
- Identify the stages of crisis resolution.
- Identify interventions that are useful for managing highly anxious clients.
- Identify interventions that are useful for managing agitated and/or confused clients.

People who experience severe disturbances in perception and in processing and expressing thoughts and feelings may be exhibiting what are called crisis responses. From a system's perspective, when the stimuli input and the demands for output exceed the capacity of the individual (i.e., a crisis is pending), then we are witnessing a deviation in communication that has clear implications for immediate intervention. People who communicate during a time of crisis reflect not only the stress of the emergent situation but also their inherent (in)abilities to cope with any challenge. People in crisis need special consideration since their abilities to communicate and receive messages are greatly altered by their crisis state.

What is "the straw that broke the camel's back?" In every crisis situation there is a precipitant that acts to offset whatever level of equilibrium that previously existed.

Precipitating or stressful events are change-producing events of special significance. These events are usually defined as accidental or situational, occurring without warning or occurring as ongoing events that are more or less anticipated. Individuals are vulnerable to a variety of both expected and unexpected events. Illness and injury can fall into either category but are almost always events that result in a great deal of imbalance.

DEFINITIONS OF CRISIS

Crisis occurs when more change or adjustment is required of an individual than he or she is capable of producing at the time. The first major false assumption about people in crisis is that they are always physically incapacitated. When we think of people whose tolerance has been exceeded and who become paralyzed, we are not talking about a simple stress response, we are talking about central nervous system overload. Crisis situations that produce less-severe responses are more commonplace. These situations are characterized by their more temporary nature and by their tendency to leave individuals less physically incapacitated.

A second major assumption about people in crisis is that the crisis is experienced within each individual, i.e., totally contained within the individual. It is true that crises are felt by individuals and that these events affect the somatic and psychological well-being of individuals as well as their actions. Individuals act out of crisis and these actions are usually significantly different from their usual behaviors, which may be exaggerated as in a person with high excitability. A bombing, fire, flood, or hurricane is called a catastrophe, though the event itself is not a crisis—how individuals respond to the event will determine whether the situation is a crisis or not.

It is also true that groups, as well as individuals, experience crises. The most obvious examples of group crises are situational events that lie outside the normal range of expectancy. These include situations like war, natural disasters, and witnessed violence. Not only do individuals who are experiencing crisis influence others with their emotions and behaviors, they are also affected by observing others who are sharing the same events. We know, for example, that mood states, such as fear, anxiety, and depression can be transmitted to others. We also know that the interactions of individuals in crisis may worsen or improve a particular individual's responses to the event. That is, parties to the same disaster may worsen each other's responses. Family members, for example, have been observed to elevate the fear and anxiety of the patient. Providers need to be cognizant of group responses to crisis because treating a person may include sheltering the patient from highly anxious or distressed family members.

A third common misconception about crisis is that a crisis leads to total psychological breakdown. We think about how we will need to care for people in crisis because we think that they are incapable of good judgment. The idea that people in crisis are psychologically helpless is also erroneous. While it is possible that some persons would respond with helplessness, poor judgment, and cognitive breakdown, many others do not, and any temporary collapse is usually corrected, at least in the majority of instances. As providers, we never bear full responsibility for individuals in crisis. Rather, we attempt to capitalize on the patient's remaining physical and psychological functional capabilities. The critical issue is to assess how and to what degree this functioning is limited.

A final common misconception is that crisis is the same as the stressor or stimulus-provoking response. While we concede that stressors or stimuli are always involved in crisis situations, these stimuli may not always cause a crisis. As previously indicated, the stimulus or catastrophic event may not elicit a crisis. In fact, there is a great deal of variability in individuals' responses to stress stimuli. This variation occurs within the same individual, over time, and across individuals with respect to exposure to the same stimuli. What, then, explains dysfunctional responses when individuals are exposed to stressful or noxious stimuli?

Dysfunctional Aspects of Communication in Crisis Situations

People in crisis are affected on several levels. They may experience extreme disorganization, which has ramifications for somatic functioning. Anxiety, erratic behavior, and inadequate decision making may occur as well as a set of physical signs and symptoms that parallel these responses.

A major factor in the imbalance that accompanies crisis is the presence of anxiety. Anxiety itself appears in varying amounts and with varying frequency. Even in a crisis situation, individuals' anxiety levels may fluctuate. Anxiety is characterized as a distressed state accompanied by diffuse feelings of uncertainty, apprehension, and sometimes imminent danger.

People in crisis also exhibit several forms of communication difficulties. They generally have difficulty perceiving accurately; their abilities to process information may be significantly impaired, and their ability to express ideas, thoughts, and emotions may be limited. They may be aware of these functional limitations and their awareness of their declined capacities may intensify their feelings of fear and anxiety. Thus, persons in crisis may become even more dysfunctional as they observe their responses to the effect of the initial stimulus.

Disturbances in perception frequently occur as a direct result of over-stimulation. Overstimulation includes rapid or excessive bombardment with stimuli or stimuli that exceeds the particular tolerance of the individual. Persons who are raped or tortured are known to endure multiple stimuli, and inherent in these situations is the fact that the stimuli exceed the tolerance level of the individual (and would do so for most people).

Although crisis is frequently associated with overload, there are circumstances where understimulation or stimulation with inappropriate noxious information also creates crisis. Is the prisoner who is in isolation experiencing crisis? When sensory deprivation is involuntary, the situation may exceed the tolerance level of the individual and therefore present a crisis to the individual.

Persons in crisis also experience the inability to process stimuli. The most common aspect of this problem is when memory fails, which is usually at the point of peak crisis stimuli. Memory fails for several reasons. First, there may be sensory overload. Flooding one's awareness with stimuli can create problems in properly sorting and prioritizing data. A second way in which memories fail us in crisis is when information is constructed or reconstructed in faulty ways because we were not expecting or have no way of dealing with the new and different signals that we received. Our decision making can be affected by either sensory overload or memory impairment. Decision-making capabilities are also affected in that our usual ways of dealing with problems do not suffice in the new crisis situation.

Crises also affect individuals' expressive communication capabilities. Crises frequently affect our ability to sleep and concentrate as well as our ability to remember and process information appropriately. Disturbances in perception and the processing of stimuli will also affect individuals' capacities to express their thoughts, ideas, and feelings in a complete and coherent manner.

In Exhibit 12–1, the various levels of anxiety are described along with their consequences for communications. The client's ability to observe, focus, and learn in crisis situations is mitigated by the client's level of anxiety at the time.

A crisis that affects groups reflects these problems in manifold proportions. Groups in crisis may behave like mobs or highly disorganized, chaotic gatherings. Additionally, groups in crisis will frequently exhibit a variety of internal changes. In response to crisis, they may change in size or composition, in reciprocity or mutuality of relationships, in symbolic or explicit goals and values, in the pattern in which information and messages flow between members and among the group, and even in how the group communicates with the external environment. Groups, including families in crisis, are dysfunctional, though not all the time. Some groups who are experiencing crisis events operate at high levels of sophistication

Exhibit 12–1 Level of Anxiety and the Client's Ability To Observe, Focus Attention, and Learn.

Level of Anxiety	Effects on Client
Mild (+)	Sensory perception and ability to focus are broad. The ability to observe oneself and what is going on is enhanced. Connections between events are made and verbalized. At this level, learning can take place. The individual who is at this level of anxiety is alert and able to function in emergencies.
Moderate (+ +)	Sensory perception is somewhat narrowed, but alertness continues to the extent that the individual is able to concentrate on a delineated focus. With some effort, concentration on relevant data is possible, and appropriate connections are made as long as the individual is able to shut out irrelevant data.
Severe (+ + +)	Sensory perception is greatly reduced. The person focuses on a small detail of an experience and is unable to make connections among scattered details. The individual is unable to get a total picture of an experience. Learning cannot take place.
Panic (+ + + +)	There is major dissociation of experience, and the person does not notice or remember major experiences. Details become enlarged and distorted. Communication is not understood by the listener, and personality disorganization is apparent. The individual is in a state of "terror." At this level of anxiety, learning cannot take place. The immediate goal is to get relief.

Source: Reprinted with permission from M.C. Smith, The Client Who is Anxious, in *The American Handbook of Psychiatric Nursing*, S. Lego, ed., p. 389, © 1984, J.B. Lippincott Company.

previously thought to be impossible. Catastrophic situations have shown that major threats to groups can actually improve group communication and functioning. Dysfunctional or disorganized family units, characterized by deficient and inappropriate relationships and role enactment, frequently exhibit crisis states because family resources are severely limited even in the precrisis stage. Marginally functional families are able to maintain minimal levels of functionality when no excessive stress is present but suffer significant disruption when demands on the family seriously exceed their resources.

STRESS THEORIES AND UNDERSTANDING CRISIS

Theories of stress provide us with a better understanding of crisis and responses to crisis.

Stress and Adaptation

Lazarus and Folkman (1984, p. 3) define stress as the demands placed on us from either internal or external sources that are perceived as taxing or as exceeding the resources of the individual. Subsequently, researchers have operationalized stress not only as responses to stressful life events (discrete episodic life events) but also as ongoing stressful conditions or chronic strain. Whenever stress is discussed, the basis for coping with stress is also addressed. In fact, a large part of what we know about stress and stressors comes from studies of coping and adaptation. Over the last decade in particular, considerable evidence has accumulated to suggest that there is a link between levels of stress and maladaptive outcomes.

A large part of the research on stress has focused on stress that results from change, hypothesizing that any change—large or small—that requires readjustment in one's life causes stress (Holmes and Masuda 1974). Even seemingly benign changes such as starting a better job and forming a new friendship was believed to lead to stress and to its negative consequences. The extent of the change or change demand was viewed as important, and it was found that many people experienced elevated risks from many emotional and physical problems when they experienced either numerous life changes or several high-demand changes within a short time period. According to the original Holmes and Rahe theory, which was substantiated in numerous research studies, a clustering of life events or a high level of change demand has been found to precede such health problems as depression, psychosomatic conditions, and suicide attempts. Additionally, it was found that the demand of events accumulates over time. The number of events that occur over a six-month or one-year period may significantly increase a person's risk for physical illness. One major criticism of this early research is that too much attention was given to events that were typical of middle-class people, to the neglect of things that happened to poor people. And although life events were viewed as important, once an analysis of these events was conducted, it was determined that the original identified events had value but so would have a number of other minor occurrences. Thus, being able to adjust to sporadic change was also seen as important. That is, the necessity of adjusting to unchanging (or slowly changing) conditions that must be endured daily are important sources of stress. This principle is important because it stimulated us to conceptualize not only major events, e.g., acute illness or injury, as stressors but also chronic illnesses as legitimate stressors. Thus, conditions such as asthma, arthritis, emphysema, and many disabilities, including paralysis, loss of hearing, and loss of vision are stressful from the standpoint of the strain, difficulties, and vulnerability associated with them.

Coping is a concept that is associated with the ways in which people deal with, adapt to, or adjust to stress. Coping has also been used to describe day-to-day problem solving as well as the strength of personality. Because coping is a general concept, there exists a broad range of domains that are considered relevant to it. These include behavioral, affective, and even physiologic response modes. What has been shown repeatedly is that coping has both immediate and long-ranging implications. That is, people try to cope with the immediate implications of a current situation and at the same time try to find meaning in the situation in order to integrate the occurrence into their ongoing lives. Additionally, the process of coping appears to be multiphasic; individuals seem to go through stages or phases in which they attempt to "digest" and manage the stress and the secondary implications of the stressful event.

Maladaptive and Adaptive Coping Responses

Traditionally, the literature on stress and coping tended to focus on coping strategies. The purpose of this research was to identify and evaluate strategies that individuals used to deal with certain stressors. The focus was twofold: first, identify individual variance in strategies across situations, and second, identify strategies used across individuals facing the same types of stressful conditions.

Earlier notions of stress and coping also implied that coping strategies were largely either adaptive or maladaptive. This basic premise predominates in current analyses as providers attempt to get patients to seek more adaptive coping strategies. Lazarus and Folkman (1984) suggest that maladaptive responses are emotionally based, while adaptive responses are problem-solving based. The fate of any coping response is highly contingent on its ability to address stressful events and their symptoms.

When people are asked about the ways in which they cope with stress (and if they are honest), they may identify one predominant method or a specific series of actions. Some methods are used infrequently, others almost all the time. The following are responses that people identify when they describe the way they cope with stress.

- seek comfort/help from my friends or family
- try to put my stress out of my mind

- try to get information that will make me less worried, less afraid
- tell myself things (self-talk) to help me feel better
- turn to my religious beliefs
- seek to be alone, withdraw, sleep
- cry, feel sad and depressed
- search for a solution to my problems
- drink alcohol, smoke, use drugs, eat more
- take out my tensions/anger on other people
- hope that things will get better
- seek out professional counseling
- use meditation, yoga, biofeedback, or other stress management programs
- exercise
- take more frequent breaks or vacations

Before advancing this discussion of stress and crisis, it is important to explore the notion that some individuals are more crisis prone than are others. Typically, the so-called crisis-prone individual is perceived as someone who cannot avail himself of certain coping resources. These individuals, for example, lack the ability to use problem solving and social supports that help people deal effectively with crisis. These individuals also may be alienated or lack meaningful, continuous relationships and usually exhibit a variety of the characteristics depicted in Exhibit 12–2.

One must be careful, however, in presuming that these deficits are solely a reflection of individual culpability because several of these factors depict certain socioeconomic conditions that place people at risk through no particular fault of their own. Studies of women in crisis have shown that low-income women with young children are at higher risk. Money stressors were correlated with several mental health indicators and with problems and feelings of stress in more areas of life than any other single variable (Belle 1982). Studies of the coping experiences of low-income women suggest that chronic and unpredictable stressors, limited options for coping, and unreliable outcomes of coping efforts significantly affect the health and well-being of these women. It is suggested that any of these factors (alone or in some combination) can considerably erode an individual's beliefs that her world is consistent and can be effectively controlled. It is a sad commentary that we criticize individuals whose place in society puts them at continued risk for crisis.

Stressors, Coping, and Stress-Resistance Resources

Coping methods are significantly affected by people's actual and perceived coping resources such as the availability of social support. It has been shown,

Exhibit 12–2 Collective Ideas about Crisis-Prone Persons

- difficulty in learning from previous experience
- history of multiple crises, ineffectively resolved
- history of mental disorder or emotional disturbance or developmental delay that make the individual particularly vulnerable
- low self-esteem, which may be masked by aggressive or provocative behavior
- a tendency toward impulsive "acting out" (doing without thinking)
- marginal income and employment, generally low socioeconomic status
- lack of meaningful, continuous social and/or family support
- alcohol or other substance abuse
- history of numerous accidents and/or injuries, particularly within short periods of time
- frequent encounters with law-enforcement agencies, either as a victim or suspect
- multiple changes in address, including homelessness

however, that the availability of resources is not always the critical factor in supporting people in stress and crisis. In actuality, people can have very extensive social support networks but experience those resources as deficient. Similarly, persons with small support systems, just one good friend, will evaluate their network as more than adequate despite the fact that there are fewer persons to turn to.

Factors that mediate emotional distress due to crisis are stress-resistance resources, e.g., social support and a tendency toward optimism and hopefulness. Stress-resistance resources refer to both the internal and the external elements that a person employs to deal with and resolve the problems that are creating stress. If coping fails to provide a solution to the problem, stress continues. It may even be heightened by the awareness of a failed capacity to handle the problem(s) or taken as perceived lack of control over an undesirable event such as in the case of incurable cancer (Abramson, Metalsky, and Alloy 1989).

Many individuals use social support as a means to cope effectively with stress. In many instances, social support can moderate stress, and the mere perception that adequate support is available can serve to buffer situational stress as much as the actual support itself. Still, studies have shown that social support can be variable and may have a mixed influence in assisting the person with stress and crisis. Researchers have studied the effects of social support on psychological symptoms and have concluded that the stress-buffering influence of social support is, indeed, complex (Cohen and Wills 1985).

Hope or hopefulness has also been addressed as an emotional prerequisite to overcoming major stressful events, especially those events outside the realm of expectancy. Herth (1989) found a significant relationship between the level of hope and the level of coping among cancer patients who were either in the hospital under outpatient care or in home-care settings. Herth suggested that mobilizing and supporting hope is important to the patient's overall coping response. While hopefulness generally refers to expectations that elicit a positive effect, hopelessness refers to low expectancies of success and, therefore, a negative effect. Vaillot (1970) speculated that when people find hope, meaning, purpose, and value in their existence, they are more effective and more capable of combating illness. Weisman and Worden (1976) found that patients lived significantly longer than expected if they had a desire to live (a positive outlook). Buchholz (1990) contends that the will to live is diminished in proportion to the degree of hopelessness.

Stress and crisis events may be more or less lethal to individuals. Research evidence strongly supports the need to evaluate specific features of the events in order to explain the individual variability in responses. Why do some people view getting a new job as very stressful and others meet this challenge with ease? The early research of Holmes and Rahe suggested that all life events, positive or negative, could be assigned units. These units were to identify the magnitude of change required of the average person. These researchers believed that one could identify all those events that an individual experienced within either a six-month duration or over a year, and from their total unit score predict with some accuracy a negative health outcome, injury, or accident. Judge panels were asked to assign unit values to events. The idea was that greater numbers of events, and the more events requiring moderate to high levels of adaptation (with moderate to high unit values), placed the individual at greater risk.

More recent research suggests that negatively viewed events are more likely to predict stress. Therefore, it is important not only for providers to know about patients' recent life events, they should understand whether the patient perceives the event as positive or negative. And, if positive or negative, what positive or negative valence would patients assign to these events.

Researchers who have studied the quality of stressors have elucidated more specifically the link between events and stress. Those events, for example, that are perceived to be outside the individual's control, to be global (that is, affecting many aspects of one's life), and to be enduring (not likely to change), are viewed as more threatening and are more likely to yield high levels of stress. Consider, for example, a patient who has been told he will never walk again. This realization is likely to put this patient in a state of extreme distress. Never being able to walk again will affect many aspects of this individual's life. The ability to ambulate or move about is now outside this patient's control. And, the problem will endure. Because his condition is perceived as enduring, uncontrollable, and global, he experiences high-level stress. The anxiety, fear, and depression that result reflect the crisis he is facing. Usually, individuals are able to correct for most of the effects of crisis, at least over time. Three to six months postevent is sometimes used as a benchmark to separate those who have learned to adapt and those who have not. In truth, we see many deviations from this range and sometimes only partial adaptation where one or more areas of personal and interpersonal functioning are affected. For example, in the case of grieving, the actual relief from distress can occur much later than a year from the event and can recur over several years.

TYPES OF CRISIS

In the literature on crisis, two types of crises have been identified. They are either (1) developmental crises or (2) situational crises.

Developmental Crisis

Individual development requires that we pass successfully through certain psychosocial task developments that correspond to our physical potential. Erickson (1963) described these tasks and later Duvall (1977) enumerated the tasks that characterize the life span of families. To understand developmental tasks as crisis points, we must first accept the idea that each developmental task has a potential for crisis. Theorists did not adequately explain this phenomena, but the idea is that elements of growth are not givens. Just how successful we are in mastering these tasks depends on our own physical and mental capabilities and our psychosocial environment. If we do not derive a satisfactory outcome, we are set up for future problems since in passing through developmental stages, previous mastery affects future abilities to adapt.

Situational Crisis

The type of crisis more familiar to most people is situational crisis and includes assaults on physical and psychological health. Natural disasters, e.g., floods, fires, earthquakes, and hurricanes, are situational crises affecting not one, but many persons. An additional type of situational crisis is man made and refers to bombings, attacks, assaults and so forth.

Developmental and situational crises have similarities. There are precipitating events, responses, attempts to cope, and changes (temporary or more prolonged) in individuals' states of equilibrium that are of concern to providers. To some degree, crisis can be likened to an acute state of stress where the individual or group of individuals reaches a state of disorganization wherein even minimal functioning is severely curtailed.

Phases of Crisis Resolution

The initial and most obvious sign that a patient presents in acute crisis is anxiety. Sometimes this anxiety is reflective of a severe state of disorganization. Anxiety may be accompanied by some level of physical exhaustion, particularly when the precipitating event(s) may have caused sleep deprivation. The thoughts, fears, and concerns of someone with a high level of anxiety are not repressed, however. In a state of hypervigilance, the patient is seeking optimum awareness to ward off perceived or actual threat.

Some clinicians view the course of response to crisis in a hierarchal manner where acute anxiety leads to withdrawal or other deviations in behavior that place the patient in danger. Responses to crisis, e.g., exhaustion, sleep deprivation, and possibly nutritional disturbances signify a decline in individuals' abilities to protect and care for themselves. A variety of protective and injury preventive interventions are needed to safeguard patients, their families, and others around them. At this stage, responses to crisis may have escalated to where the patient is a clear threat to himself—refuses to eat, exhausts himself, or injures himself—or is a threat to others through physical assault. The escalation process of crisis is complex. It usually includes a precrisis state and also a precipitating event. While past experiences of patients may sensitize them to the situational stimuli, there is always a trigger that is found in the immediate situation.

Acute anxiety attacks are common outcomes of crisis. Newly diagnosed cancer patients are not able to tolerate the amount or magnitude of the stimuli. Initial hypervigilance is exhausting and further lowers the individual's tolerance. The patient becomes disorganized. Studies of persons who are reacting to natural catastrophes, e.g., bombing, floods, and earthquakes, have given us a great deal of information about human responses to crisis. With high-level anxiety, people may become silent and tense. They may also begin to sweat, feel weak, feel tightness in the chest, and hyperventilate. They may feel like they are going to have diarrhea and may exhibit urinary urgency and frequency. If they perceive the danger as imminent, they may shake or tremble, become pale, repeat themselves over and over again, or fail to put the most elementary messages into words. The physical paralysis that is first observed may quickly change to a state of excitation or defensive striking out. The urge to do something—the fright, fight, and flight response—overpowers them and they may run, release their temper on objects around them, or attack others.

The outcomes that occur in crisis situations are several. The aim is that the patient will, as quickly as possible, return, at the minimum, to the precrisis state and preferably to a much higher level of functioning. With preventive measures during the crisis experience, restoration can usually occur without severe levels of disorganization. However, when the crisis is prolonged and intervention is not available, the patients' perception of imminent threat can result in a more severe state of disorganization. Full recovery is still possible but restoration may take longer.

MANAGING CRISIS BEHAVIORS

Early intervention in crisis situations has been effective in not only reducing the disorganization that individuals experience but also in fortifying individuals' abilities to cope effectively with the residual aspects of the initial crisis or subsequent crises.

An important, pervasive idea in encountering patients in crisis is that they will inevitably draw from the strength of the provider. Connecting emotionally with a patient in crisis will not only enable the provider to better predict the patient's subsequent reactions, it will allow the patient to take direction from the provider that, in many cases, may save the patient's life. Even from the standpoint of emotional and physical equilibrium, the provider's own organization in the presence of the patient's disorganization will restore to the patient some ability to hold together.

A supportive relationship with the provider during crisis has been likened to a symbiotic relationship that increases dependency on the stronger, reliable problem solver. The ability to connect in this way may help the patient repress or suppress the disconcerting or traumatizing perceptions and thoughts brought on by the crisis. Additionally, the partnership that the provider establishes with the patient tends to minimize the impending threat; the patient now has someone else who knows about the trauma and the threatening aspects of the crisis and feels that he or she has an ally. While the patient's fear may remain, generally, the experience of acute anxiety and alarm subsides. Patients do, however, also register the level of alarm that providers experience. When they see that the providers are not particularly threatened by the event, this acts to reduce feelings of panic and further relax their tendencies for fright, fight, and flight. Once patients have spent time with the provider, under the protective wing of professional involvement, they are able to begin to compare actual occurrences with anticipated, feared occurrences. It is the provider's role to activate and encourage this comparison. The inherent ability of patients to conduct this comparison enlists the patient's own therapeutic potential.

Many have addressed the therapeutic guidelines for helping patients in crises. These interventions sometimes parallel the hypothetical stages or phases of the crisis experience and are designated as primary, secondary, and tertiary interventions for people in crisis. In actuality, phase-based guidelines are usually most helpful in dealing with patients who are confronting situational or environmental crises.

All providers should be aware of the General Adaptation Syndrome (GAS). Stress makes demands on individuals that are physiological, social, and psychological, and these occur singularly or in combination. In the mid-1950s, Selye described the stages of stress response that together constitute a syndrome (GAS); they include alarm, resistance, and exhaustion. Crisis, in this text, is regarded as a variant of stress that is so severe that it leads an individual or group to a state of disorganization in which one's ability to function is significantly affected.

In Selye's (1952) description of crisis, the various stages of the stress response were paralleled with a corresponding level and type of disorganization. Exhibit 12–3 depicts this conceptualization:

Since crisis is also felt to be time limited, deterioration may be short-lived. Some theorists feel that it is the very severity of crisis that causes it to be temporary. This theory suggests that the subjective distress that accompanies crisis erodes the adaptational powers of the patient so much so that a continued crisis state is incompatible with continued existence—life itself. At the same time, it is believed that the extreme distress that accompanies crisis makes individuals highly amenable to change. In this way, the distress that is experienced is fought with survival instincts. Thus, the crisis event may actually act as a catalyst, stimulating adaptation to change. To clarify, then, prolonged adaptation to stressful life events or daily hassles tends to lead to pathological conditions, whereas crisis, which is more temporary, can lead to renewed strength and problem solving if addressed appropriately. A paradigm for viewing the elements of stress and coping is provided in Figure 12–1.

Exhibit 12–3 General Adaptation Syndrome (GAS)

Stage	Behavioral Response
1. Alarm	The mobilization of adaptive mechanisms occurs, e.g., with heightened awareness, perceptual acuity.
2. Resistance	The stressful event or stimuli require sustained, high-level use of adaptive mechanisms.
3. Exhaustion	Adaptive mechanisms are depleted through prolonged use; confusion, disorientation, lapse of consciousness may occur.

Eventual Restoration
or Death

Prolonged Stress

Severe Disorganiza-
tion

Stressors	Experience of Stress	Coping
(Stress	• Alarm	• Methods
Stimuli)	• Resistance	• Resources
	• Exhaustion	

Reduction of Stress

Reintegration and
Restoration of
Functioning

Figure 12–1 A Paradigm for Viewing Stress and Coping

Can you imagine making a choice between prolonged stress (e.g., driving long hours on the freeway for five years) or a temporary crisis (e.g., an abrupt unantici-pated cut in pay)? Most people would approach this decision with caution because neither is desirable. Still, most of us would say that we would choose to avoid an emergency. Emergencies are immediate and the consequences are less foreseen (Janosik 1984). Prolonged stress is generally less compelling than emergencies. There are certain events that do not bring on emergencies but do present chal-lenges that could lead to a crisis. Some providers define emergencies as any event requiring immediate intervention. Thus, if a patient is in distress but can wait 24 hours to be seen, the situation is not an emergency. Nonetheless, the situation may still be a crisis for the patient and family. In most cases, crises are unlike emergen-cies because the situations leading to the crisis have been building over time. So, unlike emergencies that respond well to remedial measures, crises are generally more complex and may involve longer-term intervention. This intervention in-cludes mobilizing a variety of coping strategies, active problem solving, and col-laborative efforts among the patient, family, and health care team.

General guidelines are helpful in dealing with patients regardless of the type of crisis. These interventions can also be practiced by crisis workers who are not professional providers. Several basic principles are key:

1. Crisis victims should not be revictimized in the process of being helped.
2. An emotional or psychological connection with the patient is critical.

3. Crises are responses to real or imagined threats—the validity of the crisis stimuli should not be challenged or underestimated in judging its potential to disorganize the individual.
4. Crisis is not merely a single event, the residual effects of crisis can continue indefinitely.

Therapeutic response modes are obviously important when communicating with people in crisis. Providers must remember that patients in crisis exhibit a number of disturbances in perception, processing, and expression.

First, and foremost, however, the provider must practice good active-listening skills. They must listen for the content in patients' messages as well as for the affective states the patient is experiencing. What does the patient say happened, is afraid of, anticipates? What feelings and effects accompany these expressions, e.g., fear, pain, generalized anxiety, depression, anger, rage?

Second, a direct, straightforward attempt to elicit information about the situation(s) causing the trauma is important. Rather than exploring past events, the focus should be on the immediate present. Explorations of why, including rationale and motives, are irrelevant and can even be injurious if communicated without compassion. Providers need to realize that this beginning exploration helps patients master their experience by organizing thoughts and feelings and that the patient's experience of the provider's approach is extremely important.

Sometimes patients and/or families will express attitudes, feelings, or thoughts that are difficult for providers to accept. These ideas or observations may conflict with their personal or professional values and standards. One family's statement that their son "deserved" to be injured—he was headed for trouble, it was a matter of time—may be difficult for providers to hear. Their immediate response may be to challenge, judge, or even condemn the family for such remarks. It should be remembered, though, that these remarks by family members are made under duress and are actually attempts to deal with the traumatic event. To argue with a parent at this point would deny the context of the parent's experience and own personal trauma.

Because patients in crisis are not focused or are not always clear in their verbalizations, they need to know that they are being heard and understood. Validating their experience, the pain and distress they must have, and expressing understanding about the impact of the event is extremely important.

Consider these two different responses toward a patient who has learned that his tumor is malignant. The physician is conversing with the patient's wife.

Physician #1: "We're not right all the time—guess this was one time when we were wrong."
Physician #2: "I know you didn't expect those results, I didn't either; I feel very badly about the outcome—I was hoping for the best."

Which of these responses validates the family member's experience and expresses understanding of the trauma? Obviously, the second disclosure demonstrates both active listening and empathetic responsiveness. The first response suggests that the physician is more concerned about being right diagnostically, and he dispassionately ignores how the news may be received by the patient's wife.

Patients in crisis do not always communicate clearly. They may fail to grasp words that accurately describe their concerns, they may express themselves incompletely, and they may even appear to contradict themselves. The use of reflection in crisis counseling is important, because it not only gives patients the experience of being heard but also provides opportunities for patients to correct or clarify their communications.

In every instance, for the patient and family in crisis, the provider needs to connect emotionally. However, connecting emotionally does not mean becoming overinvolved with the patient and family. The reader needs to recall the differences between sympathy and the therapeutic response mode, empathy. Avoiding feeling too much but at the same time clearly communicating support and caring with an understanding of the impact of the trauma is critical in managing the patient through the crisis experience and immediately thereafter.

Dealing with Highly Anxious Patients in Crisis

Sometimes patients in crisis are on the edge of total physical and/or mental collapse or exhibit self-destructive tendencies. When this is the case, the situation becomes more urgent. This is usually the case for only a brief period, however. The basic approaches to use are those of being directive and commanding, clearly communicating the protective role the provider plays in this phase of the crisis. The provider must have a full command of the clues about acute reactions to crisis.

The primary task of dealing effectively with individuals in acute anxiety is one of regulating the intensity and flow of messages. This regulatory process has been described and changes as a function of the intensity of anxiety (Ruesch 1961). According to Ruesch, in the acute or panic state, the knowledge that others are in control helps patients contain their feelings of fear and alarm. Sometimes the provider will deliberately separate the patient in crisis from others who are also experiencing high-level stress. The protective, supportive, and consoling attitudes of providers who should have their own fear and anxiety under control is essential.

After this initial phase of severe shock and when the patient is calm, open exploration of the patient's perceptions is possible. The patient needs to be helped to elaborate on his thoughts, fears, and feelings. Sometimes the patient will begin to show extreme physiologic effects of stress after the stage of panic has subsided. The patient may begin to shake, perspire, and falter even though the provider initially assessed the patient as having regained control. This is because fear can sometimes have an incubation period; the full impact of the danger may be more obvious when the danger is over. Frequently, family members who are alarmed by prognostic details will appear stunned but coherent. But, after the physician leaves the room, the nurse observes that the family exhibits signs of panic and high-level stress. Was the family saving their response until the physician left, or has the incubation factor played a significant role? Sometimes the exit of the physician stimulates heightened awareness of feelings of helplessness and powerlessness. The management of acute anxiety in patients or family members must always include close monitoring and follow-up. If the patient (or family member) is encouraged to depend on providers, is allowed to lean on others, the patient and family will recover more quickly.

Dealing with Agitated and/or Confused Patients

A separate but important issue related to dealing adequately with people in acute crisis states is the appropriate response to disturbances in consciousness. These disturbances can range from simple intellectual impairment to total loss of consciousness.

There are several causes of lapses in intellectual capabilities. Brain disease, cerebral vascular accidents, brain injuries, brain tumors or lesions, infectious diseases, toxins, and metabolic disturbances all contribute to altered consciousness. These conditions may be temporary and reversible or they may reflect progressive and irreversible disturbances. In addition to judging potential causes and prognoses for these states, the depth of disturbance must be assessed because this will influence not only the patient's ability to cooperate and communicate but will also affect the level of appropriate response from the provider.

At one end of the continuum is simple reversible intellectual impairment. This condition may consist of minor disturbances in memory and poor judgment, but orientation and reality remains intact, and hallucinations and delusions are absent.

When intellectual impairment is coupled with personality changes, the condition is regarded as more severe. Ideas of reference, mood swings, and even delusions may be present. In these instances, providers must compensate for minor intellectual impairment, and provide frequent reality checks for the patient.

Confusion commonly occurs with patients in crisis. This is a condition that includes a disturbance in orientation as well as intellectual impairment. In rare cases, delirium, a state of confusion significantly more serious, can occur and is usually accompanied by a severe state of restlessness.

Fluctuating levels of consciousness can be seen in patients under severe anxiety; however, rarely will providers see patients in stuporous states. Although stuporous states are rare, they can occur and providers must always be alert for the possibility because patients in prolonged states of fear and anxiety who have become significantly confused sometimes present in stuporous conditions. Examples include emergency situations where patients wander aimlessly, sometimes in mute states, bordering on drowsiness or potential lapse in consciousness.

CONCLUSION

In summary, both stress and crisis are becoming so predominant in our society that everywhere we turn we can witness its emergence and impact. Stress, and even crisis, is inevitable. With this recognition, we should not have to question the wisdom of teaching stress resistance and coping with crisis in our major institutions—schools, churches, and health and welfare programs. In contemporary society, although there are many sources of stress that predispose people to ill health, we pay relatively little attention to teaching crisis-stress coping skills.

Crisis theory suggests that crises are one of two types: situational (external) or developmental (maturational). Situational crises, including being party to a natural disaster are usually highly unpredictable, affect many aspects of people's lives and affect more than one person at a time. Developmental crises are usually predictable since they have a basis in the demands placed on individuals as they pass through sequential stages of development.

Patients may not always present in full-blown crisis situations. They may be acutely distressed, very worried, or experiencing chronic hassles. Providers help patients and their families weather many situations and life transitions. Just how well we do this will influence not only the current strength of our patients to master their circumstances but also their ability to deal with crisis residuals and any future crisis or stressful life events they will encounter.

Individual differences in response to stress have long been recognized. More recent research suggests that individual variability in response to stress is affected by many factors such as patients' attitudes and perceptions of stressors, perceptions of risk and danger, and perceived level of control. Ongoing life strains and daily hassles are now being recognized for their potential to be disruptive. Previously, the burden of proof rested with how many stressful life events the patient experienced within a particular time span. Studies have shown that daily life stressors are equally significant in placing individuals at risk for health problems.

CHAPTER 13

Communicating with Patients with Chronic and/or Life-Threatening Illness

The human potential for resilience in situations of extreme threat is indeed remarkable.

Judith F. Miller

CHAPTER OBJECTIVES

- Describe typical processes of dealing with illness and/or injury and the client's corresponding communications.
- Analyze the meaning of illness and/or injury to the client and/or family.
- Identify several sequential phases in the adaptation to illness or injury.
- Discuss the specific impact of responses, e.g., powerlessness, helplessness, and hopelessness.
- Discuss providers' corresponding reactions to illness and injury in clients.
- Describe several coping skills that providers may use to avert the professional stress syndrome.
- Discuss the advisability and readiness of clients who are terminally ill to receive truthful and direct information.

There is something "special" about patients who face life-threatening illness and something "different" about those who deal with chronic illness. We make these observations and subsequently categorize patients by disease and its potential impact. Yet, can we be sure that these categorizations are correct? All patients are special; all patients are different. Why do we categorize patients? We do so because there are particular things to look for with patients who have certain chronic or life-threatening conditions. And these conditions, at least theoretically, pose differences in the way patients should be cared for. Our first assumption is that patients with chronic debilitating diseases or terminal illnesses are significantly different from those with an acute disease or mild, albeit persistent, disorder.

Are there, however, differences between patients with chronic illnesses and those with life-threatening advanced disease? For example, do patients who are experiencing the debilitating effects of arthritis differ from those who are dealing with advanced stages of cancer or AIDS? One is a chronic debilitating illness; the other, a life-threatening one. Although many issues are common to both, most providers would agree that the differences between these patients raise particular concerns that make the care of each special.

In this chapter, the similarities in communicating with these two categories of patients will be discussed in depth. Issues of coping and adaptation will be described along with the responses of helplessness, powerlessness, and hopelessness. Interventions and communications that address these negative responses will be discussed, and additionally, principles of communicating with terminal patients about their diagnoses and prognoses will be explored. The stages of adaptation to illness and injury affect patients' emotional states and the character of their communications with providers as well as friends and family.

Illnesses or debilitating conditions to which these principles apply include any number of illnesses or diseases such as cancer, AIDS, congestive heart disease, cerebral vascular accidents, chronic renal or hepatic disease, arthritis, asthma, diabetes, and any number of psychiatric and neuropsychiatric conditions, e.g., depression, panic disorders, Alzheimer's disease, and Parkinson's disease. Some conditions are merely chronic and debilitating, e.g., arthritis and asthma, but they can significantly alter a patient's quality of life; infrequently do they cause death. In contrast, some cancers, e.g., lung cancer, limit a patient's quality of life and also significantly shorten their lives. Still, other diseases have both life-threatening and chronic dimensions. This would be the case with HIV, congestive heart failure, and certain nonaggressive but life-threatening cancers.

THE PROCESS OF DEALING WITH ILLNESS AND INJURY

Most beginning health care professionals do not immediately grasp the importance of understanding how patients respond emotionally to illness and injury. Some may react defensively, claiming that they are not psychiatrists or psychologists; i.e., questioning the value of this information. The overriding premise is that in our roles as health care providers we cannot adequately care for and communicate with patients unless we understand something about how they adjust to illness and injury. Patients communicate with providers in the context of their adapting to their afflictions. We are not simply communicating with anyone under any conditions, we are communicating with patients who are responding to the threatening and debilitating effects of their illnesses.

The Meaning of Chronic and Life-Threatening Illness

Patients respond to illness and injury in ways that are similar to coping with any stressful life event. In short, patients may have long histories of adapting to stressful life events and this history influences how they will respond to their current illness. They have developed their own unique lifestyles and ways of dealing with unwanted, unpleasant, and painful situations, including illnesses and injuries. Many illnesses run courses that are unpredictable and uncontrollable, and therefore are overwhelmingly threatening to life as the patient has known it. The specific coping responses that a patient chooses and the ultimate impact of these responses vary across individuals as does the intensity of the response.

Stages of Adaptation to Illness and Injury

While each patient has a unique pattern of response to illness or injury, there seems to be certain responses or series of responses that can be generalized. The process of adaptation, particularly to traumatic illness or injury events, has been studied extensively. Essentially, specific responses typify each stage of illness and injury on a time line (Table 13–1).

For example, the discovery of disease in oneself carries with it emotional reactions of denial and disbelief. Emotional reactions to acute illness and/or chronic conditions wherein repeated exacerbations occur may manifest as anger and depression intermixed with beginning resolution. And in terminal stages of illness, resolution and acceptance are commonly observed.

One well-known theorist established a conceptualization of the process of adaptation that has significantly influenced the way patients' emotional reactions are viewed. This theorist was Dr. Elizabeth Kübler-Ross. Addressing the issues surrounding death and dying, she composed a compassionate account based on her interviews with patients. These observations were published in her book, *On Death and Dying* (1969). Essentially, Kübler-Ross identified five sequential

Table 13–1 Illness Trajectory and the Adaptation to Illness Process

I. Phase or Stage of Illness:	Discovery	Acute and Chronic	Terminal
II. Event Time Line:	Diagnosis (with or without symptoms)	Symptomatic, depending upon exacerbations and remissions	Significant physical decline
III. Adaptation Stage:	Denial and disbelief	Anger, depression, beginning resolution	Ultimate resolution and acceptance

stages that patients go through once they become aware that they are dying—denial, anger, bargaining, depression, and finally acceptance. Many factors contribute both to how a patient progresses and to the intensity of any one response. Kübler-Ross documented these reactions from a composite of statements made by patients, including their affective reactions to an awareness of their illness.

Other reports followed this initial conceptual model, and today, there are many frameworks from which to choose. Many theories parallel this classic model, differing only in semantics or in the number of stages or substages that were observed.

Clinicians engaged in disease management (caring for patients with chronic illnesses) have conceptualized the adaptation process for these patients in a similar manner. Identifying the emotional reactions of patients who are facing rehabilitation, the following four categories have been used to describe specific stages: (1) fear and anxiety, (2) anger and hostility, (3) depression, (4) resolution and acceptance.

Any categorization is largely a question of semantics, and health care providers should observe and report their own observations of patients' emotional reactions and the particular sequential arrangement of stages. The most important principles to guide our observations are that (1) patients do have emotional reactions to their illnesses or injuries, and (2) these reactions change over time.

Since this beginning early research, a number of studies have addressed the process of adaptation and have suggested further guidelines for understanding patients' responses. First, it has been documented that some patients seem to harbor certain reactions longer than others; this includes the observation that some patients never demonstrate certain reactions, e.g., anger, while other patients remain in one stage, such as denial, throughout their illness. Second, unlike the original notions about sequential stages, the process of evolving emotional reactions appears to be more complex. For example, in the case of many chronic and terminal illnesses, there are a series of events that can potentially trigger additional cycles. The initial diagnosis of a terminal illness may trigger one sequence, but the reappearance of symptoms or the advent of new symptoms can trigger additional cycles. In studies of patients with cancer or HIV, there are a series of events that herald new emotional responses. The initial diagnosis can trigger a strong emotional reaction. During the course of the disease, the appearance of opportunistic infections and symptoms may trigger additional trauma. For HIV patients, a patient's appraisal of an irreversible decline in his or CD_4 count or percent can signify his or her inevitable demise and additional responses of anxiety, anger, and depression.

Fear and Anxiety

Emotional reactions to illness significantly affect a patient's communication behaviors. Fear and anxiety (mild or intense) are generated by an awareness of illness and injury. Logically, it would be presumed that minor illnesses or injuries would evoke mild fear and anxiety and major illnesses or injuries would cause severe anxiety and fear. Studies have shown, however, that objective appraisals of illness and injury events do not always parallel patients' subjective evaluations. Therefore, a minor illness may create severe distress and a major illness, mild distress. In this way, minor illnesses may create more distress and major illnesses, less distress, than they seem to warrant. Patients' expressed fears reflect their appraisal of the severity of their illnesses. They may not verbalize their fears, but they behave fearfully, such as watching every move the physician makes and listening carefully to remarks made to the physician's assistants. Will the physician reveal the real seriousness of the diagnosis to the nurse? Will the nurse display concern that is not readily apparent from the physician's demeanor?

Patients are frequently unable to put their fears and anxieties into terms that the provider can understand. Anxiety tends to lack definition, while fear is more circumscribed. That which is making the patient anxious is not readily expressed. Fears, on the other hand, e.g., "I'm afraid the doctor is not telling me everything," "I'm afraid my incision will get infected," "I'm afraid my medication will affect my sexual performance," and "I'm afraid of the pain" have specificity. While no one questions the appropriateness of the patient to experience fear or anxiety, those reactions may be underdiscussed. One reason for this is that since these reactions are considered "normal," it is not necessary to discuss them. This reaction to a patient's experience of fear and anxiety, and similarly to any additional emotional reactions, e.g., anger and depression, is nontherapeutic. It is a standing recommendation that providers openly discuss a patient's emotional reactions to his or her illness regardless of how appropriate or commonplace these reactions are.

Anger and Hostility

Anger is both a reaction to stress and a statement of protest. When patients recognize their diagnosis as something tangible, the natural response is to object. Questions such as, "Why me?" may be quickly replaced with the denial, "Not me." Patients who are reacting angrily to their diagnosis have registered the underlying meaning, i.e., a shortened life span in the case of a terminal illness or an impaired quality of life with the advent of a chronic, debilitating illness. When stressors are insignificant, the natural reaction is a milder form of anger, e.g., irritation. In the case of either chronic or terminal illness, the reaction is not irritation; the feeling is much stronger. It is inconceivable to think that patients who are diagnosed with a chronic asthmatic condition or cancer would be irritated. Whether chronic or terminal, these conditions are "earthshaking" or "life shaking." We can understand the impact of these diagnoses if we focus on the primary and secondary implications of these conditions. Depending on several factors, e.g., the patient's outlook, culture, religion, and previous history with stressful life events, these responses may be severe or modulated. Sometimes expressions of anger are present but communicated in ways wherein they go unnoticed, or they are misunderstood. For example, a patient who learned of a cancer diagnosis and recently underwent surgery and experienced dependence and confinement could react by communicating objections to the care she receives. A limited analysis would lead one to conclude that she pulled out her nasal gastric tubing because she did not like being fed this way, the tube was irritating her nasal passages, or she did not understand the necessity of the procedure. While these factors may have something to do with her behavior, this limited explanation is very shortsighted. The insult she experienced as a result of her diagnosis explains, in greater depth, her reactions and communications. Being angry at everything and everybody is a potential reaction and a real experience for many patients. Providers and family members who are targets of this anger should understand the fact that there is seldom anything personal in the patient's response. Patients have limited outlets for their frustration, stress, and misery; it is understandable that the objects of their anger may be the very people the patient needs and relies on the most. Most providers understand that patients are actually communicating frustration surrounding the indignities of their illnesses. And, witnessing this protest may be far better than observing the patient passively acquiesce and become "victim" to their condition. This is why depression, the next reaction or stage, is more difficult to observe and respond to.

Depression

Most patients, sometime during the course of their illness, will experience and report being depressed or "down." Some may admit to being sufficiently depressed to contemplate and attempt suicide. Depression can be more intense if there is an insufficient outlet for angry feelings, limited support, and intense feelings of powerlessness and hopelessness. Patients who exhibit depression along with hopelessness are prime candidates for suicide attempts and must be watched very carefully. In cases of chronic illness, the routines of treatment allow little flexibility, and a release of anger may be curtailed. In cases of terminal illness, the patient's appraisal of her powerlessness over her disease can cause more anger than she is capable of releasing appropriately. Thus, intense, suppressed anger is associated with depression. Patients who suppress anger may also hide feelings of depression. They may mask their real feelings with comments that they are "OK," "fine," or "pretty good." They may even smile and attempt to be cheerful. This veil of well-being is thin and will soon become obvious to the astute provider.

Some patients will explore their feelings with providers. They may complain that they lack energy and feel tired; they also may report bursts of crying or an overwhelming sadness, and a sense of isolation from other people. These disclosures are clues about the depth and intensity of depression, and coupled with behavioral responses, e.g., prematurely composing a will, they expose the significance of these reactions and the need to evaluate the patients' capacity to resist depressing thoughts and feelings.

Resolution and Acceptance

The acute, demanding phases of illness do not prevail. As if to give the patient a respite, whatever physical and functional decline is to occur may plateau. The crisis does not remain a crisis. One patient experiences a new opportunistic infection and gets better from it. Another patient becomes more dependent, maybe requires life support, but eventually this event recedes in importance. In both cases, stress lessened, and then the patient prepares for the next major health event. For most patients, the end of health-related stress means recovery or rehabilitation. Even if the outcome is less than what was hoped for or expected, or the prognosis remains grim, a sense of relief occurs.

Having a chronic or life-threatening illness causes one to reflect on one's life events and accomplishments. Thoughts of having "too little time" cross the minds of the chronically ill because years of healthy life will be reduced; thoughts of "too little time left" concern a terminally ill patient because the temporary nature of human existence is acutely apparent.

Maintaining a feeling of being in control and sustaining hope despite an uncertain or downward course are extremely important to these patients (Miller 1983). Averill (1973, p. 23) identified three categories of control that are important for individuals who are experiencing stress. As applied to patients, these categories are (1) behavior control—the patient's action to direct environmental demands, (2) cognitive control—the way in which the patient evaluates or interprets events, and (3) decisional control—the ability of the patient to choose courses of action from among reasonable alternatives. Chronically ill patients may find that the intrusions into their lives by the health care system threaten their personal privacy and integrity. The ability to control this environmental intrusion and maintain one's privacy can preserve a patient's sense of dignity. Additionally, communicating to patients what is happening to them and engaging them in decisions about their care and treatment (thereby promoting cognitive and decisional control) gives to patients the regulatory ability that preserves their rights to self-determination regardless of their compromised functional abilities.

As chronic health problems become more severe and limit even further the patient's ability to function, feelings of hopefulness will bolster the patient. Hope enables patients to avoid overwhelming despair. Despair may occur as a result of the roller-coaster effects of the illness when remissions and flare-ups are multiple or as a result of the decline that becomes more permanent than transient. Assisting the patient to identify realistic and immediately relevant goals helps that patient cope with feelings of despair. Not only does this augment and confirm the patient's value, it provides a necessary distraction.

Chronic and/or life-threatening illnesses create a number of condition-related stresses, particularly losses. These have been described in research studies and include fear of pain, disfigurement or body-image change, fear of dying, and loss of work and family roles. When accompanied by actual experiences of pain, fatigue, loss of energy and appetite, self-regulatory functioning, and restricted mobility, patients' adaptive capabilities are taxed at very high levels. These occurrences, collectively, present a supreme challenge for both patients and their significant others (see Exhibit 13–1). The resourcefulness of most patients is remarkable. They employ a high level of coping potential in dealing with their disease. Some patients dredge up coping capabilities that they themselves did not realize they had. Otherwise fragile individuals may demonstrate a remarkable degree of coping once they are faced with the reality of their health status. If, however, patients cannot cope with the demands of their illnesses or have difficulty accepting the realities of their decline, they may remain anxious, angry, or depressed. Consultation on cases is warranted.

In summary, all patients do not proceed through stages of adaptation to illness in the same way. The process is not one, two, and then three. In fact, the challenge to providers is that all patients do not progress in the ways that are suggested by theoretical models. No two patients are exactly alike; therefore, each one will show some unique aspect. Thus, it is always important to understand the limits of applicability in using conceptual frameworks. The advantage of such models is that they provide a point of departure; the major disadvantage is that the model inadequately describes a particular patient's experience.

Recurring Responses: Powerlessness, Helplessness, and Hopelessness

Managing the care of patients with chronic and/or life-threatening illnesses requires the provider to be intimately and knowledgeably associated with the patient's response of feeling out of control. Among the most devastating experiences of any chronic or life-threatening condition are recurrent feelings of helplessness, powerlessness, and hopelessness.

Researchers have shown that extended exposure to threat and/or harm produces a state of helplessness. When threats are outside an individual's control, are global (affecting many aspects of the person's life), and are also unpredictable, feelings of helplessness can be intense. Helplessness, then, is a condition that is both perceived by and induced in patients who are experiencing illness. Learned helplessness occurs when patients realize that despite all they do, nothing will help their situation. Thus repeated exposures may reduce an individual's overall coping capability.

What happens when patients encounter helplessness over time? Patients encountering prolonged, sustained helplessness will develop perceptions of power-

Exhibit 13–1 Losses Associated with Chronic and Life-Threatening Illness

Categories of Losses
Alteration in health-status losses
• energy and appetite
• strength-vitality
• cognitive capabilities
• ability to communicate
• muscle coordination and mobility
• bowel and bladder control
Loss of body parts, alterations in body image
• organs
• hair
• weight
Alteration in roles
• loss of occupational role
• loss of family/marital partner
Alteration in self-esteem, self-concept
• loss of control
• loss of identity
• loss of self-respect
• loss of independence
Alteration in relationship with others/loss of significant others
• loss of friends, partners, spousal support
• isolation from social networks
Alteration in quality of life
• pain
• fatigue
• diminishing finances

Source: Reprinted with permission from Inspiring Hope, in *Coping with Chronic Illness*, J.F. Miller, ed., p. 290, © 1983, FA Davis & Company.

lessness. Powerlessness is the recognition that one cannot significantly affect a specific outcome. The patient's sense of power or powerlessness is directly related to his control over his illness—both the primary and secondary consequences of his illness. A sense of powerlessness has been attributed to individual personality predispositions, and theorists will also argue that this emotional reaction is also situationally defined.

Feelings of sustained helplessness can result not only in feelings of powerlessness, but eventually, hopelessness also. Hopelessness is a feeling of despair that causes one to give up. In fact, if powerlessness persists, a state of hopelessness *will* occur. Hopelessness is also associated with depression and suicidality, and although it may be temporary, it may, nonetheless, result in a deteriorated physical and mental status.

That which alleviates helplessness will help to prevent hopelessness. The primary issue in dealing with a patient's hopelessness is to anticipate and prevent it. Once again, the three categories of control—behavioral, cognitive, and decisional—are relevant. Giving patients explanations about their decline as well as control over treatment decisions when possible can minimize hopelessness, and reminding patients that there is something or someone to live for can alter the resulting apathy.

PROVIDER RESPONSES TO THE CHRONIC AND TERMINALLY ILL

Certain patient conditions make health care providers anxious. Patients whose circumstances are perceived to be fragile certainly create anxiety. To some extent, providers can become overwhelmed with the same feelings of helplessness, powerlessness, and hopelessness that their patients experience.

Provider's Fear and Anxiety

A common retort of providers who choose not to work with these patient groups is: "I could never work with them. Isn't it just too depressing?" Fortunately, there are many who do not react negatively and thus become deeply committed to the care of these patients. Some providers who initially regarded these patients as "depressing" learn to appreciate the rewards and satisfaction that come from caring for them.

There has been a great deal of literature directed at helping providers communicate effectively with the terminally ill or with patients who are facing death. In the professions, the most challenging aspect of caring for patients is managing one's feelings about the patient's experience and the feelings of powerlessness that are subsequently evoked. With the terminally ill and their families, the task of managing one's feelings is especially difficult. For example, the care of cancer patients can create feelings of despair. But, observing how patients adapt to and integrate the basic facts of their illnesses may reveal that these patients are indeed not to be pitied. Patients learn and come to terms with the realities of decline in health and functional status but, in doing so, do not always give up hope. Physically, mentally, socially, and spiritually they are very much alive. Experienced clinicians frequently remark that they learn much about living from their patients who are dying.

Like caring for acutely or terminally ill patients, caring for chronically ill patients also lacks appeal. Sometimes the routines for caring for the chronically ill appear repetitive and boring. There is rarely any drama associated with chronic illness. With some exceptions, these illnesses are relatively predictable as is their course of treatment. Chronic illness among the elderly frequently precipitates early placement in a nursing home. The burden of repetitive home care activities is trying on families.

Coping, Counseling Skills

Coping efforts serve two main functions. First, they manage or alter the problem that is the source of stress (problem-focused coping), and second, they regulate the stressful emotions that are engendered by the stress (emotion-focused coping). Lazarus and Folkman (1984) explain that individuals who face stressful events or situations use both forms of coping. Patients, then, employ coping mechanisms to deal with the problem (their symptoms of pain and fatigue) and to alter the emotional distress they feel as a result of their symptoms (pain and fatigue). Promoting adaptive behaviors in patients necessitates our recognizing not only the symptoms (the problem) but the patient's evaluation of the symptoms that cause distress.

Guides for assessing a patient's coping status are outlined in Exhibits 13–2 and 13–3. Exhibit 13–2 outlines specific interview questions that are useful for gather-

---

Exhibit 13–2 Disease Management—Assessment of Coping Status—Patient Interview Probes

- "What concerns do you have about your illness, your treatment?"
- "What do you expect from your treatment?"
- "How do you usually reduce stress?" (When dealing with stress, people do a number of things to try to reduce the stress or eliminate the situations that are stressful.)
- "In considering how you are dealing with your illness right now, what works best? What doesn't seem to work well?"
- "Is there a support system for you? Do you feel it is adequate?" (When people are ill, they call on friends or family to support them.)
- "What barriers exist to keep you from getting the care you need or want?" (How optimistic are you about getting the care you need?)
- "Considering the symptoms you are having right now—how well are you dealing with them? To what extent are you able to control these symptoms (pain, lethargy, fatigue, etc.)?"
- "Overall, how much does your health limit you? How would you rate the quality of your life?"

Exhibit 13–3 Clinician Guide to Assessing Patients' Coping Capabilities

---

- What is the patient's current condition? Stage of illness?
- What is the patient's current knowledge of his illness and awareness of the significance of his diagnosis?
- What is the patient's present mood, affect, feelings of control, and level of self-confidence?
- What are the patient's primary coping responses (denial, anger, etc.)?
- To what extent is denial used, and what level of denial is manifested (first order, denial of facts; second order, denial of implications of facts; or third order, denial of illness outcome)?
- What and how adequate is the patient's support network?
- How available are self-help and/or home health care resources to the patient?
- What are the patient's spiritual/religious needs?
- What stressors, secondary to health status, are particularly significant—financial, loss of family/social support, stigma and/or social alienation, loss of independence?

---

ing information from patients about their coping abilities. Exhibit 13–3 identifies avenues of investigation that will help clinicians come to an overall appraisal of a patient's coping behaviors and his or her risks for maladaptive responses.

Patients who experience chronic and/or life-threatening illness will cope better if they are aware of and understand how their personal ways of dealing with their illnesses are important to their health and how they may prevent unnecessary hospitalizations.

Most patients are not aware of how their illness creates stress and how their lifestyles and beliefs about self, others, and health impact them. This lack of awareness occurs in patients who (1) lack knowledge of the stressful events and chronic strains that contribute to their health problems, (2) believe that looking at how they cope is only necessary when a crisis has occurred, and (3) believe that changing the ways in which they deal with stress and their illness will not be necessary once they feel better. Some patients believe that learning new ways of coping will cost lots of money, and if they change an aspect of their lifestyle, this may cause other problems for them and for other people around them.

The coping efforts of an individual are influenced by many factors, e.g., personal factors and available coping resources. The cognitive mediating process that is important in determining an individual's perception of threat is cognitive appraisal. The patient's perception of and processing of health-related problems will determine any given emotional reaction. If a patient does not see a health-related condition as a problem, a threat is not perceived and the patient does not call into action any additional resources to handle the problem. To understand why patients who are exposed to the same event react differently, we draw on the principles of cognitive appraisal. Through the cognitive-appraisal process, the individual's way of processing information, the patient evaluates the significance of stressful health-related events. In primary appraisal, the patient evaluates the extent to which an event is relevant or irrelevant, benign or threatening. Threatening events are deemed either immediately harmful or capable of harm. Otherwise, the patient evaluates both the immediate and the potential anticipated threat of events. In secondary appraisal, the patient evaluates the magnitude of the problem by assessing the extent to which something can or cannot be done. When the patient's reaction is one of hopelessness, an evaluation that no available options exist has usually occurred and the event is threatening.

Whether patients perceive an event as threatening, the particular coping responses they use are determined by available resources. The resources available to individuals clearly affect coping abilities (Pearlin and Schooler 1978). There are many constraints that mitigate the use of any available resources once the event has been evaluated as threatening. They include socioeconomic factors that determine access to health care resources and sociocultural values and beliefs that define illness and shape a patient's responses to actual or potential illness.

It is important to understand the impact of coping on health, mortality, and morbidity. Research has shown that the effects are significant. Coping, for example, has been shown to influence the duration, frequency, intensity, and patterning of neurochemical stress reaction. Coping can also affect health negatively by increasing the patient's risk for morbidity and mortality. Examples include patients who cope with stress by resorting to the use of lethal substances such as elicit IV drug use or even tobacco when clearly the life-threatening potential of these actions is known. Thus, engaging in any high-risk behaviors in order to cope with stressful life events exposes the patient to higher risks for morbidity and/or mortality.

Yet another very important way in which coping responses influence morbidity and mortality is the appropriateness of the response in light of the threat. We know, for example, that many patients who suspect that they have a health problem delay seeking medical care. Medical attention can also be significantly delayed when patients do not evaluate the situation as threatening or use a response that does not directly address the significance of the signs or symptoms that they are experiencing.

Understanding the use of denial to cope with health-related threats is important. Weisman (1972) describes three levels of denial pertaining to the diagnosis of life-threatening illnesses.

First-order denial is simply a denial of facts. Signs of recurrent illness may be explained away as insignificant. New breast changes in a patient with a history of breast cancer may be explained away as too minor to be upset about.

Second-order denial, according to Weisman, is denial of the implications of the facts. Thus, the patient may acknowledge the facts—breast changes—but deny the significance or meaning of these changes. In denying the significance of these changes, patients minimize the importance of their primary diagnosis. Many patients go through phases in the course of their prolonged illness wherein they "will their illness away." They are tired of being hypervigilant; they do not want the restrictions that their illness imposes. Most patients will be brought back into awareness with minimal confrontation; others may need additional support and counseling. Sometimes patients do not deny their illness altogether but "fractionate" their illness, rendering it significantly less threatening. Fractionating means that patients have cognitively broken their illness into smaller, manageable parts; while this process can be adaptive, an undesirable result is that symptoms may be evaluated as considerably less important than they really are. Or, the patient may focus on some small part of the illness, e.g., weight loss, thus minimizing the secondary implications of the serious illness, cancer.

Third-order denial, according to Weisman, is denial of the ultimate outcome of the illness or prognosis. For persons with life-threatening illness, this is a denial of eventual death. For persons with chronic, debilitating illness that is not life-threatening, it is denial of the ultimate immobility and loss of function that may occur over time. In this case, patients acknowledge the reality of their illness (diagnosis), and even recognize the immediate consequences of their condition, e.g., pain, fatigue, and weight loss. They do not, however, accept their ultimate prognosis. The issue of death is avoided. Patients may believe and talk as if they will experience little functional decline. They may even plan future events as if their state of health will remain the same.

Denial is a powerful coping response where certain perceptions are not processed in usual ways. Patients and their families use this response to control the anxiety and distress that they experience as a result of their illness and the changes they encounter throughout the course of their illness and treatment. Assisting patients to cope requires providers to intervene effectively with the presenting health problems. This means employing interventions to control symptoms and the disease process.

Intervening with presenting health problems is a partial picture of how providers must interact with patients and their families. As previously indicated, treating patients' reactions to their health problems is imperative to effective disease management. This means that providers will communicate to patients about the responses they are likely to have, how these responses change over time, and what they can do to manage any distress they experience as a result of their health-related changes. It also means providing resources and instruction to patients such that they themselves can monitor and control their conditions.

There are certain patient attitudes and beliefs that are indicative of low-level awareness about stress and chronic illness. But, how do we know when our patients need instruction about stress and coping? The following list of statements about stress and coping with illness cover basic principles that will assist all patients to cope more effectively with the impact of the illness. Patients should know that:

- stress can contribute to their inability to cope effectively
- coping effectively with their problems can help them feel more adequate as a person
- their attitudes and beliefs influence how they deal with problems
- they and the way they cope are important in their recovery
- there are more than a few ways in which they can deal with their problems
- when their resources are limited and their stress is great, they are at greater risk for a health-related crisis
- stressful life events, e.g., loss of a loved one, affect their coping abilities, but chronic strain, e.g., dealing with chronic pain, also significantly affects their coping ability
- it is possible to know how they react to problems or stress
- active coping, i.e., exercising, or asking their health care provider for advice, is more effective than avoiding the problem
- generally, when they hide their feelings, refuse to think about their problems, or dwell on them for long periods of time, they are coping ineffectively
- other people around them can either help them cope more effectively or can encourage them to cope ineffectively
- a systematic problem-solving process can help them cope more effectively
- it is possible to cope effectively with some problems and at the same time, ineffectively with others
- feeling hopeless or helpless about their problems will not help them in the long run
- ineffective coping responses, e.g., avoiding problems, can become habits and be difficult to change

Approaches to Truth Telling and Patients' Capacities To Receive Information

Providers play a significant role in balancing a patient's awareness of his or her illness and the emotional distress evoked by this awareness. It is generally understood that all patients need to maintain some level of denial in order to remain hopeful. Thus, telling patients about their illness and prognosis is guided by certain professionally shared assumptions. First, patients have the right to make decisions about their health and well-being. Depriving patients of information is denying their rights to informed choices. Second, patients' health and well-being and the condition of their bodies belong to them. Providers discover and determine facts about patients; however, these facts are for the patient, not the provider, to dispose of. While providers may recommend and conclude facts, they are not solely responsible for deciding on courses of action. And, the provider-patient relationship is based on mutual respect and trust. If providers, particularly physicians, withhold essential facts from patients, they are violating the ethical basis of the relationship.

In cases of terminal illness, providers face additional responsibilities related to truth telling. Terminally ill patients have certain responsibilities to address before death. Settling personal affairs, making provisions for significant others, and making peace in a spiritual way may be tremendously important to patients. Failing to be truthful and factual with patients denies them the opportunity to bring closure to their lives.

Providing information, then, is an appropriate function and an important obligation. Many providers, however, question the advisability of disclosing information, particularly in relation to prognoses. Providers are concerned about the emotional reactions of their patients and the consequences of adding stress. Some believe that to evade the facts is a better course of action, particularly when the prognosis is poor. Some research, however, has shown that the majority of patients feel they should be fully informed. This research reveals that among those patients who were informed, the majority were glad that they were told. Among those undergoing diagnostic testing, the majority want to be told the truth. This disparity between what providers feel comfortable revealing and what patients want to know is a serious one.

A primary concern behind providers' hesitancy to inform patients about a poor prognosis is the fear that the patient's awareness will result in negative outcomes. Providers anticipate strong negative reactions including unnecessary dependency, excessive worry, and even clinical anxiety and depression. They are concerned that these reactions will considerably alter the patient's quality of life. In some cases, concerns about patients' suicidal potential influences providers' willingness to be truthful. Although suicide is of concern, particularly in devastating illnesses, e.g., cancer and AIDS, it is also true that the potential for actual suicide is greatly exaggerated. Providers who are sensitive to patients' suicidal expressions sometimes assume that if they broach the subject of strong emotions and suicidal thoughts, they will actually provoke self-destructive responses. Yet while some patients consider suicide, many more do not. Providers must recognize that patients, in all probability, simply want an opportunity to communicate their fears, frustration, grief, and sorrow.

In contrast to perceived negative consequences of informing patients is the evidence that patients who *are* told not only prefer to know but experience positive change. The initial awareness can create an imbalance, but after the initial upsetting event, patients regain composure. The positive effects of this awareness are also observed in family members. In general, there is less tension and desperation, which can result in improved communications and feelings of serenity that can be shared by the patient and family alike.

Underlying the issue of truth telling is the fact that patients actually know a great deal more than they are told. Many patients deduce the nature of their condition without being presented with factual information. Staff frequently do not realize that patients come to conclusions that they do not disclose to providers. Providers who believe that patients only know what they have told them are underestimating the situation. As mentioned elsewhere in this text, patients gather data from the nonverbal responses of staff and significant others. Silences, efforts at evading topics, false reassurances, and pessimistic attitudes are frequently picked up and processed by patients. Patients are also able to read their own bodies and establish for themselves that they are weaker, less alert, and irreversibly dependent on others. Patients may remain silent about what they know, because they assume that the silence of providers and significant others means that they do not want to talk about the inevitable. This phenomena of each party not disclosing to the other is called mutual denial. It can appear that patients have joined a conspiracy of silence to protect those involved from feeling uncomfortable. Because patients generally know more than what they are told, providers run the serious risk of losing patients' trust and confidence by withholding any aspect of their condition. Providers must be aware of their own reactions to patients' conditions and give careful consideration to how these feelings affect their communications with patients.

Guidelines for initiating dialogue with patients regarding their diagnosis and prognosis are outlined in many professional textbooks. Because providers' responsibilities differ with respect to their professional discipline, specific guidelines should be sought from these professional textbook sources. There are, however, some general guidelines that should be followed. First, all patients should be informed about any harmful or potentially life-threatening aspects of their current condition. Second, any negative outcomes of potential treatment regimens, including surgical intervention, should be communicated clearly and stated early. In all cases, the patient should be encouraged to ask questions about the level of threat and the probability that treatment options will yield negative or positive outcomes.

When providers approach issues of negative prognosis or terminal status, the actual discussion should be thoughtfully planned in advance. These conversations should not be initiated without providing patients the opportunities to clarify and react to the information. Abrupt announcements or short-lived explanations are nontherapeutic. Some providers will ease into a conversation by first asking questions, e.g., "Well, I suppose you've been wondering just what's going on," or by leading with a disclosure, "This news is difficult for me to tell you," or "I wish I could give you better news." By easing into the subject, providers can assess the patient's tolerance and capability to pursue the subject. Because the provider has offered an opening, the possibility of a frank and open discussion is provided. Patients who feel sufficiently secure will reveal the extent to which they have assimilated the implications of the facts. In addition to offering the opportunity to discuss the facts, providers must recognize that once the subject is raised, there may be a continuing dialogue where many concerns will surface and will need to be handled patiently and repeatedly. Different concerns arise as different people and various members of the health care team are brought into the discussion.

The uncertainty surrounding a terminal status is difficult for most patients and significant others to deal with. Patients and significant others frequently ask for exact estimates of survival time. Usually providers render an estimate very cautiously because predicted survival does not always match actual survival time. Sometimes providers will err toward optimistic estimates. Such estimates, however, are not always helpful, for though they may sustain hope, this hope is unrealistic. For those families who need to coordinate the many aspects of dealing with the loved one's actual demise, e.g., gathering family members from long distances, overoptimistic predictions are a disservice to the patient and the family.

CONCLUSION

There is a growing need for advanced expertise in chronic and life-threatening disease management as conditions continue to significantly grow in numbers and proportions. In the case of the care of the chronically ill and those patients with life-threatening illnesses, the assault of these conditions on patients and their significant others is important. Managing the care of these patients requires not only knowledge of the specific disease processes but also basic principles related to the patient's process of adapting and coping. Clinicians must be aware of the cognitive and affective changes these patients experience so that they can communicate effectively with them. They must be able to conduct an evaluation of coping responses over time. The majority of these patients will receive their care almost exclusively in ambulatory care settings and in the home. Because of this, providers will be expected to comprehend patients' needs in a rich and diverse cultural, ethnic, social, and economic context.

A good deal of the care to these patients will consist of effectively communicating in order to identify risk factors and detect early signs of decline. Care to these patients involves managing symptoms collaboratively with patients and those in supportive roles around them.

The issues of chronic debilitating and/or life-threatening illness must be understood if providers are to effectively help patients and their families cope. Patients, themselves, need to understand how coping responses influence their current health and the progression of their disease. In cases of terminal illness, the communication capabilities of providers is extremely important. Providers must understand their own responses to patients' conditions, individual patient's desires for information, and how these factors influence the content of their discussions and what information they share or withhold from patients. While there are general guidelines regarding truth telling, each situation should be treated uniquely. Providers will generally lean toward truth telling for many reasons, including ethical imperatives and patients' preferences to be told. It is false to believe that patients know only what providers have explicitly told them. Under most circumstances, open, truthful disclosures best prepare patients and families to cope with the inevitabilities surrounding their illnesses.

CHAPTER 14

Communicating Effectively with Patients Displaying Significant Negative or Resistive Coping Responses

Staying grounded in emotionally charged situations is an essential aspect in working with difficult patients and families.

Judy Bluhm

CHAPTER OBJECTIVES

- Describe how situations may be multidimensional—difficult clients, difficult tasks, and difficult care contexts.
- Discuss various types of difficult client behaviors and their potential underlying communication.
- Discuss ways in which the provider can both monitor responses to difficult client behaviors and apply specific guidelines.
- Identify several selected client encounters that would be difficult and identify corresponding therapeutic communication responses.

It has been estimated that at least 50 percent of the provider's time with patients is spent in communicating. These verbal encounters include history taking, teaching, answering questions, counseling, ensuring compliance, and achieving satisfaction with care. Health providers mainly engage patients in discussions on a variety of subjects that are organized around major categories of dialogue, but there are other times when contacts are less structured. In truth, the provider is heavily influenced by the patient's condition and any associations made during the encounter. Also, regardless of the category of data, nearly all information and perceptions derived from this encounter ultimately end up being organized for the medical notes or record.

Patterns of health care provider dialogue with patients vary and with this there are differences in what providers will accept, how much irrelevant information they will permit, and how they will respond to patients they regard as "difficult."

DIFFICULT PATIENTS, DIFFICULT TASKS, AND DIFFICULT CARE CONTEXTS

In this chapter, a substantial proportion of the discussion will focus on how certain so-called difficult behaviors may be appropriately addressed (see Table 14–1). Sufficient discussion of the underlying meaning of difficult behaviors will be provided so that the rationale behind the recommended responses is clear. Some of these behaviors are atypical, e.g., aggressive and condescending behaviors. Still others, e.g., crying and denial, are common but nonetheless difficult for some providers. In this chapter, the concept of the "difficult" patient will be differentiated from "difficult care context" and "difficult tasks." Patients who are dying may be difficult to encounter because they are in a terminal stage. This is a difficult encounter because the context is uncomfortable. Sometimes the patient's behavior is easier to address than the context in which it is displayed. Such is the case, for example, of the young burn patient who cries and screams during her debridement. The patient's behavior may be difficult to encounter; however, the task of witnessing the debridement of the wound may be equally or more distressful to the provider. At other times, the context does not arouse uncomfortable feelings, but the patient's behavior does. This would be the case if the provider encountered a patient who had come for an appointment or to get a prescription and complained profusely about the service he received. Dissatisfied patients, who actually feel insecure, can be perceived by providers as being uncooperative, noncompliant, and unpopular (Raatikainen 1991).

Hypertension patients, for example, were found to have patterns of self-presentation that could present an obstacle to effective communication with providers (physicians). And this difficulty may be amplified by providers' (physicians') disinclination to probe for psychosocial concerns (Roter and Ewart 1992). The event is commonplace but the behavior arouses irritation and defensiveness in the provider. The fact that the provider did not anticipate the patient's response further aggravates the provider.

Good communication with all patients—regardless of whether they are difficult or not—is important. Increasingly, the patient-consumer will be heard and heeded, and providers will have to learn how to communicate more successfully with a broader range of patient behaviors, particularly with those that elicit disturbing thoughts and feelings.

Students will find that encounters with difficult patients will evoke more learning if they use audiotape recordings and/or written process recordings. Audiotapes capture verbal and some nonverbal aspects of the encounter. Usherwood (1993) found that students' audiotape recordings were extremely useful in changing students' communication styles. Eighty-five percent of the students felt that their interview skills had been improved and 68 percent said that listening to their own

Table 14–1 Common Negative Behaviors: Their Underlying Meaning and Therapeutic Responses

Behavior Type	Specific Manifestations of Behavior Type	Innermost Feelings/ Underlying Meaning	Therapeutic Responses
Dependent-manipulative	Controlling Passive-aggressive	Loss of control Frustration	Set limits Respond assertively, not aggressively
Aggressive	Attacking Blaming	Low self-esteem Feelings of inferiority	Set limits Respond assertively, not aggressively
Condescending	Critical Belittling	Low self-esteem Fear of rejection Frustration	Set limits Respond assertively, not aggressively
Self-pitying	Self-centered	Low self-esteem Fear of disapproval or rejection	Provide support Present reality
Complaining	Rejecting of assistance, unrealistic expectations	Fear and anxiety Frustration Feelings of futility	Set limits Clarify expectations
Demanding	Frequent requests that may also be unrealistic	Threats of loss of control Feelings of inadequacy	Set limits Express firmness in limit setting

Courtesy of Judy Bluhm, Phoenix, Arizona.

recordings had been the most helpful aspect of their course. In interviews with patients recorded at the end of the course, students asked more open-ended questions; fewer questions referring to physical symptoms; more questions referring to feelings, beliefs, or behavior; and fewer questions of a checklist type than during interviews recorded at the beginning of their course. Process recordings or sequential accounts of what the provider and patient said and did are the most traditional forms of learning to improve communication under difficult circumstances. Audiotapes can also be used to construct process recordings and help re-create encounters as they actually occurred.

Types of Difficult Behaviors and Their Underlying Meanings

The Noncompliant Patient

If there was a vote tomorrow about what kind of patient provokes the most distress in providers, many providers would answer, "patients who don't comply." In fact, one of the most frustrating aspects of provider-patient relationships is learning how to deal with noncompliance. This is true in medicine when patients passively or actively refuse to follow doctors' recommendations or orders. This is true in nursing when patients refuse medication, in dentistry when patients fail to comply with oral hygiene instructions, and in pharmacology when patients do not read the cautionary comments on prescriptions they receive.

Providers react with anger and frustration when patients ignore professional recommendations. By being noncompliant, patients cause providers to feel disconfirmed. There is frequently more at stake than just feeling that one's professional opinion is devalued. At a personal level, these patient behaviors can trigger more deep-seated issues relating to the provider's sense of self-worth. When deep-seated issues surface, providers are more likely to make additional mistakes, e.g., unleashing their anger and frustration on the patient, inducing guilt, withdrawing or moralizing, and preaching to the patient. Recognizing that these are less than desired responses, providers can experience even greater levels of frustration. These unhelpful responses also impact the patient, whose ability to trust providers is initially tentative at best.

There are still other reasons for providers to become upset with noncompliant patients. By definition, noncompliant patients put themselves and their health at risk. Patients who refuse to comply decrease their chances for optimal recovery. Providers are rightfully concerned that rather than getting better, patients will get worse despite everything they have tried to do. It is one thing to experience defeat at the hands of disease or inadequate technology, but another to experience defeat at the hands of the patient. Breaking down barriers to treatment including dealing effectively with patient resistance is as germane as establishing a medication dose and schedule that will successfully ward off infection. Nonetheless, providers are not prepared to deal with patients who are, themselves, barriers to better care.

There are many reasons for noncompliance (Exhibit 14–1). Patients may not fully understand a medical order or they may not fully comprehend the consequences of refusing to follow the order. Pharmacists now elicit from patients their signature when they pick up medications. These signatures attest to the fact that the patient received or refused to receive counseling about these prescriptions. Why should such details be documented? Obviously, these providers want some record, if things go wrong, that instruction either took place or was refused.

In addition to not fully understanding a health care recommendation, patients may fear the treatment, medication, or therapy. If they fear it, for whatever reason, they are not likely to abide by the provider's advice. Still another cause for noncompliance is a unique pattern of reasoning that results in a patient's judging the steps to be unreasonable, impractical, too costly, or in competition with another cherished goal.

Recent research in persuading people to practice safe sex, stop smoking, or say no to illicit drugs suggests that if the behavior change results in the loss of a perceived positive experience (in the case of sex, loss of enjoyment; in the case of smoking, relaxation; and in the case of drugs, an altered emotional state), the behavior is not likely to be adopted. This is true even if the risk of continuing the behavior is known. Risky behaviors have also been associated with group conformity—peers influence both substance abuse and risky sexual practices. Despite the fact that noncompliance or lack of adherence has been an issue since the advent of medicine and health care, providers frequently lack the skill to address this problem.

The Manipulative-Dependent Patient

Manipulative patients are frequently viewed as "dependent" patients. Some providers argue that with the exception of the noncompliant patient, the dependent-manipulative patient is the most frustrating of all personality types. While these types of patients are frequently thought to be of certain genders and socioeconomic status, the fact is that these behaviors can be found in patients of all

---

Exhibit 14–1 Establishing Reasons for Noncompliance/Lack of Adherence

- unconvinced of need
- language barriers
- procedures/equipment too costly
- problem in understanding (due to illiteracy, ability to concentrate, memory lapses)
- undesirable side effects of treatment/medication
- conflicts with health provider(s)
- philosophical, cultural, and religious beliefs that run counter to modern medicine

ages, genders, ethnicities, and socioeconomic classes. Unlike patients who are exhibiting dependent behaviors consistent with their disease stage and level of impairment, patients with dependent *personalities* exhibit this behavior in routine situations and in most of their human interactions and personal relationships. What is occurring dynamically is that the patient is attempting to establish control of the provider-patient relationship, usually by playing the role of a helpless, powerless patient. Their weak and passive presentation usually suggests a lack of power. It is clear, however, that the patient, through this passive role, is exercising a great deal of control, and when the provider responds in a complimentary fashion to this helplessness, the patient has actually succeeded in getting the additional needed attention. This process is marked, however, by the distinct conclusion that no intervention seems to work completely; the provider has two choices: (1) to admit defeat, or (2) to keep trying to find ways to meet these patients' needs.

Dependent-manipulative patients tend to reinforce the authority-subordinate aspects of provider-patient relationships; some providers liken this to a parent-child relationship. When providers recognize that they are caught in a parent-child relationship, they feel used and become angry. The patients in these instances usually assume no real responsibility for maintaining their health and combating the effects of their illnesses. Patients who have negotiated this role with providers are often experts in their ploy. To behave in this manner with providers is almost second nature to them. Providers who need patients to participate actively in their treatment, e.g., to follow nutritional guidelines, resume physical activity cautiously, or evaluate their own responses to medications are understandably distressed by this type of patient. Characteristically, when something goes wrong, these patients are likely to make it appear that it was due to some deficit in the delivery of care.

Consider the following dialogue between a physician and a 56-year-old female who has been hospitalized for infectious hepatitis.

Physician: "You know you're going to have to be on bedrest for some time. You'll need to notify your work."
Patient: "Yes . . . doctor will you call them? I know they'll listen to you."
Physician: "This is something you're going to have to do; if they want a letter—and you permit it —I'll write one."
Patient: "But what if they ask me questions I can't answer. Oh boy, my back hurts (*grimacing, shifting positions*)."
Physician: "What could they ask?"
Patient: "I don't know . . . anything. Could you, please? It would be better if you called. I don't think I'm up to it, anyway."
Physician: "I'm sorry, I don't have the time."
Patient: "Well, if I tell them to call you, then you don't have to call them. OK?"
Physician: "All right." (*Leaves the room somewhat frustrated by the conversation.*)

In keeping with the style of most dependent-manipulative patients, this patient asks the provider to go "beyond the call of duty," which comes as second nature to the patient, who seems not to question the appropriateness of this request. While the physician seems to agree with her request, clearly he agrees out of duress. The request is not appropriate, is something he does not customarily do for patients, and puts him in an awkward position with the employer. He may be anticipating a scenario where he is asked questions that he cannot rightfully answer. Dependent-manipulative patients frequently ask favors and demand more than other patients. Although the requests are novel and it would seem that responding affirmatively would be OK (at least once), this is usually not the case. For this type of patient, there may be a series of such requests or demands. Frequently, this behavioral pattern is a learned response, reflecting primitive ways of coping with basic needs for attention, love, and affection.

Dependent patients who suffer acute and chronic illnesses present a particular challenge to providers. Continued reliance on medical care is needed; however, self-care and individual patient responsibility for symptom management is also essential. This case is complex because providers struggle with what is the right amount of dependence. Patients such as those with asthma, hypertension, arthritis, pulmonary disease, congestive heart failure, and many major mental illnesses require a high level of compliance to keep the disease under control. Those patients with chronic, life-threatening diseases (e.g., advanced cancer and AIDS) are a subset of patients, where medical treatment is critical to patients' quality of life. Many times providers feel that they are in a double-bind where they want to avoid infantilizing patients, yet they cannot leave patients on their own to follow even the simplest directions. Providers—nurses, physicians, pharmacists, and many paraprofessionals—are not equipped to take care of patients around the clock. Many patients, particularly the elderly and the socially disenfranchised, may not have adequate support. Under these conditions, the question of whether the patient's dependency on providers is appropriate is indeed difficult to answer.

Frequently, a critical deciding factor is whether the problem or need of the patient is judged to be authentic or fabricated. Some patients seek out providers because they need human contact and attention, not because they have legitimate somatic complaints. Patients may invent complaints, call at unusual hours, or call frequently with "important" or "urgent" messages. These patients can react negatively to providers who are too busy to respond and become extremely upset by providers taking holidays. They also tend to worship their providers and expect the same level of commitment in return. They act as if the provider has no other competing commitments but to care for them.

Providers need to recognize that passive-dependent behavior is sometimes indicative of patients with defined clinical syndromes. In the Diagnostic Statistical Manual of the American Psychiatric Association (DSM-IV), dependent personality disorders are diagnosed as legitimate medical conditions requiring professional counseling.

Persons who are considered to have dependent personalities will exhibit the following behaviors:

- allow others to assume responsibility for major areas of life
- lack self-confidence, perceive self as helpless, inadequate, or stupid
- unable to make decisions
- possess fears of being alone or abandoned
- seek constant reassurance and approval from others

If providers have such patients, special precautions are necessary to avoid patient entanglements. Improvement in the patient's medical condition may be highly contingent upon the dynamics of this dysfunctional, somewhat regressive relationship. A chronic cycle of ineffective contacts is worrisome to the provider, but necessary for the patient. The provision of unending advice, opportunities for ventilation, parental guidance, and "free" counseling and education often fatigue the provider. The following steps are helpful in responding to these patients.

First, a thorough assessment of the character and appropriateness of dependent behaviors is needed. Second, inappropriate and manipulative behaviors should be recognized and differentiated from appropriate dependency. Third, providers need to set limits on the demands and requests of the patient. Finally, in assertive ways, providers need to establish the goals of treatment and expected patient behaviors. Aggressive responses fueled by frustration, anger, and resentment should be avoided.

Precautions against entanglements should also include avoiding the following:

- socializing with the patient
- honoring special requests or privileges
- accepting patients' exaggerations of their conditions and symptoms
- attempting to bargain with providers for special treatment
- encouraging the patients' desires in choosing or designing their treatment
- accepting flattery or positive reinforcement
- manipulating time, frequency, and duration of contacts

Providers who are able to analyze their personal responses to dependent-manipulative patients and check nontherapeutic replies are more likely to succeed in managing these patients appropriately. Major feelings of tension, frustration, or anxiety are clues to the provider. These feelings may be followed by feelings of dread or resistance in seeing the patient again. Frequently, providers will make derogatory remarks to other members of the team before, after, or even during an encounter with the patient. And these discussions, while they help to diffuse the tension that has accumulated, will not solve the problem. The provider may view these situations as hopeless and consequently respond in a passive-aggressive manner. Their responses can include limiting lengths or numbers of contacts or simply ignoring what the patient says or asks. Another response that is very common is for the provider to go along with the requests or demands, thinking that the requests will not be that much trouble. Finally, the provider may overreact with hostility and overt aggression. Expressions of anger can be overt, such as losing one's temper or more covert, including allowing the patient to experience some physical discomfort, anxiety, or uncertainty. These nontherapeutic responses do not address the problem and therefore contribute to rising tensions. The only viable solution at this point is to remove oneself from the situation in order to evaluate one's responses and regain a therapeutic perspective on these interactions.

The Aggressive Patient

Although less common than either noncompliant or dependent-manipulative behaviors, aggression expressed by the patient toward a provider or the health care team is troublesome. Caring for angry patients in intense encounters can be threatening for all health care professionals. Smith and Hart (1994) discovered that providers (nurses) reacted differently from doctors, based upon their perceptions of the patient's anger. When the perceived threat to self was high, nurses managed the patient's anger by disconnecting from the patient. Low or controllable threats were generally managed by connecting empathically with the angry patient.

The attitude communicated by the aggressor is one of hostility. Behaviors that are demonstrated are usually ones of condescending, blaming, attacking, or criticizing. Sometimes these behaviors take the form of insults and sarcasm; less often, patients may exhibit aggression through physical attacks including hitting, pinching, biting, spitting, and pushing. Perhaps it seems strange that patients would respond in these ways, still, these reactions do occur. Although they are abusive, they are often not intended as such. Most of the time they are results of unabated frustration that culminates in blind rage. Either patients have not assessed the consequences, or they anticipated counteraggression, which will justify their rage. It is important to recognize that aggression is a sign of unhealthy coping. Sometimes in unfamiliar, frightening, and threatening circumstances, patients' usual ways of coping may not suffice. Patients who react aggressively indicate that they are feeling overwhelmed; thus anger and aggression are secondary responses resulting from feelings of being overwhelmed or out of control.

There are times when aggression is rooted in a patient's experience of his or her illness and disease. Anger, for example, is cited as one phase of the grief response. Once denial has diminished, other primary feelings surface, and before patients reach a level of acceptance of their disease and its consequences, a state of, "Not me!" occurs. This stage of adaptation is in essence a protest against the illness. Patients who fall victim to life-threatening illnesses or injuries experience a reduced ability to cope and therefore sometimes project their anger and rage (surrounding their illnesses or injuries) onto their health care providers. Ironically, those individuals most capable of helping and of understanding the patient become targets of the patient's rage. In these cases, small problems or unexpected events can trigger the patient to "let go" a barrage of feelings and accusations. Witnessing these behaviors can be like observing a volcanic eruption: a powerful, forceful barrage of words, perhaps accompanied by movements and gestures, gush to the top, displaying intensity far beyond anything anticipated. Usually patients' angry, aggressive outbursts do not last long. While providers may fear that the patient will harm someone or damage objects in the immediate environment, this rarely happens.

When patients become agitated and potentially assaultive, avoiding confrontation is important. Providers should learn to recognize signs of escalated agitation, should practice presenting oneself as a calm, caring professional, and should maintain poise even when facing a potentially violent patient. Stevenson (1991) states that every effort should be made to provide opportunities for patients to be in control of their own behavior. Physical confrontation should always be a last resort and should be used only when there is a clear danger of immediate physical harm. It may be that the use of force is an encouragement to aggressive behavior and a hindrance to treatment. Effective use of therapeutic communication encourages patients to express their feelings and become cooperative partners in their treatment (Stevenson, 1991). While these guidelines apply particularly to psychiatric patients, they have relevance to all patients, regardless of the setting (see Exhibit 14–2).

Consider the following dialogue between provider and patient in an inpatient encounter. The patient has a history of substance abuse but is hospitalized for symptoms related to HIV and his current opportunistic infection. The patient exhibits provocative behaviors, hostile threatening gestures, and verbalizations. He appears suspicious of his caregivers.

Exhibit 14–2 Nonverbal and Verbal Signs of Anger and Potential for Violence

- body language: clenched fists, facial expressions, rigid posture
- hostile threatening verbalizations; boasts about prior abuse of others
- overt aggressive acts, e.g., destruction of objects in the environment
- increased motor activity, e.g., pacing, agitated movements, excitement, and irritability
- provocative behavior, e.g., hypersensitivity, argumentative, overreactive responses

Provider: "Edward, I hear you're having trouble with the food. We need to get you to eat better."

Patient: "Don't *force* me to eat!"

Provider: "We don't want to force you, but we need to supplement your diet. That's how we are going to get you better."

Patient: (*Emphatically*) "What good is it? I'm going to die anyway!"

Provider: "We're all going to die someday, Edward."

Patient: "That's bull s___, what does it matter?"

Provider: "It matters because we can get you better. We can't cure you of AIDS, but we can certainly get you over this disease (PCP)."

Patient: "Where the h___ did they get you? You must be new!"

Provider: "So, what would you like to eat? Whatever, we'll try to get it."

Patient: "McDonald's."

Provider: "OK. Hamburger, fries? . . . anything else?"

Patient: "A prostitute!"

Provider: (*Jumps to respond*) "I'm not talking about extracurricular activities, Edward!"

Patient: (*Coughs several times; silent; looks at provider*) "What if I spit in your eye? . . . Would you get AIDS? (*menacingly looks at the provider*)."

Provider: "No."

Patient: "Would you be scared? (*laughs*)"

Provider: "No . . . (*pause*). Edward, we're really here to get you better; there's nothing more to it—that's what we're here for."

This patient's responses were very provocative and explicitly hostile. There is a good chance that his anger toward the provider includes displaced feelings about his illness, particularly his prognosis. In attempting to set limits rather than to quiet the patients' agitation, this provider's response tends to increase the patient's agitation and induce aggressive outbursts such as the patient's threat that he will spit in the provider's eye. Had the provider slowed his own reaction time and avoided response matching the tone of the patient's replies, a somewhat different outcome may have resulted. Still, the wisdom of afterthought is not always available to us, and we say and do what first occurs to us. The provider's expression of acceptance despite the patient's unacceptable behavior is what seemed to turn this encounter toward a better course. Still, when dealing with patients who are clearly and presently abusing a substance or whose history includes violence, the provider should always be cautious about presuming too much about the patient's own internal controls. With persons prone to violent, angry outbursts, certain things are unknown, including:

- how patients perceive others
- how the environment stimulates patients, increasing their agitation
- the ability of patients to control their outbursts

- the ability of the patient to rechannel hostility into socially acceptable behaviors
- patients' level of tolerance for frustration

Because these things are unknown and/or difficult to judge, any behaviors that suggest aggression should not be underestimated. Providers who recognize the potential for every patient to respond angrily or aggressively at some point will anticipate how to minimize this possibility. Provider attitudes of acceptance (of the person, not the behavior), maintaining low levels of stimuli, and encouraging patients to verbalize feelings of frustration and to explore alternative ways of coping will assist many patients in controlling their levels of anger and hostility. In cases of potential violent outbursts, prevention is always the strategy of choice. And when prevention is not possible, securing one's physical safety and removing dangerous objects is paramount.

The Complaining and Demanding Patient

The patient who complains about the care, the cost, the providers, and the treatment regimen is clearly difficult to encounter and deal with over time. Many times this patient is demanding as well. Complaining is the expression of negativity that implies that the patient is difficult to please. This patient is thought to have unrealistic expectations, and if providers judge this patient's expectations as unrealistic, they are likely to resist any requests that seem to be out of the usual. Ignoring this patient, though, may increase the level of demand that ensues because the patient's perception is that the provider has not heard or does not evaluate the request as important enough. The feeling of loss of control triggers hostility and the need to intensify demands. Under the surface, the complainer is feeling fear and anxiety, coupled with frustration. This patient views situations as undesirable or threatening and judges that no other rational discussion of the problem will work. And, demands become expressed concerns about the lack of control. By the time the patient issues commands or demands, feelings of loss of control are usually compounded with feelings of inadequacy. As one would expect, this patient is experiencing multiple feelings that should be addressed separately. Unfortunately, these feelings do not elicit analytical replies. Unless a provider is astute and is capable of examining the underlying feelings, this patient's inner feelings will go unaddressed. A worst-case scenario is that the patient's behavior is needlessly exaggerated because the provider withdraws, tunes out, or otherwise avoids this patient. Avoidance and withdrawal responses tend to increase the patient's feelings of fear, anxiety, and concerns about rejection. This experience serves to escalate patient demands.

A subcategory of the complaining patient has been identified as one of a provider's most trying patients. This is the hypochondriacal patient. Hypochondriasis is an official psychiatric disorder (American Psychiatric Association 1994). This disorder is distinguished by the presence of physical symptoms for which there are no demonstrable organic findings or known physiologic mechanisms. Additionally, there is positive evidence, or at least a strong presumption, that the symptoms are linked to psychologic factors. Hypochondriacal patients unrealistically interpret physical signs or sensations as evidence of physical illness. These patients are usually preoccupied with the fear or belief of having not just a disease, but a *serious* disease. Unlike people who periodically wonder about small changes that they observe or experience, these patients have enduring concerns that they have a serious disease. They tend to be chronic complainers, unrelentingly complaining of physical problems. Typically, these patients will shop for a doctor or clinic who will believe them. During this search they can become virtual invalids, impairing their social and occupational functioning and interpersonal relationships. There is excessive preoccupation with the symptom(s) that are usually exaggerated out of proportion. For these patients, hardly one social encounter will occur without them focusing on the symptom. Most have a history of seeking assistance from numerous health care providers. Excessive use of analgesics with minimal relief of pain may be reported, and this person is vulnerable to addiction. Unmet dependency needs, anxiety, and the tendency to shop for cures while engaging many physicians, each responding to the anxiety with prescriptions of anxiolytic medications, increases the risk of drug dependency. As these patients cling to their symptoms, a pattern of broken provider-patient relationships characterize their history.

Providers often face a double-bind situation with these patients. Denying the patient's symptoms and their seriousness can hinder the development of a therapeutic relationship, yet not telling the patient that the symptoms have no basis communicates to the patient that they do have medical meaning and it is appropriate to consider medications, treatment, and even surgery. In fact, the more that providers seem to try to help these patients, the more important the symptoms become. The irritation that providers feel is understandable. There are so many people with real problems who are truly fighting for life, while hypochondriacal patients seem to revel in the diseases they *think* they have. Encouraging patients to focus on the stressors in their lives as well as their fears of not being cared for may provide the foundation for the patient to accept a psychologic basis for these symptoms. However, if there are powerful secondary gains associated with the patient's experience of symptoms, e.g., a reprieve from work, child care, or the demands of a significant other, the patient may exhibit prolonged use of symptoms despite beginning awareness that there is no real physiological explanation for them.

Not all functional bodily complaints are hypochondriacal. There are many reasons why some symptoms for some patients are experienced. For example, patients who are depressed, grief stricken, delusional, or who are experiencing conversion reactions may amplify their experiences of backaches, headaches, stomach ailments, and a variety of other minor aches and pains.

Providers' responses should not cause the patient to be defensive. Focusing on the patient's life situations and present feelings, including feelings the patient has toward the provider, are usually helpful. Arguing or debating a symptom usually results in the patient leaving the provider's care. Consider the following dialogue between an obese 35-year-old male and his physician.

Physician: "Your hand is just fine. I don't see any reason why you can't go back to work."

Patient: "But it still hurts, and it swells up on me."

Physician: "Well J____, I might say you are not really interested in returning to work."

Patient: "What if I injure it again? Then it would really be bad."

Physician: "Well, we don't know for sure. J____, what's going on at work? How's work?"

Patient: "Work s____. If I don't find a better job, I'm going to be put in some institution!"

Physician: "So maybe your job is the problem—not your hand."

In this dialogue the physician reframed the problem, which was not the injured hand, but the problem of going back to work. Resuming activities means going back to a job this patient dislikes.

Mistakes that the provider could have made would have been to (1) focus needlessly on the hand, (2) challenge the patient to prove the problem existed, and (3) engage in a power struggle over who knew the most. The value of this provider's response lies in the fact that the physician did not support the patient's unrealistic view of his hand. By establishing an interested, concerned tone, the physician actually met the patient's needs for support and caring.

The Patient in Denial

Denial is usually, but not always, indicative of maladaptive coping. Authors who address the various stages of adaptation to disease, illness, and injury describe denial as an early stage of eventual resolution and acceptance of one's diagnosis and prognosis. Denial is a self-protective mechanism. It defends against underlying threats that would ordinarily overwhelm the patient. Because of this, providers are always cautioned to treat denial with respect.

Problems can occur, however, when patients exhibit prolonged periods of denial or when, in denial, they avoid actions or treatments that are absolutely necessary for full recovery. Denial can sometimes be constructed so elaborately that to maintain their denial, patients process information to negate substantial aspects of their experience. This may include denial of pain (or minimization of its intensity), fatigue, stress, and impaired functioning related to vision, hearing, or motor-sensory abilities. Patients who minimize flu symptoms, pain from an injury, a prolonged cough, the stress on the job, or their inability to accurately read street signs due to impaired vision are very common.

Patients who use denial are unable at the time to deal successfully with the reality of their condition. Although they may in fact be assisted to cope effectively, their anticipation that they will not is sufficient to cause them to deny problems that are obvious to others. Denial may be accompanied by other defenses, e.g., rationalization and blocking. Rationalization is the process of justifying or rejecting feedback that would cause the patient to acknowledge reality. Thus, a patient may deny the risk of exposure to HIV and at the same time rationalize the process of denying AIDS, as everyone knows, is a problem, yet a patient can translate it in the following way: "It is not a real problem and certainly not a problem that should impinge on me (my health-related behaviors). Therefore, the threat of AIDS is not something to worry about because it is not significant (*denial*). If it is not significant, no real changes are needed (*rationalization*)."

Patients who use denial to cope may also use blocking. Blocking is the unconscious mechanism of not allowing certain facts into one's awareness. Patients who block awareness of new or different data may interrupt the provider, become inattentive in conversations, and change the subject. This occurs when they anticipate painful awareness of facts and prognoses.

Denial, as was previously mentioned, may initially be adaptive. We know that future successful adaptation may occur if people are allowed an initial period of denial. This period protects the individual from stress and sometimes the many responsibilities and activities that are required as one actively deals with illness, disease, and injury. Denial that is adaptive can be likened to a stage of respite, a period of calm before the storm surrounding recovery.

Denial is maladaptive when it interferes with appropriate treatment. The health care provider must always assess whether the patient's denial is interfering with care and placing the patient at jeopardy. While some providers would argue that denial, by definition, suggests the patient is not ready to deal with realities and should not be pushed quickly into facing the primary and secondary consequences of one's illness, other clinicians will argue the contrary. Arguments that denial should be confronted are usually supported by the following reasoning. The patient's fear of the reality may be exaggerated, i.e., the real facts are less threatening than the patient's anticipation of them. Prolonged denial contributes to unrealistic estimates of the disease and one's ability to cope. Providers can successfully address most threatening aspects of injury or illness. And, future collaborative efforts between provider and patient require a level of reality-based problem solving that is not forthcoming if the present condition of denial is permitted to continue.

Dealing effectively with a patient in denial is complex because it is intimately linked with a level of hope. Experts suggest that if denial is reduced, the patient's level of hope may also be diminished. It is unwise to be so confrontational as to bankrupt the patient's ability to be hopeful; hopefulness is recognized as integral to the process of fortifying patients' abilities to tolerate stress and pain, including negative prognoses and loss of functional abilities. Providers who are attempting to alter patient denial for the purpose of achieving better compliance or better collaborative encounters with the patient must appreciate this phenomena. Providers will need to move patients closer to reality while preserving their spirit and optimism about their quality of life and their ability to manage their illnesses, disabilities, or impairments. Consider the following dialogue between a patient diagnosed with advanced metastatic cancer of the colon and a health care provider.

Physician: "The tests don't look good, Tina."
Patient: "Well, they couldn't be too bad. I've been feeling OK, really."
Physician: "I'd like to tell you that things are OK, but they're not."
Patient: "How long do I have?"
Physician: "I can't be sure."
Patient: "A year, two years?"
Physician: "We need to think in terms of six months."
Patient: (*Silence*) "Six months?" (*Silence begins to cry.*)
Physician: "I know this is hard; you wanted more time." (*Reaches out to touch patient's hand.*)

As providers, we might point out several commissions and omissions: (1) Should the physician have been so blunt? (2) Should the physician have said something else, e.g. "We can keep your pain under control," and (3) Should the physician have asked more about her feelings? The issues are multiple. The main idea here is that the physician presented the reality of a shortened life span to the patient in concrete, simple-to-understand terms. The patient may have anticipated a more negative outcome—some patients admit that they "know" in advance. Nonetheless, the patient needed to be told and was perceived by the physician as able to tolerate the announcement. Additionally, other aspects of care were in place that were potentially supportive to this patient. First, the physician and patient have had a continuous, ongoing relationship. Second, they have had previous discussions of the gravity of the illness. Third, the patient trusts the physician's ability to empathize and understand the unique implications of declining health. It is these elements that bolster the patient's ability to manage the trauma of being told a negative prognosis.

The Depressed or Anxious Patient

There is every reason to believe that health care providers will repeatedly encounter people in distress who are experiencing significant degrees of anxiety and/

or depression. These conditions may be reactions to stress, particularly to the stressful life event of an illness or injury. This distress may be mild and time limited or the anxiety and depression that the provider observes may reflect a clinical condition.

Clinical anxiety can reflect a variety of conditions including panic disorder, agoraphobia, social phobia, obsessive-compulsive disorder, post-traumatic stress disorder (PTSD), and generalized anxiety disorder (American Psychiatric Association 1994). For example, those patients seen in emergency rooms for gunshot wounds, rape, or other forms of physical assault may be experiencing initial signs of post-traumatic stress that are related to how they were injured. When the condition does not subside, a syndromic condition will result. But for many, the signs and symptoms are indicative of less-serious prognoses. The uncertainties surrounding who, what, and when one will get medical attention may be important, but the driving force behind the patient's experience of emotional distress may be the recollections of events leading to the injury. Emergency-room staff are aware of the effect of such trauma and monitor the patient's distress with mild to moderate tranquilizers if the patient's condition permits. PTSD is a more severe condition, warranting additional attention and is characterized by the development of physiologic and/or behavioral symptoms following the psychological trauma that occurred. A PTSD-inducing event would be considered markedly stressful to almost anyone and has usually been experienced with intense feelings of fear, "terror," helplessness, and powerlessness. While many patients experience this phenomena long after the event (referred to as PTSD with delayed onset), most patients show signs early after the trauma as the shock of the event subsides.

It is understandable that all occurrences of illness or injury are events that carry anxiety for all patients. And this anxiety may be evidenced in behavioral dimensions, e.g., expectant apprehension, vigilance (for example, about one's medications and disease signs and symptoms), or perceptual scanning of the environment. Young children do not understand a hospital environment, and with loss of a parent's support are prime candidates for considerable anxiety. All patients who are subjected to hospitalization where control is lost and routines are disrupted experience some level of uncertainty and anxiety. Particular treatments can also create anticipatory anxiety. Families are vulnerable to anxiety surrounding the diagnosis, treatment, and prognosis of their significant others. Anxiety is so omnipresent in the health care delivery system that it behooves providers to be very adept at recognizing, differentiating, and intervening effectively to minimize this condition.

Like all conditions, anxiety is best addressed when the provider is more fully cognizant of the sources of anxiety, can understand both real and perceived threats from the patient's perspective, and can judge the level and magnitude of the condition. Is anxiety the predominant condition or is other distress, e.g., depression, also occurring? Do certain stimuli expose the patient to elevated levels of anxiety? Is ritualistic or compulsive behavior involved in patients' attempts to curb fear and tension? Answers to these questions will help providers assess the magnitude and complexity of the patient's emotional state.

There are clear behavioral responses that indicate that the patient is anxious. Anxiety, usually defined as a vague uneasy feeling, is different from fear where there is a specific situation or thing that is feared. Patients who are feeling anxious will not be able to state or specify the source of their discomfort. The following signs suggest that the patient is suffering anxiety: dyspnea, palpitations, choking or smothering sensations, dizziness or unsteadiness, chest pains, feeling one is losing contact with reality, hot and cold flashes, sweating, trembling, shaking, restlessness, hyperattentiveness, recurrent and intrusive fearful thoughts, and abdominal discomfort. Any combination of these signs suggests that the patient is experiencing significant anxiety and this recognition should alter provider communication.

The highly anxious patient can only comprehend the most elemental communication. In giving these patients orders or directions, clear, simple, and brief commands will often be reassuring. The patient's immediate environment is usually perceived as overwhelming, therefore it is important to remain calm, restore quiet, and speak slowly. Patients with very high levels of anxiety will lack the usual abilities to care for themselves, at least temporarily. Some patients may even significantly regress for a period of time. While it is important for providers to encourage these patients to take care of their own activities of daily living, they may initially need additional assistance from staff and family members.

Depressed patients are usually thought to be difficult to care for because they are experienced as "draining" and "time consuming." Some providers admit that caring for depressed patients makes them feel depressed. Of all emotional disorders that require psychiatric labels, depression is the most common condition that providers are likely to confront. The American Psychiatric Association (DSM-IV 1994, p. 341) states that 20 to 25 percent of individuals with certain medical conditions, e.g., diabetes, cancer, strokes, and myocardial infarctions will develop a major depressive disorder during the course of their general medical condition. And patients who do experience these depressive episodes present with complex treatment conditions and suffer poor prognoses. Major depressive disorder, however, is only one class of depressive conditions that a provider may observe. There are other less severe conditions. Depression is generally viewed on a continuum from low levels (sometimes referred to as "the blues") to more enduring episodes that fit the diagnostic criteria of a syndrome or disorder.

MONITORING AND MASTERING REACTIONS TO DIFFICULT PATIENT BEHAVIORS

All providers need to control their reactions to patients whose behaviors are difficult for them. A primary point to keep in mind is that providers should *respond*, not *react*. To respond means to thoughtfully consider the patient's messages and to formulate a careful return. To react, on the other hand, means to move quickly without forethought and sometimes in opposition to what the patient is saying or trying to say.

The primary process of responding, not reacting, to patients' communications is the process of thoughtful consideration. This consideration aims to answer the questions: What is the patient really saying? and Why is he saying it? Otherwise, the provider is looking for the underlying meaning and motives of the patient. It is easier, for example, to communicate with a demanding patient when one understands that this behavior is triggered by his or her feelings of losing control. It is easier, as well, to communicate general acceptance of aggressive patients if one understands that their behavior is a result of their feeling inferior or frustrated. Therefore, from the standpoint of increasing responsive statements and decreasing reactive responses, it is critical that providers understand the underlying meaning behind patients' presenting behaviors.

Identifying a patient's behavior and the underlying feelings that motivate the behavior, however, is only half the task. When dealing with difficult patient behaviors, it is extremely important for providers to identify their own personal "triggers." Checking out one's own feelings about the patient and the situation enables one to respond, not react, to the situation. Most responses to difficult patients will be positive if the underlying motives are addressed. But providers who are upset with, or angry at patients will fail even if they do address underlying motives. Patients need to feel that providers' responses are, in a sense, neutralized. Neutrality will encourage patients to response match with their emotions more under control. Assisting oneself and the patient to remain grounded in emotionally charged situations will help the provider to gain further insight into the patient's situation while engaging the patient in useful self-disclosure. The delicate healing relationship then has a chance to develop and move efficiently in directions that are helpful to the patient.

What To Do About Feelings

The area most confusing to providers in the majority of encounters with difficult patients is the feeling dimension of the relationship. Feelings are one of the most important ingredients in the relationship between patients and providers, and the degree to which feelings should be controlled or expressed is not always clear.

Patients look for warmth, friendliness, and understanding. They become concerned when providers appear cold, aloof, withdrawn, or critical. The reasons for this usually involve the patient's anxiety that these more negative expressions indicate that the provider does not care and will not give good enough care. People in general are very accustomed to sizing up others on the basis of their perceptions of attitudes and feelings, even if these are based upon distortions of realities. In truth, it is feelings that frequently influence our behaviors; therefore, patients' concerns are not without merit. Patients whose behaviors are difficult frequently trigger negative reactions. Providers will need to conduct a self-appraisal of their abilities to relate to difficult patients.

There are specific instances in which feelings toward difficult patients can be problematic; these include providers' (1) lack of, or withholding of feelings, and (2) expression of too much feeling (e.g., elevated feelings of agitation, frustration, and anger). In all but a few patient encounters, human drama and sometimes great tragedy unfolds before the provider's eyes. The expression of no feeling tends to minimize the reality of the circumstances and the patient's experience. Demonstration of lack of feeling may be due to the provider having no feelings or withholding the feelings the provider does have. The patient has absolutely no way of knowing which, and the expression of no feelings tends to communicate to patients that they are not getting through to the provider. If patients think that they are not getting through to the provider, their most obvious recourse is to repeat or accentuate their behavior. Whether the behavior is repeated or accentuated, the provider is still subjected to difficult behaviors that now occur on a larger scale.

The expression of no feeling is problematic, but the expression of too much feeling can be troublesome as well. Expressing too much feeling may send the provider-patient encounter into open conflict. Anger matched by anger and irritation matched by irritation tends not only to worsen chances for understanding but resolution of the emerging conflict also becomes a major issue. One of the best means of dealing with one's own feelings toward difficult patients is to try to understand how the feelings came to be. This process of self-analysis is not easy and is sometimes painful, but is absolutely essential. The circumstances in which the provider was raised—characteristics of significant past relationships—will influence providers' feelings toward difficult patients. When providers are able to understand their own feelings and to control them, they will be better able to meet the needs of their patients and deal effectively with the patient's difficult behavior.

Guidelines To Follow with Difficult Patients

While the following discussion can apply to all provider-patient relationships, the concepts and principles discussed are particularly helpful reminders when it comes to communicating with difficult patients.

Show Respect

Although the idea of showing respect seems so obvious, it is probably one of the most seriously violated principles in health care delivery systems. Delivery systems tend to violate patients' rights for respectful treatment. This occurs, for example, when patients are left waiting for long periods, are not told what and when to expect procedures or events, and are treated as if they are objects rather than real human beings. Some providers show disrespect, which is a personal problem indicative of the personality of the provider. When providers treat any patient with disrespect, these insults affect further communications. When providers treat difficult patients without respect, the consequences can be significant. Ignoring, avoiding, and depersonalizing difficult patients all tend to escalate the conflict situation to the point where communication is blocked and/or a third person, usually another provider (but possibly another patient or the patient's significant other) is brought into the interaction. Patients who are removed from their usual channels of communication patterns experience the isolation acutely. This isolation can make them supersensitive to slights, either real or imaginary. The problem is multiplied twofold if the patient has already had a poor encounter with a provider. These patients anticipate a lack of respect and frequently interpret provider responses as disrespectful even when no disrespect is intended.

Practice Acceptance

Acceptance means acknowledging the patient as a person of worth. Although it means acceptance of the patient's way of thinking, believing, and behaving, it does not mean acceptance of destructive impulses, gestures, or actions. In many small ways, patients measure the level of provider acceptance. Providers are deeply committed to sound health care practices, and patients who test providers can use this fact as the major challenge. For example, "If you accept me, you will accept the fact that I prefer to eat foods that are bad for me," is a challenge for the provider. The question is: How can the provider show acceptance but protest the behavior? Still, if acceptance is the issue that leads to compliance, the provider never wants to win the battle just to lose the war. Sometimes, bargaining for change involves persuading the patient to alter unacceptable patterns, with the understanding that the provider unconditionally accepts the patient.

Show Concern

If there is any one response that should be perfected by providers, it is the expression of concern. Caring, a feeling state related to concern, is usually an underdeveloped skill. It is important that providers care about patients and nurture this feeling with even the most difficult of patients, showing concern as an expression of preparing to aid the patient. Patients need to witness provider concern. Patients expect providers to be ready to provide them aid. Patients view providers who do not have an attitude of concern as ill-equipped, not because of their competency, but because of the fact they do not have their patient's interests in mind. Spoken or unspoken, it is the feeling of concern that patients look for when choosing a provider. It is also the dissatisfaction with providers' concern that provokes patients to dislike providers.

Practice Objectivity

Just as the show of concern is critical, the practice of objectivity is also essential. Providers' feelings should not obscure reason and good judgment. Objectivity means that the provider can stand outside the immediate situation and evaluate it from all directions. The ability to look at an encounter from all sides before responding or taking action requires self-discipline and practice.

Beginning providers usually have a great deal of difficulty extracting themselves from uncomfortable encounters with difficult patients. When faced with abusive remarks, they may take the criticism personally. They may experience hurt and rejection, and these feelings may immobilize them. Standing apart from the encounter and viewing the situation from different vantage points usually has the effect of increasing providers' insights while at the same time neutralizing the feelings they have about how they are being treated.

The process of establishing objectivity is similar to that of the role of investigator on a research project or a detective at a crime site. It is important to assemble all factual information before making a conclusion. Any conclusions must be weighed against competing theories that would prove the results invalid. Incomplete data will always hide the truth, and it is the provider's job to uncover as many plausible reasons as possible. If providers, especially inexperienced clinicians, take this position with regard to difficult patient behaviors, they will be able to maintain their objectivity. When they maintain objectivity, they will be in better positions to respond, not react, to these patients. Objectivity, however, does not mean being aloof and noncaring. Withholding concern for a patient or patient's family while trying to maintain objectivity is both unnecessary and problematic. The skill is to show concern but remain detached enough to establish the facts as they relate to the encounter.

Enhance Awareness

Being consciously aware of the patient's circumstances, including his or her state of wellness—symptoms and any changes—is the bare minimum. It is safe to say that a majority of difficult patient encounters are due to inadequate awareness on the part of the provider. Providers come across insensitively when they are not aware of patients' conditions and their responses to their changed conditions. Being unaware and approaching a potentially difficult patient or patient's family is like walking into a minefield. The risk of unsatisfactory communication is extremely high. Therefore, the provider has set himself up for difficulty and the provider's failure to become aware is clearly the provider's fault—not the patient's.

In addition to being aware of the patient's condition, both physical and psychological symptoms and changes in the symptom picture, providers must be cognizant of the special caring needs that patients have. Does the patient want tenderness or detachment? Does he want to be informed about everything or just told the essential facts? Does she want to be alone or does she want to talk? Every patient has unique needs, and these needs change as the condition changes. Sometimes these needs are communicated clearly and directly; more often than not, they are obscure and covert. In the case of difficult patients, these needs may be very obscure, and this obscurity must be matched with high levels of awareness in the provider.

SELECTED PATIENT ENCOUNTERS AND THERAPEUTIC RESPONSE MODES

Case #1

The Aggressive and Abusive Patient

Name: Edward S.

Age: 30 years

Occupation: Sales—unemployed

Marital Status: Single

Diagnosis: PCP—one week ago diagnosed HIV+

IV Drug Abuse History

Hospitalization: To control infection.

Treatment: Includes supplemental feedings, nonroutine sedative and sleeping medications, O_2 PRN by mask.

CASE STUDY

This patient has been a substance abuser and is suspected of continued illicit drug use. He is hospitalized for symptoms related to his HIV and his current opportunistic infection. The patient exhibits provocative behaviors, hostile threatening gestures, and verbalizations as well as suspicion of his caregivers.

Provider: "Edward, I hear you're having trouble with the food. We need to get you to eat better."

Patient: "Don't *force* me to eat."

Provider: "We don't want to force you, but we need to supplement your diet. That's how we are going to get you better."

Patient: (*Emphatically*) "What good is it? I'm going to die anyway!"

Provider: "We're all going to die someday, Edward."

Patient: "That's bull s___, what does it matter?"

Provider: "It matters because we can get you better. We can't cure you of AIDS, but we can certainly get you over this disease (PCP)."

Patient: "Where the h___ did they get you? You must be new!"

Provider: "So, what would you like to eat? Whatever, we'll try to get it."

Patient: "McDonald's."

Provider: "OK. Hamburger, fries? . . . Anything else?"

Patient: "A prostitute!"

Provider: "I'm not talking about extracurricular activities, Edward."

Patient: (*Coughs several times; silent; looks at provider*) "What if I spit in your eye . . . Would you get AIDS?"

Provider: "No."

Patient: "Would you be scared? (*laughs*)"

Provider: "No . . . Edward, we're really here to get you better; there's nothing more to it—that's what we're here for."

Patient: "Ha, ha, ha." (*Coughing uncontrollably*)

Provider: "You know we're here because we care. I'm offering to help you. Do you need help to the bathroom?"

Patient: "No! I don't need help. I'm a man—f___, s___"

Provider: "I know you're a man, but you need help. I didn't say you weren't a man."

Patient: "Don't get smart with me—or I'll . . . I'll slap you!"

Provider: "You need help, Edward. Let me help you."

Patient: "I told you . . . I'm a   man!"

Provider: "It takes a man to admit he needs help."

Patient: "Don't give me that phony psychology s___."

Provider: "Edward, do you need to go the bathroom?"

Patient: (*Nods yes*)

Provider: "OK, lie over on this side. Put your legs over the side. I'm going to help you get up so you can go to the bathroom."

Patient: (*Silently responds to provider's directions, somewhat confused*) "Which way are you going to sit me up? (*angrily*)"

Provider: "This way. How are you feeling now?"

Patient: "It's cold. Why don't they turn up the heat? If they really cared, they would turn on the heat."

Provider: "The heat is on, Edward. Are you dizzy?"

Patient: "I'm dizzy and I'm cold. If the heat's on, then why am I cold?!"

Provider: "You have a fever, Edward. You've got a major infection. Are you still dizzy?"

Patient: "I'm dizzy and cold!"
Provider: "If you're dizzy, I want you to lie down. Lie back down, Edward."
Patient: (*Complies and is silent*)
Provider: (*Pulls up a chair by Edward's bed*) "What's going on?"
Patient: (*Silent, curled up in bed*)
Provider: "Obviously something is bothering you a whole lot."
Patient: (*Mumbles*) "They won't let me see my son."
Provider: "They won't let you see him? Is that because of your drug problems or your diagnosis?"
Patient: "Both. I'm just tired."
Provider: "We talked before about your eating better, getting rest."
Patient: "I used to be able to jump out of bed—get going."
Provider: "You'll regain your strength once we get you over this infection. Then we can see about getting your family involved."
Patient: "What do you mean? What can you do?"
Provider: "We'll talk to the social worker—you have every right to see your son."
Patient: "I'm so tired."
Provider: "Do you still have to go to the bathroom?"
Patient: "I can't go by myself."
Provider: "I'll take you now."

(*Provider successfully gains patient's cooperation and escorts him to the bathroom.*)

ANALYSIS

This aggressive, verbally abusive, and threatening patient is experiencing a great deal of distress not only about his illness (and prognosis) but also about the functional decline that he feels is linked with his masculinity. It is manly to take oneself to the bathroom when necessary, to jump up and get going, to get your own food, i.e., to provide for yourself. His symptoms and acute infection noticeably force him into unaccustomed dependency. He does not think that the provider understands or appreciates these aspects, and he does not want to be treated as an invalid. Unfortunately, the provider, at more anxious moments, feeds into this patient's concerns by becoming directive and authoritative, perhaps making the patient feel even more infantile. The patient, facing the threat of his own incompetency, challenges the competency and sincerity of his provider. He insists on being treated respectfully but treats the provider abusively.

Abandoning the task—getting the patient to the bathroom—was needed. Focusing on feelings, "What's going on—obviously something is bothering you a whole lot," was the primary therapeutic shift in this encounter. This intervention was punctuated by pausing. The open-ended question, "What's going on?" altered the style of communication and expressed the provider's concern and readiness to be open and receptive to the patient. The reflection, "Obviously something is bothering you a whole lot," expressed empathy and a desire to become more aware of the patient's situation as he experiences it. The fact that the provider did not reject this patient by leaving the room communicated a level of acceptance that the patient needed before trusting the provider with more intimate and painful details. The provider displayed respect for both the patient's identification of his problems and his inherent rights as a parent. Much of the dialogue that had occurred up to this point was affected by the provider's own reactions to the patient's accusatory and belittling comments. The provider communicated somewhat defensively to threats, e.g., "If I spit in your eye . . . would you be scared," and "don't give me that psychological s___." At either of these points, the provider could have attempted to refocus the patient on what was really bothering him. However, several factors may have prevented earlier attempts from working; this includes both the provider's and patient's awareness that a lot is going on here—this is not just a simple task of changing the patient's eating patterns or assisting him to the bathroom. Awareness of the complexity of the situation increased the provider's level of empathy.

What is also noteworthy is that the provider's effectiveness increased with the use of various therapeutic responses. Reflection, open-ended questions, expression of concern, showing acceptance, and enhancing one's objectivity and awareness were used effectively. They assisted the provider in this difficult encounter to compose a more therapeutic intervention.

Case #2

The Demanding, Self-Pitying, Dependent Patient

Name: Marcia Y.

Age: 56 years

Occupation: Secretary, law firm

Marital Status: Divorced

Diagnosis: Acute bacterial intestinal infection acquired on vacation to the West Indies approximately two weeks ago. No other diagnosable problems.

Outpatient treatment: Antibiotics to control infection. Lomotil to control diarrhea. Encourage bed rest and adequate diet.

CASE STUDY

This 56-year-old legal secretary is off work and on bed rest for an acute intestinal infection acquired during a vacation to the West Indies approximately two weeks ago. Although she has no other diagnosable problems, she complains of a variety of aches and pains and seeks reassurance that these signs are benign. She is being followed-up in the outpatient clinic for this infection.

Provider: "Hello, Marcia. I don't think I've met you yet. Dr. S____ and I practice together."

Patient: "Oh, yes, Dr. R____, I've heard of you. Where is Dr. S____?""

Provider: "He's out of the office today. So, how have you been doing?"

Patient: "I guess OK. I don't feel well though."

Provider: "What's going on?"

Patient: "I feel weak, tired. Sometimes I have pains . . . you know, last time Dr. S____ thought I might have something wrong with my back. I get pains between my shoulders. And, . . . "

Provider: (*Interrupts patient*) "Nothing in your chart about back pain, though. Let's see how you are doing with this infection you have."

Patient: "I've been feeling really guilty."

Provider: "About what?"

Patient: "Being off work for so long. Everything is piling up at the office. I've worked really hard to get the job I have now, and now I can't do it."

Provider: "I think in another week you'll feel well enough to go back to work."

Patient: "I don't know . . . do you really think so? What if this infection goes on longer than seven more days? This is serious—I thought I was going to die."

Provider: "You were pretty sick in the beginning. Seven more days though and you'll be able to get up and feel good about going back to work."

Patient: "I guess I worry too much. There is so much to worry about . . . You know I'm not 20 anymore. I'm weaker than I used to be."

Provider: "How do you mean, weaker?'

Patient: "I can't do that much. I sleep more. When I go home, I'll probably sleep for two days."

Provider: "Two days? Don't think so (*pats patient on arm*). I'm going to have the nurse come in to talk to you about your diet."

Patient: "You've been so kind, doctor. I guess I need reassurance. Other doctors don't take me seriously."

Provider: "We take you seriously."

Patient: "Yes . . . Before you go, do you think I should have X-rays of my spine? Maybe this infection will aggravate that back problem I have. It's probably a good idea, don't you think? Women my age have bone problems, and I'm worried that I could fall down and break a hip. That's all I need—an infection and broken hip at the same time."

Provider: "Marcia, I've got to see my next patient. Let's concentrate on getting you over this infection right now. I want you to come back in a week."

Patient: "OK Doctor, thank you. You're a good doctor, too. Will I see you next time?"

(*Physician exits room and does not respond to patient's last question. It is not clear whether he simply didn't hear the patient's question or whether he chose to ignore it.*)

ANALYSIS

This patient's general presentation was friendly and appreciative. She appeared eager to cooperate. Less obvious is this patient's multiple requests that resulted in the physician's spending more time on fictitious problems than expected. This patient wanted attention and was able to hold the physician's focus through a series of pleas to consider and reconsider potential somatic ailments. It is true that most of the symptoms she addressed were legitimate, with the exception of back pains, but she was not totally convinced that the back pains were insignificant. She used these problems to hold the attention of this physician. Her expressed reluctance to return to work raised the possibility that her current illness had some secondary gain. That is, she did not want to return to work, and because she was feeling guilty about not being at work, her symptoms and delayed recovery could function to legitimize her absence. Her response to the physician's reassurance that she could return to work soon was more of disappointment than relief. This patient's last request for attention, namely, her question about whether she would see this physician again, reflected her potential to engage the doctor in a special relationship not enjoyed by most patients.

This physician's responses were very typical. Initially, the physician attempted to meet the patient's need for attention. As the encounter progressed, however, he became aware that he would fail to provide the level of support she was asking for and that her medical needs, as she described them, were a result of her strong dependency needs. It became clear that reassurance about recovery was not what the patient sought. As the physician became progressively aware of this patient's dependent personality, he began to withdraw. His response on departure was to virtually ignore her last attempt to engage him in further discussions. Although one can only guess, this physician's thoughts and feelings upon leaving the room ("Will I see you next time?") may have included *I sure* hope *not! And, sorry I can't tell you that you have* another *problem—I know that's what you want to hear!* The end result reinforces the patient's fear, that the provider will reject her and any continuation of a helpful, supportive relationship is unlikely. That is, what the patient feared—rejection—is what she managed to achieve through her demanding, self-pitying interaction with the provider.

This provider showed respect for the patient's experience and exhibited high levels of patience in soliciting from the patient descriptions about her various concerns. Even when the patient clearly held onto false beliefs, the provider did not challenge her, express intolerance, or show irritation. Rather, reality was presented firmly, and her cooperation to work on getting better from the acute infection was presented as the appropriate objective. This focus set limits on the patient's attempts to distract the provider. Not responding to the expressed compliments in ways that would encourage a special relationship was also appropriate here.

The remaining issue here is how the provider could avert the ultimate outcome, irritation and rejection of the patient's pleas for attention. The answer to this dilemma is in his reflecting exactly what seems to be going on. Initially an open-ended question may be helpful, e.g., "Marcia, what's going on? You are continuing to talk about your back pain even after I told you there is no problem." This is a reflection about the process, not the content, of the encounter. These kinds of questions generally get through to patients at deeper levels. What will probably be discovered is that the patient's view of life is that small events can be overlooked and result in tragic outcomes; therefore, her need to dwell on what seem to be insignificant issues is understandable. Using an open-ended question actually invites the patient to talk about world views and basic premises underlying her life events. It also allows the provider an opening to discuss the differences in the patient's views (fears) and the reality of the situation. Had this conversation actually occurred, the provider may have felt more in control and less a victim of the patient's strong dependency needs.

CASE STUDY

Case #3

The Complaining, Manipulative Patient

Name: Howard R.

Age: 48 years

Occupation: Institutional stockbroker

Marital Status: Separated

Diagnosis: Diagnostic screening, possible MI.

Hospitalization: Bed rest, diagnostic work-up.

This 48-year-old institutional stockbroker is hospitalized with a possible myocardial infarction. He is on bed rest and undergoing several diagnostic tests. The provider in this case is a nurse who is caring for this patient and supervising the care of 16 patients on this unit.

Provider: "Well, Mr. R_____—it looks like you can get out of bed today. The doctor wrote orders for you to get up and begin to ambulate."

Patient: "Well, tell the doctor I'll get up later (*smiles at nurse*)."

Provider: "Because I need to help you, it's better we do it now."

Patient: "What's the results of all those tests?"

Provider: "I don't know. I have a big assignment today—it's hard to keep up on everything . . . Anyway, it's your doctor who will let you know."

Patient: "And who knows when that will be! Well, what about that blood test? It has something to do with my heart—what's the results of that test?"

Provider: "I know you want to hear about the results. It just isn't my place to tell you, even if I did know."

Patient: "Well what is your 'place'? Who are you, just the bath lady? I'll get up when I know the results of my test."

Provider: "I'm not the 'bath lady,' I'm a nurse. I guess you think that if you hold out in bed here you'll get what you want, but really, Mr. R____, I need to get you up."

Patient: "It doesn't make sense—how do I know it's OK when I don't know how my tests turned out? If I ran my business like they run this hospital, I'd be bankrupt in six months! Angiogram—that's what it was they did, an angiogram—how did that turn out?"

Provider: "Yes, you had an angiogram. Remember, your doctor will tell you."

Patient: "You know *something*—you've got to. You're not a robot . . . even though you act like one. How can you work in a place like this without knowing if it is safe to get a patient out of bed?"

Provider: "I know it is safe to get you out of bed, Mr. R____. Now let me help you . . . turn your legs around now . . . over the side of the bed."

Patient: (*Sitting on the edge of the bed*) "So, you do know the results. I hate to be difficult, but you know I need to know these things."

Provider: (*Assisting patient to wheelchair*) "I'm going to get a bath blanket to put across your legs—here . . . "

Patient: "I know you're trying to help . . . So my tests turned out OK, huh?"

Provider: "Yes . . . they're probably OK. As I said, I haven't looked at your chart yet this morning. Well, anyway, your doctor will be in to see you later this morning."

Patient: "He should have seen me before I was to get out of bed!"

ANALYSIS

It is obvious from an examination of this interaction that the patient was anxious about his test results and afraid of exciting himself in ways that would put him in jeopardy. It is also apparent that control is an issue for this man, who is accustomed to running a demanding and successful brokerage firm. He is sensitive to how work is organized and the way things should be done to maximize profits and production. He is also customarily in control as he directs the efforts of a staff of several people in his firm.

The overall presentation of the patient was hesitancy. He also attempted to "bargain" for information, implying that he would cooperate if he got what he wanted (test results). He paid little attention to the nurse's statements about the scope of her practice, suggesting that he did not believe her descriptions and did not really care about protocol. He used several responses to try to get what he wanted. He complained about not being informed. He challenged the basis of the nurse's actions. He bargained, i.e., "I'll get out of bed when I find out my test results." He attempted to get the nurse to elaborate by offering suspicions and waiting for the nurse to respond.

The issue in this case is not whether the patient is correct in his judgments, rather, it is the patient's need to trust providers and hospital procedures and comply with his treatment. Patients of this type can cause an uproar on a service very quickly because they seem to have legitimate complaints and they insist that procedures be done their way.

The provider responded appropriately in several ways. First, the nurse described the role of the physician and the nursing staff in his care. Limits were set on the patient's attempts to manipulate the nurse to tell him the test results. Further, reflective statements, e.g., "I know you want to hear about the results" were used instead of angry, hostile replies. The nurse redirected the patient to the task at hand (getting out of bed) rather than being entrapped in defensive replies to insulting remarks about, for example, being "the bath lady" or being just a "robot." The patient, however, got a partial answer by deducing that he must be "OK." And while the nurse could have expressed frustration, she conceded. Who won here? Did the patient get what he wanted? Did the nurse get what she wanted? And, at what lengths did both need to go to get these results? While it could be said that the patient won out over the nurse, in reality, the nurse won because she finally got the patient out of bed and into the wheelchair, thus fulfilling doctor's orders. It is likely that this patient will continue to want to direct his care and that he will utilize similar manipulative strategies to achieve this. And with other more harried nurses the results may not turn out as they did in this case. Patients who complain and also manipulate providers can create a great deal of anger and resentment. Experience will show that angry or hostile remarks to these patients will likely result in battlefield conditions wherein control is the central issue. Providers must remember to identify the underlying meaning before choosing an appropriate therapeutic response.

CONCLUSION

Of all the provider's communications, encounters that present the most challenges are those with difficult patients. In the high-stress environment of health care delivery systems, the demands of providing care are complicated many times over by problems with difficult patients, families, and even difficult co-workers. These problems create feelings of frustration, tension, and sometimes stronger feelings of anger and disgust.

Patients and their families are facing moderate-to-severe levels of distress due to the multiplicity of stressors that accompany illness and injury. They may respond in ways far removed from their customary reactions or more negative personality attributes, and even transient long-standing psychological problems could surface. A person who is usually cooperative, receptive, and responsible may present as complaining, demanding, and difficult to please. These individuals may actually feel frightened and helpless. Still other patients who are predisposed to reactions such as self-pity and dependency will manifest these personality tendencies in heightened ways. The behaviors that patients exhibit are frequently difficult for providers to deal with and may even surprise the patients as well.

The key to dealing with difficult behaviors in therapeutic ways lies in providers' abilities to respond, not react, to the communications of these patients. The crucial condition is engaging in an analysis of the patients' behavior wherein underlying meanings (hidden thoughts, feelings, and attitudes) are understood. Replies can then reflect both a reluctance to response match and thoughtful consideration of the patients' circumstances.

Perhaps the most difficult of all difficult patient behaviors are those that provoke providers to retaliate angrily or to withdraw. Examples of these behaviors are aggression, demands, complaints, and/or manipulation. Therefore, it is important to anticipate such responses and think intelligently about how one would respond to these behaviors. Providers can prepare for these communications by observing conversations between providers and patients and by identifying specific behaviors and attitudes that have a negative impact on them. Providers can expect fearful patients to behave in demanding ways, families to be critical of their relative's care, and co-workers to be on edge. Expectations of patients, their families, and co-workers should be appropriately viewed in the context of difficult situations. Appropriate guidelines and the providers' use of therapeutic response modes will considerably decrease the toll that difficult behavioral responses have on provider encounters.

PART IV

Beyond Patient-Provider Encounters: Managing Communications within and across Relevant Constituencies

The very dynamic that makes the health care system work is the very thing that can torpedo good communication. That is, a quality health care system is a series of layers—layers upon layers upon layers. The overwhelming number of constituents in any given case is mind-boggling.

The numbers, kinds, and levels of health care providers in managed care situations are almost beyond imagination. Each has a commitment and responsibility to serve the patient. Their service is complicated by the fact that they must have a common vocabulary and must view situations similarly. And, if that were not enough, they must design appropriate means or procedures for communicating among providers and for formulating and implementing decisions. In Chapter 15, Communications within and across Health Care Provider Groups, group interpersonal communication skills are discussed. Since providers make decisions in the context of group dynamics, it is important to understand the development and character of healthy group communication. Because many providers will be both members of and leaders of these teams, skill at recognizing and averting dysfunctional group communication patterns is also important.

Chapter 16, Conflict in the Health Care System: Understanding Communications and Resolving Dispute, describes the qualities of communication that are characterized by conflict. This communication includes interactions on a continuum from minimally helpful to disruptive. Negotiation and conflict resolution are discussed as potential solutions to conflicts and as restorative steps in cases where communication seems hopeless.

Finally, Chapter 17, Family Dynamics and Communications with Patients' Significant Others, addresses the constituency that rarely simply "sits on the sidelines." Families differ a great deal in their constellation, as do support networks in their complexity. Whatever the makeup, the "family" is a relevant constituency that must be considered. It is not simply another layer; rather, the family is pivotal in achieving successful medical outcomes. As such, we must concern ourselves with how the family adapts. Significant others, particularly families, have the power to represent the patient in affairs of health and illness. Communicating effectively with families, even beyond the immediate patient-provider encounter, is nonetheless critical to the outcome of care and the dynamics of the therapeutic alliance.

CHAPTER 15

Communications within and across Health Care Provider Groups

United we stand, divided we fall.

Aesop

CHAPTER OBJECTIVES

- Discuss the pervasiveness of groups, particularly in health care delivery systems.
- Outline phases of group process and corresponding communication patterns.
- Describe functional and dysfunctional communication patterns in groups, especially in problem-solving groups.
- Identify and describe common group communication problems, e.g., conflict and the inability to solve problems.
- Discuss several ways in which communication in groups can be improved.
- Discuss the phenomena that problems occur among groups, not only within a single group.

Providers interact in the context of group relationships. The substance of group relationships is human discourse. This includes the verbal and nonverbal transmission of both explicit and implicit messages. Human discourse is made up of a series of dynamic messages that characterize both a specific level of functioning and an evolving group process. Any work group has a defined content and process.

In health care systems, we are always interacting in group contexts. These groups include peer, multidisciplinary, patient, and consumer groups. Some communications in groups are productive; they facilitate goal and task achievement and they meet members' needs for a sense of belonging. Other group communications are nonproductive; they display an inability to define and/or achieve aims. Their communication is marked by conflict, apathy, and the inability to make decisions. A dysfunctional group frustrates its members and expends a great deal of energy in nonproductive communication. Providers should be able to diagnose group communication problems, interrupt dysfunctional interactions, and facilitate functional communication patterns. As in any work group, a finely tuned team of providers can accomplish much more than the total individual efforts of its members. Professional work groups can be enjoyable and personally satisfying for most providers.

THE PERVASIVE NATURE OF GROUPS

Groups involve three or more people involved in face-to-face interactions. Typically, that which governs this interaction is the achievement of personal or commonly held objectives. The perception of interdependency among group members is the glue that keeps these individuals communicating with one another. Groups are, indeed, found everywhere. Human interaction is characterized by small-group constellations.

Types of Groups

We spend a significant proportion of our personal and work lives in groups. On the personal level, these include family, friends, neighborhoods, and communities. Reference groups are those groups to which we belong that typically represent an aspect of our personal lives. Reference groups include religious, ethnic, gender, and age groups. In our professional relationships, we belong to a number of task groups. Task groups include peer or multidisciplinary teams. Reference and task groups differ in that reference groups may not engage in specific tasks or goal achievement in the same way that task groups do. Task groups are work groups whose primary purpose is the completion of some objective. They focus on the specifics of the task(s) at hand and on getting the job done. Task groups can serve as reference groups but usually their affiliation is more transient. For example, we could say that we are members of a continuous quality-improvement committee. We may identify with the objectives of the group and, in some arenas, reflect the goals and values of this committee. This task group serves as a reference group when we develop strong identification with the group. Such groups, however, rarely serve as permanent reference groups that constitute a standard against which we evaluate ourselves. We pay particular attention to our official reference groups because of their universal and long-standing impact on our lives.

Still another way of conceptualizing groups is through the designation "formal" or "informal." Formal groups within an institutional setting are reflected in organizational charts, policies, and procedures. Informal groups function in more oblique ways such as those that influence needs, values, attitudes, expectations, traditions, group norms, and communication (the grapevine.)

Informal groups are made up of three or more individuals whose purpose is primarily to meet the affiliation needs of its members. The cliché, "people need people," describes the motivation behind the establishment of informal groups. Informal groups are always observed in organizations. If we were to investigate an organization such as a hospital or a large medical center, we would find a number of loosely formed social groups. Information, support, and a sense of belonging are generally the outcomes that motivate people to form informal groups. Within the formal structure of the organization, then, are a number of affiliations that create what has come to be known as the informal channels of communication. Informal groups can cross peer and professional lines. Because receiving and exchanging information for personal advantage is so key to these groups, informal groups rely heavily on face-to-face, regular encounters wherein they share the latest gossip, speculation about administrative decisions, and information that enhances personal power. Some group theorists attribute a great deal of influence to informal groups and informal channels of communication.

The second type of group is the formal group. Also known as task groups, these groups are organized around institutional aims. More often than not, they have specific delineated objectives and procedures for reaching their goals. They possess authority, are accountable for their actions, and are generally regarded as having both official sanction and an area of recognized influence. They also display hierarchal arrangements, governing relationships, and influence within their membership.

Phases of Group Development

Some people find that the interactions that go on in groups are very mysterious. Groups, however, can be both complex and easily understood. An important way to understand groups is through the concepts of task, process, and stages of development. A group's *task* is an important feature. The content (task) that the group is working on is usually the reason that the group exists and this purpose should be readily discernible. The second facet that is important to understand is the *process* of the group. The term *process* refers to the manner in which the group works together. The process of the group may not be readily apparent, because it refers to the interpersonal relationships within the group and the sequential interaction as it unfolds from meeting to meeting.

It is commonly understood that groups also proceed through various stages of development. Some theorists speak of phases and subphases, others of stages and substages. Inherent in this notion about groups is the observation that groups can vary a great deal depending on how long the group has been in existence. This idea is not difficult to accept at face value. Most of us, even those of us who are not sophisticated in diagnosing group process, would notice differences in communications. Those groups newly formed, we would note, remain relatively superficial in their discussions. Newly formed task groups may cling to the task, while established task groups are not threatened by an occasional discussion of the personal lives of its members.

In actuality, there are many theories that describe how groups develop over time. These theories range from complex mathematical models to theories that are grounded in the practical aspects of the behavioral sciences.

Whether one ascribes to a simple conceptual model or to a more complex multiphasal model of how groups change over time, it is important, as health care providers working on teams and task groups, to understand that communication can differ a great deal. One factor known to significantly influence the depth and nature of communications is the developmental stage of the group.

Functional versus Dysfunctional Communication and Problem Solving in Groups

Groups, and particularly group communication, can be described as functional or dysfunctional.

In all likelihood, groups perform somewhere on a continuum of functionality. Usually if a group is proceeding smoothly toward its goals and attendance and morale is high, the group is regarded as functional. In contrast, groups that appear to be in conflict are arrested in their goal achievements, and groups whose membership fluctuates significantly are categorized as dysfunctional. By definition, we know that if a task group is not successful, it is not a good working group. Groups that are not successful generally have low morale and poor attendance. Still it is difficult to say if these are the consequences of poor group functioning. They may, in fact, be precipitant. Consider, for example, a team that is established to evaluate the cost-effectiveness of using nurses to perform minor suturing in the emergency room. The hospital's administration established a task force that consists of a variety of disciplines. Only one-third of the membership, however, is truly invested in the issue. The other two-thirds of the membership believe that a task force is not necessary, really does not care about the outcomes or decisions that are reached, do not have time to meet, and/or are not directly affected by the results of any decisions made by the task force. The group is dysfunctional because attendance is poor. It is not that the members are unable to make decisions or could not deliberate successfully and suggest a proposal, this same group of individuals may have worked extremely well together on other task forces. Nonetheless, we would judge the group to be dysfunctional.

Although that which comprises a healthy group is often unclear, organizational theorists generally agree that there are several attributes that are indicative of functional groups.

- The group process encourages and enables work to be done; it does not prevent it.
- The group reflects the individual knowledge and expertise of individuals and control and influence is equally distributed.
- The members of the group are clearly supportive of the group as a whole.
- The members come up with sufficient good and novel ideas and suggestions to keep the group working successfully toward its goals.
- The members evaluate their relationships in the group as supportive and constructive.
- The leader(s) take their roles and responsibilities seriously.
- The members know the goals and procedures that will meet group aims and have the resources to reach group goals.
- The members experience an appropriate level of feedback and rewards for goal attainment.
- The member's personal effectiveness is valued; individuals grow and develop as a result of their group involvement.

DIAGNOSING GROUP COMMUNICATION PROBLEMS

The ability to judge group effectiveness is critical to our roles on teams, particularly as we establish a leadership position within these work groups.

Group problems have been described by many theorists. One conceptualization that has practical relevance to work groups is described by Bradford, Stock, and Horowitz (1978, pp. 94–104). Essentially, the three common group communication problems are identified as conflicts or fights, apathy and nonparticipation, and inadequate decision making.

Conflicts, Fights, and Disagreements

In actuality, what is meant by conflict, fights, and disagreements is not shouting matches and fist fights; rather, it is the presence of disagreements, argumentation, nasty comments, and conflict. Member encounters are uncomfortable, and usually the atmosphere is tense.

Bradford, Stock, and Horowitz (1978) enumerate eleven ways in which fighting occurs in groups.

1. Members behaving impatiently toward others.
2. Ideas are criticized before they are even completely expressed.

3. Members polarize and take sides, refusing to compromise.
4. Members disagree openly on plans, objectives, and suggestions without resolving these disagreements.
5. Comments and suggestions are forcefully presented with a great deal of vehemence.
6. Members attack each other on a personal level and in subtle ways.
7. Members discredit the group, e.g., insisting that the group does not have the ability or knowledge to accomplish tasks.
8. Members feel that there is something about the group, e.g., its size, that keeps it from accomplishing tasks.
9. Members consistently disagree with the leader's ideas or suggestions.
10. Members are openly critical of one another, particularly of their inability to understand real issues.
11. Rather than hearing and understanding comments, members hear distorted fragments of other's communications.

As these authors suggest, there may be several reasons for this dysfunctional interaction. For example, the task group may have been given an impossible goal, and members are frustrated because they feel inadequate in meeting the demands on them. Smaller groups such as committees within larger organizations may have this problem because they feel that they have too few members or the specifics have not been sufficiently made known to them. At other times, they may perceive that they have been asked to work on a problem, but they do not have sufficient power or influence to sell their ideas. Any one of these predicaments can cause frustration and irritation and promote bickering and arguments within the group.

A second explanation is that the main purpose of members attending group meetings is not to work toward goals but to "flex some muscle." That is, the main concern for members is to establish their status in the group. Consider, for example, a chief-of-staff in a multidisciplinary meeting. This physician feels the need to comment on every suggestion or issue before the group. It is as if the group cannot proceed toward closure on any issue before it hears from the chief-of-staff. Bradford, Stock, and Horowitz (1978) suggest that some members use issues to establish alignments and subgroups or to suppress the power of others. Under these circumstances, members may disagree with each other or oppose a certain solution just to flex muscle. Power struggles often predominate and stifle group movement. Group leaders are usually drawn into these power struggles, which sometimes are an attempt to dethrone the appointed group leader.

Sometimes groups are fraught with conflict because certain members are loyal to other groups that have conflicting points of view or interests. This might be the case, for example, if members of the multidisciplinary team on the emergency room task force have dual interests and are loyal to some other group. The most cost-effective solutions may not fit with the ideals and interests of the members' own professional group. If the nurses on the task force realize the best solution but evaluate it as opposing the best interests of nurses in the hospital, they may not know whether to respond as a committee member or in keeping with their professional alliance with other hospital nurses. In the group, these members may vacillate on issues or express confusing ideals. Occasionally, their expressed alliances to groups outside the task force may be made forcefully and they may be labeled as disruptive because of their irritation or stubbornness. Blatant opposition may be interspersed with expressions of passive resentment or refusals to cooperate. One response of the group may be to "blackball" these members, recognizing that it is difficult to work cooperatively alongside them.

Still, another explanation for conflict and disagreement is the honest, high-level involvement that members feel in relation to the task and their hard-working attempts to solve problems surrounding the task or goals. Rather than feeling uninvolved in the outcome, they feel that they have a really high stake in any solutions proposed by the group. Impatience, irritability, or disagreement may reflect their overinvolvement. Interestingly enough, their behavior may appear to others as disruptive of the goal. Others may come down "heavy" on their attitudes and outspokenness. To some extent, the group cannot handle emotions of these most dedicated and committed members. If other members engage these members in dialogue and the group moves further along in its goals, the group remains functional. If, however, interpersonal struggles take the place of needed problem solving, the group can fall prey to ongoing dysfunctional communication problems.

Imagine a group where some members are overinvolved and are expressing irritation in the group. And, suppose the leader or chairperson gets angry at those individuals and criticizes their behavior in the group. Not only will these members be misunderstood but it is very likely that the group will lose confidence in the leader for his or her improper diagnosis and response. Rather than express criticism, it would be important to interpret the member's concerns with acknowledgement, e.g., "Phil, I know you have a big investment in this issue—whatever we decide will affect just about everyone in your department." In this way, the leader addresses Phil's behavior with understanding and acceptance by engaging Phil in cooperative dialogue on the issues.

In assessing conflict and disagreement, leaders must decipher the underlying issues and motivation. It is these dynamics that should be addressed, not necessarily the behavioral symptoms of conflict. As suggested by Bradford, Stock, and Horowitz (1978), one cannot completely understand the behavior in a group without understanding the context; behaviors are symptoms, they are not the real problem.

Nonparticipation and Apathy

The opposite of overinvolvement in a group is, of course, underinvolvement. Underinvolvement, also evidenced as apathy, absence, and nonparticipation, is detrimental to group communication. Frequently, dysfunctional groups are typified by high levels of apathy, and unfortunately, apathy occurs more often than we would like to think. Individual members, as well as entire groups, may suffer from apathy and underinvolvement at various levels. Additionally, groups can go through "dry" periods where productivity has slowed and the group lapses into periods of inactivity. As suggested previously, not all group members will be convinced that a given task or objective is worthy or has relevance to them. Apathy can appear as complete boredom or a lack of enthusiasm or a failure to mobilize energy toward the task. Some members may show a lack of consistent action; others will appear to be content with low-level performances.

If we were to walk into a group that we had never before attended, we would quickly be able to determine both the level of apathy in the group as a whole and the level of enthusiasm in individual members. Verbal and nonverbal behaviors that suggest positive interactions might include verbal exchanges between many members and attempts to clarify communication showing interest. On the other hand, verbal and nonverbal behaviors that might suggest apathy include silence, yawning or dozing off, distractibility, absences or lateness, restlessness, frivolous decision making, failure to follow through on decisions, early adjournment, and reluctance to take on more responsibility. These groups display low levels of decision making and responsibility. We probably would label this group as "deadbeat," "boring," or "going nowhere." It is true that apathy and boredom can overtake any group. Some groups, however, seem to be more apathetic than others. An apathetic group also reflects the quality of the group leadership. Generally speaking, groups need an enthusiastic, inspirational leader—an individual with vision and direction—to establish and maintain interest and morale and to overcome periodic apathetic phases.

As with anger in the group, we should treat apathy as merely a symptom of an underlying problem. Bradford, Stock, and Horowitz (1978) identify several underlying causes for apathy in a workplace. These include: (1) lack of investment in the problem or task of the group, (2) barriers to arriving at solutions to the problem, (3) inadequate approaches or procedures to address the problem, (4) a sense of powerlessness over final decisions, and (5) prolonged conflict that has significantly affected the group over time.

In many kinds of situations, members feel that they have had no part in initiating a program or project or in establishing its priority. Under these circumstances, members approach problems as if they were imposed on them. They may regard them and the group's activity as meaningless busy work. Apathy can be even more predominant if the tasks have little or no relationship to members' perceived needs or concerns. There may be members who are more immediately involved and committed, but a core of apathetic, disinterested members can bring the whole group to a standstill.

Sometimes members are given responsibilities but feel conflicted about fulfilling them. Sometimes this is a case of subordinates making decisions that they feel would be unpopular. Consider, for example, technicians on staff who are asked to revise policies. If these policies are controversial, then any decision—one way or the other—will be met with disapproval from some professionals or administrators.

Groups rarely want to assume accountability for actions or decisions when the information or resources to solve the problem are inadequate. Group members usually see this as an inadvertent or deliberate set-up for failure. If, for example, a team of cardiologists who were interested in establishing an adequate teaching program for their postsurgery patients assigned the responsibility to their nursing staff but could not supply the task force with essential information, the group would falter. The problem would be multiplied if the physician group did not communicate with the task force because a basis for mutual understanding between the task force and the physicians would not exist.

Most of the time providers are assigned tasks they can complete. However, sometimes health care providers are assigned to task groups, but they feel that they will make no real headway on the assigned problem. This may be because their recommendations are not really valued or because the real decisions have already been made. This happened to the staff on a geriatric inpatient and outpatient service. They were to establish a project for continued quality improvement. They met to deliberate but over time grew to realize that the supervisory group was really not invested in implementing their recommendations. They became suspicious that this assignment was a response to an anticipated review by the Joint Commission on Accreditation of Healthcare Organizations (Joint Commission). They were expected to go through the motions, but no serious attempt to change patient care was intended.

Status and authority differences within a group can also create the feeling that whatever contributions members make will not be heard or heeded. On occasion, one member, and it may or may not be the officially appointed leader of the group, will dominate the group process. Sometimes, rather than a single dominant member, there will be a specific subgroup that monopolizes the group's meetings. In cases such as these, other members experience group communication as restricted because only the views of a select few will influence decisions.

In some cases, competition within the group can serve to provoke others to speak or may alienate quiet or passive members who may withdraw even further. Competition in a group can be healthy, however, but when it is prolonged, it may cause a sense of helplessness and powerlessness that leads to significant disenchantment or apathy among noncompetitive members.

Inability To Make Decisions

Decision making in a group is not always easy because communication in groups can be quite complicated. Groups seem to have to progress through stages of development that correspond to members' interpersonal needs. Sometimes satisfactory decisions come easily, other times, especially early in the life of a group, they are hard to come by. Reasons for inadequate or incomplete decision making are many. Certainly problems such as anger and apathy influence decision-making capabilities in a group.

At other times groups are confronted with decisions that are too difficult, for instance, when members are pressured to make decisions too early or when the group has not jelled sufficiently to feel comfortable with the results of their deliberations. Certainly, no group of health care professionals wants to make what is deemed "a premature decision." Premature decision making is regarded as very risky. Therefore, asking a group of providers to come to a quick decision based on inadequate data stands in opposition to their customary approach to issues. These decisions may be perceived as potentially threatening. A fear of being wrong or of creating unclear and undesired consequences can be the result.

Signs that groups are manifesting an inability to make decisions include indecisiveness, repetitive discussions, or attempts to shift the decisions to some other group. The discussion may wander or be filled with hypothetical situations. Sometimes, just as the group appears to be reaching consensus, the group will argue that no real agreement exists or some members will disown responsibility for the decisions and a new task group may be established.

IMPROVING COMMUNICATION IN GROUPS

Several important factors contribute to successful communication in professional work groups. Among many discussions of group leadership, that which seems to surface first and foremost is an awareness of self and others.

Self and Others Understanding

Self-awareness is not only extremely important in one-to-one encounters with patients, patients' families, and other providers, it is also essential to successful participation in professional work groups.

Becoming a valuable contributor to a work group is important; our leadership and membership capabilities determine the success of the group. We can actively influence movement in the group through our own self-awareness. Self-understanding includes our awareness of how we relate to others—the impact we have on others, our strengths and weaknesses, and how we use these in a group context. It is critical that we first understand our own personal reactions to key interpersonal issues. These are our feelings and reactions to interdependency, interpersonal intimacy, and authority. For example, how do we respond to others wanting to know personal details about us? If others were to attempt to shape, direct, or control our attitudes and behavior, how would we respond? If we were asked to take on a leadership position in a group, necessitating our directing others, how would we respond? Having been assigned to work cooperatively toward a group goal, what behaviors would we exhibit?

One method of analyzing our current or potential behavior is to examine how we have responded in past relationships, particularly those within small groups. Our current behavior and ways of communicating in a group have indeed been influenced by our first primary group, our family. Depending on our birth order, for example, we may or may not exhibit leadership behavior. Still, the dynamics within our family contributed to our behavior; perhaps we learned to placate authority figures in order to get our needs met. Communication within our family may have been sparse, rigid, and guarded. Or, communication among members of our family and ourselves may have been marked with openness, honesty, and trust. In either case, this experience has shaped our current communication styles in groups, and we may not be totally aware of this fact or the ways in which we reflect our early beginnings. One way of establishing self-awareness is to ask some very personal questions about early communication patterns within our families, both within the family as a whole and within specific dyadic relationships, e.g., between oneself and an older sibling.

A second approach to self-awareness in groups is to diagnose our communication in relationship to role theory. Group roles have been the subject of a great deal of social-science research. One model of viewing member roles is to classify these roles as either self-oriented or group-oriented.

Behaviors that primarily serve an individual's needs or interests without regard to the needs or interests of the group are self-oriented roles. The self-oriented member may communicate in a self-protective manner, which includes withholding data or communicating defensively. He or she may also manifest self-importance by establishing and proclaiming self-value at whatever cost. Self-adulation, then, is a predominate feature of this member's verbalizations.

In contrast to self-oriented communication styles are behaviors that are typically relevant to the fulfillment of the purpose of the group. These behaviors may be either group-maintenance or group-task focused. That is to say, both are group oriented but they differ in that group-maintenance roles tend to satisfy only the interpersonal needs of members. For example, rendering positive feedback is morale enhancing. It does not relate directly to goal or task achievement but is the important glue that keeps the group enthusiastically centered on its task. Behaviors such as initiating new topics, providing information, summarizing group opinion, and taking minutes are all directed at helping the group achieve its goal. Specifically, members who define problems; suggest procedures for solving problems; offer ideas, facts, or information to clarify ideas; explore alternatives; restate areas of consensus; and maintain a record of group ideas and suggestions move the group toward its ultimate goal. To what extent does one choose behaviors or communications that maintain the group or move it toward its stated goals?

Another approach that one can use to analyze our own and others' behaviors in a work group is to examine our responses to group leadership. Whether our work groups are teams, committees, or ad-hoc task forces, the nature of leadership influences our communications within the group. The leadership may be democratic or autocratic. Despite common belief, not all members will prefer democratic-participative leadership styles over more autocratic ones. And some group tasks are more adequately addressed by autocratic styles. Generally speaking, the more dependent one is on a leader's direction, rules, and disciplinary action, the more comfortable one will be with an autocratic leadership style. A very autocratic leader will make decisions and define rules; concomitantly, a member who is comfortable with an autocratic style finds it difficult to function without procedures and feedback from the leader. In contrast, a leader who encourages group decision making and simply acts as a coordinator will be most acceptable to members who tend to be self-starters and who do not need or seek close supervision.

Just how one responds to a leader's approach, as well as one's own leadership styles will influence interaction within a group. Understanding others' responses includes knowing their value systems and personal goals, their relevant skills and past experiences, that which motivates them, and how they perceive others in the group. Understanding the group as a whole includes knowing the experience and capability of the members, the existing interpersonal relationships among team members, the cohesiveness and morale in the group, and the group's level of functioning.

Reporting Assessments to the Group Members

Examining communication patterns within a work group is not only a common method that is used to study group behavior, it has potential sound effects on a group's process. Just what is important to observe and note?

How well a group is functioning is determined by gathering a variety of data about the verbal and nonverbal behavior that occurs in groups. The data of interest include:

- individual members' verbal and nonverbal communications

- spatial and seating arrangements that depict attitudes toward the group or selected members
- common themes expressed by the group, e.g., frustration with the task
- the pattern of communication in the group, e.g., who talks to whom and how frequently
- the quality of listening that occurs
- the level and quality of problem solving that occurs in the group

Through observing these aspects of the group's communication one can diagnose interpersonal conflict and the quality of decision making. Additionally, these observations will give insight about both the roles that members assume and the presence of competition.

To effectively monitor and facilitate group members, it is important to understand the roles that members assume. Role is the position a member takes with respect to the problem-solving process within the group. Each group role has certain expected behaviors and responsibilities. Much of what we report to a group is intimately linked with observations of role behavior. In addition to the identities that a member has outside the group, each member exhibits behavior that is typical of a group role. For example, a member may assume or be assigned the role of record keeper. Role selection and enactment is influenced by individual and group characteristics such as the individual personality or character of the member, the specific task and size of the group, the character of group interaction, and the position or status of individuals in the group. These roles can be of three kinds: (1) group maintenance, (2) group-task roles, or (3) self-oriented individual roles not related to group functioning.

There are many ways in which data can be compiled. Different kinds of observations yield different kinds of information. For example, much can be gleamed from observing who talks to whom. It is possible to diagram interactions in a group over a given period and by this method identify problems. Consider, for example, that in one 15-minute segment 45 statements were made, with the largest proportion being made by the leader of the group. Few statements were made by members and only one-eighth of the statements were members' comments to other members. Given this pattern, we might conclude that the group was in a beginning stage of development and functioning at a low level with an autocratic leadership style.

Additionally, we could study the kinds of contributions that were made by the leader and the members. Perhaps the majority of statements were made to challenge the advisability of the group's making a decision. Together with our appraisal of what happened in the group and our appraisal of the quantity and quality of work that was accomplished, we have a pretty sound picture of the level of functioning in the group at this time (see Exhibit 15–1).

Groups need to include feedback mechanisms that evaluate and improve their effectiveness. This process of feedback is facilitated by directed observations. It is not enough just to make observations, the products of these observations must be fed back to the group.

Certain guidelines are suggested for feeding information back to the group. It is important to realize that groups, like individuals, have a low tolerance for negative feedback. Also, like individuals, they may not be receptive to feedback at the time you are ready to share your observations. Bradford, Stock, and Horowitz (1978) suggest two guidelines. First, one should be sensitive to the kinds of information that the group is ready to hear. It is important to assess what will be most helpful to the group now, rather than what was the most startling or interesting observation made. Second, it is important not to overload the group with observations. If too much information is presented, a group, like an individual, will not be able to put it to good use. One should present one or two observations and let the group assimilate this information. For example, it might be important to share an observation about the group's having difficulty in making a decision and the speculation that many facts are not yet known, which prevents the group from feeling confident about any chosen direction. Once this observation is brought to the group and discussed, members may understand their barriers to decision making.

It is also important to gauge evaluative comments of a critical or rewarding nature. Critical, negative comments are usually received as judgments of below-

---

Exhibit 15–1 Information Pertinent to Group Effectiveness

1. What is the group's goal? How successful is the group in keeping to the goals and/or aims of the group?
2. Where is the group in the process of decision making: i.e., the stage of discovery, analyzing, suggesting, or testing solutions?
3. What barriers are affecting the group's task performance? How severely is the group affected by these barriers?
4. Is the group using the most effective measures and/or procedures to accomplish its work?
5. Is the membership participating equally in accomplishing goals and in taking actions, or are a small number of individuals doing the majority of the work?
6. How are members getting along together? Are they resolving differences?
7. What are members' opinions of and attitudes toward the group, its effectiveness, and the leadership?

standard performance. Sometimes those that make the comments are viewed as "superior" or "above it all." It is also possible to praise the group so much that growth does not occur. When it comes to commenting on individuals' communication styles, it is better to discuss behaviors in general as they relate to goal attainment. It is too easy for members to perceive evaluative comments as individual attacks or favoritism; thus, placing the emphasis on behaviors to accomplish goals takes the emphasis off individual shortcomings or strengths.

Planning Group Performance Change

Once one or more members presents their views of the functional capacities of the group, thoughtful consideration of what the group should do can occur. But, for this to happen, a full discussion of group strengths and limitations must come first.

The group is no different from an individual who contemplates certain weaknesses in communicating. Members should review evaluations and determine the extent to which there is group consensus about barriers in communication. The group should also be encouraged to examine the reasons for poor communication behavior. As indicated previously, many group behaviors are merely symptoms of larger, more profound problems. It is important to discover these problems. Finally, the group should move toward solutions about what to do with the communication problems that they have uncovered. What corrective measures need to be taken or what new directions should be sought? Unless the group can successfully utilize the feedback it has elicited through the observations of members who are more astute as to group process, the overall functioning of the group will not improve.

Modeling Good Group Communication Skills

What groups need most are members who can model functional communication. First and foremost, communicating effectively in groups in ways that will positively influence members depends on a particular style of interaction.

A variety of good group communication skills has already been suggested. In general, they include skills in the areas of receiving, processing, and sending. Sending clear messages, speaking clearly and thoughtfully, avoiding stereotyping, maintaining good listening posture, expressing oneself honestly, listening carefully, and qualifying or clarifying vague statements are important principles of effective communications in groups. It should be noted that *climate* or feeling tone in a group is extremely important because in general, supportive climates promote effective problem solving, while defensive or aggressive climates impede good problem solving.

The dominant motivation behind defensive communication is power and control. Defensive communication is easily recognized because it is often designed to persuade or sway the beliefs of others. Even if the member or leader appears to be friendly and open, the basic drive is to persuade or direct others. Strategy and superiority predominate.

Supportive communication, however, promotes group involvement in discussions and decision making. The dominant goal behind supportive communication is understanding. Contrasting positions on issues are not threatening because new and meaningful outcomes can be a result of different views. Members truly seek meaningful dialogue, to listen actively, and to explore and appreciate differences in opinion.

The results of supportive communication styles are very different from those of defensive styles. Rather than persuasion and control, members attempt to understand others' views. Empathy and mutual problem solving characterize members' statements. Supportive climates make room for the resolution of differences that are bound to exist in any group. Active listening in a climate of mutual trust and support not only yields good communication, it is necessary for high productivity and the achievement of group goals.

Although supportive communication styles seem straightforward and simple, they are often difficult to practice for many reasons. First, cultural training may be a major barrier. Second, emphasis on competition and individual achievement, reinforced by professional values, may inhibit one's abilities to establish supportive climates. As professional providers, we are rewarded for arriving at independent decisions, for being right. We are also rewarded for developing skills of persuasion. Although this varies across disciplines, less attention may have been given to teaching us the attitudes of acceptance and understanding. Therefore, it is important as health care providers that we nurture and protect our inherent abilities for supportive communication.

If, in fact, supportive communication occurred naturally and consistently, then we would not need to model these behaviors. In addition to our own inherent limitations, barriers exist in the context of our work environments. The chief and foremost barrier is lack of time or energy. Creating and maintaining a positive milieu takes work. The team or work group must deliberately assume responsibility for developing an atmosphere that facilitates understanding because it is often easier to respond superficially or inappropriately to what is being said or discussed. At least one member must see to it that the group responds to what is actually being said. Supportive communication also includes some risk. To the extent that we are threatened by others' opinions and communications, we will not always perceive them accurately.

Finally, it is difficult to model supportive communications when we are not feeling good about ourselves. Feelings of anger and hostility will also inhibit our abilities to genuinely express support. Our basic inclinations are to be critical and negative, which further limits mutual understanding.

There are five essentials to facilitating supportive communication. First, an environment valuing mutual exchange must be established. Second, active listening is important. Third, grasping the full meaning (both fact and feelings) of what other members are saying, though not easy, must take place because discipline and role differences as well as status and authority discrepancies can create barriers to openness in provider groups. Fourth, clarifying and checking out messages is essential. Finally, avoiding insecurities prohibits peer-to-peer exchange.

Dealing with Problem Group Members

Supportive communication is generally a sound technique in dealing with most group members. The idea is that supportive communications will facilitate group dialogue, and when response matching occurs, supportive communication will form the basis of member-to-member encounters. There are some instances, however, where supportive responses are inappropriate or not useful. When we think about members whose behavior causes problems in the group, we will want to intervene to modify this behavior. Support in such cases may serve to reinforce behaviors that we really want to change.

Steps toward changing members' response patterns begin with a self-inventory. That is, as a witness to this behavior, how do you feel and what makes you feel this way? Examining your specific reactions will help define the problem behavior, i.e., is the member distracting the group from its purpose, challenging the authority of the leadership, seeking special attention, or resisting involvement? Also, what outcomes occur as a result, i.e., is the member's behavior rewarded, punished, or simply ignored? How are other members responding to these problem behaviors? Are they reacting similarly or differently from you? And does the behavior warrant intervention, and if so, from whom?

As in dealing with specific problem behaviors in patients, there are also specific communications that are advisable in group settings with group member problems. In Exhibit 15–2 several problematic group behaviors are listed along with appropriate leadership responses. Problem behaviors included here are: (1) the aggressive, (2) the silent/withdrawn, (3) the shy to fragile, (4) the domineering/dominating, (5) the attention-getter/clown, and (6) the bored/detached member.

INTERGROUP PROBLEMS

While communication problems clearly appear, disappear, and reappear within a group, these problems transcend group boundaries. Intergroup communication

Exhibit 15–2 Problem Behaviors and Concomitant Leader Intervention

Problem Behavior	Corrective Response
Aggressive	Avoid negative confrontation. Encourage member to be concrete about personal feelings. Ask for a private conference, share feelings and ask for cooperation, point out harmful effects on others, or ask member to leave the group. Assign aggressor the helpee role on a "personally relevant" topic. (Look for clues to the aggression from the person's self-disclosure.)
Silent/Withdrawn	Avoid negative confrontation. Invite responses. Assign nonthreatening roles that require responding but do not demand self-disclosure to the whole group.
Shy to Fragile	Avoid negative confrontation. Reduce risk level by supervising one-on-one interactions and avoid group exposure. Arrange a private conference to investigate reasons for member's behavior.
Domineering/ Dominating	Avoid negative confrontation. Avoid eye contact. Reward only very significant contributions. Ask for a private conference and assess person's sensitivity/awareness of the problem, ask for cooperation. Arrange for a presentation to the group that requires appropriate, extended verbalizing.
Attention Getter/ Clown	Avoid negative confrontation. Respond to insecure feelings if present. Assign serious roles. Ask for a private conference and assess reasons for the behavior. Assist members to identify inappropriate humor.
Bored/Detached	Avoid negative confrontation. Assign responsible roles. Provide options for creative involvement. Support involvement.

Source: Reprinted from G.M. Gazda, W.C. Childers, and R.P. Walters, *Interpersonal Communication—A Handbook for Health Professionals*, pp. 50–51, © 1982, Aspen Publishers, Inc.

difficulties are frequently reflected in intergroup problems. Sometimes the tension among staff on a treatment team (intragroup problems) mirrors communication difficulties elsewhere in the system.

Organizations are composed of many groups; some are specific coalitions or alliances that compete with one another for resources. Discrepancies about goals and values fuel a number of communication difficulties among groups as do issues of esteem, control, and affiliation that are extremely relevant to intergroup dynamics. Consider, for example, a disagreement between a task force that has been assigned to choose a computer-based patient record system, the administrative group that will purchase the system, and the service center that will pilot the new system. The staff on the pilot unit wish to be recognized for their valuable practical ideas. The administrative group is concerned that the task force is exaggerating needs, which will drive costs too high, and the task force questions the sincerity of the administrative group, stating that the administrators do not have the real interests of quality-tracking systems in mind when they criticize the task force. Conflict and mistrust exist and are acted out in the relationships between the pilot group and the task force and between the administrative group and the task force.

The conflicts and disagreements between these groups may not be expressed openly. They may be acted out through various ambiguous communications. Information from the task force to the administrative group may be withheld or may be rigidly guarded. The pilot-unit staff may express their opinions obliquely, but at other times, aggressively, and all but boycott the decisions of the task force. The observable part of these intergroup conflicts is manifested in these communication responses.

Reflecting on this example, we can see that all the ingredients of conflict are present. First, an observable struggle exists where opposing groups come together periodically to interact or do so through representatives. Second, there is a clear element of interdependence. The task force relies on the pilot unit, the pilot unit on the task force, and the administrative group on both the pilot unit and task force. Third, areas of contention arouse feelings. Because needs for control, affiliation, and esteem are involved, the arousal of strong feelings is inevitable. Finally, the differences felt between these groups are deemed incompatible or are feared to be incompatible. Incompatible beliefs, values, and goals form the content of these struggles. Desires for control and status, however, may also underlie the intergroup problems. Concerns about the unequal distribution of power among groups can affect many aspects of a provider's working life, including motivation, job satisfaction, absenteeism, stress, and turnover. It is understandable that these internal struggles may have significant effects on members.

Conflicts between groups can be aided by the same interventions that are appropriate within groups. Supportive communication can replace defensive communication in these situations as well. In capacities of leadership, one's modeling supportive communication is essential but not enough. One's recognition of the problems and their underlying dynamics, including the basis for contention, is paramount. It is important to understand the political struggles that also underlie intergroup communications. Recognizing and factoring in the feelings that are motivating intergroup communication will help to tailor responses to the inner feelings of members and groups. Rather than focusing exclusively on superficial manifestations that are revealed in the content of disagreements, group leaders should also recognize and respond to the interpersonal struggles within and between groups. Additional concepts about conflict and conflict resolution are addressed in Chapter 16.

CONCLUSION

Whether they want to be or not, every provider is a member of different kinds of work groups. And whether they are aware of it or not, as group members, they have a significant impact on the functioning and processing of these teams.

There are a variety of factors that predispose a group to communicate in a particular way. The type of group (formal or informal) and the maturity (stage of development) of a group are critical factors influencing the way a group communicates. The internal functioning within any group, and this is true of professional work groups, is a result of the dynamic interaction of all members. It also includes the relationship of the group within the context of the larger institutional setting because the goals and resources available to a group are contingent on this interdependency with the external work environment. Communication within groups can be said to be either functional or dysfunctional. In truth, most groups lie somewhere on the continuum of effective functioning.

Group communication problems are manifested in a variety of ways. Conflicts, fights, disagreements, nonparticipation, apathy, and/or the inability to make decisions effectively are diagnosable features of poorly functioning groups.

Improving communications within groups not only includes knowing oneself and others but also communicating knowledge and observations back to the group so that corrective processes can begin. Practicing and facilitating supportive communications is helpful not only in dysfunctional groups but also in maintaining a state of high-level functioning in work groups that are proceeding successfully toward their goals.

Intergroup communication problems are frequently reflective of communication problems in a larger context. Power differences, autonomy struggles, insufficient interdisciplinary understanding, unshared meanings, differences in perception, and interpretation of others' behavior contribute to intergroup conflict.

Inter- and intragroup communication difficulties are everyone's concerns. We must work together effectively in small groups if we are to provide quality care to patients and their families. The spirit and practice of collegiality makes quality care possible; without it, we are at risk of putting both patients and ourselves in jeopardy.

CHAPTER 16

Conflict in the Health Care System: Understanding Communications and Resolving Dispute

Within discord there lies the dawning of harmony.

George Leonard

CHAPTER OBJECTIVES

- Describe how conflict is reflected in interpersonal interaction.
- Define and differentiate between conflict, tension, and disputes.
- Identify signs and types of conflict.
- Analyze cases of poor resolution of communicated conflict.
- Describe the process of resolving interpersonal conflicts.
- Define the mediation process.
- Differentiate between positional bargaining and interest-based bargaining.
- Identify key factors in reaching resolutions, e.g., active listening and reframing.

It has been said that conflict is inevitable, that two or more individuals will at some point express disagreement. Also, disagreements will recur, though they may differ in content. Some of these disagreements will go unresolved because without outside expertise to facilitate the resolution of conflict, some disputes may result in a deadlock, and communication may be severely curtailed. Chronic or acute communication difficulties between two or more individuals are usually evidence of unresolved conflict. In the patient-provider relationship, conflicts can result in patient dissatisfaction, the patient leaving treatment, and/or lack of adherence to treatment or impaired communication about treatment dilemmas.

It is the purpose of this chapter to focus on several key concepts and principles that are used not only to describe conflict but also to describe the process of mediation that will resolve these communication difficulties. In some cases, providers will be a party in the dispute, e.g., between a patient and themselves or between a patient's family and themselves. At other times, they may not be one of the disputants, but they are intimately affected by the presence of the conflict. In some instances, they may have a role in mediating a dispute between others, e.g., between physicians and nurses, between physicians and pharmacists, or between teaching staff and administrators. Dealing successfully with conflict requires specific communication skills. Everyone should be familiar with the dynamics and skills of conflict resolution.

In our society, conflict is inevitable. Disputes can happen at any time and are observed everywhere—in interpersonal relationships as well as in small and in large groups. Sometimes the disputes are quite apparent, but they can also be latent or emerging. In the workplace, disputes arise at all levels, between patients and providers, among co-workers, managers, and supervisors, and on occasion, they involve many other departments directly or indirectly. Because the costs of unresolved conflicts are very high and result in potentially tremendous litigation expenses, more and more attention is placed on the informal resolution of conflicts, or better yet, on preventing them in the first place.

Certain work situations may produce more conflict. Environments in which conflicts occur very frequently are those where major changes have occurred and where unclear or overlapping roles, ambiguous lines of authority, and inadequate communication occurs. These conditions may produce conflict and/or worsen conflict that already exists. Issues of diversity (gender, age, status, ethnicity, and race) are sometimes at the base of the conflict. At other times, these factors provide a unique context for the expression of the conflict.

CONFLICTS AND COMMUNICATION

Conflict is omnipresent. Everywhere we turn, we can observe conflict in interpersonal relationships. We grow up observing and participating in conflict with siblings, parents, friends, and neighbors. When we enter the workplace with its pattern of rational responses, we sometimes assume that these environments are without dispute and conflict. Or, if conflict does exist, it is circumspect and transient. In health care delivery systems, we expect this to be the case since clinical practice is an empirically defined practice and requires predictability and control. Yet, this is far from the truth. In health care delivery systems, disputes and conflicts arise regularly. On occasion, these conflicts spill over to individuals or groups who are not parties in the dispute but who are impacted directly or indirectly by the disputants. As in many other industries, health care systems become involved in large litigation suits between parties who cannot agree. Problems in the delivery of quality care may be a result of conflict; at other times, conflict results from perceptions that inadequate care was provided.

Consider the following event describing staff conflict. The nursing staff on a postpartum unit have felt long-standing tension toward the nursing staff in the neonatal-care division. Generally, the postpartum staff believe that the nursery department is staffed more generously and does not work as hard. One evening shift, a staff member from the postpartum staff observes that the nursery staff have left two newborns unattended. No one is around, and this staff member presumes that the nursery staff are on break. Angered at this apparent neglect, the nurse comments to her peers, "I'll show them." She proceeds to take the newborns from the nursery and hides them at the postpartum nursing station. The nursery staff return but do not find the babies where they left them. They learn of the retaliatory action and become enraged.

It is sometimes hard to believe that conflict would escalate to these proportions in a health care agency bent on rational practices. But since providers are human, these episodes, though rare and quite dramatic, do happen. Regardless of whether you are directly involved in the dispute or indirectly affected, e.g., a member of the physician team or the administrator in this hospital, you will soon know about the event. Likely, you will be somewhat confused about how to handle your relationships and communications with the at-war parties. Conflict and its behavioral and communicated aspects will affect the entire system including the patients.

Historically, conflict and tension were viewed as inevitable and therefore immune to any attempts to make communications otherwise. If conflict and disputes were the result of human nature, then there was little we could do to prevent them from occurring. This position led to a passive, hopeless attitude and little was done to try to understand conflict since the expectation was that nothing would make any difference whatsoever. Recently, however, with the escalation of potential conflict, multicultural work environments, and a new look at the costs of conflict, there has been renewed interest and commitment in attempting to prevent and control interpersonal conflict in the workplace. Concomitantly, with various new approaches to conflict management, it has been shown that conflict and disputes can be resolved differently and, in some cases, better.

Definitions of Conflict, Tension, and Disputes

The chief vehicle by which conflict is initiated, nurtured, and resolved is interpersonal communication. This does not mean that all conflicts or disputes are evidenced in verbal encounters. Many conflicts get played out nonverbally, e.g., in the deliberate absence of communication, in withdrawal and separation, and in posturing and facial expressions. Thus, two parties can be in conflict, but this may not be evident because many individuals hide or disguise their conflictual attitudes and opinions. Conflict that has escalated out of control frequently gets played out in silence. "She or he is giving me the silent treatment," means that the tension has escalated to the extent that an impasse has occurred and one or more parties is no longer sending or receiving verbal messages.

Conflict arises when individuals (or groups of individuals) have incompatible, or seemingly incompatible, values, ideas, or interests. Conflict would not occur if these individuals or groups of individuals were separate, distinct systems and independent of one another. Individuals, groups, and even nations, can coexist without conflict despite vast disparity in values and beliefs if they are not related in some way to one another. When the relationship changes, however, and those parties become reliant on one another, the potential for conflict surfaces when previously there was no basis for dispute. This principle is important to understand—conflicts can only occur when there is interdependence.

The second basic principle is that conflict can be either positive or negative. Up until this point, we have illustrated the potentially negative results of conflict. Although we fear the destructive consequences of conflict (and there is good reason to do so), conflict does not always have a negative outcome. Advantageous outcomes can, and do occur, and they result in better communications, enhanced problem solving, and positive changes in the individuals involved (Deutsch 1973). Still, the positive results of conflict are not necessarily forthcoming or automatic. We take the position that conflict that is avoided or ignored will result in mostly negative outcomes. To keep conflict from having destructive consequences and to elicit positive outcomes from conflicts, deliberate strategies must be employed based on a thorough examination of the cause(s) of the conflict.

Tension and stress always accompany any kind of conflict. In fact, it is these emotional components that frequently produce the negative results of conflict. Tension and stress are the affective responses to conflict that are internalized as somatic and behavioral symptoms. They can manifest as headaches, backaches, or just heightened body sensitivity. Left untreated, they tend to have direct and significant impacts on individual behavior. Poor abilities to concentrate as well as decreased abilities to express oneself and respond rationally can all occur as a result of the tension and stress of conflict. The staff's use of poor judgment in the scenario that was presented earlier in this chapter exemplifies how tension due to conflict eventually can erupt in exaggerated expressions of discontent. Incompatibilities, once present in chronic but latent proportions, escalated into the expression of one staff member's behavior toward the other parties.

Disputes are different from conflict. Although many conflicts are eventually translated into specific disputes, not all conflicts reach this stage. Disputes are conflicts in which the parties have dealt directly with their differences but are unwilling or unable to resolve the issues. Usually these problems or disagreements move into a public forum, becoming the topic of a meeting, and frequently, they involve a third party. These third parties may simply observe and monitor the quality of communication or they may facilitate the resolution of problems through specific mediation and negotiation strategies.

Consider for a moment that you are either a hospital administrator or medical director and that you are obliged to address the dysfunctional communication on the postpartum and nursery services. The specific conflict issues are unknown, but disputes about staffing and cooperation between the parties seem to be involved. These disputes have gone into the public forum in the shape of staff meetings but have not been resolved. While arbitration is a possibility, you prefer to facilitate the problem solving and closure without bringing in additional parties from outside the hospital. To skillfully handle this conflict and the underlying disputes, some of which may involve you directly, you must determine the distribution of staff per cost center and apply procedures that will maximize the probability of increasing both parties willingness and abilities to resolve their differences. In essence, you attempt to modify the dispute so that the participating parties will negotiate a resolution within the ranks. Thus, you move a dispute toward successful resolution, maintaining the parties' faith in themselves that they have the power to resolve their differences.

Signs of Conflict

If we asked 100 people how they could tell whether someone was in conflict with them, at least 75 percent would mention anger or irritation as a sign. It stands to reason that in dealing with people under tense circumstances, when individuals are expected to cooperate but have conflicting values or beliefs, anger and frustration may result.

Consider, for example, the number and kinds of words we use to describe conflict-fraught encounters.

- "He is upset with me."
- "She's *hot* about that!"
- "Let them 'cool off' for awhile."
- "Give them a 'time out' and they'll settle down."
- "He (She) is 'seeing red'!"
- "Blind rage—that's what it is."
- "He/She is 'psycho.'"

These descriptions suggest everything from mild irritation to irrational emotions of anger or rage. In conflict, as well as in other encounters where anger is displayed, the emotion of anger is secondary to other more basic emotions, e.g., disappointment, fear of loss of control, sadness, hurt, confusion, and guilt. It follows then that behavioral expressions of conflict may reflect either the primary feeling of anger or the secondary feelings that underlie anger.

What does anger look like? There are many verbal and nonverbal clues about anger and conflict. They include but are not limited to, verbal attacks, defensive responses, and even withdrawal into silence. They also include nonverbal defensive or aggressive posturing. What must also be recognized is that these clues may be complicated by expressions of other feelings, e.g., fear of lack of control. In fact, these primary feelings may predominate, but expressions of disappointment, sadness, hurt, confusion, and guilt may also be communicated. Part of the difficulty that parties have in responding to conflict is that they must sort through and prioritize among several affective states. If they choose to respond to one effect, e.g., anger, they may negate the roles of disappointment and confusion. While it is critical in conflict resolutions to appreciate all the facets of human experience, it becomes unwieldy to address every emotion. The tendency is to reduce the phenomena in order to make the situation resolvable. This tendency toward reductionism, however, is the very thing that can lead to negotiation failures.

Recognizing conflict through multiple cues about primary and secondary affective states and carefully registering verbal and nonverbal aspects of communication is only half the story. What we must remember is that individual parties will go to great lengths to hide their true feelings and reactions. Therefore, we must be cognizant of the fact that conflict is often masked, but individuals who are masking conflict will display a number of characteristics. They tend to avoid direct eye contact, to remain superficial or curt in their remarks, and to display politeness or courteous behaviors that are not really required. They appear "cool" or "cold" and mask their feelings for a variety of reasons. First, they may not want the opposing party to know that they are having any vulnerable feelings or reactions. Second, they want to hide the specific kinds of feelings they have, e.g., hurt or sadness. They may be willing to let the other party know that they are angry but not willing to let them know about hurt and sadness. The adage, "Don't get angry, just get revenge," implies that the better way to deal with conflict and betrayal is to hide or suppress feelings and take action that will ultimately hurt the other party. Talking it out, e.g., sharing unmet expectations, is ill advised. The idea is to litigate versus resolve issues with the provider.

Verbal and nonverbal masks of anger and conflict usually minimize or exaggerate. They minimize or exaggerate because the real stimulus, not the apparent stimulus, is what the individual keeps hidden. Therefore, being overpolite may actually express the fact that we do not feel like being polite, therefore, we will force it, and the other person will never know. This line of thinking is faulty because underlying feelings are always accessible, to some extent, to others. What is actually communicated is, "I don't feel like being nice, but I will be," and *you won't know* is the false assumption that we make. We become phony people.

Types of Conflict

The types of conflict reflect their source, which rest in differences in beliefs, attitudes, and values. These may be actual differences or merely perceived differences. Conflict need not reflect reality; there is usually a great deal of distortion in conflictual relationships.

These differences, however, do not need to result in conflict unless they are deemed to be in opposition. For example, if I want to ask the physician his opinion before I ambulate a patient, and you perceive that to be superfluous even though we depend on each other for help, we may experience conflict. If we perceive that our differences oppose one another, one approach will have to predominate. It is under these conditions—opposing aims—that we will dispute the appropriate course of action.

While the most common conflict is relationship conflict—strong opposing emotions—there are many other types of conflict. Technologic conflicts are opposing ideas on how some aims—the procedures, steps, and equipment to be used—should be achieved. They involve knowledge and perception of the scientific basis behind a situation and an awareness of the standards, policies, and capacities to apply technology to a given patient situation. Providers disagree frequently about the necessity of treatment, the best treatment, and the best surgical or medical intervention to achieve the desired results, though providers do not necessarily openly disagree. If one party, however, is more familiar or more knowledgeable and the less knowledgeable party does not yield, conflict can ensue.

Conflicts in life values, attitudes, and beliefs may stem from the disputants inherent differences, yet these may be actual or perceived. Differences in values and beliefs, age, gender, race, ethnicity, political and religious persuasion, and education and socioeconomic status lay the foundation for opposing views on issues. One staff member may value small talk with patients' families based on the belief that families are important to patient care. Another staff member may believe that families are disruptive to patient care. They will thus behave in opposite ways toward families. Values and beliefs are highly influenced by an individual's personal characteristics. This is one reason why it is believed that providers who come from the same ethnic or racial background as the patient deliver more compatible care. However, different values and belief systems do not have to result in conflict. People can, and do, live in peace even though they have different ideals. Major problems only result when one group attempts to impose their values on others or presumes that their values are better than other's.

Relationship conflicts, the most common type, is so common that our first inclination is to blame relationships when disputes do occur. Relationship conflicts frequently reveal differences in interests or needs. For instance, one person may want a committed relationship, the other may not. In order for relationships to

survive, both parties must perceive that a significant number of their personal interests are addressed in the relationship. This may be impossible if the real source
of conflict is not an issue in the relationship, e.g., equality, authority, or superior/
subordinant stances but is actually a conflict stemming from ideologic differences.

While conflicts may be technologic, ideologic, or relational, they can also have
sources in one or more of these dimensions simultaneously. Sometimes issues
have their origins in one source, e.g., technologic, and proceed to additional domains, e.g., relational. Additionally, relational conflicts can fuel conflicts in other
areas, e.g., the ideologic or technologic areas. The cardinal rule is to analyze conflicts carefully, keeping in mind the various categories and origins of conflict.

Poor Resolution of Conflict

It is usually not difficult to judge when conflicts are not resolved or when the
resolution is poor because the tension that originally surfaced may be only somewhat alleviated or may erupt in significant ways without much provocation. Typically, communication styles remain the same. The disputants may exhibit evasive
or avoidant gestures, express themselves rationally but also irrationally, use both
direct and indirect messages, and either display rigidity or inconsistency.

Unresolved conflicts usually come about when the different parties have
reached a stalemate or impasse. Impasse, synonymous with stalemate, suggests
the inability of the parties to move forward and settle their differences. A characteristic common to many instances of unresolved conflict is that one or both parties is attempting to resolve issues through a series of positions that are presented
as solutions to the issue. These positions may be presented sequentially—the first
position is less demanding than the second, and so forth. If parties are fixed on one
position and display rigidity in their ability to negotiate with respect to new data,
then positional bargaining is a negative process. Stalemates connote inflexibility
and rigidity with respect to positions on an issue is bound to lead to stalemate.
Parties who participate in positional bargaining that has undesirable outcomes
generally have a win-lose mentality. They perceive that the goal is "to win" and
that they should be on the offensive. The only right solution is their solution and
conceding to the other person is a sign of weakness. For these parties it is not
conceivable that both parties can benefit because their goal is to come out on top.

Negotiations may worsen conflicts when the roles of each party are confusing.
Sometimes third-party negotiators have a stake in the outcome. If this is the case,
then the outcome will be generally unsatisfactory. Consider for a moment that you
are the outside third party in a conflict between the nursery and the postpartum
staff. Let us assume that you have also disliked members of the nursery staff and
felt that they were not to be trusted. Your attitudes and previous history may significantly have an impact on the process of resolving this conflict. If your job is to

facilitate the negotiation, then you may be biased, and this will show. If your job is to decide for these groups what should be done, then your decisions will be suspect. Much will depend on your official power base, which you may or may not choose to use.

In health care delivery systems, the primary means for identifying unresolved conflict is to examine what went wrong. Since 85 percent of the time "what went wrong" is due to a fault in the system of care giving, a large part of the time the source of an error may originate in, or be complicated by, conflict. Conflict is costly—the personal resources and energy devoted to conflict is high, and the costs of errors due to conflict are also high. So, when we establish the need to resolve conflicts, we must also recognize the costs of *not* resolving conflict (Ury, Brett, and Goldberg 1988).

THE PROCESS OF RESOLUTION

Can you imagine a workplace that is totally conflict free? Most of us would agree that such a workplace does not exist and cannot be found. Certain environments may appear conflict free but, if there were an accurate appraisal of existing conditions, we would find that it is not likely to remain conflict free indefinitely. Understanding that conflict cannot be totally eradicated is important when we consider what we mean by resolution.

Resolution means to modify differences between individuals and bring disputes under control. Modifying differences does not mean forcing one party's views on the other or even forcing a third party's view on the disputants. Resolution means making the parties realize that their existing differences, which will not change, can coexist in harmony. This important principle, i.e., that incompatible values can coexist, underscores the work of many mediators or counselors who practice mediation.

When we speak specifically about conflict resolution, we are referring to the steps that one takes to bring disputes under control. While it is most important that individuals learn to deal successfully with conflict, they frequently need outside assistance. When they require outside assistance, a third party is brought into the interaction to either arbitrate or mediate the conflict. Successful negotiation involves a problem-solving process requiring each party to discuss their differences and reach a joint decision about their common concerns.

Entering Disputes

There are various ways, then, of entering conflict situations. Most of us, if given a choice, will go out of our way to avoid being entangled in conflicts and for good reason. Conflictual relationships produce a great deal of confusion and frustration and they make our difficult jobs even harder.

Nonetheless, all of us at one time or another will be drawn into a dispute between ourselves and others or into a dispute where two or more parties are involved but we are, at least initially, only indirectly affected. It is important to differentiate roles in conflict situations—the disputants themselves, the third party who may be a "volunteer," and the officials who have been designated to mediate or arbitrate (see Figure 16–1). These groups function within the larger context of the particular health care arena.

Involuntary involvement in disputes is complicated. Because we do not want to have anything to do with the dispute, we have very strong feelings about our involvement, and our resentment and irritation tend to confuse the issues further. Examples of involuntary involvement in the health care workplace could include disputes between members of the staff and patients or between staff and patients' families. They may also include conflicts and disputes between staff as well as within and between disciplines or departments. Most outsiders would walk a mile in the opposite direction to avoid being embroiled in a dispute or conflict. Not only is there anger when one is drawn in, but our tendency to withdraw from others' conflict may also play a role in the manifestation of the conflict or dispute and its resolution. The cost of merely witnessing conflict is sometimes just as frustrating. Silent witnesses suffer; the extent to which they suffer is intangible and difficult to assess.

When a provider enters a conflict or dispute voluntarily, he does so for several reasons. First, providers may understand that quite unintentionally they are a part of the problem. Second, providers may realize that their work and/or their personal lives are affected by the conflictual relationships and communications. They may

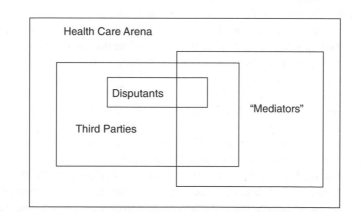

Figure 16–1 Roles in Conflicts/Disputes

perceive that quality and safe patient care are jeopardized by the conflict. A third compelling reason to enter a conflict or dispute is the personal investment an outsider has in the resolution of it. Just because we voluntarily involve ourselves in conflict or its resolution does not mean that we are the person(s) who can negotiate a compromise or arbitrate a solution. The skill of mediating disputes and conflicts requires both specialized skills and neutrality.

The Mediation Process

While it is hoped that disputing parties will resolve their own conflict or at least bring the conflict under control, the fact is that more often than not specialized intervention will be needed. This fact reflects our lack of preparation in resolving conflicts, our tendency to avoid versus pursue resolution, and the overriding impact that our feelings and attitudes have on our communications and judgments.

Given this understanding, it should not be difficult to comprehend that the mediation process must be impartial. It stands to reason that successful mediators will not only be those who are skilled but also those who can maintain neutrality. One reason that authority figures are not deemed to be effective in negotiation is that they tend to be biased, and most importantly, to have power that could be used to punish one or both disputants. Even if the authority person promises to be neutral and is capable of maintaining neutrality (a very difficult task indeed), the disputing parties may perceive (or worry about) the bias of the authority figure. Although administrators and directors have traditionally been viewed as good "referees" in disputes, in many cases today, they are viewed as inappropriate mediators.

When we speak of mediation, we may mean mediation with a small or big m— informal or formal. That is to say, when we speak of mediation with a small m, we are describing an informal process performed with and around people who are at an impasse. When we refer to mediation with a big M, we are describing a standardized formal approach to a dispute where an official mediator is asked for or appointed to help the disputants overcome the stalemate. It is clear that when mediation at any level occurs, certain interpersonal and communication skills are necessary (Lax and Sebenius 1986). These include nondefensive responses, active listening, and negotiation and/or bargaining skills. The need for these skills in formal mediation procedures remains the same. The difference is that formally appointed mediators have specialized training in negotiation, undergoing extensive education and receiving some form of certification.

Christopher W. Moore, Ph.D., with Communication/Decisions/Results (CDR) Associates (1986) defines the formal process of mediation as the intervention into a dispute wherein an acceptable, impartial, neutral third party, who has no authoritative decision-making power, assists the disputants to voluntarily reach their own, mutually acceptable settlement. Each of these elements of mediation is necessary if the disputants are to arrive at an amicable resolution. Acceptability refers to the fact that both parties agree to the presence and even the choice of the mediator, which is important if the parties are to follow the mediator's direction and guidance. Impartiality, referred to earlier as a critical element, means that one party will not be favored over the other. While it is not possible to be totally opinion free, mediators are expected to control their preferences, attitudes, and biases. Mediators do not have authority or power, so the tendency of disputants to feel threatened is lessened considerably. Mediators assist the parties in reaching mutually agreeable outcomes—neither the event of mediation nor a decision to resolve the issue are thrust upon the disputants. Mediation, whether informal or formal, is a valued process. It is expected that if the consequences of conflict can be better contained, settlements are reached more quickly, parties are more satisfied with the outcomes, and regardless the agreement, compliance is more likely. Mediation is extremely important in situations where the parties are expected to have an ongoing working relationship.

Moore, with CDR Associates (1986), carefully outlines several conditions that have led to successful mediation. These conditions, or in some cases preconditions, make successful mediation more possible. Their absence does not make successful mediation impossible, but their absence and the number of unmet conditions will, however, considerably decrease the odds that positive outcomes will be reached. These conditions include:

- The parties have a history of cooperation and successful problem solving.
- The number of parties are limited.
- The parties have been able to agree on some issues.
- The parties will have an ongoing relationship and the hostility and anger toward each other is low to moderate.

Promoting Negotiation

Promoting negotiation and resolution of conflict in work settings is each and every co-worker's responsibility. Just how well we fulfill this responsibility for others will vary and depends on several factors, e.g., our investment in the issue or potential solutions, our personal attitudes and opinions about the situation, and our beliefs about the disputing parties. Sometimes personal characteristics will also influence us, such as our age, gender, discipline, race, or ethnicity—even our marital status.

What is also clear is that each one of us has a particular conflict management style that we resort to, particularly when we are under stress. We may be primarily collaborators, compromisers, accommodators, controllers, or avoiders. The point of becoming more aware of one's inherent tendencies is to stimulate individuals to consider alternative styles. Conflict-management styles can be described on two continuums: one reflecting the individual's concerns for relationships, the second reflecting the individual's concern for personal goals.

For example, while avoidance would seem to be negative because issues may never get addressed, there are some potential uses for it. When arguments or demands get heated, avoidance sometimes provides the respite that everyone needs to reassemble their thoughts (and emotions) and come back together for more positive negotiation attempts. Similarly, compromising would seem to be a positive conflict-management style. Yet, compromising may lead to situations where solutions do not please either party and the main issues lose their value and importance.

Changing Positional Bargaining to Interest-Based Negotiations

If we were to conduct an "autopsy" on those conflict situations where no resolution was reached, we might discover an interesting phenomenon. Although there are many factors that influence whether positive outcomes emerge, there is one phenomenon that surfaces as a "vital sign" for diagnosing conflict-management failures. For the purposes of this discussion, we will refer to this phenomenon as the balance between interest-based bargaining and position-based bargaining. These two distinctively different negotiation strategies produce significantly different outcomes most of the time (Moore, CDR Associates 1986).

Interest-based bargaining is a negotiation strategy that attempts to satisfy as many interests or needs of the disputing parties as possible. It is a problem-solving technique that is used to reach a mutually satisfying solution rather than to determine an outcome in a win-lose manner. Although compromise may occur, the intent is not to compromise but to construct a solution to address the specific needs and interests of both parties. When parties are cooperative problem solvers, they do not behave as opponents. In interest-based bargaining, win-win solutions are sought. This is very different from win-lose scenarios created by positional bargaining strategies.

Positional bargaining strategies are more familiar to us. They are, in essence, what we know. Classically, our view is that if we become assertive, we will be able to verbalize our position. And, verbalizing our position will increase the odds that we will have our needs met. Positional bargaining, like interest-based bargaining, is a strategy used by one or more parties in a dispute to maximize the gain he or she is likely to make. By stating a preferred outcome up front, the parties hope to minimize concessions. Usually the parties view each other as opponents wherein a win for one results in a loss for the other. The idea is to win as much as you can. Positional bargaining strategies on the part of one party usually begets positional bargaining by the other party. The disadvantage of this mode is that compromise is not valued, and parties often reach a standoff where no resolution is immediately foreseeable.

How do we change our patterns of negotiating, and how do we assist others to change from one strategy to another? We have already implied that interest-based bargaining is, in many ways, better. Stalemates, impasses, and deadlocks are less likely to occur with interest-based bargaining. The process of changing positional to interest-based bargaining includes a sophisticated analysis of situations. For example, in any potential conflict, three elements are always present. Although we tend to view situations from the positional vantage point, i.e., what a person's position is on the issue, there is more to it than mere proposals or solutions. Each conflict contains issues, interests, and positions. Dealing with positions alone decreases the potential for resolution because there is less to discuss and more temptation to polarize.

Consider the issue of assisted suicide. What is your position? Do you believe in it and support it? Or do you oppose it? If someone says, "I support the concept," the automatic response is to agree or disagree with the position—"I don't" or "I do support it, as well." However, if we discuss the situation from the standpoint of issues, e.g., is assisted suicide appropriate for only some medical cases, or how do we define *assisted*, we have much to discuss. Because we have more to discuss, there is a greater chance that we will arrive at a consensus.

Consider the issue of having fewer patients to care for. If this situation, a potential area of conflict among staff and administrators, stays at the position level, what becomes the issue is whether fewer patients or better nurse-patient ratios are better. However, if the discussion is expanded to include all of the issues behind patient-nurse ratios, e.g., acuity of patients, quality care, and cost constraints, there is a great deal to discuss. And, if the subject of personal interests are discussed in reference to the issue, the dialogue is not only expanded further but has more of a chance to satisfy the parties. Needs or interests of the staff may include fears that they will deliver unsafe care or that their patients may be harmed and that they will be held accountable. From the management or administrative side, the interests may include wanting staff to feel supported but knowing that an already out-of-control budget must be kept in line. Mediators will generally treat positions as incomplete. They may ignore them completely, and they will generally avoid coming to solutions too early. They tend to interrupt when positions form counters to other positions, or they will make the issue and interest elements in a dispute more explicit.

In successful negotiations, issues, interests, and positions are relevant. Arguments and compromises that adequately reflect these elements are more likely to be acceptable to both parties.

Reaching Resolutions

We all have assumptions about coming to a resolution, and we also may harbor fantasies about it. In the workplace scenario presented earlier, we may have hopes and dreams that the postpartum and nursery staffs will come to realize how silly they have behaved, that each group is in some way responsible for the events, and that realizing all this and having compromised on other issues, they will change and, in fact, be *model* communicators. Such a thought is more fantasy than reality. In truth, the potential for further problems is high. However, so is the potential for successful resolution if one was reached before.

In actuality, there is a host of potential resolution outcomes, but in reality, more partial resolutions are reached. Settlements, compromises, and decisions to drop all or most of the issues are all possible products of resolution. The settlements or solution may be partial or temporary. Sometimes disputing parties will just decide to drop the issue because the time, energy, and resources are not available (at the time) to reach a satisfactory conclusion. In those instances, no resolution is perceived to be more advantageous than a partial resolution. And in those instances, stalemates may be initiated by one or more parties. Sometimes one party will initiate an impasse hoping that time or resources will change things and that they will be at a better place down-the-line to compromise.

While the level of agreement or disagreement at resolution is important, of equal importance are the attitudes and feelings of both parties. Both sides must feel that they have had an adequate opportunity to explore their issues, interests, and positions. They also must believe that although they disagree with one another, they are better able to understand and to be understood by the other party. If this is not the case, whatever resolution occurs, partial or complete, the attitudes of participants are sufficiently problematic as to undermine any future cooperative activities.

Communication Guidelines in Conflict Resolution

To some extent, conflicts are synonymous with dysfunctional communication. Associations between communication responses and level of conflict are quite strong. Does faulty communication, however, lead to conflict or does conflict lead to faulty communication? The answer is: Both are true. In fact, we can significantly interrupt conflict by changing communication patterns. It is also true that by improving communication, we can avoid conflict, or at least, resolve it more quickly.

The following discussion describes elements of interpersonal communication that are vital for avoiding conflict and resolving disputes. They are the concepts of (1) active listening, (2) reframing, and (3) assertive versus aggressive styles.

Active Listening

Active listening is a strategy or technique that is very familiar to mental-health professionals. A large part of what therapists do is engage in active listening with their patients. Active listening entails paying attention to all aspects and levels of communication—the verbal and nonverbal elements and the report and metacommunication aspects of messages. Active listeners not only perceive the explicit content of messages but also the implied emotions and views of how one individual sees his or her relationship with another.

Active listeners practice empathy. They are capable of reading beyond the expressed idea and into the feelings, attitudes, and beliefs of individuals. They are also able to articulate these perceptions in ways that increase the patient's learning and validate the patient's experience.

Because this strategy tends to legitimize the communication abilities of the other person, the process of active listening often encourages the sender to disclose more. With more disclosure comes better understanding, and better understanding minimizes the chance of conflict and controls the destruction that conflict can create in relationships.

Active listening includes a number of smaller steps to achieving more effective communication. These steps in the context of conflict resolution may include:

- listening to and observing carefully the overt content of each party's message
- perceiving the feelings, beliefs, and attitudes behind the spoken messages
- placing both the verbal and metacommunication aspects within the personal or interpersonal context in which they occur
- placing oneself in each individuals' shoes—noting messages, feelings, and context that are discrepant
- expressing in meaningful ways your understanding
- feeding back to the parties' observations about the foregoing process
- listening for the parties' clarification and responses to your stated observations
- assisting parties in forming new conclusions based on the entire process

Active listening, like most other strategies, can be both taught and learned with relatively high rates of success. Active listening reinforces this process and tends to increase the probability that it will be used repeatedly to facilitate successful communications.

Reframing

Reframing is a term that describes the strategy of redefining the issues, the importance of the issues, the investments of the parties in the issues, and the value of one or more perceived solutions.

Reframing in conflict resolution occurs when an outside third party describes a problem or issue in a different manner from how the parties are accustomed to perceiving it. Cognitive behavioral theories suggest that the way in which we cognitively construct our situations constitutes our reality. Therefore, if we offer a revised definition of a problem or issue, we are actually offering disputants new realities. Sometimes the manner in which a conflict situation is described or defined is detrimental to our negotiating solutions. For example, with the staff conflict raised earlier in this chapter, an attitude or conclusion detrimental to these parties' abilities to resolve their differences would be, "I'm not surprised; I expected something crazy would happen—they're 'psycho.'" This conceptualization of the problem is destructive, and no material that has been presented is worth discussing. Solutions to the conflict are deemed hopeless, and one has the feeling of "What's the use?"

When attitudes, beliefs, issues, or interests, or even the context of the conflict, interfere with conflict resolution, reframing must occur. Individuals and whole groups develop definitions and beliefs about situations according to their independent or collective realities. And, we know from earlier discussions of the principles of human communication that people perceive based on need and thus do not perceive accurately the stimulus that is presented. A part of managing conflict, then, is presenting a different reality, a reality that might more accurately reflect the stimuli and one than diminishes perceptions of competition and antagonism.

A good deal of what occurs in teaching people motivational or remotivational skills is teaching them to redefine and reconceptualize the problem (Bandler and Grinder 1982). Insurmountable problems are small glitches and difficult people are people who are behaviorally compromised. Notice that when we describe the postpartum and nursery staffs as "energized" instead of "crazy," we have altogether different attitudes about their actions and the prospects of their resolving their conflicts.

Assertive versus Aggressive and Passive-Aggressive Stances

In the last quarter of a century a good deal of literature has been produced to suggest that being assertive is good, being aggressive is not. Theorists have attempted to dichotomize these behaviors and project consequences if individuals behave in either manner. In truth, both aggressive and assertive behaviors make use of aggressive energy. It can be said that even passive responses are aggressive. This notion is borne out in descriptions of those behaviors that are labeled "passive-aggressive."

At one level it was believed that individuals could be classified or typed according to certain personality attributes, i.e., they were either passive-aggressive or aggressive personalities. Assertive individuals were perceived to be healthy, well-adapted individuals taking advantage of life's challenges but never at the sake of another's interests.

The issue of assertive versus aggressive behavior and the relative preference for assertive communications over either passive-aggressive or overtly aggressive styles is still an issue today. When it comes to a discussion of conflict and negotiation of differences, it is generally believed that those who can express themselves assertively without being aggressive (disrespectful of others' needs), fare better than those individuals who are either passive-aggressive or openly aggressive (Bolton 1979). Most theorists would agree, but why?

One reason is that assertive individuals bring their issues, interests, and positions to the bargaining table. They are open but not pushy, patient but not avoidant. Furthermore, aggressive individuals behave as if their issues, interests, or positions are the only ones or, at least, are the most important. For these reasons, they are not sufficiently open nor flexible enough to entertain alternatives and incorporate others' ideas.

Conflicts with a low probability of resolution generally involve one or more disputants who are either semiaggressive or overtly aggressive. Also, resolution failures are frequently complementary where one party is aggressive and the other is passive-aggressive. Some authors argue that the symmetry or complementary nature of relationships and communications rules out the possibility of assertive behavior when one party is either overly aggressive or passive-aggressive. This idea underrates the human capacity to avoid dysfunctional patterns. We know from counseling victims of domestic violence, for example, that we can change the victim's responses even if we cannot change the perpetrator. That is, we can bolster the victim to the extent that he or she relinquishes the victim role, becomes assertive, and resists the perpetrator. The idea that aggressive or passive-aggressive styles once learned can never be altered is not true. These styles can be changed, and there are many training programs that prepare individuals to become assertive in both their personal relationships and their work settings. Needless to say, conflict mediators are very interested in the capacities of parties to relinquish aggressive and passive-aggressive styles and take on assertive, respectful responses.

CONCLUSION

Communicating with people in conflict requires providers to have a sophisticated awareness of conflict as a human condition. This awareness includes knowing what spurns conflict and what resolves conflicts and disputes. Each provider will have his or her own unique conflict-management style. Whatever the style, there are always limitations and advantages in a given approach to managing conflict. Specific tactics to use in conflict situations are those that reframe situations in helpful ways and engage disputants in active listening. A general problem-solving process that encourages providers to stay grounded in the issues is important.

In the present health care climate, conflict is inevitable. These conflicts are played out in professional and bureaucratic differences, in differences in the perception of the goals of the institution, and in conflicts over roles and responsibilities (some of which may be competing). While it is possible that work conflict will reflect personality differences, there are many more potential sources of conflict. Usually, there are multiple causes behind a conflict, and a more complete understanding of the complexity of the conflict increases the likelihood that any solutions that are reached will be more than just partial settlements.

CHAPTER 17

Family Dynamics and Communications with Patients' Significant Others

Current thought about the nature of comprehensive care would view blatant disregard of the patient's family or social networks as tantamount to health care neglect.

Gwen van Servellen

CHAPTER OBJECTIVES

- Discuss how the family is a major dynamic constituency in health care.
- Differentiate between family and social network.
- Discuss potential functional and dysfunctional characteristics of the family unit.
- Identify traditional ideas about the impact of illness on families.
- List potential difficulties that providers may have in communicating with families or significant others.
- Describe the process that families experience in adapting to their member's injury or illness.
- Describe factors that affect family health and family relationships.
- Identify selected requests that patients may have regarding providers' communications with family members.
- Describe several types of difficult family responses, including provider responses that would be helpful.
- Discuss the concept of "caregiver burden" in a family coping with and communicating with an ill or injured member.

Patients do not exist in isolation, despite the fact that they may be treated that way or may feel themselves to be. Patients are members of social units, which are loosely referred to as social networks and more traditionally include formal and informal family systems.

The importance of adequate patient-provider family communications is addressed extensively in the literature. Providers are sometimes accused of forgetting or ignoring the importance of family members in all phases of the caregiving process: as informants in the assessment phase, as decision makers in the planning phase, as caregivers in the implementation phase, and as reporters in the evaluation phase. It is true that what happens to the patient happens to the family. The family may not feel the physical pain of the injury or disease, but they do suffer social, psychological, and financial consequences of significant magnitude. They become fearful, anxious, and frustrated as a result of witnessing the injury or disease that afflicts one of their members. If they adapt successfully, they are stronger for the experience; if they do not adapt, they experience prolonged and unnecessary helplessness and powerlessness. Providers can do much to alleviate the emotional pain of family members. Thus, it is important to learn to communicate compassionately and effectively with the family unit—the patient's major constituency.

Miller (1992) divides encounters into three different types, and thinking about family encounters in this way may help providers integrate family-system concepts into busy office practices. These three encounters are: routines—clinical encounters that are simple, single, and brief; ceremonies—rituals that involve covenantal style; and dramas—a series of visits concerning situations of conflict and emotion that include families' psychosocial problems.

THE FAMILY—A MAJOR DYNAMIC CONSTITUENCY

What is this thing called "family?" What real importance and meaning does this unit have in health care and how best can we communicate with this unit, the patient's primary constituency?

Definitions of Family and Social Network

The concepts of family and kinship have been revised extensively in American society. It used to be that families were units comprised of children and biological parents living together under the same roof. Today, families are defined in a variety of ways to encompass many variations of the traditional-family unit. We have single-parent, blended, nuclear, and three-generational household families. We have families not bound by any legal or blood ties that function in ways similar to traditional families and that are linked together in a system of exchange of resources and role reciprocacy.

In addition to changes in notions of what constitutes a family, the family network has also been described as fluid. Not only are individuals members of several types of family structures concurrently, some of these memberships change dramatically over the course of life. It is possible that one individual can be a child in a divorced family, grow up in a blended family, establish a nuclear family of her own and end up in a divorced-family situation. Adult members of a family are also members of their nuclear family of origin, which in some cases may itself be multiple units wherein child rearing took place. Three generations of family form the structure of still another family system. Additionally, the in-law family is a family unit that influences its members. Culturally prescribed roles and social norms shape the nature of primary and collateral family units.

The complexity of kinship and family has been further described in the notion of "everyday family." Everyday family may transcend households and extend to communities. Sussman (1982) explains that the everyday family is growing in incidence because of many factors, including lowered fertility and increased survival of persons over retirement age.

The everyday family typically consists of persons who are not related by blood or marriage, who are of different ages, who live in the same neighborhood, and who trust one another as if they were family. These families provide varying degrees of contact and intimacy. Social networks are frequently comprised of loosely or tightly bonded everyday families who serve the functions of traditional, primary family units. Although these families are not bound legally or financially, they have a significant impact on their members and should be viewed similarly to flesh-and-blood systems. These groups influence the perceptions, feelings, attitudes, decisions, and behaviors of its members in everyday living and in other matters involving the members' quality of life and life transitions.

The structure of the American family unit both is and is not intimately linked with the roles and functions of contemporary families. That is to say, the structure reflects that which a family unit will and will not provide. Still, there are some traditional functions that do not seem to change, regardless of the nuclear, extended, or blended structure.

Functional and Dysfunctional Characteristics of the Family Unit

In Chapter 15 we looked at the unit (group), giving a system's perspective. Families, also, are frequently equated with groups. With this, we are reminded to regard families as collections of individuals with subsystems. Families, like groups, are not just individuals, they are more or less cohesive systems organized for a specific purpose. Families are also affected by the suprasystems, culture, and genealogical structure in which they are imbedded. So, to understand the functional and dysfunctional aspects of families, we must first understand these rather basic principles. It is not the purpose of this text to delve deeply into theories of family pathology. If readers are so inclined, however, they may seek out such classic works as those of Bowen (1971), Satir (1974), and Minuchin (1974). These texts describe theories, each with a somewhat different interpretation, of family functioning.

A family's functioning can be, and has been, categorized to include various tasks that fulfill relational, communicative, and survival needs. Whenever the physical and emotional resources of the family are insufficient, critical family tasks and functions are threatened. When this occurs, families can become marginal or disorganized. Families who attempt to cope by appropriate but inadequate role enactment are labeled marginal, while those that engage inappropriately are labeled disorganized. In general, disorganized families tend to be more pathological and deviant than marginal families, who are functional but whose productivity is tenuous.

One way in which families have been differentiated as healthy or unhealthy has been through their functioning. That is, effective families are healthy, and ineffective families are unhealthy.

Conceptual frameworks that have made significant contributions to understanding families facing illness are those utilized to analyze families' coping with chronic illness. Four different perspectives have been represented in the literature and are divided into: (1) the resource perspective, (2) the deficit perspective, (3) the course perspective, and (4) the impact perspective (Steinglass and Horan 1987). These perspectives are briefly summarized (see Exhibit 17–1).

The Family as a Resource

The first perspective on family functioning conceptualizes the family as a resource to individuals who are coping with illness, particularly with chronic illness. Within this perspective is the notion that families are frequently the primary source of social support and comfort. As such, families serve a preventive and protective role. The family strengthens the patient's capacity to resist illness and is a major influence in patient compliance once care has been prescribed. Evidence for this aspect of the family's role comes from a series of studies indicating that family qualities such as empathy, as well as the family's own coping resources, have been associated with improvements in the medical condition and in the patient's compliance with medical treatment.

Of significant importance to providers is the potential for the family or significant other to be supportive. Social support, typically derived from close relationships, is felt to buffer or mediate the stress that is associated with chronic and/or life-threatening illness. Since most people use social support to cope with all kinds of stress, the mere perception that adequate support is available can be as important as the actual support itself (Sherbourne et al. 1992).

The Family as a Deficit

This perspective, according to Steinglass and Horan (1987), speaks not to the family as a potential helpful resource but as a potential negative contributor. In this perspective, the main influence that the family is believed to have is not its protective, buffering capability but rather its tendency to increase the incidence of illness by debilitating its members. This debilitation is believed to be a result of a

Exhibit 17–1 Perspectives on the Family and Illness

- the family as a resource (protective)
- the family as a deficit (contributor to illness)
- the family and the course of illness (adaptive or maladaptive responses)
- the family and the impact of illness (burden and stress)

Source: Data from P. Steinglass and M.E. Horan, Families and Chronic Medical Illness in *Chronic Disorders and the Family*, F. Walsh and C.M. Anderson, eds., pp. 128–135, © 1987, New York: Haworth Press

---

dysfunctional, rigid, and/or stressful family system. The classical example of this approach is the original understanding of the so-called psychosomatic family. The idea is that families in which there is a chronically ill member share certain structural properties and response styles that render the family member vulnerable. An additional set of studies looks not only at the prevalence of these characteristics in families with a chronic illness, but they also attempt to identify factors that are temporarily related to the clinical exacerbations of chronic episodic conditions such as diabetes and asthma, with psychiatric disorders, e.g., schizophrenia, and addictive disorders such as alcohol abuse.

The Family and the Course of Illness

Families are also believed to influence the course of illness. This perspective does not deal with the roles of families in the onset of illness or exacerbations of conditions, but it does address the ways in which families influence the course of illness. Because the course of chronic illness is observed to vary depending on the patient, an analysis of the differences in patients has been attributed to the family. The idea is that different illness consequences and phases of illness place different demands on the family unit. The manner in which families respond to these challenges, then, may have a substantial impact on the patient's adaptation to illness. This perspective analyzes the interface between family behavior and illness characteristics; family and illness variables may mutually reinforce one another. Questions that often get asked are: What aspects of family behavior serve to maintain symptomatic illness states? and what illness factors provoke certain family behaviors?

The Family and the Impact of Illness

The fourth and final perspective described by Steinglass and Horan (1987) focuses less on the way families influence the onset or course of illness and more on the impact of the illness on the family. Chronic medical conditions, in particular, drain families of emotional and financial resources. These conditions can significantly divert the family from its usual operating agendas to deprive it of time and energy. Studies of the indirect costs of chronic debilitating disease address the significance of this burden.

One behavior associated with family burden is, for whatever reasons, overinvolvement. Overinvolvement is of concern because it threatens social resources. And the depletion of these resources may result in psychological states, e.g., suppressed anger, frustration, and guilt that are ultimately communicated influence the patient in negative ways. Overinvolvement with the patient (or the treatment) can threaten the family's broader social life. Also, when the patient's needs predominate over all else, someone else in the family may be neglected. In the case of an adult patient, a child or spouse may suffer, and in the case of a child patient, a parent or sibling may not have certain needs met.

Family burden has been linked with family perceptions of the seriousness of the illness, whether or not the illness is as bad as the family pictures it to be. Reactions such as worry, fatigue, alterations in eating and sleeping patterns, and decreased socialization occur when families become preoccupied with their ill or potentially ill family member. Families will tell you that they do not feel like eating, do not feel like having a social life, and do not sleep well because they worry considerably about the health and welfare of their ill family member. Todres, Earle, and Jellinck (1994), in discussing how providers (internists) communicate with the parents of critically ill children, emphasize the importance of (1) the first meeting, (2) trust and understanding parental needs, and (3) coping mechanisms.

FAMILIES, ILLNESS, AND PROVIDERS

Origin Notions of the Impact of the Family

Families, like patients, express changing needs, depending on the events that occur. Because family members influence patient recovery, failure to address their needs may hinder patient recovery (Bokinskie 1992). One such need that is often expressed by family members of acutely ill patients is that of dealing with the anxiety that is generated by the hospital setting.

Originally, the stress of illness on the family was seen to be a byproduct of the disease itself. That is, the stressors on the family wherein a member has cancer were unique to the disease and different from the stressors imposed by cardiac or diabetic conditions. The potential stressors were perceived to be a function of the specific disease. The underlying assumption was that the family lay victim to the demands and stresses associated with the particular illness, and health care providers tended to support this notion. As a result, there were separate family programs for renal failure, arthritis, diabetes, stroke, cancer, and AIDS within a single medical center.

A more recent approach to the study and design of programs for families is the development of typologies of illnesses based on the psychosocial challenges affecting families with ill members. That is, families might be grouped together based on the characteristics of the onset, course, or prognosis of the condition. Thus, terminal conditions based on acute onset that involve episodes of incapacitation, e.g., with AIDS and some cancers, dictate similar psychosocial challenges for the patient and the family. Epilepsy or asthma, however, have acute onsets but are not as incapacitating or as life threatening. Still, other illnesses like Alzheimer's disease and late-onset multiple sclerosis are characterized by a gradual onset and a progressive debilitating course. In sum, illnesses vary in type of onset (acute or gradual), course (progressive, constant, or episodic), and degree of incapacitation. The prognostic time frame (crisis, chronic, or terminal) is still another variable that differentiates illnesses from one another. Illnesses in turn differentially challenge families, requiring different resources, strengths, attitudes, and behavioral changes. The overall amount of readjustment may be similar, but the manner and pace of those adjustments can be quite different. Since family adaptation is fluid and dynamic, the degree to which the family meets these challenges can affect not only the patient's adjustment to illness but the strength of the psychosocial stressors that impact the family.

Much of this approach of looking at families presumes illness to have negative effects on families. We also know that illness can and does bring out the best in families. Like individual patients, families can perceive the illness to be a challenge and then not only meet the challenge but even surpass expectations for coping. Just what makes the difference between high-level coping and low-level coping in families is not altogether clear but is probably accounted for by many factors relating to the family, the patient, the disease demand, and the treatment program.

General Difficulties Communicating with Families

With experience, providers learn about the different types of families that they may encounter and they develop a communication style suited to each. Nonetheless, their comfort in initiating interaction with families may vary a great deal. Many providers avoid direct interaction with family members—at least, as much as possible. That there are those who do not feel at ease in communicating with families should not be surprising. There is a certain ambiguity related to encountering families. First, considering all the ways in which family members can or have participated in the illness process, they are the protector, the enemy, and/or the confounding variable in the onset and course of the illness. On the other hand, the family is as much the victim as is the patient. So, how is the provider to view the family and how does one converse with such extreme possibilities?

In addition to this ambiguity about the effect of the family, there are other reasons why communicating with the family is difficult. Some providers are not trained in communicating effectively with family members or with the family as a whole. Also, some providers feel threatened. They may feel outnumbered by people who may question their competency. They may feel that families will make requests that they are unable or unwilling to fulfill. Other providers resent the time it takes to establish contact and talk with the family, especially if it is not altogether clear that this expenditure makes a difference. A final explanation for provider discomfort is that families may become another difficult variable with which to deal, and providers do not want to complicate an already challenging treatment situation. Is it any wonder that some providers, on seeing the family from a distance, might walk the other way to avoid them? Despite these generic fears and concerns that providers have, delivery systems do design, implement, and evaluate programs for families. Unfortunately, the families who need attention are not always those that are able or who choose to participate.

Families also express difficulty in communicating with providers. Northouse and Northouse (1992) explain that families have traditionally faced two problems: (1) They have minimal or limited contact with providers, and (2) their access to information about the patient's health status is limited or controlled. And as these authors point out, in spite of these shortcomings and the stress they experience, they generally receive little support from providers. On the whole, providers generate strong feelings in family members. Providers are the source of help and hope, and when the patient gets worse or better, providers' behaviors or lack of response are considered to be the reason. When things go wrong, providers are safer to blame than is the patient, and they are more tangible than is the disease. Because family members are the patient's primary constituency, they feel compelled, in some cases, to fulfill the role of advocate to the maximum. The stress they experience in their advocate role can place additional strain on their communications with providers. Providers need to provide appropriate reassurance and factual information in a caring manner with adequate follow-up in order for families to feel relief from the stress they experience (see Table 17–1).

Family Adaptation to Injury and Illness

The conditions that threaten the patient also threaten the family. As indicated previously, a number of illness- and treatment-related stressors impact families.

Families frequently experience crisis at the first sign of illness or injury. Principles that apply to working with patients in crisis, in large part, also apply to families. Families facing chronic debilitating or life-threatening illnesses are also

Table 17–1 Family Communications, Underlying Meanings, and Needs

Selected Family Communications	Underlying Feelings or Concerns	Request Value of Family Member's Statement
"Is he/she OK?" "How is he/she doing?"	Fear Worry Concern	Reassure me; tell me he/she is OK.
How did he/she get it?"	Confusion Concern	Educate me about this disease. Can I get it too?
"Will he/she die?"	Worry Concern Fear	Prepare me for what I have to face.
"Why hasn't his/her tray come/bath been given/medicines/treatments been started?"	Worry Concern Frustration	Tell me I can trust you to do what needs to be done when it needs to happen.
"Can I talk to you for a minute?"	Determination Concern	I really need more time. Can you talk to me? I need your input.
"I'm afraid I'll do/say the wrong thing."	Hesitancy Concern	Tell me how I should do this/tell me how I should conduct myself. Tell me I'm doing it OK.

believed to progress through grieflike stages in response to the illness. For a life-threatening condition, this may mean denial, anger, bargaining, depression, and acceptance. For chronic conditions, this may mean fear and anxiety, anger and hostility, depression, and resolution and acceptance.

The similarities in patient and family adaptive tasks are so great that the phenomena of adaptation is frequently attributed to both. The assumption here is that the patient and family progress through an illness process in a parallel fashion. Although this is generally the case, there are exceptions and the gap between patient and family seems to widen with time. For example, an initial diagnosis may shock both the patient and the family, and the length of time it takes to move on may be similar. By the point of acceptance, however, the gap may have widened. The patient may have reached acceptance but the family, or selected members of the family, may not have. The reverse may also be true. That is, the family may be in resolution but the patient may be primarily angry or in the bargaining mode.

Assessing Family Health and Family Relationships

History-taking relies not only on the patient's self-report but also on the information that family members give the provider. This information can be broken down into roughly three categories: (1) the family's report of the patient's condition, (2) the family's report of the health of its members, and (3) the family's report of the nature of its roles and relationships. This information is gleaned from the patient because the patient is the first line of inquiry. Families, however, are often brought into the assessment process because patients cannot or will not report certain data. In other cases, patients have given their information, but they are judged to be poor historians so family members are utilized to clarify, extend, and corroborate data that has been derived directly from the patient or indirectly from records and charts.

The family's report on the patient's current condition reveals how the patient's illness or injury is perceived from the outside. This report may reveal the patient's tendency to minimize or exaggerate symptoms. It also reveals the family's level of awareness and their own tendencies to minimize or exaggerate changes in the patient's appearance, behavior, or demeanor. Essentially, the provider wants to know what the family member has observed—the nature of the signs and symptoms, the degree of disability or impaired functioning, and how the member has processed this date and been affected by the patient's condition.

Families are informants about the family's health and can serve as a check on the reliability of the patient's report. Families are not necessarily better historians than patients, except in certain circumstances. Family members who are older, who have had recent experiences with illness, and who are (or have been) interested in health issues and familial problems are likely to be good historians. Some family members are hypervigilant about disease prevention and are able to report major illnesses (heart disease, cancer, strokes, etc.) three generations back. One by one, the provider progresses systematically through family members, accounting for major illnesses, injuries, and deaths. Where hereditary, infections, or familial conditions are concerned, extending the list of significant others beyond the immediate family is important.

The third category of data that is the subject of family interviews is specific data related to the roles and relationships in the family support network. Providers should identify which family members are most important to the patient, since their health and level of functioning will have the most bearing on the patient's current and future health status. Inquiring, "Who lives with the patient?" and "Do they have health problems? If so, what kind?" generally picks up on nonfamilial relationships that the family member may have forgotten to mention. Full information about the patient's current life situation is important. There are several basic categories of information that are derived from these conversations with family members. They include:

- active or potential dysfunction in the family
- factors that may inhibit communication in the family
- quality of communication between the patient and specific designated responsible parties
- patient's role in the family and alterations in role functioning as a result of the onset or progression of illness

There are numerous strengths and problem areas that can be revealed from this dialogue. Evidence of social isolation or alienation may surface. Evidence of impaired verbal communication, altered family functioning, and compromised family and parental role performance can be determined. Beginning evidence of actual or potential violence directed toward family members may also surface. Additionally, family-role conflict, ambiguity, role reversal, and role overload may become apparent from these initial conversations.

It is expected that families can elaborate on details, especially in areas wherein the patient was vague or where independent corroboration is needed. It is not unusual that a provider will get more information from family members than from patients themselves, particularly in areas that the patient is unaware of or reluctant to expand. For example, patients may not be aware that they had a seizure or exactly how an accident occurred. They may not realize that their behavior was irrational or bizarre. Sometimes patients not only minimize or exaggerate symptoms, they distort them in other ways as well. Providers may find that the patient was more acutely ill than the patient reported. Families can also be helpful in understanding patients' reactions to treatment and hospitalization, since members have observed both how patients have handled similar situations in the past and how they customarily behave. Sometimes providers will secure the entire history from a family member. This is the case if the patient is critically ill, demented, delirious, unconscious, psychotic, or cannot speak and/or hear.

Repeated brief contacts with family members, particularly if they are assuming caregiving functions, is important. These contacts not only allow providers to follow the patient's disease course but also reveal more about the persons concerned about the patient. Throughout the course of illness, families' involvement can change—caregivers and their caregiving duties can change. Such information is essential in planning the patient's care and managing the patient's illness. On some occasions, providers will meet conjointly with family and patient to discuss the patient's condition and plan of care. These sessions are extremely valuable but are not always possible unless the treatment program is specifically designed to actively involve family. A much more common occurrence is periodic family contact and brief conjoint encounters, a structure that permits limited education and support.

The confidentiality of family communications is very important. Personal information about family members is not communicated to the patient. Also, patients should be protected from conflictual data that is obtained from the family unless their condition requires it.

Patients' Requests with Respect to Families

As if to make the process of communicating even more difficult than it inherently is, there are other circumstances that complicate the picture. These circumstances are defined by patients themselves and include formal and informal requests.

We understand that patients typically define their own family unit. They identify a responsible person, a next of kin, and/or a parent/guardian, but these individuals are not always the same person. These individuals may not even be those persons who actually and/or legally fill these roles.

In addition to this complexity, patients establish the boundaries of communication with either their significant others or their next of kin. These boundaries include what the patient wants and does not want the family member to know. "I don't want them to know," or "I don't want them to be told," is not a rare occurrence. In some cultures, however, the role of family prevails. Some patients, typically some Latino and Asian patients, expect the family to know everything and take a major role in decision making. To maintain the patients' trust, their requests to share or withhold data from family members must be respected. In some cases, the law or absence of laws will support the provider's decision to keep information from a family. In other cases, there may be legal grounds for suspending confidentiality, e.g., the risk of self-harm.

Professional judgment may override patient requests. Professional judgment can dictate the necessity of sharing information with family members if it relates directly to the well-being of the patient. For example, the family may be instrumental in helping the patient make a decision or obtain resources. Another reason professional judgment may prevail is that discussing the patient's condition with the family or a family representative may prevent reinforcing the patient's avoidance of health care problems. Providers should not support maladaptive coping strategies, e.g., by helping patients not face their condition. Providers do not want to be placed in positions of conflict in their own clinical attempts to help patients acquire adaptive coping strategies.

For the provider to be released from the obligation of confidentiality, both patient and provider should negotiate compromises. Patients who openly express preferences do not make requests without reasons, and it is critical that providers understand the basis of the request. Providers cannot take these requests lightly. Still, by observing the patient with the family and by discussing the patients' reasoning, the consequences that are feared are usually clarified. Providers are not released from their promises of confidentiality until the patient has stated the circumstances (when and how) this confidence is to be suspended.

There are instances in which the patient's request becomes more imperative. Diagnoses and prognoses carry with them social consequences. A positive diagnosis of HIV infection, for example, produces stigma, fears, and responses that lead to social isolation and even alienation. While families may not, in reality, react negatively to information about the patient's diagnosis, the patient's concern may be deep-seated. Violation of the patient's confidence, even (or especially) with family, is prohibited in such cases.

If patients do not negotiate the release of confidentiality, the responsibility rests on the provider to determine if withholding information would jeopardize the patient's well-being. Sometimes these decisions are linked to the hindering of family rights or responsibilities. Consider, for example, the issue of teen pregnancy. If the teen patient requests that her next of kin (mother) not be told of her pregnancy, her well-being may be jeopardized. Also, withholding information about current or potential conditions from the patient's mother would be a violation of the mother's parental rights because it would significantly hinder her from fulfilling her parental responsibilities.

There are other instances in which the interface between patient and family becomes complicated. This problem is mentioned in instances of caring for terminal patients. As Cable (1991) describes, it is generally felt that caring for terminally ill patients requires effective communication with the families. Effective communication must become a regular part of the treatment. Decisions to support patients do not always have equally good outcomes for families, and vice versa, decisions favoring families may not be good for the patient. Providers find themselves in a dilemma. If they, on the one hand, do what appears to be best for the family, they may violate rights or ignore the needs of the patient. On the other hand, if they address specific needs of individual patients, they may weaken the family unit. Examples of these dilemmas also include acting on the information that patients report about the alleged abuse they have experienced at the hands of a family member or significant other.

Difficult Families and Provider Responses

Families bring with them certain characteristic ways of responding that may make providers' roles more difficult. Families who are regarded as more stressed are generally those who are more difficult to communicate with.

The following review highlights several types of families whom providers find difficult. Similar to dealing with patients who are difficult, it is important to understand the dynamics behind the family's communications and respond to these underlying issues, not just to the manifest expressions. For example, a family member who anxiously questions "Is he or she going to be OK?" is concerned, worried, and afraid. The underlying request to the provider may be interpreted as "Reassure me; tell me he/she is, in fact, OK." Questions like "How did he or she get it?" implies confusion and concern. The request behind the question is "Educate me about the disease. Can I get it too?" Communications that express concern, fear, and frustration are commonplace with family members who are or are not deemed to be difficult. Most providers will observe that if they try to understand the dynamics, they will experience less stress, more satisfaction, will achieve better overall treatment outcomes, and lower the potential for conflicts and disputes.

Howell and Schroeder (1984) identify nine separate categories of difficult families with the caveat that these categories are not mutually exclusive. Some families exhibit one or more categories or features from more than one categorical group. These categories are (1) the chaotic family, (2) the family in crisis, (3) the anxiety-ridden family, (4) the guilt-ridden family, (5) the enmeshed family, (6) the intimidating family, (7) the "split" family, (8) the psychosomatic family, and (9) the uncooperative or abusive family.

The following discussion highlights basic principles and concepts that are important in communicating with these selected categories of difficult families.

The Chaotic Family

According to Howell and Schroeder (1984), chaotic families are usually characterized by having multiple problems and multiple caregivers. They may appear to lack structure, to have no goals, and to have no designated person in authority. Their communication is confused and poor. This family looks to providers for guidance and structure. When a family moves with the same problem from one provider to another, the external authority figure, the provider, becomes disillusioned or even angry about having so much responsibility. Because of the continuous chaotic lines of communication and members' self-defeating encounters with each other, it appears that little effective problem solving will take place. And while the provider may diligently seek the origin of each problem and offer suggestions, it is best to realize that the family has a temporary plan and structure to follow but will respond with minimal compliance.

Providers must recognize the character of these families and set limited, realistic goals. Guidelines to structure communications with the chaotic family in conjoint sessions include (1) structuring the direction and duration of the interview, (2) speaking clearly and gaining and maintaining control within the family, (3) appealing to the leaders to follow up on recommendations, and (4) establishing definite time lines for future encounters.

The Family in Crisis

The family in crisis is not unlike the patient in crisis who is experiencing an unexpected incapacitating trauma. The major reason that providers have difficulty communicating with these families is that communication is boundless. Typically, they may have lost control over their emotions and/or do not synthesize instruction or information in a rational manner (Howell and Schroeder 1984). And because family members vary in their responses, providers may have multiple responses to deal with simultaneously. These include anger, rage, fear, panic, blame, and guilt. The provider can be flooded by the number of responses as well as by their intensity. The primary therapeutic response is to allow family members time to express their emotions. A central organizing figure must be assigned to deal with this family's responses and needs, and feedback should be provided in an empathic, supportive manner.

The Anxiety-Ridden and Guilt-Ridden Families

Families who are in crisis over illness or who are facing uncertainties that accompany the illness process may be anxiety ridden or guilt ridden. Typically, the anxiety-ridden family is extremely tense, is upset about the status of the patient, and is frequently overinvolved in the patient's care. These families may be awaiting test results or the outcome of treatment or surgery. They are frequently anxious because they lack information that would calm them down or at least limit their worst fears. They also seek reassurance and information but utilize information poorly. It is important to be clear, to say the same things to all family members, and to avoid false reassurance.

Guilt-ridden families can be draining. This family's communications are motivated by the desperate need to make restitution, to pay for injustices, or to deal with unresolved feelings toward the patient (Howell and Schroeder 1984). Some guilt may be internally generated because a family wants to know that they did all they could do. These families may become desperate when they realize that the patient may be so incapacitated (or may die) that their desires for restitution will be thwarted. Whether their guilt is justified or not, if it is exaggerated out of proportion, they can become difficult to converse with. Another characteristic is this family's inability to control anger and their negative feelings. The consequence of this is that they may project their guilt onto someone else, typically the provider(s). Unreasonable demands made of providers are often a reflection of the guilt the family experiences.

The Enmeshed or Disengaged Family

Enmeshment and disengagement refer to distinctly different structural properties of families (Howell and Schroeder 1984). Enmeshed families appear to be overinvolved and individual member autonomy is either severely limited or nonexistent. It appears as if no boundaries exist in this family and whatever happens to the patient happens to them. While anxiety and guilt may account for these behaviors, some families have long histories of relating as enmeshed units.

In contrast, disengaged families have rigid boundaries, the experiences of one member seem to cause no response in others. These family members may be incapable of feeling or sensing the needs of the patient. Structurally, they may also have minimal contact and minimal interactions with the patient.

Responses to enmeshed families include setting limits and clarifying boundaries. These families may not respect provider boundaries. Therefore, clarifying professional roles and expectations, and maintaining autonomy for one's own clinical decision making are important. In contrast to the enmeshed family, the disengaged family typically must be brought closer together. Projecting feelings and discussing typical responses to injury or illness also help to encourage a revelation of feelings that can make these families more empathic toward the patient.

The Intimidating and Uncooperative Family

Two additional family types that providers find difficult to encounter are the intimidating and the uncooperative family (Howell and Schroeder 1984).

The intimidating family can be one of the most distressing types because there is an element of threat that looms in the background. These families' communications may be characterized as abusive. By putting providers down, by making providers feel that their actions could be questioned, and by alluding to the fact that complaints or suits may be forthcoming, they become threatening. Some families ask for extensive details about treatment, question providers' judgments, and when they do not get the response that they need, become rude or belligerent.

Guidelines for communicating with this family include establishing a clear treatment plan that is constructed similarly to a contract. Providers must also resist the anger these families provoke in them and focus on the underlying dynamics that explain the power struggles that these families tend to evoke.

Uncooperative families who clearly are problematic are those who exhibit very little or no real concern for the patient. They may also be very resistant to speaking with providers as well as carrying out any suggestions or recommendations. Some families in this category abandon the patient, leaving the patient to fend for himself. This type of family may also not be helpful in the assessment and history-taking process. They may even be secretive and somewhat paranoid about being addressed in an official capacity. Establishing communication with these families requires careful analysis of underlying issues and assessment of how the families responses will affect the outcome of the patients' care and treatment.

The Phenomena of Caregiver Burden

While the stress of caregiving has been widely reported among health professionals, less has been reported about the stress of caregivers who are not professionals. Professional caregivers have been educated and trained and it is presumed this knowledge and skill helps them cope with the stresses of caregiving. Informal family caregivers typically lack the skill, knowledge, and experience that providers have. Still, the number of informal caregivers is increasing significantly. These informal caregivers receive variable amounts of support and education with which to accomplish similar tasks. While their responsibilities are typically limited to one patient, these responsibilities can be 24 hours a day, seven days a week. Both professional and informal caregivers experience stress and burnout, perhaps for different reasons, but the expressions of stress are similar.

First, families experience stressors unrelated to specific caregiving tasks. Some of the most compassionate reports of caregiver stress have appeared in the last decade and come from family members of cardiac, cancer, HIV, and Alzheimer's disease patients. These family stressors are many and occur in significant magnitude to place the family at high risk for further problems and afflictions. These include social and emotional costs, physical exhaustion, financial drain, and in some cases, stigma and alienation.

In most cases, the stressors related to the patient's illness and treatment are also many. But, among those that are of most concern to families who are giving care are the cognitive and emotional changes both in the patient and, potentially, in themselves.

Cognitive impairment in patients can include memory loss, disorientation, impaired concentration and judgment, impaired perception, confusion, mental slowing, and the inability to engage in abstract thinking. These problems can occur in patients with senile dementia, HIV, depression, and in patients with mental and addictive disorders. In addition to cognitive impairment, emotional changes and disturbances occur in patients who have mental illness, the elderly, persons with HIV, substance abusers, and in medical illnesses such as cardiac disease and cancer. Patients who experience these disturbances can be bothered by sleep and eating disturbances, fatigue, generalized apathy, irritability, low self-worth, hopelessness, and suicidal or homicidal ideation and/or risk.

Typically, the informal caregiver is faced with the same situations that confront the professional. That is, the informal caregiver must learn to give instrumental care (administer medications, treatments, etc.) and emotional support and these must be accomplished in cases where the patient's ability to cooperate or render self-care may be minimal and variable. The difference is that informal caregivers must organize these responsibilities in and around their own activities. Thus, the social and occupational lives of informal family caregivers are threatened, sometimes considerably.

Informal caregivers' reports of emotional exhaustion indicate that the burdens that they experience are significant and not easily modified. To understand the informal family member's experience of emotional exhaustion, a list of potential reactions are provided in Exhibit 17–2.

Exhibit 17–2 Caregiver Burden: Emotional Exhaustion in Family Caregivers

- feeling physically and emotionally drained from caring for the patient
- feeling angry and frustrated by the prospect of endless caregiving responsibilities
- feeling frustrated by the program of caregiving and the numerous demands without clear signs of improvement or progress
- feeling powerless over the disease, its course, and their ability to make changes for the better
- feeling angry at the patient for significantly altering their quality of life

CONCLUSION

Dealing with families during illness implies a challenge to patient and family by an altered set of circumstances for which adaptive resources may not readily be available (Kercher 1991). Adequate intervention implies an evaluation of the resources within the individual and an evaluation of the resources among those who surround the individual in the family and the community.

Families are not just "those people" who "ask stupid questions" or "get in the way"; they are special patient constituencies who significantly impact and are impacted by the patient, the treatment, and the treatment institution. Providers need to enlist families in formal and informal ways to get the best of any illness or condition. Because of their importance, it is critical that providers understand family communications and how best to converse with the family members. A small part of this time will be spent in taking a social or family history; the large part of the investment will be the use of the family in understanding and helping the patient.

Families have been associated with the onset and outcome of diseases, particularly chronic conditions, in a number of ways. Research has focused on the protective role of families, particularly in their ability to buffer illness-related stressors. Studies have also isolated instances in which families may contribute to the occurrence of disease or at least worsen the probability of adequate adaptation. More-recent research has addressed the interdependent nature of the patient's illness and the adaptive capabilities of the family. Finally, we have a model that addresses the significant burden that families endure as a result of an ill family member. With the broad range of possibilities—to help or to hinder and sometimes both simultaneously—the family should be approached with appropriate caution.

Families who are most difficult to communicate with, e.g., the anxiety, guilt-ridden, or uncooperative families, can be managed. The key is to understand that the behavior is amenable to change if the underlying issues are approached and resolved.

Families are currently faced with burdens of caregiving that they never before expected to see. This is, in part, an outcome of the many delivery-system changes that have moved caregiving from inpatient intensive care settings to outpatient facilities and the home. In a study by Davis-Martin (1994), it was found that the needs of long-term, critical-care patients' families do not subside. The desire for information remained the number-one need. This is not the time to abandon the family because it is difficult to communicate with family members or the unit as a whole. Rather, as providers, we must embrace the family with all its rough edges, strengths, and limitations. Next of kin, parents or guardians, responsible persons, and everyday families (broader social units acting like families) are a part of the picture. Patients may need to rely on these constituencies for extended periods. Some, but not all, will deliver aspects of care. As such, they constitute the greatest potential health care resource that we have today and that we will have in the future.

In spite of the growing recognition of the influence of interactions with health care providers on how patients and family members respond to illness, the level of research about families and their roles is deficient (Knafl et al. 1992). More research is needed.

PART V

Ethics and Communication in Health Care

Instruction in the skills and concepts of applied communication in health care would be incomplete without a discussion of the important ethical and legal concepts that shape and limit providers' communications with patients and families. Stipulations about the nature of the professional patient-provider communications underscore a good deal of what is considered ethical. Some rules and norms are not only standards of professional practice, they are displayed in statements of patient rights, in statutes, and in laws. It is important to understand the issue of patient rights in its fullest. Patient rights govern what patients have a right to know and what protection they have against others' knowing, that is, what will be communicated to them, but not to others.

In Chapter 18, The Privileged Nature of Patient and Provider Communications: The Issue of Patients' Rights, the concepts of informed consent and informed choice are discussed. These concepts are applied to research- and nonresearch-based clinical practice. They are basic in intent, but their assurance is far from simple; thus problems in securing informed consent and informed choice are identified and discussed.

In addition to patients' basic rights to informed consent and informed choice, there are specific stipulations that protect patients from exposure. One such stipulation governs issues of confidentiality—that which providers can ethically and legally divulge, to whom, and under what conditions. In Chapter 19, The Privileged Nature of Patient and Provider Communications: Issues of Confidentiality, Anonymity, and Privacy, the rules around confidentiality are presented. Two related concepts, that of anonymity and privacy, are also discussed.

It has been said that today we need to be more concerned than ever before with the ethical and legal foundations of health care communications. The flagrant abuse of patients' rights can be observed in many arenas and in many different ways. Certainly, the flippant disrespect of patient confidentiality is among the most serious. Policies that protect patient rights and afford patient control must be uppermost in our minds. Providers' commitment to ethical practices in the realm of written and verbal communications to and about patients must be fostered and reinforced.

CHAPTER 18

The Privileged Nature of Patient and Provider Communications: The Issue of Patients' Rights

This declaration of patient rights (AHA Patient's Bill of Rights) is even more important in today's health care environment, in which cost containment efforts so often seem to be driving most organizational decision-making, including patient care decisions.

Anne J. Davis and Mila A. Aroskar

CHAPTER OBJECTIVES

- Define the principle of client-informed choice.
- Describe the process of obtaining client-informed consent.
- Discuss providers' legal duty to care for clients.
- Discuss dynamics under which providers refuse to provide care and identify how they communicate refusal to clients.
- Identify selected times in which clients do not have personal choices about communication.
- Identify which factors make informed consent difficult to obtain.
- Identify various client groups for which informed choice and informed consent are especially difficult to obtain. Identify alternatives.

The privileged nature of patient-provider communications is played out in the specific encounters we have with patients and patients' families. It is understood that patients who enter into relationships with providers are protected by a set of norms that outline, at least in part, how the roles of provider and patients are to be enacted and exactly what privileges and responsibilities it is that these roles entail. The reality of practicing as a health care provider includes risks as well as rewards. In this era of malpractice controversies and the emerging legal considerations of managed care, these risks become more than just hypothetical circumstances or philosophical debates. The rights and privileges of patients regarding their care and communications with providers should be taken very seriously.

Many kinds of legal and ethical issues confront health care providers. These vary from what seem to be straightforward issues of informing patients of their diagnosis to more complex issues related to extending patients' lives. From a legal and ethical standpoint, we are concerned with liability, incident reports, and malpractice. From a communication perspective, we are concerned with the basic challenge of effectively communicating with patients in order to maximize their privileges of choice and execute our responsibilities. There are several sources of pressure that influence our actions. Licensure and accreditation of health care facilities sanction practices that are not respectful of patients' rights. These sanctions range from very severe to merely warnings. Providers' own professional licensure requirements, however, strongly enforce adherence to basic fundamental patients' rights.

Additionally, legal systems have evolved in elaborate ways to address the complexity of provider-patient encounters. Federal and state laws regulate practice through professional-practice acts. Each state must assume the responsibility for developing these guidelines and for providing regulatory measures to ensure that professional standards are upheld. This legislative authority is both ethically and legally binding. It is important to note that providers are expected not only to practice within standards, but they are also expected to protect patients from abuses within the health care system. It is this latter area that can create dilemmas that are not easily resolved. Many providers are clear about their own level of practice; however, when the system and/or other providers are involved and place the patient at risk, indirectly or directly, the fundamentals of practice and of protecting health care systems becomes complex. These conflicts raise a number of professional consequences that create stress in providers. Thus, the role of providers in protecting patient rights is influenced by many factors. The communication and interpersonal competencies of providers are intimately connected to safeguarding patients' rights.

ISSUES OF PROFESSIONAL-PATIENT PRIVILEGE

Perhaps the most noteworthy examples of professional-patient privilege are embedded in the concepts of informed choice and informed consent. The underlying belief behind the issues of informed choice and informed consent is that in health care arenas, the balance of power rests with providers. After all, the patient is ill or otherwise incapacitated and is at the mercy of the system's definition of when, where, what, and how actions will be taken. By virtue of this inequitable power distribution, patients' rights for self-determination must be protected. Inherent in this objective is the standard to act and communicate in ways that respect the dignity and worth of every patient. We, as health care providers, are morally obligated to respect human existence and the individuality of all patients who are recipients of our care, but our values may run counter to traditional treatment measures. Resolving these conflicts is not easy; an entire science of bioethical decision making has emerged in the last two decades to assist us with these complexities.

Informed Choice

In each and every health care situation, providers have a duty to offer patients choices and participation in decisions that are germane to their case. These choices are always reflective of the medical technology and resources available. A provider cannot offer an alternative surgical procedure if that procedure is contrary to hospital policy or is not available due to lack of medical and professional resources. Providers are, however, obligated to describe the alternatives that are available. Informed choice requires providers to clearly communicate about the treatment of choice, but also about other less-favored approaches. Sometimes, clarity is severely lacking and options may go undiscussed altogether.

Haas et al. (1993) reported on the barriers that providers had in discussing resuscitation with AIDS patients. In this study, the majority of persons with AIDS had not discussed their preferences for life-sustaining care with their physician, despite their desire to do so. Health care providers need to be well-informed about advance directives for medical care in the event that a patient becomes incapacitated. The Patient Self-Determination Act requires that all patients be advised of their options at the time of hospital admission (Goldstein et al. 1991). Whereas attitudes toward advance directives are positive, many providers have little knowledge of the Durable Power of Attorney for Health Care Act and are poorly equipped to discuss it with patients, not only out of ignorance, but because of their own personal discomforts.

In cases where providers must offer informed choice, a number of factors influence the process. These include the historical and technological treatment patterns as well as the philosophical and even religious background of providers. These factors often explain why providers may hold different attitudes about the same issue and why some providers are more comfortable in their communication than others.

Some providers come from cultural backgrounds that do not place much value on principles of autonomy and self-determination. We might expect these providers to understand and practice informed-choice procedures somewhat differently.

Without accusing or critically evaluating these providers, we can say that their approach to informing patients of treatment choices may be influenced by their underlying belief system. For example, they may fail to address all potential treatment choices, or they may overemphasize their authority in directing patients' choices. On a more subtle level, they may verbally present *choices* but nonverbally suggest that their *opinions* should be followed. Their encounters with patients may also suggest that if patients do not follow their advice, there may be negative repercussions. A patient's fear of retaliation, real or imagined, can influence whether he or she will exercise his or her autonomy. Fear of retaliation could be fear that the treatment they receive will be withdrawn, that they will suffer unnecessary pain or discomfort, or that they will even experience some form of interpersonal abandonment in their relationship with providers. For these reasons, patients may be very sensitive to any variances in the context of discussions of choices. They may react to perceptions of the providers' bias or preference, or even imagine what those biases might be.

Despite this subtle, and not so subtle, interplay between providers' preference and patients' choices, one thing must be generally clear: The patient is the primary decision maker. With the advancement of the science of bioethical decision making, there has been a renewed concern for patients' roles in their care and their personal freedom to direct this care. It is generally maintained that patients should retain significant control over health care decisions that affect their welfare, and they can only do this if the communications between the provider and patient are open and fluid.

In 1983, the President's Commission for the Study of Ethical Problems in Medicine and Biomedical and Behavioral Research issued a recommendation with regard to patients' roles in health care decisions (Thompson and Thompson 1985). This document supported the important concept that patients with the capacity to make decisions be permitted to do so. The Commission, however, indicated that the process is based on mutual respect and shared information, though this choice is not absolute. For example, patients cannot expect health care providers to render services that violate standards of practice or the providers' moral beliefs. This deliberation also touched on the issue of reasonable rights; that is, the patient cannot insist on services that draw on limited resources to which the patient has no binding claim.

We could say, for example, that expensive one-to-one nursing care, although demanded by a patient, is outside the realm of possibility—the patient has no binding contract with the facility to receive this type of care. This clarification of the limits of patients' choice in health care is made on a case-by-case basis. The institution's rights may predominate, but this is not just an issue of providers' maintaining power over patients. Rather, it provides some protection to the health care facility and provider groups as they attempt to balance patient autonomy with instances in which it is inappropriate to let patients make the final choice.

What remains critical here is that regardless of the request, respectful discussions, where information is provided in ways the patient can comprehend it, must be ensured.

Informed Consent

The era of automatic acceptance that physicians and nurses are competent in ethical decision making is said to be coming to a close (Thompson and Thompson 1985). One reason for this is that clinical and technical skill and expertise cannot be easily generalized to ethical decision making. Rees (1993) suggests that political, legal, ethical, social, economic, and technological changes in the twentieth century have profoundly changed the way in which providers and clients communicate. As patients now assume two identities, health consumers and active participants in medical decision making, they are more and more concerned not only about symptoms, disease, and treatment, but they are also equally preoccupied with issues about cost of, quality of, and access to health care.

There are many more decisions to be made in health care practice than there were a century ago; even within the last decade, technological advances have made bio-behavioral medical decision making exceedingly complex. This advancement in technology has created choices and options in patient care that did not previously exist.

The issue of informed consent is derived from the value of self-determination wherein information is the prelude to informed choice. That is, under normal circumstances, informed patients are capable of making decisions about their care. Exceptional circumstances are those in which families make decisions and many times providers fail to communicate effectively with the family.

There are many difficulties in achieving patient informed consent; these difficulties cause us to consider whether informed consent can in actuality be met. First, patients, families, and providers frequently come to decisions with dissimilar values and beliefs. Even if these values and beliefs appear compatible, their translations may be quite different. For example, both patient and provider may want the best possible surgical intervention and on the outside, their views seem compatible. When these views are translated to specific steps and "surgical cuts," however, we find that the provider's views are more radical than the patient's. Because values and beliefs are always subject to individual interpretation, they are best presented by the patient and not simply inferred from what the patient has said. If the patient is unable to verbalize the specifics, then the provider can address gaps or problems in understanding by qualifying, clarifying, or offering the patient multiple-choice options.

Knowing the views of the patient requires time and this time is not vacuous—it is time within the context of a therapeutic relationship. Does the provider have the time that is required to learn the views of the patient? Some providers feel that too much time spent in extracting patients' views may inhibit decision making rather than facilitate it. They are concerned that the process can get bogged down. In extended communications of this sort, it is common that many options are raised. Sometimes these options are impractical or have never been tried before. Too many options can contribute to the confusion of what decision to make. The patient, family, and provider may have already had difficulty with only two options for action; now the situation is complicated with still additional choices.

Most providers would agree that the time spent in learning to understand the patient's concerns, personal beliefs, and cultural beliefs is worthwhile. There are many of us who would say that this process is not only valuable, it is an imperative. That is, providing the best care possible rests on our knowing our patients well.

Patients' rights for self-determination include their protection from deception. Deception in health care is a type of manipulation that subverts patients' capacities to exercise rational and deliberate choice. Deception, when translated into specific acts, includes withholding information, deliberately making the information unclear or difficult to understand, minimizing important aspects, and presenting an unbalanced picture. Historically, providers have considered that less information leads to greater satisfaction, at least in the short run. This point of view is highly inconsistent with current thinking. It is currently held that with each act of deception, however minor, there is a corrosive effect on the patient-provider relationship. The trust that is necessary in patient-provider relationships suffers with even the most minor instances of deception.

Given the importance of truthfulness in the professional provider-patient relationship, it may come as a surprise to realize that the codes of professional ethics have not always presented a strong case for truthfulness. Bok (1978), cited in Benjamin and Curtis (1992), points out that professional oaths and codes as well as the writings of physicians have made little to no mention of the need to be truthful.

For whatever reasons the issue of truthfulness has not been stressed early on, the current shift away from paternal dominance to individual rights through knowing is both a serious and important shift. The Patient's Bill of Rights, endorsed by the American Hospital Association in 1992, clearly recognizes the importance of a high level of honesty in patient-provider communications (see Exhibit 18–1).

This bill of rights recognizes the patient's right to complete, current information concerning his or her diagnosis, treatment, and prognosis in terms that the patient can be reasonably expected to understand. Except in emergencies when the patient

Exhibit 18–1 Patient's Bill of Rights, American Hospital Association (October 21, 1992)

1. The patient has the right to considerate and respectful care.

2. The patient has the right to and is encouraged to obtain from physicians and other direct caregivers relevant, current, and understandable information concerning diagnosis, treatment, and prognosis. Except in emergencies when the patient lacks decision-making capacity and the need for treatment is urgent, the patient is entitled to the opportunity to discuss and request information related to the specific procedures and/or treatments, the risks involved, the possible length of recuperation, and the medically reasonable alternatives and their accompanying risks and benefits. Patients have the right to know the identity of physicians, nurses, and others involved in their care, as well as when those involved are students, residents, or other trainees. The patient also has the right to know the immediate and long-term financial implications of treatment choices, insofar as they are known.

3. The patient has the right to make decisions about the plan of care prior to and during the course of treatment and to refuse a recommended treatment or plan of care to the extent permitted by law and hospital policy and to be informed of the medical consequences of this action. In case of such refusal, the patient is entitled to other appropriate care and services that the hospital provides or transfer to another hospital. The hospital should notify patients of any policy that might affect patient choice within the institution.

4. The patient has the right to have an advance directive (such as a living will, health care proxy, or durable power of attorney for health care) concerning treatment or designating a surrogate decision-maker with the expectation that the hospital will honor the intent of that directive to the extent permitted by law and hospital policy. Health care institutions must advise patients of their rights under state law and hospital policy to make informed medical choices, ask if the patient has an advance directive, and include that information in patient records. The patient has the right to timely information about hospital policy that may limit its ability to implement fully a legally valid advance directive.

5. The patient has the right to every consideration of his privacy. Case discussion, consultation, examination, and treatment should be conducted so as to protect each patient's privacy.

6. The patient has the right to expect that all communications and records pertaining to his/her care will be treated as confidential by the hospital, except in cases such as suspected abuse and public health hazards when reporting is permitted or required by law. The patient has the right to expect that the hospital will emphasize the confidentiality of this information when it releases it to any other parties entitled to review information in these records.

7. The patient has the right to review the records pertaining to his/her medical care and to have the information explained or interpreted as necessary, except when restricted by law.

continues

Exhibit 18–1 continued

8. The patient has the right to expect that, within its capacity and policies, a hospital will make reasonable response to the request of a patient for appropriate and medically indicated care and services. The hospital must provide evaluation, service, and/or referral as indicated by the urgency of the case. When medically appropriate and legally permissible, or when a patient has so requested, a patient may be transferred to another facility. The institution to which the patient is to be transferred must first have accepted the patient for transfer. The patient must also have the benefit of complete information and explanation concerning the need for risks, benefits, and alternatives to such a transfer.

9. The patient has the right to ask and be informed of the existence of business relationships among the hospital, educational institutions, other health care providers, or payers that may influence the patient's treatment and care.

10. The patient has the right to consent to or decline to participate in proposed research studies or human experimentation affecting care and treatment or requiring direct patient involvement, and to have those studies fully explained prior to consent. A patient who declines to participate in research or experimentation is entitled to the most effective care that the hospital can otherwise provide.

11. The patient has the right to expect reasonable continuity of care when appropriate and to be informed by physicians and other caregivers of available and realistic patient care options when hospital care is no longer appropriate.

12. The patient has the right to be informed of hospital policies and practices that relate to patient care, treatment, and responsibilities. The patient has the right to be informed of available resources for resolving disputes, grievances, and conflicts, such as ethics committees, patient representatives, or other mechanisms available in the institution. The patient has the right to be informed of the hospital's charges for services and available payment methods.

Source: Reprinted with permission from the American Hospital Association, Chicago, Illinois, © 1992.

lacks decision-making capacity and the need for treatment is urgent, the patient is entitled to the oppurtunity to discuss and request information related to the specific procedures and/or treatments, the risks involved, the possible length of recuperation, and the medically reasonable alternatives and their accompanying risks and benefits.

Perhaps the most dramatic example of the shift to provide patients with information is seen in the following example. Not more than two decades ago it was unthinkable for a patient to exercise his rights to the extent of requesting copies of everything in his medical record, including notes, lab-test results, doctors' orders, and so forth. Today, this request occurs, albeit infrequently, and while the entire chart is not usually provided, excerpts of the contents of the record are summarized for the patient. This request is not only for the purpose of completing referrals, it is in response to a direct request of the patient to have access to and therefore to be able to pursue and deliberate, for himself and under conditions he chooses, aspects of his illness and treatment.

The process of informed consent becomes even more deliberate when the patient is involved in research studies. Research studies are usually of two kinds: (1) those focused on specific medical experiments, e.g., studies involving experimental drugs or devices, and (2) those focused on nonmedical research, e.g., studies in the social sciences that study behavioral responses to illness through the use of surveys and interviews.

Research studies involve several issues around patient's rights and, therefore, undergo a great deal of scrutiny in institutional review boards (IRBs) and human subject protection committees (HSPCs). Issues of concern to review committees include (1) risk (minimal and major) of physical and/or emotional injury, (2) physical and/or emotional (mental) discomfort or pain related to the research process, (3) loss or invasion of privacy, dignity, and/or autonomy by consenting to participate, and (4) the time and energy required to participate. In any research study, these issues must be addressed clearly and truthfully by researchers. Under review, these issues are extensively examined, including the clarity of the investigators' descriptions. An approval issued by an IRB or HSPC always means that the risks of the study outweigh the benefits and that any conditions placing the patient at risk have adequately been communicated by the investigator.

Additionally, IRBs will expect to be assured that specific issues related to subject recruitment, procedures for obtaining informed consent, and protecting confidentiality are addressed. They are concerned with how subjects will be selected and contacted as well as what subjects will be told on the first contact. IRBs are concerned about whether subjects and data about subjects will be identifiable by name, and if patients are identified by name, what procedures will be used to collect, process, and store data that will protect patient identity. Review boards expect patients to be informed of the purpose of the study, the expected duration of their participation, and the reasonably foreseeable immediate and long-term discomforts, hazards, risks, and potential consequences. Every consent must include certain guarantees; these vary from institution to institution but generally include stated reassurances that (1) the patient may refuse to participate or may withdraw from participation at any time without any negative consequences, (2) no information that identifies the patient will be released without the patient's separate consent (except as specifically required by law), and (3) if the study, design, or use of data is changed, patients will be informed and their consent reobtained. The informed-consent forms inform the patient whom to contact with concerns or questions about the study and how to proceed if this avenue does not satisfy the patient. A copy of the written consent along with a statement of the Patient's Bill of Rights is provided to each subject. In the case that a subject is unable to sign, e.g., in the case of minors, a signature (and date) is obtained from a parent or guardian. If the patient cannot sign because of physical disability or illiteracy but is otherwise capable of being informed and of giving verbal consent, a third party not connected with the study (a next-of-kin or guardian), would be asked to witness the discussion, sign, and state the reason for standing in for the patient. When a subject's native language is one other than English (or the person is poorly versed in English) an accurate translation must be used.

Studies of a medical nature involving treatment of disease or illness, e.g., those involving experimental drugs or medical devices, must provide additional information to patients. Studies of this kind must include a statement that describes any appropriate alternative procedures or treatment that might be advantageous, including both risks and benefits.

THE LEGAL STATUS OF THE PATIENT-PROVIDER RELATIONSHIP

Health care providers are confronted with many legal and ethical issues, but medical technology is not the sole reason for this circumstance. Health care delivery has become exceedingly complex. The emerging system of managed care brings a myriad of important issues to the surface that includes who decides, who gives care, and who, ultimately, is accountable for outcomes. A good deal of this complexity is played out in one-to-one encounters with providers. Accountability, responsibility, and subsequently, liability, is understood or misunderstood in the specific context of patient-provider relationships.

Just about every ethical and/or legal issue reflects the inadequacy of patient-provider communication and the trustworthiness of the relationship. Refusal or withdrawal of treatment, for example, occurs in the context of patients' and providers' understanding of one another's roles and beliefs. When "push comes to shove," patient dissatisfaction and/or the decision to pursue litigation reflects, in large part, the poor quality of communication within the patient-provider relationship.

Legal Duty To Provide Care

Duty to the patient, including a breach of duty, underlies standards of practice for all health care professionals. When health care professionals enter into a relationship with a patient, a duty or obligation that is recognized as a legal relationship ensues. This legal relationship holds the professional accountable for practicing within established standards of care. When this duty includes providing care as well as protecting patients from harm, the legal relationship becomes even more complex. Clearly, one can comprehend the circumstances of a particular provider neglecting the patient and performing below standards, which is grounds for malpractice.

Providers, however, are also commonly confronted with situations that impinge on, or have the potential to impinge on, patients' rights. The four basic consumer rights outlined by the American Hospital Association (AHA) are (1) the right to safety, (2) the right to be informed, (3) the right to choose, and (4) the right to be heard. What happens if the provider witnesses infractions of these rights by others in the health care system?

Most clearly, our legal duty includes protecting patients from harm and from violations of their rights. Consider, for example, a particular patient who is not warned of the consequences of research protocol or of a drug trial. Let us also say that another provider, or even a group of providers, is aware of this problem. It is obvious that the provider who is prescribing the treatment is at risk for malpractice through negligence. Still, are the providers who are aware of the problem and who do not intercede also negligent? We could argue convincingly that this is the case; in truth, however, malpractice claims are usually levied against the institution as well as the individual practitioner. Is this because the attorney understands that the institution has more money than does the individual provider? Maybe. But, the real issue here is that other professionals were aware of the situation and did not correct it. As providers, we have a moral, ethical, and legal duty to intervene.

Providers Who Refuse To Provide Care

Essentially, providers have the right to refuse to provide care if the interventions to be used stand in opposition to the provider's ethics or values. Additionally, if the provider feels incompetent to care for a patient, this refusal is supportable. If providers assume care that they are not competent to perform, they may be disciplined for incompetence or negligence.

There are other circumstances that may also surround providers' refusals to provide care. These include (1) physical risk (when there is strong evidence to suggest more than minimal risk to self), (2) rendered care that violates patient autonomy and rights to self-determinations, and (3) religious and/or moral issues that cause the provider to object. Most institutions will support a provider's personal objections provided that these are stated well in advance and result in no harm or negative consequences for patients.

While the duty to provide care is quite clear, providers' refusals to provide care are not infrequent occurrences. Early on in the AIDS epidemic, many providers expressed their fears, and even distaste, about caring for patients with AIDS. These fears, expressed as fear of AIDS contagion, were questioned because the chance of a provider contracting HIV infection was extremely small. These fears were often worsened by conflicting values and underlying prejudice against persons or groups who practiced risky behavior. As the epidemic has spread into the heterosexual population, attitudes have shifted somewhat; still, the ways in which the majority of people contract HIV in the United States (through intravenous drug use, unprotected sex with an intravenous drug user, or male homosexual sexual encounters) fuel a great deal of negative reaction in providers who cannot accept those lifestyles.

A provider's reluctance to care and refusal to care are frequently communicated to patients. This reluctance may be blatantly disloyal and may take the form of refusal to enter a patient's room, exaggerated protective measures, and even direct comments to patients, implying that they have some form of character weakness. It may also be covert (e.g., in little time spent with the patient and minimal communication responsiveness). Historically, provider refusal to provide care was viewed as unethical. Ethical codes focused on patients' rights, ignoring providers' values and beliefs, but times have changed. The shift toward recognizing providers' limits to providing care have largely been regarded positively, since forcing them to provide care would be detrimental to both patient and provider.

Limitations on Patients' Personal Choices

The so-called doctrines of personal choice and informed consent originated largely from malpractice litigation. Historically, patients' rights to informed consent were blatantly violated; patients knew little of the nature of their treatment, outcomes, or alternative procedures (and/or the outcomes of no intervention). There was no conceivable way in which they could enter into a personal cost-benefit analysis. To correct this situation, numerous changes occurred, but the outcomes of these changes did not respect the limitations of patient decision making. The President's Commission for the Study of Ethical Problems in Medicine and Biomedical and Behavioral Research (1983) recognized that patients' choices were not absolute. This limitation was described as irregularities in patients' requests such that they violated standards of practice or overtaxed clinical resources.

There are specific circumstances wherein providers' recommendations clearly need to be heeded in spite of contrary beliefs of patients. In these cases, it is appropriate for providers to make the final decision for action. Perhaps the most obvious situation is when the patient clearly and directly requests the provider to make the decision. In this case, it is important for providers to understand why the patient or patient's family has requested that the provider decide. There is at least one problem area. This is in respect to the traditional deference given to providers. Some cultural groups are more likely to defer to authority figures. When their request is an unnecessarily dependent one, the provider has an obligation to engage the patient or patient's family more actively in the decision-making process. In any case, providers should not take the relinquishing of decision making by the patient lightly.

THE PROBLEMS WITH INFORMED CONSENT AND INFORMED CHOICE

Assumptions about Patients

The concept of informed choice and informed consent is based on the important assumption that the patient (and/or family) is adequately informed. Prerequisites are that the patient is willing, capable, and competent to receive the information. Questions that must be satisfied include:

- Does the patient have the ability to hear or read?
- Is the language used appropriately for his understanding?
- Is the method used to present the information respectful of the patient's age and educational level?
- Is the patient's attention span and memory sufficient enough to allow him to process the information?
- Will the patient clarify the information he cannot fully comprehend?
- Does he understand his rights to decide even if his decisions run counter to those of the provider?
- Does he have the ability to communicate his decisions and preferences?

Special Problems with Certain Patient Groups

It is important to recognize that all patients have handicaps in one or more of these areas. Patients' willingness to be informed, their abilities to receive and to process data, and their abilities to express themselves are due to many factors. These factors include illness, the effects of treatment, the psychological responses to illness and injury, trauma and crisis states generated by the awareness of a guarded prognosis, recency of diagnosis, and other personal demographic factors, including age, education, and sociocultural background. Historically, certain groups have been recognized because of their special limitations. These groups include the mentally impaired and developmentally delayed, the mentally ill, children, and the elderly. These groups are known to have limitations in one or more areas of communication (reception, processing, and/or expression of thoughts and feelings). A group that is particularly vulnerable to infringement of personal choice are those individuals who are institutionalized or imprisoned. In these cases, the freedom that patients can exercise in making choices, even if they are fully informed and communicated competently, may be severely restricted. Coercion, in the form of implied or expressed threat, is considered to be a factor in restricting choices, and, therefore, is an actual or potential threat to individual rights.

The problem that engages any patient groups who have known impairment is complicated further by instances in which patients belong to more than one group. For example, the elderly, mentally ill, and children with mental impairments may not be able to participate in the informed-consent, informed-choice process. Usually, family or court-appointed guardians represent patients in instances wherein health care decisions must be made.

Some providers, even when they attempt to fully inform patients, observe that patients do not want to know everything, and they prefer to defer to the provider. Although this may, in fact, be the case, it is not adequate justification for short-circuiting the process of informed consent. In many situations, short-circuiting can occur despite full and appropriate procedures to engage patients in the informed-consent process because informed consent forms can be prohibitive. They may be very long (three to eight pages), and they may express ideas in legal jargon unfamiliar to the patient. These elements add to a patient's resistance to hear and/or read in a comprehensive manner all of the information contained in the consent. For this reason, patients are always provided with their own copies of both the signed consent form and a copy of the Patient's Bill of Rights.

CONCLUSION

A lack of effective communication between providers and patients is at the root of the violations of patients' rights. Whether the problem is one of informed choice or informed consent, a lack of effective communication can lead providers into serious ethical, moral, and legal problems. Providers have an obligation to care and also to protect patients from harm. When the problems in communication are not a result of their interactions but involve encounters with other providers, there remains the obligation to intervene and change existing circumstances. If a patient does not know about treatment options, is not aware of the consequences of a chosen treatment, or feels that the choice provided is not a "real choice," patients' rights are in jeopardy.

Issues of standard communications are increasingly important in cases of informed choice and informed consent because of the medical and legal implications (Sharpe 1994).

But more than this, professionals are members of a moral community. This community is made stronger by the support of and adherence to standards of practice that protect patients' rights. The privileged nature of patient and provider relationships derives meaning from the morality of the health care system.

CHAPTER 19

The Privileged Nature of Patient and Provider Communications: Issues of Confidentiality, Anonymity, and Privacy

In the area of the confidentiality of patient's communications, what may be "right" in most instances, may be terribly wrong in others.

Gwen van Servellen

CHAPTER OBJECTIVES

- Discuss the rules and regulations surrounding the principle of provider-client confidentiality.
- Describe ways in which the provider-client communication is privileged.
- Discuss the advisability of this principle.
- Discuss how anonymity and privacy can be maintained.
- Discuss the one common dilemma that rests with the inability to provide absolute client protection.
- Discuss alternatives to absolute confidentiality.

In the last 30 years, a great deal of attention has been given to the issues of privileged communications in relationships between patients and providers. The majority of this discussion has been sparked by two important and related issues: the confidentiality of the research process and infractions of patients' rights that reached the level of litigation. The issue of privileged communications in health care is extremely important in regard to patient-provider relationships. Many states have granted statutes that guarantee privileged communication for health care professionals. Still, these statutes have been challenged by arguments against privileged communication. A case in point centers around the threat of societal exposure to HIV. The argument centers around the issue of social good versus individual rights. That is, it is deemed essential to reveal certain information that would otherwise be held confidential because reporting it is essential to protect society. A most notable example where the rights to confidentiality were challenged was in a landmark case in California (Tarasoff *v.* Regents of the University of California, 1976). This case established that it was a therapist's duty to warn endangered parties if the patient intended to harm them.

In truth, the issue to disclose or not and protection of individual versus societal rights is not as straightforward as we could hope it to be. Each individual case must be evaluated with respect to the particular facts and consequences that surround the case. Absolute confidentiality, anonymity, and privacy cannot be guaranteed; however, protection of patient information must be respected and provided. Practices that do not reflect a conscious effort to provide for these rights are subject to severe ethical and moral scrutiny.

THE SACROSANCTITY OF PROVIDER-PATIENT COMMUNICATIONS

When patients seek medical intervention, they reveal very intimate details about themselves and their families. In fact, effective patient-provider relationships rely on the patient's willingness and ability to talk frankly and openly about their situations. The information may be denunciatory or incriminating. For many patients, this information has rested in the realm of secrecy. It is data that may not have been shared with any other individual. A great deal of the time, the information that patients divulge, because it is related to problems, causes them distress. It is generally argued that professional health care providers have an explicit obligation to hold all information in confidence with the understanding that the patient's welfare and trust could be jeopardized by the disclosure of this confidential information (Stern 1990).

Confidentiality

Confidentiality as it relates to professional patient-provider communications has the sole purpose of protecting the patient from unauthorized disclosures (Taylor and Adelman 1989). This ethical principle is concerned with privacy, with secret knowledge, and with knowledge known only to a select few. Confidential communication refers to personal or private matters that are revealed to a provider who cannot be compelled by law to repeat this communication or be a witness against the patient. Codes of professional ethics address the issue of confidentiality explicitly. Essentially, patients should be able to assume or be explicitly assured that their private communications with the professional will not be passed on to others except in a few specific situations. Exceptions include the need for professionals to seek other professional opinions about the patient in consultation.

A field of practice that has addressed the issue of privileged communication in detail is that of mental health. There are precise stipulations governing conditions under which information can be disclosed. In specific situations, e.g., psychiatric-patient encounters, the provider must disclose any threats that the patient has made to him- or herself or others. Generally, however, the guideline is that the provider should disclose that which is needed and specifically requested. That is, the provider should keep in confidence those disclosures that are immaterial or irrelevant (Stern 1990).

On the issue of confidential written records, the provider has the obligation and duty to maintain patient records in a manner wherein there is no reasonable chance of their getting lost, stolen, or falling into the hands of unauthorized persons.

Confidentiality, it would seem, is like anonymity, privacy, and other such phenomena. There are specific differences, however, and these differences have been addressed (Shah 1970a). Essentially, confidentiality protects the client from unauthorized disclosures of any sort by the professional without the informed consent of the patient.

Examples wherein providers may be at liberty to reveal details to family members are cases of interest. Consider, for example, a terminally ill patient who expresses a desire to commit suicide, or a woman who unbeknown to her husband, admits that she has had two therapeutic abortions; or a cancer patient who pulled her nasogastric tube out. To what degree is it the provider's obligation to keep this information confidential? The ethical codes of professional organizations aim to safeguard the patient's right to confidentiality, even though it could be argued that the patient's significant other(s) may have an equal right to know this information. Professional ethics would support the sanctioning of any health care provider who violated the patient's rights to confidentiality in these instances.

A specific instance in which rules of confidentiality are taken extremely seriously is in cases of research in which patients are the subjects. In research studies, the issues of confidentiality are clearly stated. Research subjects should not be identifiable by name, rather, another procedure, e.g., a code number, should be used. On the chance that identifiable data is obtained, the researcher must explain the specific procedures that will be used for collecting, processing, and storing data, including who will have access to the data and what will be done with the data when the study is completed.

Privileged Communication

Historically, the doctrine of privileged communication simply meant that patients have a legal right by law to have their communications protected. That is, the patient has the legal right where that right exists, to not have his confidences revealed publicly from a witness stand during legal proceedings without his expressed permission. Through judicial interpretation, this protection can be extended to legislative and administrative proceedings as well. Privileged communication statutes exist to govern patient-provider communications in many, but not all, states. Currently, the physician-patient privilege is a recognized statute in 33 states and the District of Columbia. And, in states not having statutes, the right to privileged communication can be affirmed by common law on a case-by-case basis.

When we speak of privilege, we are confining our definition to the patient; that is, the privilege belongs to patients, and they alone have the right to employ it. The privilege does not extend to the family or provider and may not be used in any way to enhance others. This privilege, however, is not absolute. Once the patient has waived this privilege or compromised it with his own actions, the provider has no obligation to withhold relevant information even if statutes about privileged communication exist. These conditions include the patient's own disclosure of both diagnosis or prognosis.

The history of privileged communication dates back to early English law where the responsibility to testify in a court of law was the issue. Despite the stated duty to provide witnessed data, it was argued that some relationships were of sufficient importance that communications originating in these relationships should be privileged. Recent cases, such as those related to the AIDS epidemic, have reaffirmed the need for strict statutes pertaining to privileged communication. Arguments in favor of privileged communication include the need to promote patient disclosure not only to adequately care for the patient but to ultimately reduce threat to others. It is logical, taking this argument into account, that the provider-patient interaction be protected to inspire trust and confidence both for the good of the individual and society at large. Under these conditions, confidence in providers is nurtured and a full account of symptoms is made available to the providers.

As has always been the case, the issue of privileged communication involves our striking a balance between two important social values: (1) society's right to access information critical to fact finding, and (2) the individual's right to privacy. But (as has been inferred) these principles are far from simple to apply in selected instances.

Anonymity and Privacy

Shah (1970b) states that the United States Supreme Court first recognized the "right to privacy" as an independent constitutional right in the case of Griswold *v.* Connecticut in 1965. This case concerned the unsuccessful attempt by the state of Connecticut to prevent by statute anyone, including married couples, from using contraceptive devices. In their decision against Connecticut, some of the Supreme

Court justices claimed that the right to privacy was not to be found in any specific constitutional amendment but in the implications cast by several amendments (first, third, fourth, fifth, and ninth amendments). But how many times have health care providers themselves witnessed infractions of the principle of patients' rights to anonymity and privacy? The infractions occur so frequently that providers sometimes become insensitive and oblivious to them. Anonymity refers to the right of patients to have their identity protected from its being known to others. Privacy more generally refers to the right of the patient to limit any knowledge of others about himself or herself.

Consider, for example, the pharmacist who speaks loudly to a person in the presence of several other people about such things as his diagnosis, the names of his medications, the patient's social security number, and the spelling of his first and last name. Consider also the medical resident or student nurse who discusses the details of a patient's case (revealing the patient's name) in a clinic or hospital elevator. If you watch such events you will notice that onlookers waiting nearby will turn their heads and look down or look away. People are aware that this data about another person is privileged and that they are not really entitled to know this information. The provider, however, appears oblivious to the situation. When this occurs, most people feel anger and concern, but what good does it do to complain when their complaints may bring even more attention to their identity or to the identity of the patient being discussed? The damage has been done. People waiting in line for their medications worry that this will happen to them and they may speak softly or withhold verbalizing information in hopes of decreasing the likelihood that their rights to privacy and anonymity will be preserved. Assertive providers, bystanders in the elevator scenario, may pull the violators aside and reprimand them for their misconduct.

There are many examples of this same infraction. Consider the patient in an outpatient clinic who is awaiting diagnostic-testing procedures. The receptionist broadcasts the name of the patient to the room of six to seven patients and family members. Having not obtained all the information initially, she requests the patient to call back to her (behind the desk) the reason for the diagnostic test, where the patient lives, and home and work phone numbers.

Can we say that the information that is revealed publicly in these situations should not be confidential? Unlikely, given the rights of patients for anonymity and privacy. These infractions are serious ethical errors. Could the patient legally sue the provider, assistant, and/or health care facility? The answer is "yes." Would the patient win? That answer is complicated. Issues of privacy and anonymity are complex and the exact legal interpretation of the boundaries is still evolving.

In general terms, the concept of privacy acknowledges the freedom of patients to pick and choose for themselves the time, circumstances, and particularly, the extent to which they wish to share or withhold their identity, attitudes, opinions, beliefs, and current, past, or future behaviors. The right to privacy is not just the entitlement to have the curtain pulled during a physical exam or medical procedure, it is an affirmation of the importance of the uniqueness and individuality of patients and their desired freedom from unreasonable intrusion by others.

COMMON DILEMMAS AND ALTERNATIVE RESPONSES

The Lack of Absolutes

Responsible actions by providers need to reflect the fact that with issues of privacy, confidentiality, and the privileged nature of patient-provider communications, dilemmas will always arise. In fact, as stated earlier, these issues are not translated into absolute terms. The particular facts and consequences of each individual case must be considered. Additionally, patients' bills of rights, professional codes of ethics, and the legal statutes of a specific state will influence the resolution of the dilemmas.

Alternatives

Because absolute confidentiality and privacy cannot be guaranteed, certain suggestions have been generated as potential alternatives. Stern (1990), for example, offers three alternatives with which to provide patients some protection of personal information. First, the patient can be offered anonymity. This would necessitate obscuring identifying information on records. Second, the patient can be provided access to records in order to correct inaccurate information and to make decisions about the dissemination of the record. Finally, abridgement of patient records can occur. This would delimit the contents of records so that extraneous and irrelevant written data would be inaccessible to others. These provisions would considerably reduce the risk that patient information will fall into unauthorized hands or be disseminated and misapplied and/or used in unauthorized ways.

CONCLUSION

Patients who seek treatment reveal important intimate information that is known to very few or, often, to no one else. Some of this information or the meaning of the information may be out of the patient's immediate awareness. Thus, patients could be revealing not only data no one else knows but also data previously unknown to them. Since the provider uses techniques to promote patient self-disclosure, the chances of the patient revealing personal and private information are very high. Many times, the contents of this private and personal communication can be distressing or even self-incriminating. Therapeutic relationships with providers rely on both the patient's willingness to self-disclose as well as on the provider's skill in promoting patient self-disclosures. There are inherent professional obligations in patient-provider encounters to hold patients' communications, both written and verbal, in confidence. Although not absolute, these principles of confidentiality, anonymity, and privacy characterize professional-patient relationships. The patient's welfare and trust may be severely compromised by the disclosure of information provided in confidence or by the disclosure of identifying information to others outside the immediate circle of health care providers responsible for the patients' care. Exceptions do occur, particularly when the welfare of others is in question.

A full and detailed discussion of the principles and skills of therapeutic communications is appropriately closed by the affirmation of the special professional obligation that underlies the treatment of patient self-disclosures once they are effectively elicited.

APPENDIX A

Glossary

Accessibility: Access problems in health care generally refer to the fact that health care is not provided equally to all citizens. The major deterrent is usually identified as a lack of adequate insurance coverage. It includes problems of certain persons being either uninsured or underinsured.

Accountability: Accountability in health care delivery refers to the process of knowing and controlling for outcomes. The issue refers to both efficiency and effectiveness of services.

Active Listening: Active listening is the process of understanding fully what another is communicating. It enables providers to be fully attuned not only to what the patient is saying, but also to what the patient feels.

Advisement: The act of disclosing what you think another person should feel, think, or do. Less direct advice and providing rationale generally makes advice more palatable.

Affective Sensitivity: This term is sometimes used synonymously with the term *empathy*. It refers to the ability to sense, at a feeling level, the experience of another.

Affordability: Affordability of health care services refers to the relative costs of rendering care as a portion of the Gross National Product (GNP). When accusations are made about health care costs being out of control, the context of the discussion includes not only percentage increases in expenditures but how this increase measures up in terms of increasing the proportion of the nation's GNP.

Aggression: This is a common negative stance that is displayed in blaming and/or attacking behaviors. Low self-esteem and feelings of inferiority may underlie behaviors of aggression.

Analogic Communication: When we refer to objects as representations or likenesses and observe and respond nonverbally and contextually, we are using our analogic communication capacities.

347

Anonymity: Anonymity refers to the privacy rights of patients wherein their exact identity is not made known to others.

Arbitration: Arbitration is one solution to settling disputes. It involves an impartial third party who has been given the authority to present solutions.

Attribution Theory: Attribution theory includes concepts and principles that explain the process of assigning meaning and character to events.

Autonomic Nervous System: The nervous system that is responsible for regulating the functioning of internal organs is the autonomic nervous system.

Bargaining: Bargaining is the process of making trade-offs or coming to mutual compromise. It is one aspect of negotiation.

Biofeedback: By providing sensory feedback, it is believed that internal bodily responses, e.g., stress, can be controlled.

Case Management: Case management includes case assessment, treatment planning, referral, and follow-up to ensure comprehensive and continuous services and coordinated payment and reimbursement.

Chronic Illness: Chronic illness refers to conditions that will not be cured by brief intervention. Chronic illnesses frequently have a downward course despite multiple remissions.

Classical Conditioning: Classical conditioning refers to the Pavlovian principle of establishing a conditioned response by pairing a conditioned stimulus with an unconditioned stimulus.

Closed-Ended Questions: Questions that are phrased to evoke a narrow range of possible responses and that frequently elicit one-word or "yes"/"no" responses are closed-ended.

Coding: Coding is a term in neurophysiology that is used to describe the correspondence of some part of a stimulus and some aspect of action in the nervous system.

Coercion: Solutions reached through coercion have occurred because the alternatives have been severely restricted and fear or threats have underscored the process.

Commands: Like orders, commands are directives that must be followed. They are different from orders in that they demand immediate action.

Competition: Competition occurs when one disputant pursues his or her own interests, neglecting to consider the needs of the other.

Complainer: This is a common negative stance. Patients frequently exhibit unrealistic expectations, and fear and anxiety are often the inner feelings of dependent complaining patients.

Compliance/Noncompliance/Partial Compliance: Compliance is the act of following medical orders as they are prescribed. Noncompliance refers to ignoring medical orders, at least the essential aspects. Partial compliance is inconsistency or incompleteness in following orders.

Compromise: A compromise is a solution that produces relatively the same losses and gains for both parties.

Conciliation: Conciliation is a state or condition that is established to shortcut substantial discussion of issues wherein conflict could escalate.

Confidentiality: Confidentiality in health care communications implies that the patient may either assume or be explicitly assured that his private communications with the provider will not be transmitted to others except in specific instances. Providers have a moral, ethical, and legal responsibility to protect the confidentiality of these communications.

Confirmation: Confirmation is a way of communicating acknowledgment and acceptance of others. Confirming-communicative responses acknowledge and validate the other person.

Conflict: Conflict exists when two or more interdependent parties have opposing interests or positions on an issue. Conflicts can be latent, emerging, or manifest. They are characterized by disputes between two or more individuals. Whether latent or manifest, they are communicated.

Confrontation: Confrontation is the act of presenting differing observations. Patients may, for example, say one thing and do another. Telling patients that their behaviors are discrepant is an act of confrontation.

Consensus: Consensus refers to reaching an agreement on issues through the process of blending each party's views.

Coping: Coping refers to that which an individual thinks and/or does in a particular stressful situation. It refers to efforts that help the individual to master, tolerate, or reduce the problem that is creating the stress and/or the emotional response to the problem.

Coping (Maladaptive and Adaptive): Coping, in crisis theory, refers to the sequential development of specific responses to stress and crisis. Crisis resolution is contingent on the development of effective adaptive responses. When these responses do not diminish the tension and anxiety or result in effective problem-solving behaviors, the responses are usually described as maladaptive.

Coping Resources: Coping resources refer to both internal and external facilities that individuals in crisis have at their disposal. For example, they may possess a sense of hopefulness (an internal resource) or be recipients of social support (an external resource). Coping resources enhance individuals' abilities to deal with crisis situations. It is generally believed that individuals with low levels of resources will fare worse in crisis situations than persons with adequate resources.

Corpus Callosum: The two hemispheres of the brain are connected by a large network of axons called the corpus callosum.

Crisis: The impact of stress can produce a state of crisis, placing an individual or entire family off balance. While emergencies are sudden, unforeseen, isolated incidences, crises may have been gathering momentum over time.

Cultural Blindness: While not as serious as cultural destructiveness and cultural incapacity, some individuals ignore cultural differences. These individuals are perceived as "unbiased" because they believe that "culture makes no difference"; they practice cultural blindness.

Cultural Competence: Cultural competence refers to the capacity to function in an effective manner within the context of a multicultural society. Individuals who are culturally competent accept and respect differences, continually conduct self-assessments, pay attention to the dynamics of difference, and continually expand their knowledge of different groups.

Cultural Destructiveness: Cultural destructiveness is one phase in the process of developing cultural competence. At the most negative end of the continuum, it refers to blatant attempts to destroy the culture of a given group. There is the assumption that one race or group is superior and that all others are inferior.

Cultural Diversity: While there are many commonalities among, between, and within groups, there are also vast differences in individuals' communications and life views.

Cultural Incapacity: Certain individuals do not intentionally seek to be culturally destructive but still lack the capacity to be responsive to differences. Ignorance and unrealistic fears are often the basis of the problem of cultural incapacity.

Cultural Precompetence: Cultural precompetence implies movement toward cultural sensitivity. Characteristic of this phase is the active pursuit of knowledge about differences and attempts to integrate this information into the delivery of services.

Cultural Proficiency: Cultural proficiency is represented at the most positive end of the continuum. Individuals at this end of the continuum hold cultures in very high esteem and are regarded as specialists in developing culturally sensitive practices.

Culture: The word *culture* refers to the integrated pattern of human behavior that includes the customs, values, beliefs, communications, and actions of a specific group. This group can be distinguished along racial, ethnic, religious, or social dimensions.

Deadlocks, Stalemates, or Impasses: These terms are used to refer to the state of inertia that is experienced by disputants. They are unable to move forward in resolving their issues and/or disagreements.

Decoding: The process of deciphering the meaning of a message is known as decoding. The receiver decodes messages.

Defensive Communication: Defensive communication is that which addresses issues of personal interest in a rigid manner.

Denial: Denial is a coping response; it is also the first stage in the process of adaptation to illness. Denial helps patients minimize the threat (and, therefore, the painful, emotional reactions) associated with illness.

Digital Communication: Humans utilize both digital communication and analogic communication; digital communication refers to perceiving and expressing oneself in concrete terms, e.g., referring to things by their names.

Directives: Directives are absolute statements made to patients about the preferred course of action. Providers expect directives to be followed. Directives are simply statements that tell patients what is expected of them. Directives are different from advice. Advice is offered without explicit expectations; directives describe what you want patients to do.

Disconfirmation: Disconfirmation denies the value of another's existence. Disconfirming-communicative responses are frequently irrelevant to the other person's communication. They cause the other person to feel devalued.

Disorganized Families: Disorganized families are those in which appropriate role enactment is rarely attempted and never maintained. Dysfunction is more apparent in disorganized families than in marginally functioning families.

Double-Barreled Questions: This question format asks for one answer to multiple and separate questions It is impossible to answer adequately with one response, although this is what is evoked.

Dysfunctional Communication: Dysfunctional communication may occur as a result of transient conditions or more permanent defects. Disturbances in perception, processing, or expression are manifested.

Dysfunctional Families: In the broadest context, dysfunctional families are those that fail to be effective along various dimensions. Their communication and decision-making capacities are extremely limited.

Emotional Knowing: Emotional knowing, often used to describe empathy, refers to the process of establishing objective awareness of another's thoughts and feelings through the process of entering the experiential world of the other.

Empathic Understanding: Empathic understanding refers to the condition of knowing the other person through insight achieved in the process of identifying what it must be like to be that person.

Encoding: This is the process of forming a message that transmits a specific meaning. The sender encodes messages.

Feedback (Feedback Loop): Feedback generally refers to sensory information stemming from actions or activities; this information is fed back to affect sequential perceptions and actions (thus, the notion of a loop).

Functional Communication: Functional communication is characterized by an absence of disturbance in perception, processing, and expression; it usually contains a great deal of clarification and qualification.

General Adaptation Syndrome (GAS): GAS refers to a specific description of the sequential responses to crisis events. Each of three stages, according to Selye (1978), have a corresponding level and type of behavioral disorganization. These stages, representing acute behavioral responses, include (1) alarm, (2) resistance, and (3) exhaustion.

Group Content: In contrast to the process of the group, the content refers to the explicit tasks that the group addresses.

Group Maintenance: Behavior in a group may be directed toward maintaining and encouraging the group. These behaviors include gatekeeping and harmonizing. Both behaviors encourage members to sustain their participation.

Group Process: Group process refers to the dynamic unfolding of interaction within a group sequentially, over time. Stages of group development depict the process of the group at any one point in its history.

Health Care Delivery System: Health care delivery system describes the major way in which health care has been provided. One classical analysis is to consider the institutions in which the majority of services occur, e.g., inpatient or outpatient home-care programs.

Health Maintenance Organizations (HMOs): HMOs are comprehensively designed structures for financing and delivering health care. These organizations provide services to enrollees within a geographical area through a panel of providers.

Health Promotion: Health promotion versus disease prevention is an issue that is addressed in general health care policy. It is generally agreed that the ideal goal of the American health care system should be reflected in an increase in the years of healthy life of its citizens. This approach requires an investment not only in the treatment of disease but also in the prevention of illness.

Hemisphere: Hemisphere refers to either the right or left sphere of the brain; each sphere has decidedly different functions.

Hypochondriasis: This disorder is one form of a somatoform disorder. It includes excessive preoccupation with one's physical health. As with somatoform disorders in general, these somatic symptoms have no basis in a physical disorder.

Informed Choice: It is generally understood that patients who have the capacity to make decisions about their care must be permitted to do so. Patient choice is not absolute.

Informed Consent: Informed consent is the permission from the patient to conduct a test, treatment, or procedure after the provider has fully informed the patient, in ways that the patient can understand, about the actions that will be taken. Informed consent can be obtained in writing or orally. Some conditions require written consent, e.g., in the case of research studies.

Informing: Informing refers to the process of offering data that is pertinent to the problem(s) that are confronting the patient.

Interest-Based Bargaining: With interest-based bargaining, as many needs or concerns as are presented are attempted to be addressed.

Interpersonal Group Problems: Interpersonal group problems refer to discontent across groups. These problems also frequently include issues of power, status, and affiliation.

Interpersonal Space: One way of conceiving of silence is to conceive of it as interpersonal space. This refers to a hypothetical, changing degree of psychosocial distance that occurs whenever two or more individuals communicate.

Interpretations: Convey an understanding of the individual that is not within his/her immediate awareness. In therapeutic encounters, interpretations are offered less frequently than reflections and when substantial data has been gathered.

Interresponse Boundary: Interresponse boundary refers to the space after a speaker makes a statement and before another speaker replies or the same speaker talks again.

Interresponse Time: The period of time that elapses after a speaker makes a statement and before another speaker replies or the same speaker talks again is the interresponse time. Interresponse times can vary; they include pauses as short as one to two seconds or therapeutic silences lasting up to ten seconds.

Interruptive Response: Interruptive responses are disruptions of another individual's speech that generally have the impact of cutting short the expression of the person's thoughts and feelings.

Intragroup Problems: Health care delivery systems consist of many professional task groups that address larger organizational goals. Intergroup problems also reflect issues of power, status, and affiliation with groups.

Joint Commission on Accreditation of Healthcare Organizations (Joint Commission): The Joint Commission is a private, nonprofit organization whose purpose is the accreditation of hospitals and other provider facilities. The Joint Commission sets standards for the quality of health care by publishing national standards, evaluating facilities on request, and granting accreditation to those facilities that meet the standards.

Limbic System: The limbic system is responsible for emotional experience and expression; it consists of a set of subcortical structures in the forebrain that includes the hypothalamus, hippocorpus, amygdala, olfactory bulb, septum, part of the thalamus, and the cerebral cortex.

"Loaded" Questions: Loaded questions are those that restrict or influence responses. The wording of these questions suggests which answers are appropriate or desirable.

Managed Care: Managed care is an approach to providing a range of health services in such a way that both the services and the resulting costs are carefully scrutinized and controlled.

Manipulator: Manipulative patients generally have self-centered attitudes. They attempt to control providers' actions, sometimes in passive-aggressive ways. Manipulators anticipate loss of control and are usually fearful.

Marginal Families: Marginality refers to families who function below par due to illness, injury, or disability. Family needs exceed family resources. The family can function appropriately, but their level of functioning is tenuous.

Mediation: Mediation refers to the process by which an impartial third person with authority assists disputants to reach mutually acceptable solutions.

Metacommunication: Metacommunication is simply communication about the communication or message. It directs the receiver as to how to receive the content portion of the communication.

Metadisclosure: Metadisclosures are disclosures about a disclosure. An example would be, "I just told you that to see what you'd say."

Mistrust: Mistrust and trust can be viewed on a continuum. Mistrust can occur because providers are viewed as lacking competence. Mistrust can also occur if providers are deemed to have other than the patient's best interests in mind.

Multidimensional Communication: The assumption that communication occurs on multiple levels, e.g., the verbal and nonverbal levels, exemplify that interpersonal communication is indeed complex.

Multimodal Strength: Modes refer to channels of communication; multimodal strength refers to exhibiting strength in more than one modality at a time, e.g., having strength in visual and auditory channels simultaneously.

Multiple-Choice Questions: These questions are phrased to evoke a response to simultaneously presented choices. One choice is made between two or more options, e.g., "Would you like to take your medication with or without juice?"

Mutual Denial: When both the patient and the provider seem to enter into a conspiracy of denial about the prognosis of an illness, they exhibit mutual denial. One party's denial is dependent on the other party's need to avoid reality as well.

Nondirective Advice: Advice that is offered tentatively, as in the form of options or alternatives to be examined jointly by provider and patient and that refrains from projecting the provider's view onto the patient, is nondirective.

Nontherapeutic Communication: Nontherapeutic communications are those that generally limit patients' expressions and cause patients to have negative reactions.

Nonverbal Communication: Not all communication is expressed in the verbal exchange of messages and responses. A good deal is expressed through posture, facial gestures, spatial positioning, and the like; these components are aspects of nonverbal communication.

Open-Ended Questions: Questions that are phrased to evoke a wide range of possible responses and that frequently begin with "what" phrases are open-ended.

Opinions: Opinions are expressions of thoughts or feelings about health care situations affecting patients and their families. Expressing opinions is not telling patients what to do, rather, it is offering them information and the benefit of the provider's professional views.

Orders: Orders are directives that the patient must follow. Giving orders is a critical aspect of providers' roles.

Overtalk Response: Overtalk occurs when both parties in a conversation speak simultaneously. It can occur at the beginning of a conversation, at the midpoint, or near the end of an expressed thought when these expressions trigger impulses in the other to respond. Overtalk usually indicates defensiveness in individuals, is rarely productive, and usually culminates in frustration for those trying to communicate.

Paraphrasing: Paraphrasing consists of selecting among several statements that the patient has made, summarizing these statements, and giving them meaning in another form.

Parasympathetic Nervous System: This neuro-network to the internal organs tends to work to conserve energy and produce relaxation.

Patient's Bill of Rights: There are several conceptual models of patients' rights that depict ethical and legal parameters for health care providers. Among the most well-known is the American Hospital Association's "Patient's Bill of Rights."

Position-Based Bargaining: Position-based bargaining occurs when one or more disputants negotiate with a solution that satisfies that party's needs or interests.

Preferred Provider Organizations (PPOs): PPOs are managed care approaches that contract with independent providers (physicians, ancillary providers) for negotiated fees for services.

Principle of Utility: The principle of utility refers to the tendency of human needs to structure perception.

Privacy (and Communication): The concept of privacy refers to the right of the patient to limit the knowledge of others about himself.

Privileged Communication: Privileged communication refers to the legal right by statute that is provided to the patient from having confidences revealed publicly, e.g., from the witness stand without his expressed permission (Shah 1969).

Process Disclosure: Process disclosures describe reactions to the immediate interaction within the helping process. Process disclosures are helpful in clarifying patients' communications. "I notice that you interrupted me when I asked about how the treatment was working" is a process disclosure reflecting on the confusion that the provider has about the patient's reaction to treatment.

Projection: Projection applies to listeners' conscious or unconscious attempts to place on another their own thoughts and/or feelings. These thoughts and/or feelings, while they may be cogent, usually do not describe the patient's experience accurately. They have originated from the provider, not from the patient.

Reception: Reception refers to the absorption of physical energy, e.g., light and sound.

Reflections: Responses that direct back to the patient the patient's ideas and feelings about the verbal content (as well as the verbal content itself).

Reframing: The strategy of reframing is used to substantially alter disputants' views on an issue. It is used to move parties out of a stalemate and toward new solutions.

Resolution (Acceptance): Resolution is the last stage in the adaptation-to-illness process. In the case of death, it is a peaceful period wherein patients accept their impending demise. They no longer resist their diagnosis or prognosis and usually have given up hope that their illness will reverse its course.

Response Burden: "Response burden" refers to the level of demand that is placed on the respondent to address a particular question format. Each question format requires of the respondent time, energy, and certain competencies. Questions that require a great deal from the respondent would be deemed high–response-burden questions; while those requiring little thought, time, or energy would be regarded as low–response burden questions.

Response Matching: Response matching refers to the tendency of the receiver to imitate the sender's level of disclosure.

Restatement: Stating again what the patient has said, or using a slightly different wording to reiterate what the patient has said, is making restatements. Restatements are limited to the expressed content. They do not require reference to the feelings that the patient is either expressing or may have expressed.

Role Reversal: Role reversal is the reversal of the helper-helpee relationship wherein the provider is seeking assistance from the patient by disclosing some personal issue or problem. It is nontherapeutic and can lead to the patient's distrust of the provider.

Self-Disclosure: Refers to instances of openly sharing personal information including personal preferences, experiences, attitudes, and feelings. They should be used judiciously by the provider and be purposeful.

Self-Reference Statements: Self-reference statements are usually spontaneous and reveal a limited amount of personal data. Self-disclosure is not the aim.

Settlement: Settlements are those agreements that come with resolution. Settlements can be either binding or nonbinding decisions.

Significant Other (SO): "Significant other" refers to individuals who may or may not be related by blood or marriage but who act as family members.

Social Network: Social network refers to the structure of social relationships of an individual.

Social Penetration: Social penetration is a process in which the depth and breadth of personal disclosures increases over time.

Social Support: Social support is a generic term that specifies emotional and/or instrumental support provided by others.

Split-Brain: This term is used to refer to conditions wherein a portion of the corpus callosum has been damaged or destroyed.

Stress: Almost any event can pose a threat to the needs or goals of an individual. Every stressful event or situation does not lead to a crisis; a great deal depends on the meaning of the stress to the patient and the extent to which the stressful situation taxes the individual's current capabilities to cope.

Stressors: Stressors are specific stimuli that cause stress. In crisis situations, they are often referred to as stressful events or precipitating events. Newer ideas about stressors suggest that daily hassles and major strains may be as lethal to individuals as the occurrence of major stressful life events.

Sympathetic Nervous System: The sympathetic nervous system includes the neuro-network to the internal organs; this system prepares the body for vigorous activity, e.g., running, lifting, exercising.

Sympathy: This is a term used to refer to the act of feeling the feelings or needs of another. It is usually accompanied by responses of sadness or pity.

Temporal Continuum: Self-disclosures can be categorized by their temporal characteristics. Self-disclosures about one's present experience include such statements as, "I feel cold"; or about immediate or distant past experiences such as, "I remember feeling very nervous when I found out my diagnosis."

Therapeutic Communication: Therapeutic communication can occur between any two persons; health care providers employ it intentionally to give support, present reality, elicit full descriptions from patients, and so on.

Transduction: Transduction refers to our capacities to change the energy from the physical stimulus to an electrochemical pattern in the brain's neurons.

Trust: Trust is the reliance on the veracity and integrity of another individual. In patient-provider relationships, it includes both confidence in providers' competence and perceptions that providers have patients' best interests in mind.

Underlying Meaning: Underlying meaning refers to the context in which behaviors occur; they include not-so-obvious thoughts, feelings, and attitudes that explain behavioral responses.

Victim Patient: Patients who present as victims are generally self-pitying. They appear somewhat immobilized by a perceived real or anticipated threat. They exhibit low levels of self-esteem and fear rejection. Patients who take on the role of victim without a clear and present threat should be distinguished from those who have been victimized.

Wellness versus Illness: The goal of health promotion stresses the number of years of healthy life that individuals experience. It does not rely heavily on estimates of mortality, or even morbidity, to judge the adequacy of care, since these measures minimize quality-of-life indicators.

APPENDIX B

References

Abramson L. Y., G. Metalsky, and L. Alloy. 1989. Hopelessness depression: A theory-based subtype of depression. *Psychological Review* 96(2):358–72.

Acosta, Frank X., Joe Jamamoto, and Leonard A. Evans. 1991. *Effective psychotherapy for low-income and minority patients*. New York: Plenum Press. (Epigraph from p. vii)

Agosta, L. Quoted in J. Lichtenberg, M. Bornstein, and D. Silver, eds. 1984. *Empathy*. London: The Analytic Press. (Epigraph from p. 49)

Allred, C. A., P. H. Arford, Y. Michel, R. Dring, and V. Carter. 1995. Case management: The relationship between structure and environment. *Nursing Economics* 13(1):32–41.

American Psychiatric Association. 1994. *Diagnostic and statistical manual of mental disorders (DSM-IV)*. 4th ed. Washington, D.C.: American Psychiatric Association.

Arnold, E., and K. Boggs. 1995. *Interpersonal relationships: Professional communication skills for nurses*. 2nd ed. Philadelphia: W. B. Saunders Co.

Auvil, C. A., and B. W. Silver. 1984. Therapist self-disclosure: When is it appropriate? *Perspectives in Psychiatric Care* 22(2):57–61.

Averill, J. 1973. Personal control over aversion stimuli and its relationship to stress. *Psychological Bulletin* 88:29. Cited in J. D. Miller, *Coping with chronic illness—overcoming powerlessness*. Philadelphia: F. A. Davis, 1983, p. 23.

Bakan, P. 1971. The eyes have it. *Psychology Today* 4(11):64–67.

Bandler, R., and J. Grinder. 1982. *Reframing: Neurolinguistic programming and the transformation of meaning*. Moab, Utah: Real People Press.

Barbara, D. A. 1958. *The art of listening*. Springfield, Ill.: Bannerstone House.

Barbe, W. B., and M. N. Milone, Jr. 1980. Modality. *Instructor*, 44–47.

Bateson, G. 1972. *Steps to an ecology of mind*. New York: Ballantine Books.

Beck, C. K., R. P. Rawlins, and S. R. Williams. 1988. *Mental health-psychiatric nursing: A holistic life-cycle approach*. 2d ed. St. Louis, Mo.: C.V. Mosby Co.

Belle, D. 1982. *Lives in stress*. Beverly Hills, Calif.: Sage Publications, Inc.

Bernstein, L. S., and R. S. Bernstein. 1985. *Interviewing: A guide for health professionals*. New York: Appleton-Century-Crofts.

359

Bertakis, K. D., D. Roter, and S. M. Putnam. 1991. The relationship of physician medical interview style to patient satisfaction. *Journal of Family Practice* 32(2):175–81.

Bilu, Y., and E. Witztum. 1994. Culturally sensitive therapy with ultra-orthodox patients: The strategic employment of religious idioms of distress. *Israel Journal of Psychiatry and Related Sciences* 31(3):170–82.

Blackburn, J. A. 1992. Achieving a multicultural service orientation: Adaptive models in service delivery, and race and culture training. *Caring* 11(4):22–26.

Bluhm, J. 1991. *How to work with difficult people.* Phoenix, Ariz.: Judy Bluhm Seminars.

Bluhm, J. 1991. *The healing triangle in working with difficult people.* Santa Clara, Calif.: California (Epigraph from p. 6)

Bok, S. 1978. *Lying: Moral choice in public and private life.* New York: Pantheon, 32. Quoted in M. Benjamin and J. Curtis, *Ethics in nursing,* 3d ed. New York: Oxford University Press, 1992, p. 32.

Bokinskie, J. C. 1992. Family conferences: A method to diminish transfer anxiety. *Journal of Neuroscience Nursing* 24(3):129–33.

Bolton, R. 1979. *People skills: How to assert yourself, listen to others, and resolve conflicts.* New York: Simon & Shuster.

Book, H. E. 1991. Is empathy cost efficient? *American Journal of Psychotherapy* 45(1):21–30.

Booth, T., and W. Booth. 1994. The use of depth interviewing with vulnerable subjects: Lessons from a research study of parents with learning difficulties. *Social Science and Medicine* 39(3):415–24.

Bowen, M. 1971. The use of family theory in clinical practice. In *Changing families,* edited by J. Haley. New York: Grune & Stratton.

Bradford, L. P., D. Stock, and M. Horowitz. 1961. How to diagnose group problems in communication and group process. In *Group development,* edited by L. Bradford. Washington, D.C.: National Training Laboratories, National Education Association.

Bradley, J. C., and M. A. Edinberg. 1990. *Communication in the nursing context.* Norwalk, Conn.: Mosby Year Book.

Brock, C. D., and J. V. Salinsky. 1993. Empathy: An essential skill for understanding the physician-patient relationship in clinical practice. *Family Medicine* 25(4):245–48.

Brodal, A. 1981. *Neurological anatomy.* 3d ed. New York: Oxford University Press.

Brown, S. J. 1995. An interviewing style for nursing assessment. *Journal of Advanced Nursing* 21:340–43.

Buber, M. 1957. Distance and relation. *Psychiatry* 20:97–104.

Buchholz, W. 1990. A piece of my mind: Hope. *JAMA* 263(17):2357–58.

Cable, D. G. 1991. Caring for the terminally ill: Communicating with patients and family. *Henry Ford Hospital Medical Journal* 39(2):85–88.

Cade, J. 1993. An evaluation of early patient contact for medical students. *Medical Education* 27(3):205–10.

Carkhuff, R. T. 1969. *Helping and human relations: A primer for lay and professional helpers.* Vol. 1, *Selection and training.* New York: Holt, Rinehart, & Wilson.

Carkhuff, R., and J. W. Rordan. 1987. *The art of helping.* Philadelphia: W. B. Saunders Co.

Clark, K. B. 1980. Empathy: A neglected topic in psychological research. *American Psychologist* 35(2):187–90.

Cohen, S., and T. A. Wills. 1985. Stress, social support, and the buffering hypothesis. *Psychological Bulletin* 98(2):310–57.

Cole-Kelly, K. 1992. Illness stories and patient care in the family practice context. *Family Medicine.* 24(1):45–48.

Coleman, J. R. 1990. HMOs and individual case management. *The Case Manager* 1(3):55–61.

Collins, M. 1977. *Communication in health care: Understanding and implementing effective human relationships.* St. Louis, Mo.: C.V. Mosby Co.

Coser, L. 1956. *The function of social conflict.* New York: Free Press.

Cournoyer, B. 1991. *The social work skills workbook.* Belmont, Calif.: Wadsworth Publishing Co.

Cross, T. L., B. J. Bazron, K. W. Dennis, and M. R. Isaacs. 1989. Towards a culturally competent system of care. Washington, D.C.: CASSP Technical Assistance Center, Georgetown University Child Development Center.

Crowther, D. J. 1991. Metacommunications. A missed opportunity? *Journal of Psychosocial Nursing and Mental Health Services* 29(4):13–16.

Curtiss, F. R. 1989. Managed health care: Managed costs? *Personnel Journal,* June, 12–85.

Davidhizar, R., and J. N. Giger. 1994. When your patient is silent. *Journal of Advanced Nursing* 20(4):703–6.

Davis, A. J., and M. A. Aroskar. 1991. *Ethical dilemmas and nursing practice.* 3d ed. Norwalk, Conn.: Appleton & Lange. (Epigraph from p. 80)

Davis, C. M. 1990. What is empathy, and can empathy be taught? *Physical Therapy* 70(11):707–11.

Davis-Martin, S. 1994. Perceived needs of families of long-term critical care patients: A brief report. *Heart and Lung* 23(6):515–18.

Day, M. E. 1964. An eye movement phenomenon relating to attention, thought, and anxiety. *Perceptual and Motor Skills* 19:443–46.

Del Mar, C. B. 1994. Communicating well in general practice. *The Medical Journal of Australia* 160(21):367–70.

Denny, M. R., and S. C. Ratner. 1970. *Comparative psychology: Research in animal behavior.* Rev. ed. Homewood, Ill.: Dorsey Press.

Deutsch, M. 1973. *The resolution of conflict.* New Haven, Conn.: Yale University Press.

Dilts, R. B., in J. Grinder, R. Bandler, J. DeLozier, and L. Cameron-Bandler. 1979. *Neurolinguistic programming.* Vol. 1. Cupertino, Calif.: Meta Publications.

Duvall, E. M. 1977. *Marriage and family development.* 5th ed. Philadelphia: J.B. Lippincott, Inc.

Ehvmann, V. 1971. Empathy. Its origin, characteristics and process, *Perspectives in Psychiatric Care* 9(77). Cited in S. J. Sundeen, G. W. Stuart, E.A.D. Rankin, and S. A. Cohen, *Nurse-client interaction—Implementing the nursing process.* St. Louis, Mo.: Mosby Yearbook, Inc., 1994, p. 176.

Enthoven, A., and R. Kronick. 1989. A consumer-choice health plan for the 1990s: Universal health insurance in a system designed to promote quality and economy. *New England Journal of Medicine* 320(1):29–37.

Erikson, E. H. 1963. *Childhood and society.* New York: Norton, Inc.

Evans, B. J., R. O. Stanley, and G. D. Burrows. 1993. Measuring medical students' empathy skills, part 2. *British Journal of Medical Psychology* 66:121–33.

Evans, D. R., M. T. Hearn, M. R. Uhlemann, and A. E. Ivey. 1989. *Essential interviewing: A programmed approach to effective communication.* Pacific Grove, Calif.: Brooks/Cole.

Feldstein, J. C., and G. A. Gladstein. 1980. A comparison of the construct validity of four measures of empathy. *Measurement and Evaluation in Guidance* 13:49–57.

Findlay, S. 1993. The case for a new cooperative spirit. *Business and Health* 11(11):66–68.

Fisch, J. M. 1994. The self in psychotherapy. *Israel Journal of Psychiatry and Related Sciences* 31(2):71–77.

Fisher, R. C. 1992. Patient education and compliance: A pharmacist's perspective. *Patient Education and Counseling* 19(3):261–71.

Fleishman, P. R. 1989. *The healing zone: Religious issues in psychotherapy*. New York: Paragon House.

Fordham, Christopher C., III. 1994. Issues of trust in medicine. *Southern Medical Journal* 87(7):770. (Epigraph from p. 770)

Garvin, B. J., and C. W. Kennedy. 1986. Confirmation-disconfirmation: A framework for the study of interpersonal relationships. In *Nursing research methodology,* edited by P. Chinn. Gaithersburg, Md.: Aspen Publishers, Inc.

Gazda, G. M., W. C. Childers, and R. P. Walters. 1982. *Interpersonal communication: A handbook for health professionals*. Gaithersburg, Md.: Aspen Publishers, Inc. (Epigraph from pp. 141–42)

Geschwind, N., and W. Levitsky. 1968. Human brain: Left-right asymmetries in temporal speech region. *Science* 161:168–187.

Gladstein, G. A. 1987. Counselor empathy and client outcomes, in *Empathy and counseling: Explorations in theory and research*, edited by G.A. Gladstein. New York: Springer-Verlag. Cited in S. J. Sundeen, G. W. Stuart, E.A.D. Rankin, and S. A. Cohen, *Nurse-client interaction—Implementing the nursing process*. St. Louis, Mo.: Mosby Yearbook, Inc., 1994, p. 178.

Goffman, T. E., and L. Dachowski. 1992. The strategic management of serious news. *Military Medicine* 157(8):424–26.

Goldman, J. 1967. A comparison of sensory modality preference of children and adults. Ph.D. diss., Yeshiva University, New York.

Goldsmith, J. C. 1992a. The reshaping of health care (Part I). *Healthcare Forum Journal,* May/June 19–27. (Epigraph from p. 27)

Goldsmith, J. C. 1992b. The reshaping of healthcare (Part II). *Healthcare Forum Journal,* May-June, 34–41.

Goldstein, M. K., R. P. Vallone, D. C. Pascoe, and C. H. Winograd. 1991. Durable power-of-attorney for health care. Are we ready for it? *Western Journal of Medicine* 155(3):262–68.

Goodman, G., and G. Esterly. 1988. *The talk book: The intimate science of communicating in close relationships*. Emmaus, Penn.: Rodela.

Gordon, D. 1978. *Therapeutic metaphors: Helping others through the looking glass*. Cupertino, Calif.: Meta Publications.

Grinder, J., and R. Bandler. 1976. The structure of magic II. Palo Alto, Calif.: Science and Behavior Books. Cited in G. M. Gazda, W. C. Childers, and R. P. Walters, *Interpersonal communication: A handbook for health professionals*. Gaithersburg, Md.: Aspen Publishers, Inc., 1982, p. 35.

Gur, R. E. 1975. Conjugate lateral eye movements as an index of hemispheric activation. *Journal of Personality and Social Psychology* 31:751–57.

Haas, J. S., J. S. Weissman, P. D. Cleary, J. Goldberg, C. Gatsonis, G. R. Seage, F. J. Fowler Jr., M. P. Massagli, H. J. Makadon, and A. M. Epstein. 1993. Discussion of preferences for life-sustaining care by persons with AIDS: Predictors of failure in patient-physician communication. *Archives of Internal Medicine* 153(10):1241–48.

Hames, C. C. and D. H. Joseph. 1986. Basic concepts of helping. In *Communications in nursing,* edited by S. B. Smith. St. Louis, Mo.: Mosby Year Book, 1992.

Hammer, E. F., ed. 1968. *Use of interpretation in treatment.* New York: Grune & Stratton, pp. 1–41. (Epigraph from p. 6)

Hanes, C. C., and D. H. Joseph. 1986. *Basic concepts of helping: A holistic approach.* Norwalk, Conn.: Appleton-Century-Crofts.

Haynie, N. A. 1981. Systematic human relations training with neurolinguistic programming. Unpublished doctoral dissertation. Cited in G. M. Gazda, W. C. Childers, and R. P. Walters, *Interpersonal communication: A handbook for health professionals.* Gaithersburg Md.: Aspen Publishers, Inc., 1982. p. 35.

Hein, E. C. 1980. *Communication in nursing practice.* 2d ed. Boston, Mass.: Little, Brown & Co.

Herth, K. 1989. The relationship between level of hope and level of coping response and other variables in patients with cancer. *Oncology Nursing Forum* 16(1):67–72.

Hicks, L., J. M. Stallmeyer, and J. R. Coleman. 1992. Nursing challenges in managed care. *Nursing Economics* 10(4):265–76.

Hill, C. E., and F. Gormally. 1977. Effects of reflection, restatement, probe, and nonverbal behaviors on client affect. *Journal of Counseling Psychology* 24(2):92–97.

Holmes, T. H., and M. Masuda. 1974. Life changes and illness susceptibility. In *Stressed life events: The nature and effects,* edited by B. S. Dohrenwend, and B. H. Dohrenwend. New York: John Wiley & Co.

Howell, J. B., and D. P. Schroeder. 1984. *Physician stress: A handbook for coping.* Baltimore, Md.: University Park Press.

Jackson, S. W. 1992. The listening healer in the history of psychological healing. *The American Journal of Psychiatry* 149(12):1623–32.

Janosik, E. H. 1984. *Crisis counseling: A contemporary approach.* Monterey, Calif.: Wadsworth Health Sciences Division. (Epigraph from p. 5)

Jourard, S. M. 1971. *The transparent self.* New York: Van Nostrand Reinhold.

Kalat, J. W. 1988. *Biological psychology.* 3d ed. Belmont, Calif.: Wadsworth Publishing Co.

Kaplan, R. M. 1991. Achieving wellness for all Californians: The general health policy model. Wellness Lecture Series, U.C., San Diego (October 29, 1991).

Kercher, E. E. 1991. Crisis intervention in the emergency department. *Emergency Medicine Clinics of North America* 9(1):219–32.

Kimura, D. 1961. Cerebral dominance and the perception of verbal stimuli. *Canadian Journal of Psychology* 15:166–71.

Kissick, W. L. 1994. *Medicine's dilemmas: Infinite needs versus finite resources.* New Haven, Conn.: Yale University Press.

Kleinman, A. 1988. The illness narratives: Suffering, healing, and the human condition. New York: Basic Books.

Knafl, K., B. Breitmayer, A. Gallo, and L. Zoeller. 1992. Parents' views of health care providers: An exploration of the components of a positive working relationship. *Childrens Health Care* 21(2):90–95.

Korzybski, A. 1958. *Science and sanity.* 4th ed. New York: Science Press.

Krashen, S. D. 1977. The left hemisphere. In *The human brain,* edited by M. C. Wittrock. Englewood Cliffs, N.J.: Prentice-Hall, Inc.

Kübler-Ross, E. 1969. *On death and dying.* New York: Macmillan.

Laing, R. D. 1967. *The politics of experience*. New York: Pantheon Books, Inc.

Lax, D., and J. Sebenius. 1986. *The manager and negotiator*. New York: Free Press.

Lazarus, R., and S. Folkman. 1984. *Stress, appraisal and coping*. New York: Springer Publishing.

Leonard, G. 1994. *Words* in Dawnpoint. R. May, D.R. Brown, A. Ellis, W. Schultz, D. South, A. Maslow, G. Leonard. San Francisco: The Association for Humanistic Psychology, p. 3.

Lipps, T. 1935. Empathy, I . . . , Imitation and Sense. Feelings. In *A modern book of esthetics: An anthology*, edited by M. M. Rader. New York: Henry Holt.

McCleary, R. A. 1966. Response-modulating functions of the limbic system: Initiation and suppression. In *Progress on physiological psychology*, edited by E. Steller and J. M. Sprague. New York: Academic.

MacLean, P. D. 1962. New findings relevant to the evolution of psychosexual functions of the brain. *Journal of Nervous and Mental Disease* 135:289–301.

MacLean, P. D. 1970. The limbic brain in relation to the psychoses. In *Physiological correlates of emotion,* edited by P. Black. New York: Academic, pp. 129–46.

MacLean, P. D. 1973. *A triune concept of the brain and behavior*. Toronto: University of Toronto Press.

Mallett, J. 1990. Communication between nurses and post-anaesthetic patients. *Intensive Care Nursing* 6(1):45–53.

Martyres, G. 1995. On silence: A language for emotional experience. *Australian and New Zealand Journal of Psychiatry* 29(1):118–23.

Maslach, C. 1982. *Burnout: The cost of caring*. Englewood Cliffs, N.J.: Prentice-Hall.

Matthews, D. A., A. L. Suchman, and W. T. Branch Jr. 1993. Making "connexions": Enhancing the therapeutic potential of patient-clinician relationships. *Annals of Internal Medicine* 118(12):973–77.

Miller, G. A. 1956. The magical number seven, plus or minus two: Some limits on our capacity for processing information. *Psychological Review* 63:81–97.

Miller, J. F. 1983. *Coping with chronic illness: Overcoming powerlessness*. Philadelphia: F. A. Davis Company. (Epigraph from p. 15)

Miller, W. L. 1992. Routine, ceremony or drama: An exploratory field study of the primary care clinical encounter. *Journal of Family Practice* 34(3):289–96.

Minuchin, S. 1974. *Families and family therapy*. Cambridge, Mass.: Harvard University Press.

Moore, C. W. 1986. *The mediation process*. Boulder, Colo.: Communication/Decisions/Results (CDR) Associates, pp. 1–87.

Mullally, L. 1977. Educational cognitive style: Implications for instruction. *Theory Into Practice* 16:238–42.

Nebes, R. D. 1977. Man's so-called minor hemisphere. In *The human brain*, edited by M. C. Wittrock. Englewood Cliffs, N.J.: Prentice-Hall, Inc.

Northouse, L. L., and P. G. Northouse. 1985. *Health communication: A handbook for health professionals*. Englewood Cliffs, N. J.: Prentice-Hall, Inc.

Northouse, L. L., and P. G. Northouse. 1992. *Health communication—Strategies for health professionals*. 2d ed. East Norwalk, Conn.: Appleton and Lange.

Norton, B. A., and A. M. Miller. 1986. *Skills for professional nursing practice*. East Norwalk, Conn.: Appleton-Century-Crofts.

Novack, D. H., G. Volk, D. A. Drossman, and M. Lipkin Jr. 1993. Medical interviewing and interpersonal skills teaching in U.S. medical schools. Progress, problems, and promise. *JAMA.* 269(16):2101–5.

Nunnolly, E., and C. Moy. 1989. *Communication basics for human service professionals*. Newbury Park, Calif.: Sage Publications.

O'Brien, M. J. 1978. *Communication and relationships in nursing*. 2d ed. St. Louis, Mo.: C.V. Mosby Co.

Olnick, S. L. 1984. A critique of empathy and sympathy (chapter 6). In J. Lichtenberg, M. Bernstein, and D. Silver, eds. *Empathy* Vol. 1. London: The Analytic Press, pp. 137–166.

Pearce, W. B. 1974. Trust in interpersonal communication. *Speech Monographs* 41:236–44.

Pearlin, L., and C. Schooler. 1978. The structure of coping. *Journal of Health and Social Behavior* 19:2–21.

Pettigrew, J. 1990. Intensive nursing care: The ministry of presence. *Nursing Clinics of North America* 2(3):503–8.

Pinderhughes, E. 1989. *Understanding race, ethnicity and power: The key to efficiency in clinical practice*. Southfield, Mich.. National Center for Special Needs Adoption.

President's Commission for the Study of Ethical Problems in Medicine and Biomedical and Behavioral Research. 1983. *Securing access to care*. Vol. 1. Washington, D.C.: U.S. Government Printing Office.

Raatikainen, R. 1991. Dissatisfaction and insecurity of patients in domiciliary care. *Journal of Advanced Nursing* 16(2):154–64.

Rees, A. M. 1993. Communication in the physician-patient relationship. *Bulletin of the Medical Library Association* 81(1):1–10.

Reik, T. 1951. *Listening with the third ear: The inner experiences of a psychoanalyst*. Garden City, N.J.: Garden City Books. (Epigraph from p. 144)

Riccardi, B. M., and S. M. Kurtz. 1983. *Communication and counseling in health care*. Springfield, Ill.: Charles C. Thomas Publisher.

Rice, D. 1988. Do we get full value for our health dollar? *Hospitals* 62(6):18.

Ridsdale, L., M. Morgan, and R. Morris. 1992. Doctors' interviewing technique and its response to different booking time. *Family Practice* 9(1):57–60.

Roberts, G. W. 1994. Nurse/patient communication within a bilingual health care setting. *British Journal of Nursing* 3(2):60–64, 66–67.

Rogers, C. 1951. *Client-centered therapy*. Boston: Houghton-Mifflin Co.

Rogers, C. 1957. The necessary and sufficient conditions of therapeutic personality change. *Journal of Consulting Psychology* 21:95–100.

Rogers, C. 1961. *On becoming a person: A therapist's view of psychotherapy*. Boston: Houghton-Mifflin Co.

Rogers, C. 1980. *A way of being*. Boston: Houghton-Mifflin Co.

Rooda, L. A. 1992. The development of a conceptual model for multicultural nursing. *Journal of Holistic Nursing* 10(4):337–47.

Roter, D. L., and C. K. Ewart. 1992. Emotional inhibition in essential hypertension: Obstacle to communication during medical visits? *Health Psychology* 11(3):163–69.

Roter, D. L., and J. A. Hall. 1992. *Doctors talking with patients/patients talking with doctors—improving communication in medical visits*. Westport, Conn.: Auburn House.

Rowland-Morin, P. A, and J. G. Carroll. 1990. Verbal communication skills and patient satisfaction: A study of doctor-patient interviews. *Evaluation and the Health Professions* 13(2):168–85.

Rubin, F. I., M. M. Judd, and T. A. Conine. Empathy: Can it be learned and retained? *Physical Therapy* 57(6):644–47.

Ruesch, J. 1961. *Therapeutic communication.* New York: W. W. Norton. (Epigraph from p. xiv)

Satir, V. 1967. *Conjoint family therapy.* Palo Alto, Calif.: Science and Behavior Books.

Schatz, I. J. 1995. Empathy and medical education. *Hawaii Medical Journal* 54(4):495–97.

Selye, H. 1978. *The stress of life.* New York: McGraw-Hill.

Shah, S. A. 1969. Privileged communications, confidentiality and privacy: Privileged communications. *Professional Psychology* 1:59–69.

Shah, S. A. 1970a. Privileged communication, confidentiality and privacy: Confidentiality. *Professional Psychology* 1:159–64.

Shah, S. A. 1970b. Privileged communication, confidentiality and privacy: Privacy. *Professional Psychology* 1:243–52.

Sharpe, N. F. 1994. Informed consent and Huntington's disease: A model for communication. *American Journal of Medical Genetics* 50(3):239–46.

Sherbourne, C. D., L. S. Meredith, W. Rogers, and J. E. Ware, Jr. 1992. Social support and stressful life events: Age differences in their effects on health-related quality of life among the chronically ill. *Quality of Life Research* 1:235–46.

Sherover-Marcuse, R. 1987. Liberation theory: A working framework. Unpublished manuscript. San Francisco: Unlearning Racism Workshops, Inc.

Short, P. F. 1990. National medical expenditure survey: Estimates of the uninsured population, calendar year 1987: Data summary 2. Rockville, Md.: National Center for Health Services Research and Health Care Technology Assessment.

Short, P. F., A. Monheit, and K. Beauregard. 1989. National medical expenditure survey: A profile of uninsured Americans: Research findings I. Rockville, Md.: National Center for Health Services Research and Health Care Technology Assessment.

Sieburg, E. 1969. Dysfunctional communication and interpersonal responsiveness in small groups. Ph.D. diss., University of Denver. Abstract in *Dissertation Abstracts International,* 1969, 30(2622A).

Siminoff, L. A. 1992. Improving communication with cancer patients. *Oncology* 6(10):83–87.

Singer, L. L. 1976. *Daydreaming and fantasy.* London: George Allen & Unwin, Ltd.

Smith, M. E., and G. Hart. 1994. Nurses' responses to patient anger: From disconnecting to connecting. *Journal of Advanced Nursing* 20(4):643–51.

Smith R. C., and R. B. Hoppe. 1991. The patient's story: Integrating the patient- and physician-centered approaches to interviewing. *Annals of Internal Medicine* 115(6):470–77.

Smith, S. 1992. *Communications in nursing.* 2d ed. St. Louis, Mo.: Mosby Yearbook.

Spiro, H. What is empathy and can it be taught? *Annals of Internal Medicine* 116(10):843–46.

Steinglass, P., and M. E. Horan. 1987. Families and chronic medical illness. In *Chronic disorders and the family,* edited by F. Walsh and C. M Anderson. New York: Haworth Press, pp. 127–142.

Stern, S. B. 1990. Privileged communication: An ethical and legal right of psychiatric clients. *Perspectives in Psychiatric Care* 26(4):22–25.

Stevenson, S. 1991. Heading off violence with verbal de-escalation. *Journal of Psychosocial Nursing and Mental Health Services* 29(9):6–10.

Stumpf, S. H., and K. Bass. 1992. Cross-cultural communication to help physician assistants provide unbiased health care. *Public Health Reports* 107(1):113–15.

Sullivan, H. S. 1953. *The interpersonal theory of psychiatry.* New York: W.W. Norton & Co.

Sundeen, S. J., G. W. Stuart, E. A. D. Rankin, and S. A. Cohen. 1994. Nurse-client interaction—Implementing the nursing process (5th Ed). St. Louis, Mosby Co.

Sussman, M. B. 1982. Family-organizational linkages. In *The psychiatric hospital and the family*, edited by H. T. Harbin. Jamaica, N.Y.: Spectrum Publications, Inc., pp. 277–96.

Tappen, R. M. 1991. Alzheimer's disease: Communication techniques to facilitate perioperative care. *AORN* 54(6):1279–86.

Taylor, L., and H. S. Adelman. 1989. Reframing the confidentiality dilemma to work in children's best interest. *Professional Psychology: Research and Practice* 26(2):79–83.

Thomas, R. K. 1981. Personal communication, August 6, 1981. Cited in G. M. Gazda, W. C. Childers and R. P. Walters, *Interpersonal communication: A handbook for health professionals*. Gaithersburg, Md.: Aspen Publishers, Inc., 1982, p. 27.

Thompson, J. E., and H. O. Thompson. 1985. *Bioethical decision-making for nurses*. Norwalk, Conn.: Appleton-Century-Crofts.

Todres, I. D., M. Earle Jr., and M. S. Jellinck. 1994. Enhancing communication: The physician and family in the pediatric intensive care unit. *Pediatric Clinics of North America* 41(6):1395–1404.

Tong, K. L., and B. J. Spicer. 1994. The Chinese palliative patient and family in North America: A cultural perspective. *Journal of Palliative Care* 10(1):26–28.

Truax, C. B., and R. Carkhuff. 1967. *Toward effective counseling and psychotherapy*. Chicago, Ill.: Aldine.

Ury, W. L., J. M. Brett, and S. B. Goldberg. 1988. *Getting dispute resolved: Designing systems to cut the costs of conflict*. San Francisco: Jossey-Bass.

Usherwood, T. 1993. Subjective and behavioral evaluation of the teaching of patient interview skills. *Medical Education* 27(1):41–47.

Vaillot, M. C. 1970. Hope: The restoration of being. *American Journal of Nursing* 70(2):268–73.

van Servellen, G. 1986–1988. The stresses of hospitalization in the AIDS patient, University of California, Universitywide Task Force on AIDS (W-P860623).

Wada, J. A. 1977. Fundamental asymmetry of the infant brain. In S. J. Dimond and D. A. Blizard, eds., *Annals of the New York Academy of Sciences*, 299, 370–79.

Wade, C., and C. Tauris. 1990. *Psychology*. 2d ed. St. Louis, Mo.: Harper and Row.

Watzlawick, P. J., J. Beavin, and D. D. Jackson. 1967. *Pragmatics of human communication*. New York: W.W. Norton & Company, Inc. (Epigraph from p. 13)

Webber, G. C. 1990. Patient education. A review of the issues. *Medical Care* 28(11):1089–1103.

Weisman, A. D. 1972. *On dying and denying: A psychiatric study of terminality*. New York: Behavioral Publications.

Weisman, A. D., and J. W. Worden. 1976. *Coping and vulnerability in cancer patients*. Boston: Project Omega, Harvard Medical School.

Wilson, L. 1982. The skills of ethnic competence. Seattle: University of Washington. Resource paper.

Witelson, S. F., and W. Pallie. 1973. Left hemisphere specialization for language in newborn: Neuroanatomical evidence of asymmetry. *Brain* 96, 641–46.

Wolfe, G. 1995. Case managers: The natural leaders in disease management. *The Journal of Case Management* 1(2):8.

Index